"This book is very important for the *whole* field of education. It is essential reading for anyone wanting deeper understanding of the extraordinary education project of Reggio Emilia, delving into its underpinning pedagogy, politics, ethics, culture and philosophy as well as the 'competent system' that enables it. It contests the impoverished education of the neoliberal hegemony, with its standardised criteria and predetermined outcomes. It leaves the reader with hope that another world is possible as that hegemony passes."
    Peter Moss, *Emeritus Professor, UCL Institute of Education*

"A *city that cares* and *collective research* – these enchanting concepts are the opening words and ethos of this book that describes the role of the *pedagogistas* in Reggio Emilia. However, the book does not only describe the role of the *pedagogistas*, it also demonstrates how this role is constantly put into play, into the not-yet – '*mettersi in gioco*' – through the *pedagogistas*' lived experiences together with the children, the teachers, the parents, and engaged others. In tune with Reggio Emilia's tradition of systemic and pragmatic thinking, the role of the *pedagogista* is placed in an ecology of practices, which opens up towards speculative pragmatic thinking; towards events, affect and minor gestures, and towards life in its widest sense. The book also sends a message of hope and a call for an *education commons*, which is so important when education systems internationally are experiencing the dissolution of collective action."
    Gunilla Dahlberg, *Emeritus Professor, Stockholm University*

THE ROLE OF THE *PEDAGOGISTA* IN REGGIO EMILIA

The Role of the Pedagogista *in Reggio Emilia* offers unparalleled insight into dialectic encounters between teachers, *pedagogistas*, and *atelieristas* in the world-renowned municipal early childhood services of the city of Reggio Emilia. It sheds light on the system and culture that cares for and sustains an enduring educational experience, for the common good.

Emerging from a collaborative research project with Reggio Children and the Preschools and Infant-toddler Centres – Istituzione of the Municipality of Reggio Emilia, this book features in-depth observations of *pedagogistas*, teachers, and *atelieristas*, as well as interviews with key figures in Reggio Emilia. Children's learning is thoughtfully emphasised, as the authors render the inextricable connection between theory-practice-research, framing documentation and *progettazione* as artful collective experimentation.

The authors illuminate how Reggio Emilia's system sustains reciprocal professional formation through *progettazione*, contesting dominant marketplace discourses of early childhood education as a commodity and re-imagining settings driven by values of reciprocity, artistry, culture, and the common good.

By troubling conventional views on education and care, professionalism of teachers, and educational leadership, this book will appeal to all those who long for something different and hope to shift the field of possibility for early childhood education culturally, socially, pedagogically, and politically. It will be a key resource for teachers, leaders, policy makers, and scholars in the whole field of education.

Stefania Giamminuti, Senior Lecturer in Early Childhood Education at Curtin University, Australia, cultivates an enduring research collaboration with Reggio Emilia.

Paola Cagliari, *Pedagogista*, formerly Director of the Preschools and Infant-toddler Centres – Istituzione of the Municipality of Reggio Emilia, collaborates with Reggio Children on research projects and *formazione*.

Claudia Giudici, Psychologist, formerly President of Reggio Children, where she is currently responsible for the Research Area, is Professor in Psychopedagogy at the University of Modena and Reggio Emilia.

Paola Strozzi, *Pedagogista*, former member of the Pedagogical Coordination of the Preschools and Infant-toddler Centres – Istituzione of the Municipality of Reggio Emilia, collaborates with Reggio Children on *formazione*.

Contesting Early Childhood

Series Editors: Liselott Mariett Olsson
and Michel Vandenbroeck

This ground-breaking series questions the current dominant discourses surrounding early childhood, and offers instead alternative narratives of an area that is now made up of a multitude of perspectives and debates.

The series examines the possibilities and risks arising from the accelerated development of early childhood services and policies, and illustrates how it has become increasingly steeped in regulation and control. Insightfully, this collection of books shows how early childhood services can in fact contribute to ethical and democratic practices. The authors explore new ideas taken from alternative working practices in both the western and developing world, and from other academic disciplines such as developmental psychology. Current theories and best practice are placed in relation to the major processes of political, social, economic, cultural, and technological change occurring in the world today.

The Decommodification of Early Childhood Education and Care
Resisting Neoliberalism
Michel Vandenbroeck, Joanne Lehrer and Linda Mitchell

Becoming Pedagogue
Aesthetics, Ethics & Politics in Early Childhood Education & Care
Liselott Mariett Olsson

The Role of the *Pedagogista* in Reggio Emilia
Voices and Ideas for a Dialectic Educational Experience
Stefania Giamminuti, Paola Cagliari, Claudia Giudici and Paola Strozzi

For more information about this series, please visit: www.routledge.com/ Contesting-Early-Childhood/book-series/SE0623

THE ROLE OF THE *PEDAGOGISTA* IN REGGIO EMILIA

Voices and Ideas for a Dialectic Educational Experience

Stefania Giamminuti, Paola Cagliari, Claudia Giudici and Paola Strozzi

LONDON AND NEW YORK

Designed cover image: *Air in the leaves* (detail). Drawing by 5-year-old children of the Robinson municipal Preschool, Reggio Emilia © Preschools and Infant-toddler Centres – Istituzione of the Municipality of Reggio Emilia, Italy

First published 2024
by Routledge
4 Park Square, Milton Park, Abingdon, Oxon OX14 4RN

and by Routledge
605 Third Avenue, New York, NY 10158

Routledge is an imprint of the Taylor & Francis Group, an informa business

© 2024 Stefania Giamminuti, Reggio Children and Preschools and Infant-toddler Centres – Istituzione of the Municipality of Reggio Emilia, Italy

The right of Stefania Giamminuti, Paola Cagliari, Claudia Giudici and Paola Strozzi to be identified as authors of this work has been asserted in accordance with sections 77 and 78 of the Copyright, Designs and Patents Act 1988.

All rights reserved. No part of this book may be reprinted or reproduced or utilised in any form or by any electronic, mechanical, or other means, now known or hereafter invented, including photocopying and recording, or in any information storage or retrieval system, without permission in writing from the publishers.

Extracts of archival documentation presented in Chapters 4 and 6 (texts and images by *atelieristas*, teachers, *pedagogistas* and children) are from the Reggio Emilia municipal infant-toddler centres and preschools. Images and extracts from interviews and encounters in Reggio Emilia, presented in Chapters 1, 3, 5, 7 & 9, are from the research project led by Stefania Giamminuti.

Trademark notice: Product or corporate names may be trademarks or registered trademarks, and are used only for identification and explanation without intent to infringe.

British Library Cataloguing-in-Publication Data
A catalogue record for this book is available from the British Library

ISBN: 9781032019246 (hbk)
ISBN: 9781032019215 (pbk)
ISBN: 9781003181026 (ebk)

DOI: 10.4324/9781003181026

Typeset in ITC Galliard Pro
by KnowledgeWorks Global Ltd.

*To all the adults and children who participate
in new horizons of hope
for early childhood education and care.*

CONTENTS

Acknowledgements	*xvi*
About the authors	*xviii*
Series editor foreword	*xx*
Glossary	*xxii*
Preface	*xxvi*

> *A city that cares: lively ethographies for educational research xxvi*
>
> *Researching together: dialectics, reciprocity, participation xxix*

1 Reciprocal *formazione* and collective care   1

Introduction 1
International unease 2
Reciprocal formazione *and collective care 6*
   Formazione: *amateur scholarship and teachers as intellectuals 6*
   Obligation to care: a collective response 12
Conclusion: storying values and ethics 15

2 Reciprocal *formazione* in Reggio Emilia   21

Introduction 21
The Italian education and schooling system 22
   The Italian state and administrative decentralisation 22
   Compulsory schooling 22

xii Contents

0–3 educational services and 3–6 scuole dell'infanzia *23*
0–3 educational services and 3–6 scuole dell'infanzia
  directly managed by municipalities: constraints
  on employment 25
Clarifying the term pedagogy *26*
Pedagogista, équipe pedagogica, *coordinators,*
  and pedagogical coordination 27
  Brief historical notes on the profession of pedagogista *27*
  Pedagogical coordinators of early childhood services: the
    genesis of a profession 28
  The role of coordinator and the birth of pedagogical
    coordinations 29
  The pedagogical coordinator and pedagogical
    coordinations: the case of Emilia Romagna 32
The experience of 0–6 services in Reggio Emilia 35
  The équipe pedagogica *and the* pedagogistas:
    historical notes 35
  Choosing the Istituzione *as a form of management*
    for 0–6 educational services 38
  Organisms of participation and co-responsibility as
    outlined in Indications *(the new Rulebook) 38*
A diffused pedagogical system 40
  Nido d'infanzia and *scuola dell'infanzia 41*
  City Childhood Councils and the City Intercouncil 44
  The équipe pedagogica *46*
  System resources 47
  Administrative offices 48
  The Reggio Emilia Approach system and the Loris
    Malaguzzi International Centre 48
  The varied geographies and articulations of the
    formazione *system 49*
Innovation and research 50
Institutional identity: between local and global 51
Conclusions 51

3 The value of relationality and an ethic of dialectics   56

Introduction 56
The value of relationality 57
  The value of relationality: affect and reciprocity 58
  The value of relationality: worlds seen through care 68

Contents **xiii**

*The value of relationality: solidarity, freedom,
    and democracy 72*
An ethic of dialectics: confronto *and participation 76*
Conclusion 84

4 Dialectical encounters in Reggio Emilia   86

Introduction 86
Dialectics in daily contexts in Reggio Emilia's municipal
    nidi *and* scuole dell'infanzia *87*
*Fragment 1: the classroom door of the new three-year-old
    children 90*
Fragment 2: a portrait of yellow daisies 108
Concluding notes: dialectics and progettualità *125*

5 The value of artfulness and an ethic of making   127

Introduction 127
Progettazione *as an elusive concept 128*
Progettazione, pensiero progettuale *and documentation 130*
    From programmazione *to* progettazione: *welcoming
        complexity and participation 132*
    Progettazione *and documentation:
        Theory-Practice-Research 137*
    Pensiero progettuale in daily life *142*
The value of artfulness *in Reggio Emilia 146*
Pedagogy, architecture, and the potential of constraints 150
An ethic of making: craftsmanship and the real 155
Conclusion 163

6 *Pensiero progettuale* and educational research in
  everyday contexts in the *nidi* and *scuole dell'infanzia*
  of Reggio Emilia   167

Introduction 167
Pensiero progettuale *and research in everyday
    contexts 168*
Everyday contexts and routines 170
The example of setting the table 170
    Collective aggiornamento *(the whole school working
        group and the* pedagogista*): writing the school's
        declaration of intents 173*

xiv Contents

Class aggiornamento *(class C teachers, auxiliary colleague, teacher educator,* pedagogista*): writing the class declaration of intents 176*
Collective aggiornamento: confronto *with initial documentation 177*
Class aggiornamento*: analysis of ongoing documentation 183*
Collective aggiornamento: from setting the table to representations of setting the table 185
The group continues its work (Cristian, Francesco, and Lorenzo) 198
The following day ... 207
Class aggiornamento*: evaluation of work in progress 210*
The next appointment with the children 212
The following day ... 214
An unexpected relaunch 218
Conclusion 219

7 The value of culture and an ethic of research   223

Premise: the words we choose 223
Introduction 224
Culture and the posthuman convergence 226
  Children as knowing subjects 227
  Thinking that takes place in the world 235
  Affirmative ethics and conceptual creativity 238
Culture as correspondence 241
An ethic of research: the creation of the new 243
  Research as movement 246
  Research as collective experimentation 248
  Research as thinking in the making 251
Conclusion 253

8 Education Commons: History, choices, and tools for rendering a utopia concrete   256

Introduction 256
Nidi and scuole dell'infanzia: *vital nucleus of a broader educational system 257*
The city of Reggio Emilia's cultural "revolution" 258
Education Commons: *policies and actions for realising a utopia 261*

The 0–6 integrated public system 262
The Consulta *265*
Territorial pedagogical coordination 265
Reggio Children and The International Network;
    Fondazione Reggio Children; The Loris Malaguzzi
    International Centre Project 266
Participation: an unrenounceable value and strategy
    of an Education Commons *267*
Conclusions 271

9 The value of the commons and an ethic of alliances   275

Introduction 275
Privileging immaterial goods in dangerous times 276
The marketplace and early childhood education
    as a commodity 277
A political stance: living an Education Commons *280*
The value of the commons: micropolitics and the
    unimaginable 283
An ethic of alliances: "always more than one" 287
    Collective platforms for experimentation 289
    Expanding alliances and micropolitics 296
Final musings: "the minor gesture" 301

Epilogue   305

Nidi *and* scuole dell'infanzia *in Reggio Emilia,*
    a commons 305
The discourse on education, between pedagogy
    and politics 307
Frequenting the future in a dimension of community
    and collegiality 309
A different and possible way of doing school
    and education 311

Index   *314*

ACKNOWLEDGEMENTS

To the teachers, *pedagogistas* and *atelieristas* who participated in interviews and meetings, and to all those who contributed to creating a culture of welcome for this research project – thank you for your intellectual generosity and enduring collegiality.

To the Preschools and Infant-toddler Centres – Istituzione of the Municipality of Reggio Emilia and to the children who appear in our book – thank you for consenting to the use of documentation from the *scuole dell'infanzia,* enabling us to illuminate reciprocal dialectical relationships within the educational experience of Reggio Emilia.

To the pedagogical coordination of Reggio Emilia, with sincere gratitude for the warm welcome and openness to dialogue, and in recognition of the invaluable contribution that their collective work over many decades has offered to our thinking and writing in this book.

To the Reggio Emilia Australia Information Exchange – for the generous gift of a grant which allowed us to engage translator Jane McCall in a thoughtful collaboration. Jane's skill and care in translating chapters from the Italian provided an additional lens to our work through which we all emerged with new knowledge.

To Annamaria Mucchi (Reggio Children publishing) – for her graceful and attentive contribution to our editorial efforts. Annamaria's considerable care and skill in coordinating our work significantly enhanced our collaboration and smoothed the path towards publication.

To Rolando Baldini (artistic direction, Reggio Children) – for his thoughtful and generous insight in optimising the design elements that give life to our narratives.

To our editor Alison Foyle and *Contesting Early Childhood* series editors Liselott Olsson and Michel Vanderbroeck – thank you for your patience, insight, and guidance.

To Cristian Fabbi, Gigliola Venturini, Nando Rinaldi, and Maddalena Tedeschi – thank you for contributing generous Epilogues, highlighting the importance of this work locally and globally.

To all the children, families, citizens, teachers, *pedagogistas*, and *atelieristas* who tirelessly participate in Reggio Emilia's educational project – thank you for sharing new horizons of the possible with the world.

The co-authors
Stefania Giamminuti, Paola Cagliari,
Claudia Giudici, and Paola Strozzi

ABOUT THE AUTHORS

Paola Cagliari, *pedagogista*, has worked in the municipal *scuole dell'infanzia* of Reggio Emilia since 1978, first as a teacher and then, from 1985, as a *pedagogista*. She was Director of the Preschools and Infant-toddler Centres – Istituzione of the Municipality of Reggio Emilia, from 2010 to 2019. Paola is a member of the Italian ministerial commission for the 0-6 integrated system, and she has authored several journal articles and chapters in edited volumes. She collaborates with Reggio Children on research projects and *formazione* in Italy and internationally, and she curates exhibitions and publications. Paola has engaged most deeply in the areas of: children's religious and moral education; educational *progettazione*; digital technologies; and participation and multiculturalism.

Stefania Giamminuti is a bilingual Italian/Australian Senior Lecturer in Early Childhood Education, Curtin University, Western Australia. Formerly an early childhood teacher in Rome (Italy), she draws on two decades sustained research collaboration with Reggio Children and the Preschools and Infant-toddler Centres – Istituzione of the Municipality of Reggio Emilia, to investigate possibilities for early childhood education and care as the common good. Stefania privileges research projects where educators, children, and community members are valued co-researchers engaging in collective experimentation through pedagogical documentation. Her international research collaborations question boundaries between theory, research, and practice and are informed by philosophy and by aesthetic-ethico-political concepts.

Claudia Giudici, psychologist, has worked as *pedagogista* in the *scuole* and *nidi d'infanzia* of the municipality of Reggio Emilia since 1995. From 2009 to 2016, she was President of the Preschools and Infant-toddler Centres – Istituzione of the Municipality of Reggio Emilia, and from 2016 to 2022, she was President of Reggio Children, where she is currently responsible for the Research Area. Claudia coordinates research projects and curates exhibitions and publications; she also presents at conferences and seminars in Italy and internationally. She has engaged most deeply in the areas of: children's religious and moral education; educational *progettazione*; and pedagogical documentation and participation. Claudia is Professor in Psychopedagogy in the Degree of Psychological Sciences and Techniques at the University of Modena and Reggio Emilia, and since 2022 she is the Regional Guarantor of Childhood and Adolescence of Emilia-Romagna.

Paola Strozzi, *pedagogista*, was a teacher in the municipal *nidi* and *scuole dell'infanzia* and in the Documentation and Educational Research Centre of the Preschools and Infant-toddler Centres – Istituzione of the Municipality of Reggio Emilia, from 1976 to 2004. From 2007 to 2018, she was *pedagogista* with the Pedagogical Coordination of the Istituzione. Paola has engaged most deeply in the area of *pensiero progettuale*, also in relation to children with autism, and in approaches to mathematics in the *nidi* and *scuole dell'infanzia*. She has coordinated and curated many educational research projects and professional learning pathways within the Preschools and Infant-toddler Centres – Istituzione of the Municipality of Reggio Emilia, with whom she continues to collaborate.

SERIES EDITOR FOREWORD

Michel Vandenbroeck

The pedagogy of the municipal early childhood system in Reggio Emilia has a worldwide reputation and – maybe perhaps partly due to its global reputation – it has also often been misunderstood, mistranslated, and even recovered by "those who cling to conventional pedagogies and predictable approaches in educational settings". The ways in which the pedagogy of Reggio has been used and misused, often reduced the work of the *pedagogistas* and the concepts of *formazione*, *progettazione*, *pensiero progettuale*, or documentation to a series of techniques. And all too often, such a technification of pedagogy serves a narrow focus on defining quality, a concern with predictability and control of results, rather than embracing ambivalence and unpredictability. It considers pedagogy as a theory of "what works", waiting to be translated to practice, rather than a way to "firmly chip away at the boundaries that separate those who practice from those who think from those who do research". Rather than serving "what works", this book serves, in the words of its authors, the obligation towards care as a political, ethical, and affective act, and as a catalyst for engaging with the responsibility of imagining the possible in places other than Reggio Emilia.

The *Contesting Early Childhood* series, has, from its origins opposed the reduction of pedagogy into a technique; its obsession with predictable outcomes and conformity to econometric reasoning. The aims of this series have always been to document alternative pathways and therefore has often referred to the work and the thinking of the municipal services to children, to families, and to the community in Reggio Emilia. In the very first book of this series, Peter Moss and Gunilla Dahlberg (*Ethics and Politics in Early Childhood Education*) have referred to Reggio Emilia as a possible alternative for the mainstream discourse on what "quality" in early childhood is about. Since then, several books

Series editor foreword **xxi**

in this series have further documented the work of Reggio Emilia and made it accessible to a whole generation of early childhood scholars, practitioners, activists, and students. In 2010, Vea Vecchi published her book on *Art and Creativity in Reggio Emilia* in this series; in 2016, a wonderful compilation of translated texts by Loris Malaguzzi was edited by Paola Cagliari, Marina Castagnetti, Claudia Giudici, Carlina Rinaldi, Vea Vecchi, and Peter Moss and recently, a second edition of Carlina Rinaldi's *In Dialogue with Reggio Emilia* was published in this series.

The present book is a welcome and necessary addition to the series. It speaks of the unique work of the *pedagogistas* as a guarantor of permanent and reciprocal *formazione*. It provides a thorough historical and political as well as administrative background, developing deep insights in the relations between politics, ethics, and care in education. In elaborating on the essence of the *pedagogistas*, the authors reflect on novel concepts of professionalism. In their view, professionalism goes way beyond and above concepts of individual competences, in line with Reggio Emilia's tension towards collectivity and cooperation in education and civic life more broadly, as it is exemplified in the words of former Mayor Graziano Delrio, quoted in this book, who states that: "we understand that the purpose of education is not related only to *you* but it is also related to *us* – to the community, to other people". Early childhood education is, as Musatti and Mayer, also quoted in this book, term it, a sector in which the cultural implications of creating policies are more obvious, and in which the concept of quality immediately has a broader connotation, that goes beyond satisfying user needs, and expands out into *social quality*.

Stefania Giamminuti, Paola Cagliari, Claudia Giudici, and Paola Strozzi are all very familiar with the work of the *pedagogistas* as part of a complex pedagogical system where knowledge is both personal and collective. They elaborate in theoretical as well as very concrete ways on the inextricable connection between theory-practice-research that enlivens daily life in the municipal *nidi* and *scuole dell'infanzia*, framing *pensiero progettuale* as both an "artful" collective project and as a praxis of "making". With their carefully worded chapters they offer a unique contribution to this series, and to all those of us, who reflect on what Peter Moss has titled *Alternative Narratives in Early Childhood*.

GLOSSARY

In sharing this glossary with our readers, we would like to convey our delight in the exchange [*confronto*] that characterised our work together, and particularly the heated intellectual debate that could ensue over one word. Each term/word, while possessing corresponding translations in various languages, assumes locally acquired meanings within different geographical, social, and cultural environments and in relation to different disciplines; Reggio Emilia is no exception. Mindful of this, we all shared a firm belief that the minutia of one mis-translated word can upend decades of hard-fought beliefs and practices. Therefore, we elected to maintain several terms in Italian throughout this book. We do not contend that our final selections are perfect, nor are they in fact final or even our own (the echoes of all those who have attempted to translate or not can be heard here in our own deliberations), but they do reflect value-based decisions behind which lie deep and extended discussions around alternatives and what they might entail. Also, the terms delineated here are not exhaustive nor representative of what could be termed the "Reggio Emilia discourse"; rather we have chosen to emphasise only a few of the many meaning-full words that belong to the experience of Reggio Emilia, focusing on those that were often most used in discussing the topic at hand, and therefore most at risk of misinterpretation.

Aggiornamento The term *aggiornamento* (which translates literally in English as *update*) refers to a particular kind of meeting that occurs regularly between staff in the municipal *nidi* and *scuole dell'infanzia* of Reggio Emilia. This term is generally accompanied by an adjective that qualifies who participates in said *aggiornamento*. The *aggiornamenti* (plural) that occur within *progettazione*, always implicating documentation as a key player, are quite

Glossary **xxiii**

different from what the generic term *aggiornamento* (*update*) might suggest; in fact, the term has come to assume a specific locally acquired meaning over time and in relation to its intents. We prefer, where possible, to maintain the term *aggiornamento* in Italian. Where the term *meeting* works equally well, we will substitute to avoid any unnecessary complication.

Assessore *Assessore* is a term used to describe a member of an executive body of local government, whether municipal, provincial, or regional. An *assessore* generally has responsibility for a particular department or policy area, such as education. We have maintained this term in Italian because systems of local government are different in all contexts, and we did not wish to cause confusion by using a term that might be misconstrued.

Atelierista This term relates to an educator with a background in the arts, who is part of the working group of each municipal *scuola dell'infanzia* in Reggio Emilia. It has never been translated, and we keep to this tradition to also honour the uniqueness of this role, which was effectively invented in Reggio Emilia. To indicate a plurality, we have used the Anglophone term *atelieristas*, which does not exist in Italian but is clearer for the reader.

Confronto *Confronto* is a daily experience of practical and theoretical knowledge-sharing, dialectic exchange, and mutual support amongst educators and children. Within *confronto,* the sharing of critiques, comments, and diverse perspectives leads to reciprocal enrichment, improvements, and advancements in knowledge and actions. It is therefore a generous attitude, which refutes indifference, and has a fundamental ethical value. It is a term so frequently in usage in Reggio Emilia that we feel no English term can quite convey its cultural energy. In Chapter 3, we explain our reasons more fully.

Consulta The *Consulta* is the organism constituted by representatives (families, staff, and citizens) of the management bodies of all the *nidi* and *scuole dell'infanzia* belonging to Reggio Emilia's public integrated system. For some time, it was known as *Interconsiglio Cittadino* [City Intercouncil], and it is thus termed within the 2009 *Regolamento* [Rulebook]. The *Consulta* has often been translated into English as "General Committee Meeting", generating misunderstandings about its nature and purpose. In fact, this organism is a stable body, formally constituted, of the city's educational system – it is not simply a form of meeting. For this reason, we decided it is best to avoid translating this term, maintaining instead the Italian *Consulta.*

Équipe pedagogica The term *équipe* refers to the collective group of *pedagogistas* who together coordinate the municipal *nidi* and *scuole dell'infanzia,*

xxiv Glossary

also known as *coordinamento pedagogico,* which we translate as "pedagogical coordination".

Formazione The term *formazione* is frequently used in Reggio Emilia to define processes of collective and systemic research, knowledge-building, and professional learning. In this book we will maintain the Italian term *formazione*. In Chapter 1, we explain our reasons in significant detail.

Nido d'infanzia *Nidi d'infanzia* (services welcoming children from birth to age 3) were born at the beginning of the 1970s in Italy, and at the time were given the name of *asilo nido* – a somewhat untranslatable combination of *asylum* and *nest*. Beginning in the new millennium in Reggio Emilia, and from 2015 in Italian educational policy documents, these educational services are largely referred to as *nidi d'infanzia*. In dialogue with an English-speaking audience, this Italian term has been translated for a very long time as *infant-toddler centre*. In this book, we generally prefer to maintain the Italian term *nido* (singular) or *nidi* (plural).

Pedagogista The term *pedagogista* is the heart of this book. It is a term we find impossible to translate, hence the reader will find it in Italian throughout. To indicate a plurality, we have used the Anglophone term *pedagogistas*, which does not exist in Italian but is clearer for the reader.

Progettazione, Pensiero progettuale, and Progettualità In this book, we often refer to *progettazione*. the associated concept of *pensiero progettuale*, and the approach of *progettualità*. For reasons that will become evident in Chapter 5, we have chosen to privilege the Italian terms, whilst occasionally utilising the literal English translation *design thinking/designerly thinking*.

Reggio Emilia Approach/Reggio Emilia educational project/Reggio Emilia experience The experience of Reggio Emilia is widely known internationally as the "Reggio Emilia Approach". When referring to the experience as a whole we also use the terms "Reggio Emilia experience" (*esperienza)* or "Reggio Emilia educational project" (*progetto educativo)* which are most frequently used in discourse in Italian and reflect the collective effort to sustain the project's livelihood, which extends to all citizens of Reggio Emilia.

Sistema pedagogico diffuso *Sistema pedagogico diffuso*, which translates literally and coherently as *diffused pedagogical system,* is a term of fairly recent elaboration and usage in Reggio Emilia. Chapter 2 will explore its qualities in significant detail. In this book, we use the Italian and English terms interchangeably.

Scuola dell'infanzia In this book, we have also chosen to maintain in Italian the term *scuola dell'infanzia* (plural *scuole dell'infanzia),* or the abbreviated form *scuola,* when referring to services welcoming children aged from 3 to 6 years. There are historical and value-laden reasons for this choice, which relate not only to our own reticence towards the English equivalent *preschool,* but also to honouring the hard-fought change from the mainstream Italian term *scuola materna* to *scuola dell'infanzia,* spearheaded by Loris Malaguzzi and the Reggio Emilia educators. *Scuola materna* translates literally as *motherly school,* implying thus that the main purpose of school is to substitute the mother. The term *scuola dell'infanzia* (which translates literally as *school of childhood*) instead recognises children's right to a school of their own.

Working group and Collettivo The *working group* is composed of all those who work within a *nido* or *scuola dell'infanzia* in Reggio Emilia. It is also known as *collettivo* (*collective* in English); we explore the significance of this term, which we have chosen to maintain in Italian, more fully in Chapter 2. Throughout this book, the reader will find both *working group* and *collettivo,* and the terms are intended as synonymous.

PREFACE

A city that cares: lively ethographies for educational research

Stefania Giamminuti

> Driving together through the city of Reggio Emilia, familiar landmarks outside the car window. The bustling Via Emilia, then the subdued old train station where all visitors to the city used to arrive and be welcomed, departing then with their hopes for something different in the places from whence they came. With the new fast train came the futuristic Reggio Emilia AV station; this surprising structure now heralds an unusual arrival into the city's outskirts, with visitors emerging both stunned and rushing amongst the trains flying by as if speed *must* become a general concern. The station signals a collective tension towards the future in a city that has always welcomed the contemporary, whilst giving value to its illustrious, cooperative, and turbulent past – a city that is an emblem of resistance and progressiveness. As we leave the old central train station and the elegant piazzas behind, the city landscape begins to give way to the gently inhabited countryside, where the echoes are felt of the resistance to fascism and of the fervent advocacy of women who wanted more for their children and for themselves. We arrive at a *scuola dell'infanzia* named after the date of the Liberation of Italy, or Anniversary of the Resistance – XXV Aprile – and we snap a nostalgic photo at its entrance, in front of a plaque that reads: "Men and Women together, we built the walls of this school because we wanted it new and different for our children".
>
> (memories and notes from a research journal,
> Stefania Giamminuti)

The new and different, while inherently familiar and dear, accompanied me for several months as in Reggio Emilia I shadowed Paola Strozzi, and occasionally other *pedagogistas*, for our co-participated research project on the role of the

Preface **xxvii**

FIGURE 0.1 From the left: Gilda Tomasini, Stefania Giamminuti, *atelierista* Mirella Ruozzi, and *pedagogista* Paola Strozzi posing at the entrance to *Scuola dell'infanzia* XXV Aprile.

pedagogista. This book, drawn from our research, could thus be the story of one or two, the shadowed and the shadower, instead it is a storying of many protagonists across time. Driving and walking together across the city; forming new questions and new ideas; being welcomed together into *nidi* and *scuole dell'infanzia* and beyond into other forums that matter; listening and questioning; being alongside while observing. In traditional qualitative research, "like the good fieldworker-*cum*-ethnographer" (Britzman, 2000, p. 33), I could be perceived as "following" those whose lives were of interest to me – mostly silently observing perhaps, recording objectively maybe, finally representing here a "true" story through my/our writing. The readers of this book may hence be justified in expecting a manual for how to *be* a *pedagogista* and how to call themselves such no matter where they live and work, for the promise of ethnography is that it …

> […] takes the reader into an actual world to reveal the cultural knowledge working in a particular place and time as it is lived through the subjectivities of its inhabitants. Such access persuades readers that they can imaginatively step into this world and act like a native, or, at the very least, understand the imperatives of cultural assimilation […] The reader learns to expect cultural secrets and may well suppose that outsiders can become vicarious insiders.
> *(Britzman, 2000, pp. 27–28)*

It may disappoint to know that such a seductive promise is far from our intention in this book as we story the experiences of *pedagogistas*, teachers, *atelieristas*, cooks, children, families, city, materials, places, all of whom participate in the educational project of the city of Reggio Emilia. Rather we concur with Britzman (2000) when she suggests that "the authority of ethnography, the ethnographer, and the reader is always suspect" (p. 28). This book is made of many such "authorities", with myself as the academic "outsider" being the most "suspect" of all despite my decades of encounters and dialogue with the city of Reggio Emilia. I *was* there, but as Britzman (2000) exhorts the aspiring or experienced ethnographer to remember, "being there does not guarantee access to truth" and also "my own telling is partial and governed by the discourses of my time and place" (p. 32). Hence, as we welcome the reader to join in to our multi-layered and multi-voiced storytelling, we also extend an invitation to what Britzman (2000, p. 30) calls "reading with suspicion", reminding of "the impossibility of telling everything" (Britzman, 2000, p. 38) and thus encouraging all those who encounter us in this book to open their minds and hearts to the stories not told and to the possibilities these might engender, to know and learn with the silences as well as the spoken and told.

This book engages with "an ethic that refuses the grounds of subjectification and normalization and that worries about that which is not yet" (Britzman, 2000, p. 39). We do not normalise what it means to be a *pedagogista*, and we extend an invitation to worry about and pursue the not yet in places other than Reggio Emilia. We bring many voices and experiences to this storying; our own as authors and those of the people, places, and non-human others who accompany us in our thinking and doing in the past, the present and towards the future. The entangled and "messy" (Law, 2004) echoes of all these beings, thinkings, doings, are to us what St. Pierre (2018) refers to as "The Too Much" in post qualitative inquiry:

> The too strange is, however, the provocation, the knot, the world kicking back, the too much that demands experimentation. Inquiry should begin with the too strange and the too much. The rest is what everyone knows, what everyone does, the ordinary, repetition. (p. 607)

The too much and too strange is a force we rely upon, and thus the "participants" in the research project narrated in this book are incalculable. Meanwhile, we purport that, rather than a traditional ethnography, the research project on which this book is based might be perceived as a "lively ethography" (van Dooren & Bird Rose, 2016), in its aspiration to be "a mode of knowing, engaging, and storytelling that recognizes the meaningful lives of others and that, in so doing, enlivens our capacity to respond to them by singing up their character or ethos" (van Dooren & Bird Rose, 2016, p. 77). In this book, collectively we "become witness" to the entangled lives of an educational system through "grounded acts of care, of witnessing and careful storytelling" (van Dooren & Bird Rose, 2016, p. 79).

Ethnography has traditionally attempted to capture the ways and experiences of humans, conceptualising "culture" as human-centred – defined, constructed, and experienced by humans in isolation. While it may appear at first glance that this is also our own primary concern as we seek to story the role of the *pedagogista*, we do so in the constant company of non-human others and we feel a kinship for ethography's underlying ethical obligation towards "taking others seriously in their otherness – whether cultural, biological, geologic, chemical, or something else entirely – and consequently learning to ask and to see how we might be called to respond" (van Dooren & Bird Rose, 2016, p. 87). This attitude of taking others seriously in their otherness coupled with a capacity for response is an invitation we wish to set out to our readers from the very beginning, in recognition of Reggio Emilia's fundamental "alterity" (Rinaldi, 2006). We hope our readers will be "drawn into new connections and, with them, new accountabilities and obligations" (van Dooren & Bird Rose, 2016, p. 87), and we put forth an invitation to care, for "care is omnipresent, even through the effects of its absence. Like a longing emanating from the troubles of neglect, it passes within, across, throughout things. Its lack undoes, allows unravelling" (Puig de la Bellacasa, 2017, p. 1).

As we trouble the state of early childhood education and care locally and worldwide, we ask whether a lack of care might undo us all – children, families, educators, citizens and non-human others together. How can we counter a state of unravelling in our educational thinking and doing, and might collective care as a political, ethical, and affective act – such as in the enduring experience of Reggio Emilia – offer a way for re-imagining our common endeavours? As Puig de la Bellacasa (2017) invites us to consider, "caring here is a speculative affective mode that encourages intervention in what things could be" (p. 66). Our collective witnessing and storytelling bring forth speculations for what things could be, as we energise possibilities for thinking, acting, and resisting in alliance with Reggio Emilia.

Researching together: dialectics, reciprocity, participation

Paola Cagliari, Claudia Giudici, Paola Strozzi
Translated by Jane McCall

We believe that research has much to do with care as defined by Puig de la Bellacasa (2017). To care means to take to heart, to look after something or someone, and to attend to them, nurturing them in the physical and metaphorical sense to preserve their existence and integrity as they evolve, change, and go on to inhabit the future. To care, therefore, is not to maintain the existing as it is now, but rather to accompany its growth and change. For living beings and institutions, change is the fruit of constant [re]search into new adaptations, new equilibriums, and new arrangements that come with

xxx Preface

the desire for more and better understanding of who one is, what one is doing, and the directions one's existence is taking. Care is a sensitivity towards change, towards relations. Keeping eyes and minds open, being constantly in doubt and therefore researching.

It is because of this vital dynamic connected with change that research, understood as caring for adults' thinking and caring for children's open and permanently under construction thinking, is a signature of the experience in Reggio Emilia's *nidi* and *scuole dell'infanzia*. We have built our entire professional journey, and a large part of our human journey, on this vital living dimension of permanent reflection and openness to change. However, research requires alliances. It is possible to research alone, but we frequently surrender because as human beings we are limited and can often only see what is already known or very proximal to the already known. It is the multiplicity of gazes and exchanges of perspectives and knowledges that opens our minds. They can be virtual exchanges at a distance; points of view we encounter (and that open our minds) in books, articles, films, and conferences. Or they can be in-person exchanges (we like to have many of these in Reggio Emilia while not disdaining other kinds) made up of dialogue in close proximity, where we look each other in the eyes and compare points of view – sometimes, often, in lively discussions. When external elements are introduced into the exchange between colleagues, schools, and centres, or in the *équipe pedagogica*, the discussion broadens, ideas multiply, and different perspectives – bringing other people's stories into our lives – create disorientations that then lead us to enriched ways of seeing things.

This is the richness of research with partners in other countries and other cultures. We cannot always accept the many proposals we receive, because research that involves *nidi* and *scuole dell'infanzia* must respect the values and practices of the protagonists of our educational experience. Therefore, dialectics, reciprocity, and participation must be the methodological premises of any research, in all its phases. When these premises exist, we accept with enthusiasm, always mixed with concern and a strong sense of responsibility, but confident we will learn something new together. This research, in which we have participated, on the role of the *pedagogista* in Reggio Emilia's educational project, has let us view this role through eyes that, though external, already possessed deep knowledge of our experience. Much is being wagered in Italy today on the role of the *pedagogista*, as decree-law 65/2017 identifies pedagogical coordination as one of the most strategic interventions for defining, maintaining, and expanding the quality of 0–6 Years Public Integrated Systems. A reality then, and at the same time, a hope.

Investigating the *pedagogista*'s role – not only in its public expressions, visible to all, but also in the daily action alongside teachers during the processes of designing, interpreting, and constructing new contexts, in relations with families, in the multiple relations that weave together to shape the multiple social, cultural, educational, and institutional systems in which *nidi* and *scuole dell'infanzia* function and operate – has been a stimulating adventure. It is through the figure of the *pedagogista* that readers, together with us, will encounter a complex pedagogical system, highlighting the impossibility of separating what exists, what is thought, and what is enacted, as intrinsically interconnected. In fact, as Loris Malaguzzi states:

> [...] our choices have been in the direction of currents of thinking that define children first and foremost as disposed to and active in constructing the self and knowledge through social interactions and interdependencies: [...] as much as possible we have tried to hold together processes that are biological, political, cultural and – in the spirit of the times – also ecological. [...] Indicators emerge from these contributions – or can arise if we are competent – that help us without any kind of obligation to try out educational strategies and attempt responses that are more farsighted and just – the most democratic and progressive – to the problems, demands and troubling questions posed by the society of our times, and above all the ethical and civic repercussions they bring with them.
> *(Malaguzzi, 1990, in Cagliari et al., 2016, pp. 377–378)*

References

Britzman, D. P. (2000). The question of belief: Writing poststructural ethnography. In E. A. St. Pierre, & W. S. Pillow (Eds.), *Working the ruins: Feminist poststructural theory and methods in education* (pp. 27–40). Routledge.

Cagliari, P., Castagnetti, M., Giudici, C., Rinaldi, C., Vecchi, V., & Moss, P. (Eds.). (2016). *Loris Malaguzzi and the schools of Reggio Emilia: A selection of his writings and speeches, 1945–1993*. Routledge.

Law, J. (2004). *After method: Mess in social science research*. Routledge.

Puig de la Bellacasa, M. (2017). *Matters of care: Speculative ethics in more than human worlds*. University of Minnesota Press.

Rinaldi, C. (2006). *In dialogue with Reggio Emilia: Listening, researching and learning*. Routledge.

St. Pierre, E. A. (2018). Writing post qualitative inquiry. *Qualitative Inquiry, 24*(9), 603–608. https://doi.org/10.1177/1077800417734567

van Dooren, T., & Bird Rose, D. (2016). Lively ethography: Storying animist worlds. *Environmental Humanities, 8*(1), 77–94. https://doi.org/10.1215/22011919-3527731

1
RECIPROCAL *FORMAZIONE* AND COLLECTIVE CARE

Stefania Giamminuti

Introduction

In this chapter we introduce our co-participated research project, arguing that whilst conventional qualitative research concerns itself primarily with methodology (Manning, 2015; St. Pierre, 2021a), from the beginning of our encounters to the time of writing we were far more entangled with theory and practice than troubled by methods, thus aligning our work with the spirit of post qualitative inquiry (St. Pierre, 2021a, 2021b). In this project, we not only think with philosophers and scholars such as Loris Malaguzzi, Gunilla Dahlberg, Peter Moss, Rosi Braidotti, Tim Ingold, Erin Manning, Brian Massumi, Maria Puig de la Bellacasa, Henry Giroux, Elinor Ostrom, and Elizabeth Adams St. Pierre, we also take a broader view of the meaning of "theory", encompassing the theory-practice-research of the *nidi* and *scuole dell'infanzia* of Reggio Emilia as fundamental interlocuters. We hope to open possibilities for thinking research differently, as we set ourselves out to firmly chip away at the boundaries that separate those who practice from those who think from those who research.

In setting the scene for our research, we trace the international debates and local/global policies that regularly seek to position early childhood teachers as lacking, then we illustrate how our growing unease with these discourses led to our project, and finally, we consider hopeful and concrete alternatives to such despairing scenarios. We conceptualise "reciprocal *formazione*" as a tension towards collective care that is constructed within complex knowledge-practice relations. We believe any notion of educator professionalism – a term that, as we outline below, sparked our research but which we are no longer sympathetic to – demands attention to systemic possibilities and collective care

DOI: 10.4324/9781003181026-1

2 Reciprocal *formazione* and collective care

rather than a focus on isolated individual qualities (or professional standards, another term we are hardly sympathetic to). We conclude this chapter with a brief reflection on what is meant by "values" and "ethics", terms and concepts we have used to orient our thinking and writing, and that helped us go somewhere we hadn't imagined.

> I learned to trust writing to take me somewhere I couldn't go without writing.
>
> *(St. Pierre, 2018, p. 605)*

International unease

The storying this book concerns itself with is drawn from a co-participated research project entitled *The role of the pedagogical coordinating team in the educational project of Reggio Emilia: A study of educator professionalism in early years settings*. This project was approved by the Curtin University Human Research Ethics Committee and was imagined and conducted in close collaboration with Reggio Children and with the Preschools and Infant-toddler Centres – Istituzione of the Municipality of Reggio Emilia.[1] As foregrounded in the Prologue, this research may be conceived as a "lively ethography" (van Dooren & Bird Rose, 2016); a "witnessing" and "singing up the ethos" (van Dooren & Bird Rose, 2016) of an educational experience that has gained considerable attention and acclaim globally. While certain kinds of apparently conventional data such as interviews, fieldnotes, and transcripts of meetings are conveyed within this book, our view of data is far more encompassing of broader lives, encounters, and thinking through places and times. Our respective entanglements with the city of Reggio Emilia and its citizens lead us to feel a kinship with the confounding experience of St. Pierre (2018) during her doctoral studies:

> My hometown was officially the field of my study, the natural setting. But my school friend and I both remarked during that lunch that we felt we were in the past as much as the present. When was the field? During fieldwork, I was, indeed, in the past–present–future – time was untimely. I'd been studying that small tobacco town since I moved there from Yankee country as a child of five. It had borne my never-ending scrutiny because I had been the Other there, never quite fitting. I had 35 years of field notes and interviews to work with, and, as I wrote, I strayed far from "official" data, overwhelmed with a lifetime of the real. So I made the field as I wrote. I laid out the field in sentence after sentence in all the writing spaces I could find […] Data became irrelevant and data analysis was writing and thinking and laying out of the field of the text, moving. (p. 606)

This experience of dialoguing with "a lifetime of the real" as opposed to neatly categorising fieldwork "data" is particularly notable for the authors of this book who have worked within the educational project of Reggio Emilia for many decades. Humbly though, we purport that this feeling of not properly being able to grasp the time of "the field", and of making the field as we write, is shared by us all, and it is in the writing that "the field" is laid out here. Our hope is that, through our writing, "data get lived in new ways" (Lather, 2013, p. 639), thus engendering not an appropriation of an educational experience but rather an obligation to respond, a necessity to transform education and care elsewhere, whilst being attuned to the places we live in. Far from aiming to provide "hard evidence" of how the experience of Reggio Emilia operates, so that it may be "applied" elsewhere, ours is an invitation to, as Ingold (2013) suggests, "take [...] counsel from the world itself":

> Disguised as social scientists we enter this world either by stealth, feigning invisibility, or under false pretences by claiming we have come to learn from teachers whose words are heeded not for the guidance they have to offer but as evidence of how they think, of their beliefs or attitudes. Then, as soon as we have filled our bags, we cut and run. This, in my estimation, is fundamentally unethical. It is to turn our backs upon the world in which we live and to which we owe our formation. With all the data at our fingertips, we think we know what can be known; yet knowing all, we fail to see or take our counsel from the world itself. (pp. 5–6)

We caution those whose research practices are premised on entering by stealth, thinking that they know what can be known. Rather, we share Ingold's (2013) aims "to restore knowing to where it belongs, at the heart of being" and "to refute the division between data collection and theory building that underwrites normal science" (pp. 5–6), hoping that our readers might not search for "evidence" with which to cut and run, but rather believing that they might wish to turn to their own worlds and respond to them, creating new possibilities within their daily lives with children.

Our research project was born of many conversations and sparked by feelings of unease with deficit portrayals of early childhood teachers in political discourse and in educational policy and reform. At the time we were first envisaging this study, our international colleagues were called upon to define and rethink professionalism of early childhood teachers, or "what it means to be, to become and to act professionally in working with young children, families and communities" (Urban, 2010, p. 2). We fundamentally agree with Urban (2010) when he states that concepts such as "profession" and "professional" are a "highly efficient means of control and normalisation of diverse individual practices, which, in turn, provokes resistance and non-compliance from practitioners" (p. 4). Our unease can be traced also to the fact that the "emphasis

4 Reciprocal *formazione* and collective care

on "professionalism" in education often refers to increased accountability and outcome-focused approaches to teaching" (Duhn, 2010, p. 49).

In engaging with this theoretical work at the time, we were drawn in particular to Urban's (2010) notion that professionalism "is necessarily systemic, democratic and political" (p. 5). As such, we hoped that our burgeoning study might contribute to understandings of professional identity as "provisional and discursively produced" (Ortlipp et al., 2011, p. 57), as we engaged with conceptualisations of professionalism as "relational" (Lazzari, 2012; Urban, 2008) whereby professional identities are constructed within complex systems of reciprocal relationships. We aimed to reconceptualise early childhood educators' professional identities within "competent systems" (Urban et al., 2012) such as the municipal system of Reggio Emilia, in order to contribute to the understanding of professionalism as "an attribute of the entire system, to be developed in reciprocal relationships" (Urban, 2008, p. 149). Thus, our study focused on the role of the *pedagogista*, which we felt had not been adequately explored elsewhere, possibly leading to misconceptions about the role of the system in the educational project of Reggio Emilia.

In the course of our research, we found ourselves returning to Peter Moss' (2010) cautioning: "in an attempt to critically reinvent professionalism for educators, might we not end up reconceptualising the concept of professionalism so much to accommodate what is important, such as the idea of multiple knowledges and democratic practice, that we render the concept meaningless?" (p. 17). In feeling a kinship with Moss here, we also recognise that the notion of being a professional is hard fought and preciously guarded, particularly for women working in infant-toddler centres who are historically perceived as lesser, and who continue to work across the world in conditions that privilege discourses of masculinity and power (Osgood, 2006) whilst perpetuating deficit images of women, children, and the practice of educating in the early years. Being a professional, with recognition of its accompanying deep specialist knowledge, could be perceived as a weapon against such deficit positioning, but it does buy into the dominant marketplace narrative, and thus brings with it many risks for, as Ingold (2021b) purports: "professionalism [...] is not what it was. In its capture by corporate and managerial interests, the accusations levelled against it have become self-fulfilling" (p. 158). We caution therefore that professionalism is a culturally situated construct, and hence to be construed as a professional in individualistic societies governed by neoliberal values and marketplace ideals can be quite different to owning an identity as a professional within collectivist societies informed by democratic values.

Our own discomfort with the term professionalism and the neoliberal tensions it elicits, and our desire to avoid rendering the concept meaningless, have led us to prefer the Italian term *formazione*, which is widely used in Reggio Emilia. In choosing to use this term, we also resist similar tensions and assumptions that relate to widely used (and misused) terms such as "professional development" and "professional learning" which might be readily applied to the experiences we convey in this book. While the direct translation of *formazione* as "formation" in English may conjure images of unyielding humanist paradigms and passive learning, such hierarchies are eschewed in Reggio Emilia in favour of collective thinking, doing, and experimenting. In an effort then to avoid associations with such conventional paradigms as might arise in the mind of the reader when encountering the English term "formation", we choose to privilege the Italian term, and specifically its usage within the Reggio Emilia discourse. The following words, spoken by Loris Malaguzzi at a conference in Modena in 1971, offer some insight into his understanding of *formazione*:

> It is a great effort, a brave act of honesty towards herself, an exhausting autonomous desecration of things in which until now she has in good faith believed in, that which we ask of the teacher so that together with children and then with young people and families and citizens she may participate in the construction of school as a lively centre of open and democratic culture. That she may be enriched and nurtured by those roles and those social exchanges that will not only allow her to overcome her false and equivocal autonomy and her historic detachment but will enable her to finally be free of ideological leanings and authoritative indoctrination.
>
> *(Malaguzzi, 1971, p. 149 [our translation])*

In choosing *formazione*, we recognise that "subject formation is never static" (Arndt et al., 2018, p. 102) and we fundamentally agree that "now is the time for solidarity" (Arndt et al., 2018, p. 112). In fact, years on from our initial conversations about our research project, as we write and gaze onto the international landscape, we cannot say that our unease with a dominant stance of mistrusting teachers has been allayed. Rather, we cling to solidarity as we are confronted by, for example, Henry Giroux's (2014) lament of schools in the USA becoming "dead zones of the imagination" as neoliberal market-driven educational reforms "exhibit contempt for teachers and distrust of parents, repress creative teaching, destroy challenging and imaginative programs of study, and treat students as mere inputs on an assembly line" (p. 492). In her scathing review of the effects of neoliberalism on early childhood education and care, with a particular focus on the Australian context, Margaret Sims (2017) presents a similarly despairing picture when she suggests that "what is valued has increasingly become compliant employees who have the skills and knowledge to perform the job required without asking questions" (p. 1). Furthermore, there is cross-national agreement on the fact that the early childhood workforce is in peril, compounded by challenges such as incommensurate pay, workplace stress, and limited career opportunities (Cameron & Moss, 2020; Cumming et al., 2015).

6 Reciprocal *formazione* and collective care

However, we would rather not dwell on despair; instead, we join Cameron and Moss (2020) in sighting glimmers of hope arising from the devastation of the COVID-19 global pandemic, when "after years of derision and disregard, we have been reminded of the value of the social state, of collective action and of the caring professions" (Cameron & Moss, 2020, p. xv). Believing deeply in the possibility of transformative change, and recognising the urgency of such change, we caution that such possibilities in Reggio Emilia are premised on the construction of "an intelligent organisation[2]" (Dahlberg, in Cagliari et al., 2016, p. x); this focus on a coherent organisation enabled the experience of Reggio Emilia to elaborate a recognisable identity as a system, and hence to remake pedagogy whilst being deeply in tune with its times and always foreseeing possibilities for the future (Malaguzzi, in Cagliari et al., 2016).

Reciprocal *formazione* and collective care

We now delve deeper into our unease with the notion of "professionalism" as we offer two alternative intertwined concepts that emerged whilst writing and thinking with others – both Reggio Emilia educators and international scholars: *reciprocal formazione* and *collective care*. These concepts are introduced here in order to counter the powerful neoliberal discourse of professionalism, positioning ourselves within a new conceptual space that invites openness to other, different, and more democratic ways of thinking the roles and identities of teachers, *pedagogistas, atelieristas*, educational leaders, and educational systems.

Formazione: *amateur scholarship and teachers as intellectuals*

> How does the intellectual address authority? As a professional supplicant, or as its unrewarded amateurish conscience?
>
> *(Said, 1993)*

> Ours is the "profession of uncertainty", but life is a profession of uncertainty.
>
> *(Malaguzzi, 2021, p. 30)*

Our discomfort with the notion of professionalism can be traced back to nothing more occult than the undermining of teachers. This seemingly useful construct, intended to elevate the status of (mostly) women in an undervalued profession, has perversely led to educators being afforded the "status of specialized technicians within the school bureaucracy, whose function then becomes one of managing and implementing curricular programs" (Giroux, 2013, p. 461). Lack of trust in teachers, combined with a dominant managerial ethic, has led to professionalism itself being captured. Several decades ago, Said (1993) bemoaned that the greatest threat to intellectual life in our times comes from the attitude of "professionalism" and the ensuing expectations of "professional behaviour": "not rocking the boat, not straying outside the accepted paradigms or limits, making yourself marketable and above all presentable, hence uncontroversial and unpolitical and objective". In referring to his own discipline and to the risks of specialisation/professionalism within it, Said goes on to suggest that "to be a specialist in literature too often also means shutting out history, or music, or politics. In the end, as a fully specialised literary expert, you become tame and accepting of whatever the so-called leaders in the field will allow" (Said, 1993).

Loris Malaguzzi, also several decades ago, similarly lamented the risk of teachers being or becoming "melancholy implementers", beholden to "a school which talks and acts only on commission, thus neglecting its functions of critique and reform" (nd, as cited in Strozzi, 2014, p. 39 [our translation]). Paulo Freire (2005), of a similar time, despaired of teachers being "enslaved" and "domesticated" by "prepackaged educational materials produced by some experts in their offices to unequivocally demonstrate their authoritarianism" (p. 15). Melancholy, enslaved, tame, accepting, domesticated, marketable technicians and supplicants, shutting out the arts and politics and more; the scenario of teacher identity was/is dire indeed. Anthropologist Tim Ingold (2021b, p. 155) asks: "how, then, can we rescue intellectual life from the threat of its professionalisation?" He goes on to rely on Edward Said's notion of "amateurism": "the desire to be moved not by profit or reward but by love for and unquenchable interest in the larger picture, in making connections across lines and barriers, in refusing to be tied down to a speciality, in caring for ideas and values despite the restrictions of a profession" (Said, 1993). This to us seems to encapsulate many of the qualities of the work of the *pedagogista*, as illuminated in the words of Simona Bonilauri:

> The *pedagogista* – and the pedagogical coordination – has never been conceived as a specialist. Rather, the *pedagogista* takes many core aspects into consideration: organisational; managerial; pedagogical; cultural; social; and political. The *pedagogista* embraces all these functions and is not reduced to simply a technical role.
>
> *(Simona Bonilauri*, pedagogista[3], *interview with*
> *Stefania Giamminuti, Reggio Emilia)*

In considering the restrictions of the profession of educational leader elsewhere, it is likely that such varied connections across lines and barriers (pedagogical, managerial, cultural, political, and so forth) would be perceived as unrealistic, whilst caring for ideas and values might be seen an unattainable luxury. In Reggio Emilia instead this collective attitude of "amateur scholarship" (Ingold, 2021b, p. 153), informed by knowledge, interest, care, and curiosity, is of the essence in re-configuring professional roles within the system, and in re-imagining the meaning of education itself. Furthermore, the

8 Reciprocal *formazione* and collective care

notion of "amateur scholarship", with its focus on the ability to wander in mind and body, can contribute to unsettling dominant views on the role of research across all levels of pedagogical practice, for, as Ingold (2021b) laments, "professionalised regimes of research leave little room for wandering" (p. 153). In the chapters that follow, we narrate several experiences where teachers and children follow "the urge to wander along with that which captures their attention" (Ingold, 2021b, p. 153); this right to wander is of the essence in educational research and *progettazione*, and is overlooked in any rigid definition of professionalism, whether of an early childhood teacher or scholar.

We are aware together with Ingold (2021a) that "this appeal to amateurism is not without its pitfalls" (p. 11), and thus we caution that to welcome the concept of "amateur" into one's daily practice is not a concession to thoughtlessness. In fact, in our own co-author musings on welcoming this terminology, we shared dismay and concern at the direct translation of the term "amateur" into the Italian *dilettante*, which conjures unappealing prospects of educators being flippant, unqualified, and unprepared for the job at hand. Rather, in aligning the notion of amateur scholarship with the field of early childhood education and care, we wish to recognise as essential: educators' ethical commitment to resistance and political/professional activism (Fenech et al., 2010); their desire to be uncertain, to wander along lines of flight (Haraway, 2016); and their right to experience unease in research-practice (Giamminuti et al., 2021). Importantly, Ingold (2021a) refers to the "rigour" of amateurs, likening it to "a softer and more sympathetic approach, one that both answers to the call of the subject and is in turn answerable to it. The response is tinged with responsibility, curiosity with care" (p. 12). Amateur rigour, he goes on to qualify, "is flexible and in love with life, by contrast to the professional rigour that induces rigidity and paralysis" (Ingold, 2021a, p. 14).

We thus liken amateurism to an intellectual curiosity that is enamoured with learning and research; a right for teachers to call upon their knowledge in dialogue with others (adults, children, materials, places, non-humans), and to act with responsibility, care, and curiosity. In the words of teacher Francesca Forenzi: "our challenge is to maintain this curious gaze, this gaze that enables a different way of doing things" (interview with Stefania Giamminuti, Reggio Emilia). Therefore, rather than proposing an abstract notion of the *dilettante*, we engage with the concept of "an amateur scholarship that is both practically activist and potentially transformative" (Ingold, 2021b, p. 153), which in our view bears a strong relationship to the Italian notion of *mettersi in gioco*: literally, to "put oneself into play". No such term exists in English to convey this activist, experimental, transformative, and rigorous attitude to life and work, as *pedagogista* Elena Giacopini suggests:

> To create, but also to be able to see oneself again, to re-listen, re-think, to return to a context that can be similar but also different, and with the possibility of revisiting questions. This is to conceptualise experience.

Reciprocal *formazione* and collective care **9**

For adults, experience is to be able to return and reflect on what you have done, to discuss it again, to interpret and to re-think possibilities for where this might lead, and what else you might *mettere in gioco* [put into play]. And look, the terminology *mettersi in gioco* doesn't actually exist in many languages …

(Elena Giacopini, pedagogista, interview with Stefania Giamminuti, Reggio Emilia)

The experience of *mettersi in gioco* was frequently discussed in interviews with *pedagogistas, atelieristas,* and teachers, for whom transformative possibilities, rather than the strictures of a profession, were prerogatives:

For me, being a teacher within our *nidi* and *scuole dell'infanzia* allowed me to escape being defined, to be constantly growing within conditions of evolution, of openness, of dynamicity. And for me this was such an important value, for who I was and for my image of school, for how I intended to learn how to become a teacher. This possibility of *mettersi in gioco* all the time, to be able to transform, to ask myself questions, to make mistakes, to experiment, to measure myself within very diverse situations.

(Loredana Garofalo, teacher, interview with Stefania Giamminuti, Reggio Emilia)

What is evident here is not only the possibility of amateur scholarship that is inherent in the practice of *mettersi in gioco*, but also the fundamentally different positioning that *mettersi in gioco* presents to what is variously, in the dominant English educational discourse, called "training" or "professional development" or more specifically "continuous professional development". In critiquing the construct of continuous professional development, Moss (2018) refers to "formazione" in Reggio Emilia as "a process of self-formation […] of continuous evolution […] evolving is about responding unpredictably to contingencies, 'a-rythmic and discontinuous', rather than the 'uniform, regular advance' implied by 'development'" (p. 84). An attitude of *mettersi in gioco*, or of amateur scholarship, requires openness to challenges, tension towards bravery both individual and collective, that is inherent both in the notion of *formazione* and in the act of "playing", as opposed to the predictability and linearity of development.

Our preference for the term *formazione* in opposition to "professionalism" is not simply a virtuosity in wishing to retain the Italian term, though we admit to such a necessity as does Peter Moss himself, given the very unsatisfactory, laden, "narrow and prescriptive" (Moss, 2018, p. 84) English alternatives. Rather, our linguistic preference is a way of resisting the linearity, conformity, and obedience that both "professionalism" and "development" belie. As Said (1993) argues, "specialisation also kills your sense of excitement and discovery, both of which are irreducibly present in the intellectual's

10 Reciprocal *formazione* and collective care

makeup". Excitement and discovery are fundamental qualities of *mettersi in gioco*, as is evolution (evidenced in Loredana's words above), and valuing uncertainty and the unexpected:

"Formazione", from Malaguzzi's perspective, is an integral part of the everyday pedagogical work, an attitude of mind, a way of thinking and being, a part of life, an inseparable element of what it means to be an educator. Valuing uncertainty and wonder and with the concept of evolution in mind, Malaguzzi would have hoped for and welcomed surprising and unexpected consequences, the creation of thought, understandings and knowledge.

(Moss, 2018, p. 84)

Hence, we promote an image of teachers as public intellectuals, we choose *formazione* over professionalism, and we privilege amateur scholarship and *mettersi in gioco* in preference to the managerial strictures evoked by the concept of professionalism. We wish to reclaim for all early childhood educators the possibilities that arise from a more lively, transformative, and radical way of envisaging themselves:

The intellectual spirit as an amateur can enter and transform the merely professional routine most of us go through into something much more lively and radical. Instead of doing what one is supposed to do, one can ask why one does it, who benefits from it, how can it reconnect with a personal project and original thought.

(Said, 1993)

This lively intellectual spirit, its connection to a personal project, and the originality it entails are highlighted in the words of teacher Annalisa Rainieri:

I feel in constant transformation, in constant *formazione*, and it's beautiful. I love how you never feel as if you have arrived. I believe it is within our role, knowing that you have this responsibility of being in *formazione*, to study.

(Annalisa Rainieri, teacher, interview with Stefania Giamminuti, Reggio Emilia)

The practice of questioning, rather than doing what one is supposed to do, and of contributing to collective original thought, is evident also in teacher Lucia Colla's experience of constructing knowledge through *pensiero progettuale* and documentation:

Whether it is your own documentation or that of another colleague, or perhaps a *nido* sharing its documentation, you try to have that *progettuale* lens.

And here each one of us brings her own share of knowledge; knowledge that you have constructed through time by being part of this experience, but also theoretical knowledge, and also more often knowledge that has been generated within exchange with others.

(Lucia Colla, teacher, interview with Stefania
Giamminuti, Reggio Emilia)

Pedagogista Elena Giacopini emphasises that such knowledge is both personal and collective when she states that: "we are working towards the construction of a body of knowledge of a system" (interview with Stefania Giamminuti, Reggio Emilia). In relation to this practice of exchange and knowledge co-construction, teacher Annalisa Rainieri goes on to emphasise the need for intellectual curiosity: "I leave these research meetings with questions, then I go home and I start searching, it becomes a personal curiosity, you begin to follow exhibitions, it's a way to personally *mettersi in gioco*". (interview with Stefania Giamminuti, Reggio Emilia). Teacher Marina Castagnetti also aligns knowledge and curiosity with research and transformation: "if you welcome the importance of knowledge, of curiosity, the dimension of research should be constant, in order to respond to a world that is continually in transformation" (interview with Stefania Giamminuti, Reggio Emilia).

Our invitation to praise amateur scholarship in early childhood education and care is therefore far from an exhortation to reduce those working with young children to an unqualified workforce devoid of knowledge; in contrast, the image proposed is that of a teacher as intellectual, a lively, curious, inventive and knowledgeable researcher and radical activist intent on transformation of self and system, desirous to continuously *mettersi in gioco*. In the words of teacher Giulia Ovi: "a curious teacher, a teacher who is prepared to *mettersi in gioco*, a teacher who tries, who experiments" (interview with Stefania Giamminuti, Reggio Emilia).

Moss (2018) further clarifies that "for Malaguzzi 'formazione' is a means of enacting political choices and indeed also making and clarifying those choices" (p. 84). In fact, in a speech to the *Partito Comunista Italiano* (Italian Communist Party) Federation of Reggio Emilia in 1975, while advocating for greater universal access to the *scuole dell'infanzia*, Malaguzzi recognised that "the need for renewal requires the kind of teacher who is a new type of intellectual, a producer of knowledge and connected with organised social demands" (Cagliari et al., 2016, p. 210). As noted above, the traditional framework of professionalism instead privileges a tame individual who determinedly (or forcibly) eschews any engagement with politics. Rather, as Malaguzzi recognised and as Giroux (2013) suggests, "central to the category of public intellectual is the necessity of making the pedagogical more political and the political more pedagogical" (p. 463). Loredana (interview excerpt above) made clear in her memories that becoming a teacher in Reggio Emilia

12 Reciprocal *formazione* and collective care

meant "to escape being defined" and "to experiment"; this experience reflects a view of teachers "as public intellectuals [who] should develop a discourse that unites the language of critique with the language of possibility" (Giroux, 2013, p. 464).

Finally, as an alternative to melancholy, enslavement, tameness, and marketability, we propose activism, inventiveness, the production of knowledge, renewal, critique, political thought and action, liveliness, curiosity, possibilities, and openness to wandering – for all those working with young children. We now turn to emphasising that such hopeful alternatives are only possible when educators are not left on their own, for "the life of the intellect is carried on not in isolation but in a milieu that is intrinsically social – and not just social, I would add, but more widely ecological" (Ingold, 2021b, p. 160). In Reggio Emilia, this milieu is exemplified by the educational system, particularly in its tension towards collective care.

Obligation to care: a collective response

> Amateurism: literally, an activity that is fuelled by care and affection rather than by profit and selfish, narrow specialization.
>
> *(Said, 1993)*

> I think for me the greatest richness, as a teacher, has been to never feel lonely. I have not felt lonely from an intellectual point of view or from a cultural point of view, because I have always felt a sense of belonging not only to a *nido*, but also to a system and to a city.
>
> *(Manuela Pederzoli, teacher, interview with Stefania Giamminuti, Reggio Emilia)*

Reggio Emilia's tension towards collectivity and cooperation in education and civic life more broadly is exemplified by the words of former Mayor Graziano Delrio (2012) who states that: "we understand that the purpose of education is not related only to *you* but it is also related to *us* – to the community, to other people" (p. 84). We will return to this purpose, with a more intentionally political lens, later in the book when we discuss the value of the commons and an ethic of alliances.[4] What is important to us here is to frame both *formazione* and care as endeavours of collectivity, and hence to emphasise how in encountering this educational project one must be prepared to welcome a collectivist stance in daily educational thinkings and doings.

In the Prologue, we briefly introduced the question of our obligation towards care as a political, ethical, and affective act, and as a catalyst for engaging with the responsibility of imagining the possible in places other than Reggio Emilia. We wish to illuminate here how an underlying ethic of care renders a collectivist perspective – both in thought and action, in theory and practice – the premise for daily life in Reggio Emilia, where teachers like Manuela whom we quoted above (who has taught in a municipal *nido* for more than 30 years), and Marika (who taught in a *nido* for 15 years prior to becoming a *pedagogista*) never feel lonely:

> The other thing that is part of my history is to never ever be lonely. This collegial work with my colleagues, with the *pedagogista*, but with the system as well.
>
> *(Marika Lorenzani, teacher, interview with*
> *Stefania Giamminuti, Reggio Emilia)*

It is not by chance or simply by virtue of location that such lack of loneliness exists in the lives of these teachers. Rather, to eschew loneliness for teachers and *pedagogistas* is a determined organisational choice, a revolutionary one in the 1970s when Malaguzzi wrote, in a letter to a friend, of the decision to have two teachers together within each classroom "in a permanent break with the impossible and inhuman relations teachers have when they are left alone to experience problems, and the individualistic solitary schema that result" (Malaguzzi, in Cagliari et al., 2016, p. 223). Similarly, while in other Italian municipal contexts *pedagogistas* mostly act and think in solitude, in Reggio Emilia the organisational choice has been to enable the collective, thus safeguarding the system:

> The pedagogical coordination was never conceived as one person, it was always conceived as a group, with all its complexities, difficulties, and beauty. This dimension of *équipe* safeguards educational services, safeguards the system; no educational process can be done in solitude.
>
> *(Daniela Lanzi, pedagogista, interview with*
> *Stefania Giamminuti, Reggio Emilia)*

This unbounded capacity for collectivity, an antidote to the loneliness that affects so many teachers and educational leaders elsewhere, is enabled by the systemic nature of the educational project of Reggio Emilia, as evidenced in the words of Manuela, Marika, and Daniela. The system is alive, protagonist, competent interlocuter, and protected. In this sense the system is characterised by tension towards solidarity, ongoing responsibility to the historical roots of civil cooperation in the region of Emilia Romagna, commitment to collective organisational principles of collaboration, strenuous upholding of education as the common good, and unfaltering efforts towards participation. Collectivity is thus woven into experience and is felt and valued by all, including the *pedagogistas* who experience belonging to all *nidi* and *scuole dell'infanzia*: "my schools are my schools, the ones I coordinate directly. But when you enter another school, you never feel like a stranger, you always feel part of a context that is known to you" (Daniela Lanzi, *pedagogista*, interview with Stefania Giamminuti, Reggio Emilia).

14 Reciprocal *formazione* and collective care

We acknowledge that for those readers whose daily lives take place in cultural contexts that value individuality over collectivity, or profit over care, and whose daily experience of teaching and leading is more akin to loneliness, such an encounter with the experience of Reggio Emilia, and such a premise to their own work may appear an insurmountable barrier. As Maria Puig de la Bellacasa (2017) acknowledges, "relations of care are made more difficult when we are under the pressures of managerial and output-oriented time constrains" (p. 208). Such reciprocal relations of care would thus seem unimaginable in places where the construct of professionalism, with its image of tame teachers and its pressures for outputs in the form of obedient consumer children, holds unrelenting power over concepts such as amateurism and intellectual liveliness. However, we concur with scholars such as Puig de la Bellacasa (2017) and van Dooren (2014) who argue that care is more than a choice, it is an "immanent obligation".

Furthermore, in order to encounter the experience of Reggio Emilia not as a method to replicate, it is essential to engage in what Puig de la Bellacasa (2017) calls "a politics of speculative thinking", or "a commitment to seek what other worlds could be in the making through caring while staying with the trouble of our own complicities and implications" (p. 204). To be aware of one's own complicities and implications (both of self and context) is a premise to dialoguing with Reggio Emilia; hence we place this invitation here before we take the reader with us to the places our writing has brought us. There is an urgency felt by many early childhood educators to seek other worlds, or democratic alternatives (Fielding & Moss, 2011); this hope of transforming their own educational settings is often what drives those who visit Reggio Emilia once or multiple times. Imagining other worlds through the lens of care could bring closer the possibilities of re-making educational practices in relation with Reggio Emilia, for as Van Dooren (2014) notes, "the question is how placing care at the centre of our critical work might remake ourselves, our practices and our world" (p. 294).

We do not suppose that such an obligation is either easily understood or unproblematically shared, or in fact that it should be blindly applied. Rather, we acknowledge that care "remains an ongoing matter of struggle and a terrain of constant normative appropriation" (Puig de la Bellacasa, 2017, p. 8). Normative appropriation is most active in the field of early childhood education and "care" – where the construct of care is historically and culturally-contextually value-laden, predominantly associated with a highly gendered workforce of low status and little power, poor pay, and increasingly challenging working conditions within mostly dysfunctional systems (Cameron & Moss, 2020). Care in the early years is also invariably associated with the highly-contested construct of "quality" (Dahlberg et al., 2013; Elwick et al., 2018; Fenech et al., 2020; Giamminuti, 2013), with its powerful regulatory gaze and neo-liberal governing practices (Dahlberg, 2016). Moss (2016), in lamenting why we can't seem to get beyond it, conceptualises quality as "a technology of normalisation", "a technology of distance" and "a technology of regulation" (p. 10). He goes on to bemoan that under the influence of neoliberalism "our vocabulary has withered, limiting our capacity to imagine and talk about a different sort of society and a different sort of early childhood education" (Moss, 2016, p. 14). It is hence imperative for us to mention that far from providing a model of care, or offering simple solutions for collective caring, ours is an invitation to imagine a new vocabulary, to question what grounds everyday relations in early childhood settings, and to collectively strive towards transformative practice.

> We will need to ask "How to care?" in each situation, without necessarily giving to one way of caring a role "model" for others. It means too that as a doing, I look into caring as a transformative ethos rather than a normative ethics.
>
> *(Puig de la Bellacasa, 2017, p. 67)*

We offer no normative solutions in this book, but rather we propose the bold hope of embracing a transformative ethos in early childhood education and care beyond Reggio Emilia.

Conclusion: storying values and ethics

The chapters that follow convey fundamental values and ethics in the experience of Reggio Emilia, for "behind every school, there is a choice of values and ethics" (Dahlberg & Moss, 2005, p. 120). We choose to story values of *relationality, artfulness, culture,* and *the commons* in this book because of their capacity for summing up the character and aliveness of an educational system, whilst positing possibilities for other contexts. The choice to illuminate ethics meanwhile enables us to emphasise the situational stories of a place (Reggio Emilia) and its people, whilst welcoming uncertainty and eschewing judgements of others, wherever they may be, for as Massumi (2015) suggests, ethics "is completely situational. It's completely pragmatic" and furthermore "ethics is about how we inhabit uncertainty, together. It's not about judging each other right or wrong" (p. 11).

Environmental humanities scholar Deborah Bird Rose (2004) also emphasises that "while ethics can be talked about with some degree of abstraction, ethics are properly always situated" (p. 8). She goes on to suggest that "situatedness poses significant challenges for our New World societies. Our immersion in concepts of disconnection, our future-orientation, our seeming indifference to the losses that colonisation entail – these and other specificities of our way of conceptualising and actualising time and place ensure that ethics place particular, perhaps unique, demands upon us" (Bird Rose, 2004, p. 8). We are not intimidated by these demands; rather, we consider them essential

16 Reciprocal *formazione* and collective care

to a transformative view of education. In defining something as an ethic – in our case *dialectics, making, research*, and *alliances* – we intend to emphasise the need for an ethical response to the encounter with Reggio Emilia. Bird Rose (2022) cites philosopher Emmanuel Levinas when she notes that "to be enmeshed is to bear responsibility" (p. 5); for those who become enmeshed in the experience of Reggio Emilia, it is essential to bear responsibility for pedagogical, cultural, and organisational transformations.

While we expounded earlier on the notion of data, it is worth reiterating that we did not approach analysis through a traditional coding lens and that those concepts we grapple with as values and ethics do not reflect a thematic separation; they are in fact fundamentally inseparable, and we have wondered at times whether a value was an ethic, or an ethic was a value. Our values and ethics cannot really contain or close off meaning, they do not "describe" what is a complex and layered experience, and they are fundamentally available to rupture and re-thinking (St. Pierre, 2011). We do believe however that the international dialogues around how the experience of Reggio Emilia can propel new possibilities elsewhere (or make them inevitable) require rigorous debate, and that such values and ethics as we propose can be the catalyst for collective responses that are not predetermined, expected, or generalised. Such responses, led by an ethic of caring, might create situations whereby "a very small intervention might get amplified across the web of connections to produce large effects" (Massumi, 2015, p. 43). While this book concerns itself with local actions, we have every hope that these might produce large effects for the benefit of all those involved in the education and care of young children in places beyond our imagination.

Chapter 2, by Paola Cagliari, offers a historical, political, and cultural overview of Italian education and care systems, placing the role of the *pedagogista* within the broader context of the evolution of the Reggio Emilia experience. The chapter also invites a deeper understanding of *formazione* as permanent and reciprocal. Chapter 3, by Stefania Giamminuti, stories the value of relationality and an ethic of dialectics in Reggio Emilia, inviting an obligation to affect, solidarity, and participation elsewhere. Chapter 4, by Paola Strozzi, extends the discussion on the ethic of dialectics by relaying two fragments of everyday experiences in Reggio Emilia: the first illuminates dialectic decision-making around welcoming new children and families to the *scuola dell'infanzia*; and the second emphasises how *confronto* relies on offering differing points of view within a collegial space open to critique and solidarity.

Chapter 5, by Stefania Giamminuti, renders the inextricable connection between theory-practice-research that enlivens daily life in the municipal *nidi* and *scuole dell'infanzia*. In this chapter, *pensiero progettuale* is framed as both an "artful" (Manning, 2016) collective project, and as a praxis of "making" (Ingold, 2013). Chapter 6, by Paola Strozzi, illuminates the relationship between *pensiero progettuale,* research, and daily life by narrating in depth the lively experience of "setting the table" in the *Scuola dell'infanzia* Diana. This detailed documentation of learning emphasises the relational dynamics between the different professional roles in the working group of the *scuola dell'infanzia*, highlighting the practice of "relaunching". Chapter 7, by Stefania Giamminuti, considers the value of culture as a guiding question for further exploring the role of the *pedagogista* and for speculating how all educators in Reggio Emilia "come to know what they do" (Ingold, in Angosto Ferrandez, 2013, p. 299) by engaging in "correspondences" (Ingold, 2021a). Furthermore, the chapter conveys how an ethic of research as movement and experimentation permeates all aspects of daily life in Reggio Emilia.

Chapter 8, by Claudia Giudici, frames the experience of Reggio Emilia within the concept of *Education Commons*. The chapter brings the system to the fore, illuminating how political, pedagogical, and cultural choices have led to rendering a utopia concrete and emphasising the "unrenouncable strategy" of participation. Chapter 9, by Stefania Giamminuti, dwells further on the value of the commons, framing it within the overtly political stance of the educational project of Reggio Emilia and counterposing it to dominant marketplace views of early childhood education and care as a commodity. In conceptualising the alliances that give life to the everyday work of *pedagogistas*, this concluding chapter draws on the notion of "collective individuation" (Manning, 2013) and the concept of "always more than one" (Manning, 2013).

Our hope is that by storying our own research and by going with our writing places we ourselves might not have imagined, we may open possibilities and obligations for others to think anew the meaning of education in the places whence they come from. As Massumi (2015) contends, "there is no such thing as starting from scratch. Everything re-begins" (p. 51).

And so, we re-begin.

Notes

1 All participants in this research project provided signed informed consent and all adults approved the use of their full name in this book. Consent to utilise archival documentation, which we share in Chapters 4 and 6, was obtained from the Preschools and Infant-toddler Centres – Istituzione of the Municipality of Reggio Emilia and from the individuals involved. For the children who appear in this book, first names – original or non-original – have been used.
2 We will illustrate further the elements of what makes an intelligent organisation in Chapter 2.
3 It is important to note here that when the words of *pedagogistas, atelieristas,* and teachers have been cited in this book, their role is recorded as it was at the time of the event (research interview or *aggiornamento*). Several years have passed in the writing of this book, and roles may have changed and evolved, with some moving into institutional roles, others retiring, and others moving from teacher roles to teacher educator or *pedagogista* roles. We believed it was more coherent and respectful to cite the roles at the time the contribution was offered.
4 Chapters 8 and 9.

References

Angosto Ferrandez, L. F. (2013). Ways of living: Tim Ingold on culture, biology and the anthropological task. *Revista De Antropología Iberoamericana, 8*(3), 285–302. https://doi.org/10.11156/aibr.080302e

Arndt, S., Urban, M., Murray, C., Smith, K., Swadener, B., & Ellegaard, T. (2018). Contesting early childhood professional identities: A cross-national discussion. *Contemporary Issues in Early Childhood, 19*(2), 97–116. https://doi.org/10.1177/1463949118768356

Bird Rose, D. (2004). *Reports from a wild country: Ethics for decolonisation.* University of New South Wales Press.

Bird Rose, D. (2022). *Shimmer: Flying fox exuberance in worlds of peril.* Edinburgh University Press.

Cagliari, P., Castagnetti, M., Giudici, C., Rinaldi, C., Vecchi, V., & Moss, P. (Eds.). (2016). *Loris Malaguzzi and the schools of Reggio Emilia: A selection of his writings and speeches, 1945–1993.* Routledge.

Cameron, C., & Moss, P. (Eds.). (2020). *Transforming early childhood in England: Towards a democratic education.* UCL Press.

Cumming, T., Sumsion, J., & Wong, S. (2015). Rethinking early childhood workforce sustainability in the context of Australia's early childhood education and care reforms. *International Journal of Child Care and Education Policy, 9*(2), 1–15. https://doi.org/10.1007/s40723-015-0005-z https://doi.org/10.1007/s40723-015-0005-z

Dahlberg, G. (2016). An ethico-aesthetic paradigm as an alternative discourse to the quality assurance discourse. *Contemporary Issues in Early Childhood, 17*(1), 124–133. https://doi.org/10.1177/1463949115627910

Dahlberg, G., & Moss, P. (2005). *Ethics and politics in early childhood education.* Routledge.

Dahlberg, G., Moss, P., & Pence, A. (2013). *Beyond quality in early childhood education and care: Languages of evaluation.* Routledge.

Delrio, G. (2012). Our responsibility toward young children and toward their community. In C. Edwards, L. Gandini, & G. Forman (Eds.), *The hundred languages of children: The Reggio Emilia experience in transformation* (pp. 81–88). Praeger.

Duhn, I. (2010). 'The centre is my business': Neo-liberal politics, privatisation and discourses of professionalism in New Zealand. *Contemporary Issues in Early Childhood, 11*(1), 49–60. https://doi.org/10.2304/ciec.2010.11.1.49

Elwick, A., Osgood, J., Robertson, L., Sakr, M., & Wilson, D. (2018). In pursuit of quality: Early childhood qualifications and training policy. *Journal of Education Policy, 33*(4), 510–525. https://doi.org/10.1080/02680939.2017.1416426

Fenech, M., Harrison, L. J., Press, F., & Sumsion, J. (2020). Using metaphor to illuminate quality in early childhood education. *Australasian Journal of Early Childhood* (2), 197–210. https://doi.org/10.1177/1836939120918482

Fenech, M., Sumsion, J., & Shepherd, W. (2010). Promoting early childhood teacher professionalism in the Australian context: The place of resistance. *Contemporary Issues in Early Childhood, 11*(1), 89–105. https://doi.org/10.2304/ciec.2010.11.1.89

Fielding, M., & Moss, P. (2011). *Radical education and the common school: A democratic alternative.* Routledge.

Freire, P. (2005). *Teachers as cultural workers: Letters to those who dare to teach.* Westview Press.

Giamminuti, S. (2013). *Dancing with Reggio Emilia: Metaphors for quality*. Pademelon Press.

Giamminuti, S., Merewether, J., & Blaise, M. (2021). Aesthetic-ethical-political movements in professional learning: Encounters with feminist new materialisms and Reggio Emilia in early childhood research. *Professional Development in Education*, *7*(2–3), 436–448. https://doi.org/10.1080/19415257.2020.1862277

Giroux, H. (2013). Neoliberalism's war against teachers in dark times. *Cultural Studies - Critical Methodologies*, *13*, 458–468. https://doi.org/10.1177/1532708613503769

Giroux, H. (2014). When schools become dead zones of the imagination: A critical pedagogy manifesto. *Policy Futures in Education*, *12*(4), 491–499. https://doi.org/10.2304/pfie.2014.12.4.491

Haraway, D. (2016). *Staying with the trouble: Making kin in the Chthulucene*. Duke University Press.

Ingold, T. (2013). *Making: Anthropology, archaeology, art and architecture*. Routledge.

Ingold, T. (2021a). *Correspondences*. Polity Press.

Ingold, T. (2021b). In praise of amateurs. *Ethnos: Journal of Anthropology*, *86*(1), 153–172. https://doi.org/10.1080/00141844.2020.1830824

Lather, P. (2013). Methodology-21: What do we do in the afterward? *International Journal of Qualitative Studies in Education*, *26*(6), 634–645. https://doi.org/10.1080/09518398.2013.788753

Lazzari, A. (2012). Reconceptualising professionalism in early childhood education: Insights from a study carried out in Bologna. *Early Years: An International Research Journal*, *32*(3), 252–265.

Malaguzzi, L. (1971). La nuova socialità del bambini e dell'insegnante attraverso la esperienza della gestione sociale nelle scuole dell'infanzia. La gestione sociale nella scuola dell'infanzia, Modena.

Malaguzzi, L. (2021). *Design/Progettazione in infant-toddler centres and preschools: Research open to wonder, between the possible, probable, and unpredictable*. Reggio Children.

Manning, E. (2013). *Always more than one: Individuation's dance*. Duke University Press.

Manning, E. (2015). Against method. In P. Vannini (Ed.), *Non-representational methodologies: Re-envisioning research* (pp. 52–71). Routledge.

Manning, E. (2016). *The minor gesture*. Duke University Press.

Massumi, B. (2015). *Politics of affect*. Polity Press.

Moss, P. (2010). We cannot continue as we are: The educator in an education for survival. *Contemporary Issues in Early Childhood*, *11*(1), 8–19. https://doi.org/10.2304/ciec.2010.11.1.8

Moss, P. (2016). Why can't we get beyond quality? *Contemporary Issues in Early Childhood*, *17*(1), 8–15. https://doi.org/10.1177/1463949115627895

Moss, P. (2018). What might Loris Malaguzzi have to say? *European Journal of Education*, *53*(1), 82–85. https://doi.org/10.1111/ejed.12256

Ortlipp, M., Arthur, L., & Woodrow, C. (2011). Discourses of the early years learning framework: Constructing the early childhood professional. *Contemporary Issues in Early Childhood*, *12*(1), 56–70.

Osgood, J. (2006). Deconstructing professionalism in early childhood education: Resisting the regulatory gaze. *Contemporary Issues in Early Childhood*, *7*(1), 5–14. https://doi.org/10.2304/ciec.2006.7.1.5

Puig de la Bellacasa, M. (2017). *Matters of care: Speculative ethics in more than human worlds*. University of Minnesota Press.

Said, E. (1993). *Professionals and Amateurs*. The Reith lectures 1993: Representations of the intellectual. http://palestine.mei.columbia.edu/said/edward-said-lectures

Sims, M. (2017). Neoliberalism and early childhood. *Cogent Education, 41*(1). https://doi.org/10.1080/2331186X.2017.1365411

St. Pierre, E. A. (2011). The critique and the coming after. In N. K. Denzin, & Y. S. Lincoln (Eds.), *The Sage handbook of qualitative research* (pp. 611–625). Sage.

St. Pierre, E. A. (2018). Writing post qualitative inquiry. *Qualitative Inquiry, 24*(9), 603–608. https://doi.org/10.1177/1077800417734567

St. Pierre, E. A. (2021a). Post qualitative inquiry, the refusal of method, and the risk of the new. *Qualitative Inquiry, 27*(1), 3–9. https://doi.org/10.1177/1077800419863005

St. Pierre, E. A. (2021b). Why post qualitative inquiry? *Qualitative Inquiry, 27*(2), 163–166. https://doi.org/10.1177/1077800420931142

Strozzi, P. (2014). I nidi e le scuole dell'infanzia come luogo della ricerca e del pensiero progettuale: Appunti per una ricostruzione storica dell'idea e della pratica della progettazione. *Bambini* Marzo, (3), 39–42.

Urban, M. (2008). Dealing with uncertainty: Challenges and possibilities for the early childhood profession. *European Early Childhood Education Research Journal, 16*(2), 135–152.

Urban, M. (2010). Rethinking professionalism in early childhood: Untested feasibilities and critical ecologies. *Contemporary Issues in Early Childhood, 11*(1), 1–7. https://doi.org/10.2304/ciec.2010.11.1.1

Urban, M., Vandenbroeck, M., Van Laere, K., Lazzari, A., & Peeters, J. (2012). Toward competent systems in early childhood education and care. Implications of policy and practice. *European Journal of Education, 47*(4) 508–526.

van Dooren, T. (2014). Care: Living lexicon for the environmental humanities. *Environmental Humanities, 5*, 291–294.

van Dooren, T., & Bird Rose, D. (2016). Lively ethography: Storying animist worlds. *Environmental Humanities, 8*(1), 77–94. https://doi.org/10.1215/22011919-3527731

2

RECIPROCAL *FORMAZIONE* IN REGGIO EMILIA

Paola Cagliari
Translated by Jane McCall

Introduction

The *formazione* that gives us the title of this chapter is an indispensable action for the qualification of educational services (0–3 years) and schools (3–6 years). Until the 1960s, *formazione* fundamentally took place at the start of people's working lives, making it possible to obtain the necessary qualification to teach in various levels of school. This corresponded to a conception of knowledge as static, and of learning as consequent on teaching. In the 1970s, in the climate of cultural, social, and scientific renewal that defined the era, UNESCO produced the "Learning to Be" Report (Faure et al., 1972), and proposed the concept of *formazione permanente* or "permanent" lifelong learning that would prove fundamental in all social and working environments. Reggio Emilia's municipal *scuole dell'infanzia*, in search of a new cultural, social, and pedagogical identity from the start, had posited permanent *formazione* as a fundamental lever, and this imposed the need to organise structurally, introducing a role into the staff scheme that would be its guarantor: the *pedagogista*.

In this chapter, we would like to propose some broad cultural, political, and social arguments to frame the role of the *pedagogista* in Reggio Emilia's experience, offering a deeper understanding of *formazione* as not only permanent but also reciprocal. We begin by briefly outlining the administrative structure of a decentralised Italian state, and certain distinctive aspects of education and instruction in Italy, describing, albeit synthetically, the national, regional, and city contexts in which the *pedagogista* operates. As authors we feel this framework to be necessary; in fact, no professional role can be defined without reference to its own micro (local) and macro (national) contexts. We also feel it is important to provide a brief introduction to the role of the *pedagogista* in Europe, and the development it had in Italy in the initial experience of

DOI: 10.4324/9781003181026-2

22 Reciprocal *formazione* in Reggio Emilia

municipal *scuole dell'infanzia* in certain northern and central Italian regions, and how it then continued on specific pathways in various areas of Italy and in other international contexts. In particular, we will discuss Emilia Romagna, which as well as being the region in which the city of Reggio Emilia is located, is also the region that developed and contributed most to elaborating and expanding the role of pedagogical coordinator. This, in fact, is the term many regional laws have used to denominate the professional role. From the start, the name used for the role in Reggio Emilia was, instead, *pedagogista*, for reasons that will become clearer as we proceed with our arguments.

All this information is intended to allow readers to assign a fuller, more precise meaning to the terms *pedagogista* and reciprocal *formazione* in the context of the Reggio Emilia experience, which will be discussed in the latter part of the chapter, and to terms related to concepts and organisation introduced in Chapter 1: the relation between theory, practice, and research; the tension towards collective care; "systemic, democratic and political" (Urban, 2010, p. 5) professionalism; "competent systems" (Urban et al., 2012); ethical commitment and transformative ethics.

The Italian education and schooling system

The Italian state and administrative decentralisation

Administrative decentralisation is a fundamental and democratic principle in Italy, enshrined in the Constitution, the purpose of which is to enable effective participation of the collectivity in the exercise and care of all possible aspects of public life. Local Authorities have decentralised powers, but these are coordinated in a balanced and non-hierarchical way with the interests of the State. Italy therefore presents with strongly pluralist institutions, although they are regulated by coordination mechanisms that tie their autonomy to a coherent vision. In local governments, both regional and municipal, a president (region) or mayor (municipality), both directly elected by the people, are the heads of a *giunta* or cabinet made up of city (or regional) *assessori* or officers who could be defined as the equivalent of ministers in a central government, and who are entrusted with *assessore* offices with specific tasks, including schools, public works, welfare, budget, and so on. Simplifying, we might say that the regional legislative assembly or the municipal council, which have functions of steering and supervision, are local counterparts of national parliament.

Compulsory schooling

Italy's school system includes a compulsory period of ten years (from 6 to 16 years). Compulsory school in Italy is free, as laid down in article 34 of the Constitution. Coherent with school provision laid down in the Constitution, the Italian state has provided for the building of a universal state school system. Non-state schools are a small percentage of the compulsory school sector and may have parity status, or be private. Parity or "equivalent" schools have a public function and issue qualifications with the same legal value as those given by state schools.[1] However, private schools are not part of the system of instruction, do not receive state funding, and issue qualifications without legal value. The employment of staff in state schools is guaranteed through public competitions that take into consideration qualifications (years of study and of school service) and exams (one written and one oral usually). The assignment of teaching posts and transfers is managed through league tables in which the main criterion is the score for years of service.

In-service *formazione* is a complex and articulated issue for state schools of every kind and age level, and has undergone different phases. In-service *formazione* has generally been oriented, with varying degrees of emphasis, by voluntary engagement, individuality and pay over and above the normal salary, and linked to the possibility of career development. Although it has been considered a teacher's right and responsibility since 1974, only recently has it been the focus of planning with related funding, by a *Collegio Docenti*[2] (Teachers' Board) in each *Istituto Comprensivo*[3] (Comprehensive Institute) and therefore an integral part of qualifying their *Piano della Offerta Formativa*[4] (Educational Offer Plan). Moreover, state school staffing does not include roles with a pedagogical background or function.

0–3 educational services and 3–6 scuole dell'infanzia[5]

Italy's integrated system of education and instruction for 0–6 years was instituted in 2017 by decree-law 65 and has a different history to the rest of the school system, which explains its different complexities and iterations. Educational services for 0- to 3-year olds were established by law 1044/1971 which gave regions the task of designing networks of services in their territories, defining the general criteria for building, running, and supervising their *asili nido* (as they were called at the time), and distributing State funds to their various municipalities, which were then entrusted with building and running the services. Law 1044/1971 considered spending for 0–3 services to be part of the Ministry of Health's budget. After changes in legislation the services passed first to the Ministry of Employment and then to the Ministry for Families. In 2017 the 0–3 services were definitively assigned to the Ministry for Instruction after approval of decree 65.

For almost 50 years (from 1971 to 2017), 0–3 educational services developed above all in regions of northern and central Italy where municipalities were committed to directly managing them, accompanied by actions on the part of other, private, bodies who, through public bids in which they compete

24 Reciprocal *formazione* in Reggio Emilia

by presenting a pedagogical project and organisational and financial plan, take responsibility for running a *nido*, and are allocated premises, furnishings, and funds by the municipality. A Convention[6] or agreement of this kind, has a duration of three years, and is renewable for up to six, after which a new bidding process must be announced. Conducting educational services in this way is called "indirect management by a local authority" (*gestione indiretta dell'Ente Locale*). In regions where there is a shortage of places and demand cannot be met, which happens mostly in the south of Italy, private providers work by the municipality's side, and sometimes even replace it. The percentage of children aged 0–3 currently attending educational services in Italy is 24.7%, and 51% of all provision is accounted for by public ownership. The educational system for children aged 3–6 years has roots that go further back and comprises:

- Private schools with a Catholic orientation, which were already operating at the end of the 1800s in Italy.
- Municipally managed schools established in the late 1950s, after initial projects from the 1900s were closed down under Fascist rule in the 1930s.
- State schools, the most prevalent in Italy today, instituted in 1968 after law 444 was passed.

Periodically gathered data describes a situation that is articulated in the following way:

> The *scuola dell'infanzia* is widespread throughout Italy and with 94.4% of all 4-year-olds attending falls just short of the objectives defined in the European Strategic Framework (ET2020). The majority of provision at this age is delivered directly through the State, is part of the national framework of school administration, and was attended by 63% of students aged 3–6 years in the year 2017–2018, flanked by municipally run schools (9%), and parity-status private schools (28%).
>
> (*Gruppo di lavoro per la Convenzione sui diritti dell'Infanzia e dell'Adolescenza, 2020, p. 135, [translated by Jane McCall]*)

Italy's system of education and instruction for children aged 0–6 is therefore made up of a plurality of providers, who can elaborate their educational projects autonomously, within the limits dictated by general standards. Providers therefore bring differences with them that can become an added richness for collaboratively working on projects when they come together as part of one dialogue, or are integrated, which is what has happened in Reggio Emilia's experience and what is laid down in decree 65/2017. Every municipality that has the responsibility of supervision on schools' compliance with the requested parameters is responsible for this integration. The municipality of Reggio Emilia has fully developed its cultural autonomy, as laid out in the national Constitution, developing a unique educational, cultural, and political project, and directly managing a significant network of 0–6 educational services, of *nidi* and *scuole dell'infanzia*. These two conditions have made it possible for the municipality to respect differences, while growing the function of supervision into a tool for raising quality through the system, and offering other 0–6 city schools the cultural references, knowledge, and lived experience gained through its experience of direct management.

To conclude, the Italian system of education and instruction is public but includes several private providers, particularly for children aged 0–6. Public authorities (the State, the Regions, the Municipalities) coordinate policies for education and schooling, and evaluate compliance with the quality parameters that are used to define whether an entity is eligible to belong to the system, or not, and the consequent funding.

0–3 educational services and 3–6 scuole dell'infanzia *directly managed by municipalities: constraints on employment*

Municipalities are an expression of the Italian Republic, and as such are subject to laws on matters of staff costs, qualifications, permanent and non-permanent employment contracts, inclusion of staff in contract categories and their related salaries, overtime, and production awards. The public nature of municipalities therefore makes their autonomous management of *nidi* and *scuole dell'infanzia* subject to certain legislative limits, established by parliament and the ministries (of Instruction, Finance, Interior, and so on). This requires directors to identify non-financial forms of professional recognition or career development, and the people who work in them to pay attention not only to the pedagogical dimension, but also to the political dimension, keeping them connected in dialogues they develop during *progettazione*, and in meetings of *formazione* and participation. Educational services for 0- to 3-year olds and *scuole dell'infanzia* directly managed by municipalities must comply with similar laws on staff employment as those for state services: cooks, auxiliaries, teachers, *atelieristas*, and *pedagogistas* cannot be recruited directly but must go through public competitions or exams with scores for qualifications. Qualifications for professionals in *nidi* and *scuole dell'infanzia* have been defined by different laws at different times, but we only see a framework for defining progressive qualifications consistent with roles and positions in the staff structure with the budget law of 2017.

For auxiliary staff,[7] the completion of compulsory schooling is required; for the role of cook, a secondary school leaving diploma; for educators in 0–3 services, a three-year degree in Sciences of Education (since 2019); and for *scuola dell'infanzia* teachers, a five-year degree in Sciences of *Formazione* (since 2001). This last degree is valid for *scuola dell'infanzia* and elementary school. Previous to these dates it was sufficient for *nido* and *scuola dell'infanzia* teachers to have a three-, four-, or five-year diploma from a secondary high school.

26 Reciprocal *formazione* in Reggio Emilia

For the role of *atelierista* (not included in state legislation), a secondary school leaving diploma or a degree is required, both in the arts.

The state only began to legislate on qualifications for the profession of *pedagogista* in the 2017 budget law. Previous to this date the only reference was the regional law on the *nido*. Currently, *pedagogistas* are required to have a *magistrale* degree (a two-year masters level specialisation after completing a first-level degree) in one of the following courses: programming and management of educational services, adult education sciences and continuous *formazione*, pedagogical sciences, theories and methodologies of e-learning and media education. The *pedagogista's formazione* is dependent on achieving appropriate educational knowledge, abilities ("skills"), and competencies ("responsibility" and "autonomy") at level 7 of the European Qualifications Framework for lifelong learning (European Commission, 2018, pp. 18–19).

Clarifying the term pedagogy

At this point we feel some clarification is needed on the term that gives us the name *pedagogista*: "pedagogy", a term that is frequently misunderstood and used less and less frequently in the Italian academy for its descriptions of study courses (as readers will have noticed in descriptions of qualifications required for staff in *nidi* and *scuole dell'infanzia*). Piero Crispiani, professor of general didactics and special pedagogy at the University of Macerata, notes that in the late 1980s:

> Pedagogy was affected by the more international movement of disaggregation in the direction of "Educational sciences" […] which in the 1970s and 1980s positioned a fragile epistemological image of pedagogy, with a fragmentation of related *formazione*. Pedagogy remained as an indistinct discipline, separated from the [various] "educations" and other professional forms, vaguely nudged towards being a sub-heading in a disciplinary specialism. It was inevitably subjected to the invasiveness of other disciplines such as psychology and sociology.
>
> *(Crispiani, 2017, pp. 124–125, [translated by Jane McCall])*

Losing the term pedagogy was accompanied by a process of emphasis on the pragmatic aspects of education, on quantitative evaluations of learning, and the priority of teaching disciplines as opposed to reflections on human identity, human rights, and potentials in various phases of development, and the dynamics of relations and communication. There was a celebration of the technical, and a rejection of the philosophical. These words of Loris Malaguzzi might be useful for us to counter this culture of simplification:

> We need to accept and consciously go in the direction of complicating our themes. Primarily I think this is a question of habit, style, and merit. […]

I believe complication to be a very civilized term, with a high degree of rigour. Complication in the sense of no longer accepting reductions, or imaginary, illusory simplifications of situations that are part of our reality, instead trying to face them with our capabilities in very pragmatic terms, with precise and timely readings, with the capacity for accessing our tools of intelligence and the orientation of our politics and ideals, the capacity for interpreting, in constant and timely ways, what direction facts and events are taking. [...] We need to read more, read the meaning of life more closely, and shifts that are taking place in individual subjectivities and the great objectivity of things: large things, large changes, large questions, and large worries that accompany our reflections and attempt at reasoning in these times.

(Malaguzzi, 2021, pp. 15–16)

We will return later to Reggio Emilia's experience, and how it opted for the primacy of pedagogy.

Pedagogista, équipe pedagogica, coordinators, and pedagogical coordination

Brief historical notes on the profession of pedagogista

The role of the *pedagogista* has deep roots, referencing names sometimes known to the general public, such as Jean-Marc Gaspard Itard, Edouard Seguin, Ferrante Aporti, Frederick Froebel, and Maria Montessori: intellectuals who, from the 17th to the early 20th century, worked with education for children over the age of three, or with institutions for children with cognitive, psychological and physical difficulties. Their experiences "highlight the constant and untiring commitment *pedagogistas* have always held towards people in difficult conditions, and are a clear example of the knowledge, abilities and openness that this professional must be acknowledged with" (Pesci & Bruni, 2006, p. 24, [translated by Jane McCall]). In the early 1900s, the pedagogical-medical institutes run privately, or by charitable institutes, and later affiliated through conventions with the ministry for public instruction and the universities, included the presence of *pedagogistas*, as did the psycho-pedagogical medical centres[8] opened by municipalities 40 years later.

Through their professionalism *pedagogista*s, have [...] always occupied important roles in structures for education, re-education, and rehabilitation, such as medical-pedagogical and medical psycho-pedagogical institutes. They worked as the directors of welfare institutes, were called up as affiliated specialists in rehabilitation and training centres, given positions in

28 Reciprocal *formazione* in Reggio Emilia

public services such as municipalities, and in private organisations, as independent consultants.

(Pesci & Bruni, 2006, p. 52, [translated by Jane McCall])

In terms of educational institutions for children aged 3–6, the *pedagogista*s who chose to work with them founded schools in which their ideas could be applied, places where they could refine their ideas and evolve them. This is how the Froebel and Montessori methods, to name but a few, came to be developed.

Pedagogical coordinators of early childhood services: the genesis of a profession

The role of the pedagogical coordinator dates back to the 1960s and the establishment of early childhood educational services by municipalities. The opening of the first municipally-managed *scuole dell'infanzia* in the late 1950s and early 1960s was a significant challenge for local administrations. Urged by the women's movements this commitment was an affirmation of municipal provision in the field of education for under six-year-olds, an area that had always belonged exclusively to the Catholic world, and anticipated the State legislation that only arrived in 1968 after many vicissitudes. Faced with the necessity of managing these new institutions, the municipalities took one of two different paths. The first was that of "entrusting a completely new administrative post to a municipal employee with, by chance, a past as an educator in the services, or a background in pedagogy or psychology" (Musatti & Mayer, 2003, p. 19).

The second path, mostly pursued in the capital cities of provinces in the Emilia Romagna region, was to ask the principals of elementary schools, or prominent figures in the world of pedagogy, to direct the new schools: "these administrators and experts [who] were distinguished by their solid social and political ideals, their great educational and cultural tension, and their profound humanity" (Campioni, 2003, p. 33, [translated by Jane McCall]) committed personally to breathing life into networks of services (*scuole dell'infanzia*, and then in the early 1970s *nidi*) that responded to women's need for emancipation, while at the same time offering experiences of progressive democratic education to children. The contribution made by these *pedagogistas* was that of constructing schools with high pedagogical value going beyond the idea of the then *asilo nido*. They were Loris Malaguzzi in Reggio Emilia, and for a short time in Modena, Bruno Ciari in Bologna, Enea Bernardi in Rimini, Duilio Santarini, and later Giancarlo Cerini in Forlì, to name but a few.

[These] personalities had the capacity to envision new worlds and realities with non-banal perspectives (Bruno Ciari used to say, "It is always necessary to have something to 'fight' for, and not something simple and easy") strongly rooted in the local area: characters who invented the role of coordinator, or better, of the "non-bureaucratic school director", which was the first step towards the role of coordinator.

(Campioni, 2003, p. 33, [translated by Jane McCall])

The 1960s were a period of great ferment. Returning to the innovative ideas first proposed by authors such as Friedrich Fröbel and sisters Carolina and Rosa Agazzi in the late 1800s, and Maria Montessori, John Dewey, and Célestin Freinet in more recent years, these new *pedagogistas*, through their *confronto* with the Movement of Cooperative Education,[9] the CEIS (Centro Educativo Italo Svizzero)[10] founded by Margherita Zoebeli in Rimini, Gianni Rodari,[11] Ada Gobetti,[12] and others, and the idea of child being revealed in Piaget's work, situated all this thinking within the country's re-birth, trusted in the values of a democratic and participatory society and "in the absence of a history in the Italian context of educational *nidi* or *scuole dell'infanzia* that were not of a charitable or scholastic nature" (Campioni, 2003, p. 34, [translated by Jane McCall]), breathed life into a pedagogy that was active, democratic, and secular. All this constructed experiences that are:

> an exemplary case of management close to services for the people, of modalities and journeys through which an efficient management of the public sector can be effected in offering quality services. The early childhood education sector is one in which the cultural implications of creating policies are more obvious, and in which the concept of quality immediately has a broader connotation, that goes beyond satisfying user needs, and expands out into *social quality*.
>
> *(Musatti & Mayer, 2003, pp. 17–18, [translated by Jane McCall])*

Almost all municipalities, particularly those without a stable charismatic figure, entrusted the pedagogical framework of these schools and *formazione* of the teachers to universities, and for many of them *formazione* has remained assigned to universities. This first phase, situated in the cultural background described, and which mainly involved certain regions in the north and centre of Italy that include Emilia Romagna and Tuscany, later led, after the 1971 law on the *nido d'infanzia*, to the unfolding of very different stories.

The role of coordinator and the birth of pedagogical coordinations

The decision by municipalities to make pedagogical coordination part of their organisation, and the construction of the role of pedagogical coordinator as part of the municipal staff, was taken at different times, from municipality to municipality. The municipalities of capital cities in the various provinces in the Emilia Romagna region established their own pedagogical coordination

30 Reciprocal *formazione* in Reggio Emilia

during the 1970s, though this took place at different times and with different characteristics. In other regions in the north and centre of Italy –Tuscany, Umbria, Lombardy, and others – the capital municipalities of provinces moved in a similar direction. Research by Musatti and Mayer (2003) attests that only 8 of Italy's 22 regions mention pedagogical coordination or pedagogical coordinators in their regional laws on the *nido*. As well as graduates in pedagogical disciplines or similar (psychology, sociology, literature, etc.), educators and teachers with several years of experience also qualified for the profession and were allocated to carrying out the role on a temporary or alternating basis. This latter choice was criticised because it was considered to be a loss of knowledge and continuity of experience for coordination.

In all the regions, and in almost all the municipalities (including those in Emilia Romagna), educational services for children aged 0–3 came under the city office for welfare, in a similar way to organisation in the national ministries, while *scuole dell'infanzia* came under the city office for schools. A consequence of this was that where regional legislation required the establishment of the role of coordinator for children aged 0–3, smaller municipalities also gave this person coordination of the *scuole dell'infanzia*. In larger municipalities two distinct coordinations were created, one for 0–3 years, and one for 3–6 years. However, these answered to different management and to different city offices. At the time of writing, the situation, even in Emilia Romagna, is still organised in this way, despite the approval of legislation in 2005 instituting an "Integrated System of 0–6 Education and Instruction" and assigning both the 0–3 educational services and the *scuole dell'infanzia* to the Ministry of Instruction. In 1984 a conference of the Permanent National Work and Study Group on the *Asili Nido*[13] dedicated a session to the role of the *pedagogista*. In her speech, Umbrian *pedagogista* Laura Cipollone (1984) analyses (although not in a systematic way) the functions of *pedagogistas* and the problems they encounter in their work; she outlines a complex professional role at the intersection between municipal administrations and individual 0–3 educational services and *scuole dell'infanzia*, whose autonomous decision-making powers and responsibilities are not precisely or clearly defined:

> Significant problems related to the bureaucratic apparatus of local authorities have been raised in regards to the decision making of coordinators, because often it is impossible for them to carry out the function of activating decisions, for reasons of institutional rigidity and the difficulty of connecting knowledge with actions.
>
> *(Cipollone, 1984, p. 57, [translated by Jane McCall])*

Cipollone (1984) also comments on the difficulty coordinators experience in detaching from the role of director, leading in many cases to the activation of "direction models more attentive to checking and supervision, and less dialectical both towards workers and towards the direction of administrative policy" (p. 57, [translated by Jane McCall]), while underscoring that the complexity of the role requires "a continuity of the coordinator's presence, a condition often not met given that working conditions are not homogeneous" (p. 57, [translated by Jane McCall]).

Significant changes were introduced in the 1990s. The Public Administration Reform of 1993 created a clear separation between political and administrative powers, and gave managers direct personal responsibility for achieving objectives, defining projects and the transparency of procedures, through autonomy in spending, organisation of human and instrumental resources, and supervision. This caused a shift of attention and responsibility in the coordinating bodies, from cultural aspects only, to administration and managerial aspects. In 1997 law 285, "Dispositions for the promotion of rights and opportunities for childhood and adolescence", led to a new era in 0–3 educational services by allocating early childhood socio-educational services with funds for experimentation and innovation, both in terms of new forms of organisation (attending occasionally, weekly, monthly, a few hours a day, packages of hours, and so on) and from a managerial point of view. With this prospect local authorities were given a role prevalently of systems governance, underscoring how residual the role of direct management has become.

In a country where the *nido* had been instituted in 1971 with law 1044, but only developed in a few regions, offering the possibility of creating less onerous structures in terms of cost and organisation, these new dispositions and consequent funding oriented the policy of several municipalities and suggested a re-think of the pedagogical coordinator's role. A role no longer tied to the pedagogical themes of *nidi* and *scuole* but with a more social leaning, in socio-educational services such as children-parent centres (*centri bambini e genitori*), play spaces (*spazi gioco*) games rooms (*ludoteche*), all gathered under the name of integrated services and mostly run by private entities in conventions with the local authority, with age groups beyond 0–6. Although consensus for the legislation was high, there was also concern for educational policies and some dissent. In one of many conferences dedicated to pedagogical coordinators by the Emilia Romagna region, these aspects were debated, as Anna Bondioli[14] recounts:

> The founding "philosophy" of the [new] law situates the entire range of interventions for early childhood in a familial and privatised perspective that contradicts, in manifest ways, the basic assumptions that have promoted the qualitative growth of early childhood services over the last thirty years [...] The tasks of local authorities are being re-drawn, and they are asked to work on promoting, coordinating, supporting and supervising

32 Reciprocal *formazione* in Reggio Emilia

interventions whose management is only partly offered and entrusted to the local authorities, the regions, and the State, and increasingly offered to the "private social sector". [...] the new functions of pedagogical coordinators, on whom the task of translating "systems governance" into operational terms falls more than on others, appear more obscure and confused than ever. It is not possible at this moment to attempt a definition of these tasks in more precise terms, if first we do not define the type of role that local authorities intend to take for themselves. And this is an eminently political issue.

(Bondioli, 2001, pp. 135–136, [translated by Jane McCall])

The debate is an open one, producing different considerations, as Maura Forni[15] affirmed in the same seminar:

For a pedagogical coordinator to extend their competences [...] "between care and education" could also lead to disadvantages and difficulties. The first that comes to mind is that of becoming a *tuttologo* (someone who knows a bit of everything), but perhaps we can get around this by maintaining specific knowledge of a certain topic, and having diffused knowledge of the rest; or thinking that one person could perhaps be dedicated to the overall "services network" and another to various different services in a more specialised way.

(Forni, 2001, p. 96, [translated by Jane McCall])

As Crispiani (2017) suggests, "all this testifies to how the profession of pedagogical coordinator is one that has been affirmed in the field, thus suffering from the same many-sided and uneven history as the science its name refers to" (p. 123, [translated by Jane McCall]).

The pedagogical coordinator and pedagogical coordinations: the case of Emilia Romagna

An analysis of pedagogical coordinators carried out in the late 1990s underscores certain critical aspects connected with their new tasks:

The new managerial assignments and responsibilities conferred on coordinators, corresponds, at least in certain realities [...] to a separation in relations with the 0–6 services. Centralised technical experts have increasingly found themselves planning and organising services, making decisions on courses of *formazione*, and setting up experimental projects, without the systematic feedback of constant relations with their group of educators, rarely able to account directly for the educational climate or personally listen to the problems, difficulties and successes of the daily work. Their pedagogical competence continues to be spent on the general level of planning, but has lost any possibility of accompanying and supporting operational realities from close up.

(Musatti & Mayer, 2003, p. 77, [translated by Jane McCall])

In 2000, regional law 1/2000, "Regulations on early childhood educational services" dedicated three articles to pedagogical coordinators, defining their qualifications (degree in socio-pedagogical or socio-psychological subjects) and tasks.

Specifically, Article 34 notes:

1 As part of the objectives defined by authorities and providers, pedagogical coordination is the tool suited to guaranteeing connections between the early childhood services that are part of a local educational system, based on principles of continuity and consistency of educational initiatives, and homogeneity and efficiency on the organisational and managerial levels, contributing, on a technical level, to defining criteria and directions for the development and qualification of the system of early childhood services.

2 Pedagogical coordinators also have the task of technically (educationally) supporting and guiding the work of (school) operators, including permanent *formazione*, promoting and evaluating the quality of services, together with monitoring and documenting experience, experimenting with innovative services, intersecting with educational, social, and health services, and collaborating with families and the local community, including the aim of promoting a culture of childhood.

The commitment made to coordinating services for 0–3 years in the Emilia Romagna region can be seen in the biennial regional meetings on the theme, presenting findings from periodical surveys of pedagogical coordinators working in the region. The data from 2001 reveals some of the contradictions accompanying the profession's development. Pedagogical coordination is present in 56% of the total of 330 municipalities in the Emilia Romagna region. Of this total number of coordinations, 72% are made up of only one person. Although pedagogical coordinators are employed on the basis of legislation for 0–3 educational services, almost all of them also coordinate private, affiliated, and/or municipal *scuole dell'infanzia* for 0- to 6-year olds, sometimes as many as 11 different centres. Moreover, 62.4% of coordinators are also occupied with issues of an administrative and managerial nature. With a view to qualifying an "integrated system" for early childhood, defined as such on account of the plurality of institutions and organisations cited above, the Emilia Romagna region used regional laws 26/2001 and 12/2003 to pose

34 Reciprocal *formazione* in Reggio Emilia

the objective of supporting providers to employ pedagogical coordinators in *scuole dell'infanzia*. These new laws paved the way for trying the role out in the private sector, and state-run *scuole dell'infanzia*, in which they are still absent on the national level to this day.

From the 2013 survey data (the latest on the Emilia Romagna region's website), we can appreciate some of the results that have been produced by the region's commitment to promoting the pedagogical coordinator's role. In 2013, there were 440 coordinators, compared to 175 in 2001, of whom only 42.4% had contracts with a local authority – full-time permanent contracts for the most part – the remaining 57.6% were employed by private bodies, mainly with short-term part-time contracts of periods between 1 and 25 hours of work per week. Although these conditions are an improvement on a total absence of coordinators, they do not allow for a continuity of the experience which alone can guarantee the fruition and capitalisation of coordinators' knowledge of educational centres and the experience matured. The Emilia Romagna region's commitment also led to supporting the creation of a Provincial Pedagogical Coordination in each province, an experience that began in the 1990s as an initiative of the municipality of Reggio Emilia: a structure for *confronto* and an important connector, especially in consideration of the number of pedagogical coordinations made up of only one person. Provincial Pedagogical Coordinations were given recognition and support in 2002, in the region's Annual Plan, with hours for periodical exchange and *confronto* on a regional level. Here, Viviana Tanzi[16] (2001) describes its functions:

> The way in which Provincial Pedagogical Coordination is structured is a precious opportunity for providing a network and authoritative seat of *confronto* and consultation [for *pedagogistas*], in which to formulate proposals, explore themes more deeply, debate issues, and dissect problems: a place in which everyone's participation, as well as providing beneficial solidarity, allows us to export and rationalise the competences present in our territory. Further, it represents a useful source of consultation for the Provincial Administration, which has several new obligations to fulfil, and finds this provincial group to be a seat of concerted work and *confronto*.
>
> *(p. 31, [translated by Jane McCall])*

In 2016, changes related to the decentralised government bodies led to the Provincial Pedagogical Coordinations taking the new name of Territorial Pedagogical Coordination "with the task of *formazione, confronto* and exchange of experience, promotion of innovation, experimentation, and the qualification of services, as well as support for monitoring and evaluating the pedagogical project".[17] The establishment of these new territorial coordinations was entrusted to municipalities. During this passage important changes were officialised, coherent with the national legislation instituting an Integrated

System of Education and Instruction from birth to 6 years[18]: the 0–6 nature of coordination, and the presence of representation by all providers in the integrated 0–6 system (state, municipality, private, third sector). As previously noted, on a national level the profession of *pedagogista* was only regulated in December 2017 in budget law 205, which references the areas of education and schooling, and indicates the qualifications necessary for entering the profession. In this law, the *pedagogista* is a:

> Professional who works in the area of education, *formazione* and pedagogy related to any kind of activity carried out formally, non-formally or informally in the various life phases, in a perspective of personal and social growth […] [The *pedagogista*] operates within socio-educational and socio-welfare services and presidiums, with people of every age, and with priority for the following areas: education and *formazione*; schooling; social welfare, limited to socio-educational aspects, and, with the aim of reducing costs, social-health and health centres and presidiums limited to socio-educational aspects; parenting and family; cultural; juridical; environmental; sporting and motor skills; integration and international cooperation.
>
> (law 205, 27 December 2017)

The experience of 0–6 services in Reggio Emilia

The équipe pedagogica *and the* pedagogistas: *historical notes*

Reggio Emilia municipality's experience of the *équipe pedagogica* can be situated against the national and regional backdrop described above. The name *équipe pedagogico-didattica* was used in the 1972 *Regolamento* or "Rulebook" (Municipio di Reggio nell'Emilia Assessorato Scuole e Servizi Sociali, 1972), and formally instituted by Reggio Emilia that same year: it was preceded by a period of commitment (initially a collaboration) on the part of Loris Malaguzzi who, as we have seen, had been working in the municipality's Psycho-Pedagogical Medical centre since 1963, and by Carla Rinaldi's employment as a *pedagogista* in 1970. French for unit or team, "équipe" was a term used in the 1950s and 1960s in psycho-pedagogical medical centres to describe a group of persons pursuing a common end, or collaborating in the same sector of activity, sometimes intellectual. In the early 1970s, the term was taken up in the social and health fields. The meaning of the word *coordinamento* (coordination) on the other hand, as well as the idea of integrating, refers to actions such as organising, creating order, supervising, and achieving an end. To us it seems that in identifying this term, a deliberate choice of field was made.

Reggio Emilia's municipal *équipe pedagogico-didattica* was shaped in 1973–1974 with the employment of some *pedagogistas* alongside a strong

36 Reciprocal *formazione* in Reggio Emilia

commitment by the municipal administration to opening new educational services. By the end of 1975 and Loretta Giaroni's term as *Assessore* for schools and social services in the city, the network of services was made up of 20 *scuole dell'infanzia* and 2 *nidi d'infanzia*. In this context, "the *Rulebook* translated many of Reggio Emilia's "irregularities" into "rules", choices which have often been seen to be capable of generating innovation in the Reggio Emilia experience" (Cavallini et al., 2010, p. 105). These changes had built up gradually through experimenting with ways of organising and professional profiles not immediately visible in the city's administrative acts: School City Committees, the *Consulta*[19] of Asili *Nido* and municipal *Scuole dell'Infanzia* (the make-up of which is described in detail), the staff in each school to include two co-titular teachers for each class, one additional teacher specialising in expressive and graphics activities to conduct ateliers-*atelierista*, one cook with auxiliary staff[20], hours of *aggiornamento* as part of every professional profile's working week, and the work "collective". Furthermore, employing male teachers in *scuole dell'infanzia* was deemed possible for the first time. The 1972 Rulebook (Municipio di Reggio nell'Emilia Assessorato Scuole e Servizi Sociali, 1972) defined the *équipe pedagogico-didattica* as "an organism for coordinating pedagogical and didactic experiences in the *scuola dell'infanzia* and *asilo nido* [...] made up of operators (with a degree in pedagogy, or expert in issues of infant education) in a ratio of 1:8–10 class groups" (art. 8). It also indicates the functions of the *équipe* as follows:

> The *équipe pedagogico-didattica*, refusing all bureaucratic, administrative, and inspectorate functions, will take responsibility for creating an instrument of work and research, of study, constant verification, and above all collaboration with the staff, parents, and citizens, involved in the school experience.
>
> *(Municipio di Reggio nell'Emilia Assessorato Scuole e Servizi Sociali, 1972, art. 18)*

It is particularly significant that the Rulebook does not institute the role of *pedagogista*, but rather the body of an *équipe pedagogica* or pedagogical team, made up of operators in the pedagogical area, who are called *pedagogistas* from the outset. This underscored particular qualities it wished to assign to the professional role: not school directors, or autonomous workers, but part of a collegial body that elaborates pedagogy, framed with a role that is non directorial but collaborative with all the protagonist subjects of the educational project. Moreover, from the beginning the *équipe pedagogico-didattica* was housed in the city's *assessore* offices with just one director/manager who coordinated both the *scuole* and the *nidi*, which were being opened in those years and are considered in the Regolamento (Municipio di Reggio nell'Emilia Assessorato Scuole e Servizi Sociali, 1972) in a dedicated article (art. 3 – "Organisational and pedagogical convergences with the municipal Asili Nido") as well as in the *Consulta degli Asili Nido e delle Scuole Comunali dell'Infanzia*.

The *équipe pedagogico-didattica* was made up of graduates in pedagogy, psychology, sociology, literature, and philosophy, and teachers with long-standing experience, all with the function of *pedagogista* whatever their qualification. It is in fact pedagogy, the science of education, this inter-disciplinary area, that unites and creates relations between the knowledge of these different figures. Pedagogy that is not closed within itself, but instead open to the multiple influences of other areas of knowledge that "bring it down from an Olympian elitism, from always being over and above, always on the outside, from ignorance and faked neutrality. They want to give educators a new sense of their task and power, and lead them to finally taking a position – in a word to living their profession critically, politically" (Malaguzzi, 1971, in Cagliari et al., 2016, p. 179). Pedagogy that is "dynamic and not mummified", and that either "like all the human sciences – is remade, reconstructed and updated based on the new conditions of the times, or it loses its nature, its function, its proper capacity to correspond to the times it lives in, and above all to foresee, anticipate and prepare the days of tomorrow" (Malaguzzi, 1969, in Cagliari et al., 2016, p. 143). Malaguzzi further notes that:

> The real problem is that pedagogy […] must, as it were, walk with flat feet. It has to proceed with patience and caution, with doubt and conjecture, must place itself in different points of view, see much and listen much, ask itself if what is taking place is external to it, if the rhythms and qualities of its work are capable of meeting with children's expectations, motivations, their levels of maturation, their requests for affect and socialisation. Before being a court of judgement, pedagogy is the preliminary hearing, the inquiry, the reflection and the unclosed parenthesis.
>
> *(Malaguzzi, 1990, in Cagliari et al., 2016, p. 379)*

Opting for pedagogy is in itself a choice of field: a refusal of specialisms and predictive or diagnostic attitudes, and the opening up to investigation and dialogue with the complexity of the life contexts of children and the adults who participate with them in the adventure of growing. A dimension at once political and existential. The presence in the *équipe* of teachers with long experience – a path, as we have seen, that other municipalities also took but which Reggio Emilia interpreted as giving permanent assignments above all to people in possession of the qualifications required by law – made it possible for the group to always benefit from a plurality of sensibilities, from different points of view and areas of knowledge, from constantly refreshing their criteria for reading and interpreting experiences and problems, through gazes positioned at different distances from everyday life in the *nidi* and *scuole dell'infanzia*, and from their protagonists.

38 Reciprocal *formazione* in Reggio Emilia

Choosing the Istituzione *as a form of management for 0–6 educational services*

The municipality of Reggio Emilia, after a participatory process involving *nidi* and *scuole dell'infanzia* staff, families, and union organisations, chose in 2003 to manage its 0–6 educational services through the Preschools and Infant-toddler Centres – Istituzione of the Municipality of Reggio Emilia, a functional municipal body with cultural, pedagogical, and managerial autonomy. The purpose of this choice was to maintain the public management of *nidi* and *scuole dell'infanzia*, while at the same time constructing a body that was strongly centred on the educational services, and their identity and needs, thus with greater guarantees for daily life and quality in the *nidi* and *scuole dell'infanzia*. The *Istituzione* has the competences necessary for managing all operational and administrative aspects of the *nidi* and *scuole dell'infanzia*: a finance office, human resources office, enrolments office, repair and maintenance offices, as well as a pedagogical coordination, all with one Director.

This is conducive to more rapid decisions and actions, making it possible to overcome the difficulties of *pedagogista*s in several other municipalities in Italy who have reported (Cipollone, 1984) on institutional inflexibility, and difficult relations with a bureaucratic apparatus that has the power of decision over the essential functions of a service (personnel and premises for example) without direct knowledge of them, and rationales that are different from those of education. The establishment of the *Istituzione* has reinforced and qualified relations with Reggio Children and the Loris Malaguzzi International Centre project, creating favourable conditions for a closer weave of *progettazione* and opportunities for *formazione*.

Organisms of participation and co-responsibility as outlined *in* Indications *(the new Rulebook)*

In 2009, six years after the birth of the *Istituzione*, a new Rulebook of *Nidi* and *Scuole* dell'infanzia (Scuole e Nidi d'Infanzia – Istituzione del Comune di Reggio Emilia, 2009) – called "Indications" in the English translation (Preschools and Infant-toddler Centres – Istituzione of the Municipality of Reggio Emilia, 2010) – was deliberated. Its content is the fruit of a participatory journey, that had been initiated some years before, involving parents and staff in each *nido* and *scuola dell'infanzia*, the Director of the *Istituzione*, the *équipe pedagogico-didattica*, and representatives of municipal administration and Reggio Children. It lists a series of "organisms of participation and co-responsibility" (Preschools and Infant-toddler Centres – Istituzione of the Municipality of Reggio Emilia, 2010, pp. 15–17). One of these is the *équipe*, which has now been given the name "pedagogical coordination". *Indications* dedicates an article to this, maintaining continuity with the previous *Rulebook* while integrating it with functions introduced by new strategy, management, and administration contexts:

> The pedagogical coordinating team serves as a cultural and pedagogical link between the many aspects of the educational project at the local, national and international levels. It promotes and qualifies the educational participation in conjunction with the City Childhood Councils, the Interconsiglio, the quality support and other resources of the scholastic and territorial system. It organizes the annual professional development project for the personnel and develops it in relation to the emerging project priorities in the services and to the cultural stimuli offered by the contemporary world.
>
> *(Preschools and Infant-toddler Centres – Istituzione of the Municipality of Reggio Emilia, 2010, pp. 16–17)*

Among various bodies that were formalised in the 2009 *Indications* Rulebook is another tool of collegiality and reciprocal *formazione* that had been set up by Loris Malaguzzi in 1978, with particular importance for the identity of the *nidi* and *scuole dell'infanzia* system: the *équipe allargata*, or expanded *équipe*, which is a "context for periodic meetings between the representatives of the Preschools and Infant-toddler Centres *Istituzione*, the pedagogical coordinating team, and representatives of the personnel of the municipal and the public-private educational services and of the administrative offices" and "contributes to the construction of the educational project and to the discussion of the choices related to the network of the services" (Preschools and Infant-toddler Centres - Istituzione of the Municipality of Reggio Emilia, 2010, p. 17).

The *Indications* of 2009 include the *Consiglio Infanzia Città*, the *Interconsiglio*, class meetings with parents, and the working group among the system's participatory organisms. In this way the work elaborated within these organisms, which has its roots in the lived experience of the *nidi* and *scuole dell'infanzia*, is officially endorsed and made explicit. The organisational choice of having multiple places for local and system collegiality is a particular characteristic of Reggio Emilia's experience, and substantiates the educational project's principles: the value of human beings from birth; the right of participating in constructing the contexts they are part of; acknowledgment of the competencies, knowledge, creativity, and intelligence of all persons; valuing subjectivity and differences in our relations; and the sense of belonging to a community. This idea is the foundation of the *diffused pedagogical system*, in which no one profession owns, or is characterised, by particular competencies, but rather these exist in every one of us and contribute, through participation and dialectic encounter, to constructing the experience and its evolution.

It will not have escaped the reader that the vocabulary of the new *Indications* Rulebook has changed, in interpreting new sensibilities and cultural

40 Reciprocal *formazione* in Reggio Emilia

change. The term "collective", with its echoes of specific, politically-oriented, bodies of the 20th century, has become "working group", maintaining its characteristics of co-responsibility, participation of all professionalisms, and autonomy of elaboration, although the word "collective" is still used in *nidi* and *scuole* in spoken Italian (so the two words are used interchangeably). The *équipe* has become *coordinamento* or "coordination" and lost the specification *didattica* (didactic), which in Italian can have a connotation of prescriptive programming and the teaching of formalised knowledge. The *Consiglio* (Council) which "represents the basic democratic structure that promotes and contributes to giving public, organized form to the whole of the processes of participation and co-responsibility" (Preschools and Infant-toddler Centres - Istituzione of the Municipality of Reggio Emilia, 2010, p. 15), has replaced the previous *Comitati* (Committees), which in Italian are linked to ideas of struggle and the demand for rights.

These changes of name correspond to updating the various bodies but always with continuity of values, roles, and content. In fact, the name "pedagogical coordination" has replaced *équipe*, but not in Reggio Emilia's everyday language where it is still used today. Nor has it changed the name of the coordination's single members, who continue to be called *pedagogistas,* and not pedagogical coordinators as in the rest of Italy. This is a choice that substantiates their role, because although they also carry out functions of coordination, these are effected from a predominantly pedagogical point of view, tending towards elaboration and research, rather than control, monitoring, and conformity with norms. Pedagogical coordination in Reggio Emilia has always maintained its specific role with the *nidi* and *scuole dell'infanzia* directly managed by the municipality in a vision of complex relations expressed through horizontal continuity with the educational services of other providers and social, cultural, and health services on one hand, and vertical continuity with primary school settings on the other.

A diffused pedagogical system

Little has been written about the role of Reggio Emilia's *pedagogista*s. In *I Cento Linguaggi dei Bambini* (Italian edition of the book *The Hundred Languages of Children*), Simona Bonilauri and Tiziana Filippini state that:

- The role of the *pedagogistas* can only be grasped by going beyond the confines of pedagogy and of didactics, confirming once again the interdisciplinary and political nature of education.
- [Our] understanding will be more effective if we are able to consider it not so much [in terms] of its autonomous function but of its reciprocal interdependence with other protagonist subjects of educational events (Gandini, 2017, p. 193, [translated by Jane McCall]).

Reciprocal *formazione* in Reggio Emilia **41**

This reciprocal interdependence and reciprocal *formazione* creates a diffused pedagogical system articulated on different levels, in which *pedagogistas* bring their professionalism into play and reciprocal *formazione*, participation, and co-responsibility become lived practice, shaping the democratic idea of schools involving all subjects identified as protagonists: teachers, auxiliaries, children, and families; and through them the social, cultural, and political context. A competent system learns from the experience and contributions of the plurality of subjects who are involved, through a close weave of instruments, meetings, and groups that represent them all, and oriented by the project for *formazione* and an annual plan of commitments concerted between all the subjects. We now turn to examining the various levels of which the system is composed.

Nido d'infanzia and *scuola dell'infanzia*

On this first level, we will investigate the single *nido* and *scuola dell'infanzia*. In the words of Malaguzzi:

> Our *scuola dell'infanzia* also has to rapidly change its internal organisation, and above all its methodologies. In the first instance by appealing to the responsibility of teachers and auxiliary staff. What has been lived in segments, in separate different spaces and autonomous actions, must be lived in a seamless common dimension, taking teachers from the deforming solitude old pedagogy gave us (and continues to give us) and situating them in shared constructions, work that calls for exchange, confrontation, updating, that constantly brings into play both personal and private experience; and through this reciprocal dialogical growth and enrichment, brings them to a human and professional awareness of the group.
>
> *(Malaguzzi, 1971, in Cagliari et al., 2016, p. 171)*

In Malaguzzi's words there is a vision of people who, before being teachers or auxiliary staff, are human beings. Human beings who live through their relations, crossing several different private and public contexts, and who seek to give meaning and unity to their experience. Human beings who participate, or rather, have the right to participate, to make their contribution, and to have it recognised by others in all the contexts they live in. It is an idea of ties, relations, interdependencies, and roles that go beyond the single school or person, and thread through the whole of society. Teachers, cooks, *atelieristas,* and auxiliaries, like children and parents, do not leave their lived experience as persons at the door but bring into school all the dimensions of their lives, contributing to a group elaboration that through co-responsibility, and with each person in their own role (which finds new definitions in this situation) shapes an educational context. Rather than execute or adapt to predefined programs, these people are all asked to interpret shared values, in a collective dialectic, and

42 Reciprocal *formazione* in Reggio Emilia

shape original journeys of learning, socialisation, and construction together. Meeting with staff on the day after the 1972 Rulebook of municipal *scuole dell'infanzia* had been approved, Malaguzzi stated:

> We must make a great commitment to changing and improving the tasks and roles of auxiliary staff. Auxiliary staff must have higher levels of participation in educational matters and be able to organise times, alongside their specific tasks, when they can be part of educational activities, discussions and decisions taken by their school. It is important that staff abandon attitudes of supposed inferiority, the feeling of being incapable or daunted, and be aware they represent an educational model and belong to an adult collective whose efforts must come together to create ever improving life experiences for children. One of the conditions that can make this happen is for staff to actively participate in *Comitati di Scuola e Città* and all the internal and external events affecting their school. We believe the adult collective should reflect on how they can help each other reciprocally and organise a plan to connect the work of teachers and auxiliary staff, even create situations of co-presence together in the same classrooms.
>
> *(Malaguzzi, 1972, in Cagliari et al., 2016, p. 188)*

This conception of the professionalism of auxiliary staff references the transversal values of reciprocity, care, and solidarity running through Reggio Emilia's educational experience. Only the idea and practice of staff and working group roles designed in this way can make the *pedagogista's* role imaginable and practicable. In fact, *pedagogista*s, who are functionaries of public administration, have a position that could be defined as hierarchical within the municipal organisation. The *pedagogista* has responsibility for authorising leave, staff holidays, and changes in timetable. It is the *pedagogista* who makes the final decisions about organisational aspects; the matching of teachers and auxiliaries with class groups, the organisation of daily tasks and times, the monthly planning of *aggiornamenti* and family meetings, and is accountable for these to the Director or President of the *Istituzione*, the *Assessore* for Education, the city council and, in the final instance, the city itself. Denying this aspect would be a falsification, and would impoverish the value of a role which, as we tried to illustrate earlier in the chapter, has been decisive for the dialectical dynamic with administrators, citizens, parents, and staff working directly with children, for elaborating a new pedagogy of early childhood, and for constructing, evolving, and consolidating educational organisation for children aged 0–6 years.

It is important for readers to be aware of this aspect of the pedagogista's responsibility, however, it should be considered and interpreted within the culture of a working group that is collectively co-responsible for constructing the educational project it offers to children and families. The *pedagogista's* role of responsibility is therefore expressed through reciprocal relations and *formazione*, in a never-finished construction of authoritativeness towards staff, parents, the Director, the President of the *Istituzione*, and the city, which derives from the capacity for fusing her own learning with the learning of others, and with real contexts, in all their dimensions: educational, workers' unions, cultural, political, and social. The *pedagogista* learns from and with teachers and other staff, in *aggiornamento* and through every type of *formazione* or *progettazione* meeting the working group holds, all the while contributing with her own knowledge to advancing everyone's awareness and making that awareness a lived reality for daily life. When necessary, the *pedagogista* takes responsibility for decisions by synthesising the multiple contributions that have been provided by the working group.

In terms of organisation, the perspective of reciprocity both presupposes and promotes a sense of belonging and the value of co-responsibility. Although it is the *pedagogista* who is asked to answer for forms of organisation used in the field, the process of elaborating the decisions involves all the school personnel, in a dimension of self-organisation that is at once shared and coherent with the system as a whole. With a perspective of reciprocity, *formazione* lays its foundations on the idea that learning does not take place through teaching or transmission, but is a subjective construction that takes place in the context of relations. *Formazione*, therefore, is always a self-*formazione*, that is to say, the conscious activation of working for our own elaboration and comprehending the points of view of others. *Formazione* is also the moment in which theory, praxis, and research meet together in a fuller way. Theory does not dominate praxis, nor is praxis unaware of the implicit theory every praxis carries inside it: it is a circular relation, a dynamic of research that, starting with documentation of contexts inhabited with children, and in which the teacher herself is a protagonist, promotes a development of reflection, interpretation, and reading that are cultural, psychological, sociological, and methodological, increasing the knowledge of each person and of the group, while promoting the *progettazione* of successive actions. In the words of Malaguzzi:

> What should we do? First, put aside any rush to categorise. Secondly, vary, multiply, intensify, re-invent and re-listen to children's activities, behaviours, words and languages. Support and make use of their interests, their forms of learning, choosing and communicating. In short, widen the net that we and the children use to fish the sea. The more we extend the range of experience, the greater the possibility of producing encounters with the whole range of genetic specificities and potentialities: those ready and eager to germinate, those that are undecided, and those that are sleeping and need a shake.
>
> *(Malaguzzi, 1990, in Cagliari et al., 2016, p. 379)*

44 Reciprocal *formazione* in Reggio Emilia

In a working group, the *pedagogista* carries out the same role as a teacher carries out with children. Teachers have the responsibility for how learning contexts evolve. But rather than leading children down pre-planned paths, with a *progettazione* perspective they construct conversational contexts, in a dialogue with children's ideas, curiosities, theories, and hypotheses, opening up and walking through possibilities of new research, new because it will be constructed in *this* context with *these* children and adults, and all members of the group will converge on it with their own subjective modalities. In Reggio Emilia's educational experience, adult *formazione* moves along with these same characteristics. *Pedagogistas* situate themselves in a dialogue with their background of knowledge and bring their point of view on equal terms with others; however, at the same time they have responsibility for the conducting of the dialogue, the direction of the *confronto*, the quality of the exchange, the refreshing of cultural references, and the synthesis of the ideas and opinions that emerge. Each member of staff takes away their own considerations and elaborations, but the group must have a point of shared synthesis to relate to. This is vital to the coherence of the educational project that is offered to children and families. *Pedagogista*s also have responsibility for making choices, when different opinions on "what to do" have not coalesced into a negotiated decision. This dynamic, between subjective and inter-subjective and between individual and collective dimensions, is highly delicate and always in search of equilibrium on both organisational and educational levels, although it remains permanently unstable. It is another responsibility of the *pedagogista* to give value to individual subjectivities while constructing a consensual and shared process that brings the whole working group together, and builds innovation as it strengthens the institutional identity of that particular *nido* or *scuola*.

The *pedagogista's* authoritativeness is decisive for promoting consensual processes that go towards elaborating points of synthesis among the different kinds of "souls" in the working group. These convergences become a compass and a map, for evaluating actions that have been played out, and projects that are unfolding. While not denying their role as coordinator of the *scuola* or *nido*, or their role in being knowledgeable about and specialising in the ages of childhood (*età evolutiva*), *pedagogistas* participate and present in the class meetings with families[21] with the same interlocutory and dialectical qualities, making it possible to construct a journey of knowledge about the life of that particular group of children in that *nido* or *scuola*, with everyone's reciprocity and contribution.

City Childhood Councils and the City Intercouncil

City Childhood Councils (Preschools and Infant-toddler Centres - Istituzione of the Municipality of Reggio Emilia, 2003), are bodies of democratic participation present in every *nido* and *scuola dell'infanzia*. Elected every three years, every staff member and the *pedagogista* have the right to be part of a City

Childhood Council, and any willing parent or citizen can offer their candidacy and be elected. The work of the councils is to promote participation and to contribute to the educational project of their *nido* or *scuola dell'infanzia* by putting together proposals, projects, and actions that interpret questions arising from the context, the children and the families. *Pedagogistas*, by right, are part of City Childhood Councils in the *nidi* and *scuole* they coordinate; they participate in meetings and always contribute to the analyses and elaboration of council projects, in a dynamic of dialectic and reciprocity. *Pedagogistas*, in particular, by virtue of their participation in several places internal to the education system and to the city, have a responsibility to provide members of City Childhood Councils with elements of knowledge that can lead the analysis and reflection emerging from children and families in that specific *nido* or *scuola* to a broader context, while also learning from the more detailed analyses and reflections contributed by council members concerning the specific context. Listening in this way makes it possible to avoid the trivialising procedures of the kind that Malaguzzi warns against:

> We rise from the ground in a hot-air balloon ... until the earth is completely flat ... Then we use the same discourse for children and things that are not the same ... Speaking "scientifically" this process began before Galileo. We produce a general concept and do not allow it to be contested; if necessary, we trivialise and change the terms of the contestation.
> *(Malaguzzi, 1971, in Cagliari et al., 2016, p. 177)*

Instead, a dynamic of reciprocal learning tends not to annul differences in favour of a generic vision, but to value differences as part of a collective elaboration. As previously highlighted, City Childhood Council meetings are therefore also opportunities for *formazione* for *pedagogistas*, teachers, and auxiliary staff, increasing their competency and sensibility towards social and political citizenship. *Pedagogistas* are members of the *Interconsiglio cittadino* (City Intercouncil)[22], an organism comprising representatives of all the City Childhood Councils:

> The *Interconsiglio* serves as a liaison with the city administrators in relation to school policy; it has functions of consulting and making proposals with regard to the main educational, management, and administrative choices of the *Istituzione*; it promotes the qualitative and quantitative development of the educational services and contributes to the construction of a culture of childhood.
> *(Preschools and Infant-toddler Centres - Istituzione of the Municipality of Reggio Emilia, 2010, p. 15)*

Pedagogistas work together in meetings of the *équipe* and participate in preparing City Intercouncil meetings during which they offer the Director

46 Reciprocal *formazione* in Reggio Emilia

and President of the *Istituzione*, and *Assessore* for Education the opportunity to reflect on issues emerging within local contexts: they speak on specific aspects in turn and when they consider it opportune, they intervene in the debate in an individual capacity. The City Intercouncil is a co-responsible and participatory body, in which *pedagogista*s have a role that brings together their responsibility towards the *nidi* and *scuole dell'infanzia* and the fact of being citizens. The meetings are places of debate, consultation, and information that amplify participants' social, political, and educational awareness in a dynamic of dialectics and *confronto*. It is, therefore, a place of *formazione* for *pedagogista*s, staff, and city administrators.

The équipe pedagogica

Pedagogistas are therefore required to have a high level of competence, a solid professionalism, and a sensibility for the dimension of politics. The *pedagogistas'* primary place of *formazione* is in the *nidi* and *scuole dell'infanzia*. So where can they develop meta-reflexive thinking on their own actions, update their own cultural references, and increase their sense of belonging to a system, with shared values and knowledge? This function is carried out by the *équipe pedagogica*, otherwise known as the pedagogical coordination. The Director of the *Istituzione* and heads of administrative offices also attend the *pedagogista* group's weekly meetings, a place where people belonging to the same profession, who manage the same responsibilities, engage in *confronto* on all issues related to their role, share cultural updates, construct interpretations, and discuss trajectories for work throughout the system. During these weekly meetings, managerial and administrative aspects that have to be governed inside each *nido* and *scuola dell'infanzia* are also discussed. These reflections renew the knowledge and opinions of *pedagogistas* and officials, enriching them with other people's points of view. Thanks to the presence of heads of office in local administration at *équipe* meetings, elaborations of managerial aspects discussed collegially become a standard of reference at every level, and make it possible to maintain the unified nature of the system of *nidi* and *scuole dell'infanzia*, with due respect for local specificities. This represents a fundamental node for maintaining, in a context of change, an institutional identity that is coherently interpreted in local seats (individual *nidi* and *scuole dell'infanzia*) and at all levels of the system.

Not only does pedagogical coordination fuse together pedagogical and administrative-operational aspects, but it is also a place of participation and co-responsibility in which the pedagogical and political levels are integrated into reflections and initiatives. In the weekly meetings, which are periodically attended by the *Assessore* for Education and the President of the *Istituzione*, *pedagogistas* engage in *confronto* related to city council debates on educational policy, the political direction of the city *giunta*, and reflection on city-wide, national and international debate of educational themes. Key figures from administrative offices and system resources, and representatives of Reggio Children and the

Fondazione Reggio Children – Centro Loris Malaguzzi are also regularly invited to sit at the *équipe* table. This way of working defines the *équipe* table as a place of junction and connection for the city's educational system (*Istituzione*, Reggio Children, *Fondazione*, the integrated public system and other social, health, cultural, and school educational structures) and makes it possible to annually construct a *formazione* project and plan of commitments that, as well as involving all staff in the *nidi* and *scuole dell'infanzia*, includes a system plan for family participation and acts as a compass and framework orienting the specific commitment plans and *formazione* and participation projects of each *nido* and *scuola dell'infanzia*. The *formazione* project is therefore offered in this way, as an open map, that involves and connects all subjects, both internal and external.

System resources

The *Istituzione*'s system resources have a vital role in the organisation of the network of *nidi* and *scuole dell'infanzia* as a diffused pedagogical system. The resources are comprised of the Documentation and Educational Research Centre, the Gianni Rodari Theatre Laboratory, and the Video Centre: all structures that are also city services, each with their own specific competencies and different histories.

The Documentation and Educational Research Centre opened in 1990 and was developed from an initial project document dating to 1987. It archives documentation produced in the *nidi* and *scuole dell'infanzia*, and pedagogical and cultural documents that continue to be elaborated and produced by the *Istituzione* and Director's offices. It is, therefore, the repository of a vital documentary legacy that records the history of Reggio Emilia's educational experience: a corpus of documentation circulated by the Centre through its open hours to the public, *formazione* offered as part of the annual municipal *nidi* and *scuole formazione* plan, and a dedicated programme for the general public. The Gianni Rodari Theatre Laboratory dates to the 1970s, when the Reggio Emilia municipality distinguished itself in Italy by making Mariano Dolci, a puppeteer who had already collaborated with Reggio Emilia's Municipal Theatre, a municipal employee. The Laboratory promotes learning and *formazione* opportunities for the city's teachers and families on the themes of storytelling and drama, carries out research that explores and refreshes these themes, and founded and promotes *Reggionarra*, an annual city initiative dedicated to the art of narrative and storytelling, that has had led to national and international developments. The Video Centre started its activities in the mid-1980s, first with young volunteers, and then, in 2000, with its own permanent stable staff. The Video Centre informs reflection on video documentation, enriches its production, shares context *progettazione* with teachers, and fosters *formazione* and research on the use of video language's communicative and expressive potential. These three systems resources today have premises at the Loris Malaguzzi International Centre and are open to the public.

48 Reciprocal *formazione* in Reggio Emilia

In the year 2000, the new role of teacher educators was added as a further resource. These are teachers and *atelieristas* with several years' experience who work alongside the everyday life and experience of certain classes in the *nidi* and *scuole dell'infanzia*, enriching their *progettazione* and extending the strategic and cultural tools of teachers and *atelieristas* who work with the children on a daily basis. These resources all have their own reference *pedagogista* for *progettazione* and coordination, who takes care of their connections with the *équipe pedagogica*, and guarantees their reciprocity, circularity, and solidarity with each other and with the rest of the system.

Administrative offices

The *Istituzione* offices, whose purpose is to constantly qualify and update the cultural and organisational vision of the *nidi* and *scuole dell'infanzia*, have developed forms of organisation that concretely manifest the choice of putting collegiality at the centre of their way of working. As previously mentioned, the administrative offices of the *Istituzione*, which is part of the municipality, are dedicated to 0–6 educational services in the city's entire integrated public system, towards which the *Istituzione* holds diverse responsibilities: direct management of municipal *nidi* and *scuole dell'infanzia*; cultural, organisational, and economic management of conventions with centres which are indirectly municipally managed; financial management of conventions and nurturing of connections with private centres.

Pedagogistas have a constant relationship with administrative offices, both as individuals representing the requirements of the *nidi* and *scuole* they are primarily responsible for, and also as members of the *équipe pedagogica*. The *équipe*'s reflections and initiatives and the presence of administrative staff in meetings of participatory co-responsible bodies, such as the expanded *équipe* and city inter-councils, in situations of *formazione*, and other meetings with a more specific focus, together promote a vision of the educational system as not simply bureaucratic and administrative but as living, with a vital dynamic, and that requires procedures and solutions that administration can provide, giving it the legs to proceed with quality. Here again, solidarity, common values, transformative ethics, and interpreting constraint as possibility are attitudes and forms of awareness the system tends to in the ways daily work and reciprocal *formazione* are framed.

The Reggio Emilia Approach system and the Loris Malaguzzi International Centre

In 1994, following the impetus of Loris Malaguzzi, who worked on the project until his sudden death, the system of *nidi* and *scuole dell'infanzia* gave life to the new reality of Reggio Children. Initially presented as a public limited company (s.r.l.) and the Friends of Reggio Children voluntary association, it was newly organised when the Loris Malaguzzi International Centre opened in 2006, and in 2011 when the Friends of Reggio Children transformed into the *Fondazione Reggio Children – Centro Loris Malaguzzi*, now an ETS (Ente del Terzo Settore), or social non-profit. The Reggio Emilia Approach system (*Istituzione* of *Scuole* and *Nidi d'infanzia*, Reggio Children s.r.l. and *Fondazione Reggio Children – Centro Loris Malaguzzi*), with the municipality as its motor and promoter, is a visible manifestation of the city's investment in education. Built on a broad platform of participation, it represents a new form of public-private organisation that has the objective of giving greater cultural and economic strength and autonomy to Reggio Emilia's experience of education. The different parts are connected by relations based on conventions, periodically renewed to accommodate their evolving relations and shared *progettazione*, and maintain the vitality of the overall project.

In the system, the Loris Malaguzzi International Centre is a physical and metaphorical place of *formazione*, research, and exchange between professionals and citizens on educational themes. This research is an attitude that makes educational places truly respectful of children and their ways of learning, legitimising the *nidi* and *scuole dell'infanzia* as primary constructors of a culture of childhood. The Malaguzzi Centre is offered as a research centre that has the network of municipal public *nidi* and *scuole* that welcome children and families every day as its laboratories. The activities of research, *formazione* and exchange co-promoted by the system's three elements, are an integral part of the *nidi* and *scuole*'s annual project for *formazione*. Simultaneously, activities at the Malaguzzi Centre propose to a wide network of interlocutors working around the world an idea of practices that produce knowledge, and of the necessary relations between theory, practice, and research. For *pedagogista*s, teachers, parents, and children, these three parts of the system amplify their places of participation and co-responsibility, qualifying and augmenting the pedagogical, cultural, and economic dimension of the *nidi* and *scuole dell'infanzia*, in a virtual circle of reciprocity.

The varied geographies and articulations of the formazione system

As we have illustrated, the *formazione* system is articulated across multiple places that have variable geographies and compositions, and which include:

- Inter-collective *aggiornamenti* of *nidi* and *scuole* coordinated by the same *pedagogista*, or different *pedagogista*s.
- Thematic reflection groups with representatives of *nidi, scuole,* and other bodies in relation to internal research, or with external partners in collaboration with Reggio Children.
- *Équipe allargata* or other kinds of meetings with representatives from every *nido* and *scuola*, systems resources, administration offices, the Reggio Children system.

50 Reciprocal *formazione* in Reggio Emilia

- Mass staff assemblies for all members of staff.
- Meetings with experts that are open to parents and the citizenry.
- *Progettazione* and connection meetings between *nidi, scuole, équipe pedagogica,* and the Reggio Children system.

It is a system of *formazione* with certain stable bodies – the collective *aggiornamenti, équipe pedagogica,* and mass staff assembly – and others that vary with the kind of *progettazione* we want to undertake, the issues that are necessary to discuss, and the objectives that have been set. Some of these bodies re-propose the same dynamic of *formazione* as working groups, extending reflections beyond the research conducted within a single *nido* and *scuola,* in an attitude of dialectics and reciprocal *formazione*. Others are places where the reflections of the pedagogical coordination or of groups of *nidi* and *scuole dell'infanzia* can be contributed, with the aim of sharing a local (school) *progettazione* that has led to innovation and could advance the whole system. Afterwards, in working group aggiornamenti, each *nido* and *scuola* has time for meta-reflection, exchange, deeper exploration on these presentations, and their own local interpretation of possible new experience. In this way, the research and innovation that is carried out within individual classes in the *nido* and *scuola dell'infanzia* fuses with the research and innovation of the whole system.

Innovation and research

Innovation and research are over-used terms today. Therefore, it is important to share definitions pertinent to our own educational context. First and foremost, research is the way all children, from birth, encounter the world and gradually give it meanings, thanks to their relations with both adults who care for them and other children with whom they have possibilities of sharing experiences. Researching and socialising are human beings' way of knowing, growing, participating, and living.

Research is the life motion of every living being towards the unknown. Research is the challenge to self, it is curiosity, liberty, the desire to go beyond the confines of conformity and banality. Research is openness towards otherness, towards subjects (a child, colleague, parent, object, discipline, and so on) that never completely reveal themselves, and that bring unique and complex identities.

From this tension and this desire – which are in the child, and in teachers when they discover the rich humanity making up the group they are responsible for – innovation takes on life as a horizon. Innovation for individual teachers when they discover new possibilities, and innovation for the working group when a discovery generates wonder and new shared practices. *Progettazione* is an innovative dynamic in itself, always producing new and unexplored paths, in that they bear the signature, and fingerprint, of the protagonists of that particular process of learning. Not all of this is necessarily innovative in the absolute sense. But through these micro-innovations, shared in a vision of reciprocity, in places that bring staff together from different *nidi* and *scuole dell'infanzia*, the system constantly self-innovates, acquiring new knowledge and leading to scenarios that are more capable of interpreting the contemporary world the children, teachers, and families live in.

Institutional identity: between local and global

How then can the responsibility and creativity of an individual be co-joined with that of a *nido* or *scuola dell'infanzia*, or moreover, of a system of *nidi* and *scuole*, or an international system like Reggio Children's? How can the innovation each working group strives towards become innovation for the whole system without the system losing its identity? An institution's identity, much like a personal identity, is not a given, defined once and for all, but rather a process of constant reconstruction and re-signification. We could say identity is a narrative, that offers itself as a thread of continuity, coherence, and predictability within the permanent process of change that living and being propose and impose. Places of education and instruction, which continuously engage in *confronto* with new person-subjects (children, young people and families), and with evolutions in knowledge, forms of communication, ways of accessing information, and with new discoveries, are particularly affected by this process-dynamic of redefining their institutional and pedagogical identity. Institutional (or school) identity, like personal identity, is therefore made up of a stable core (the developmental age it is intended for, the values and ethics it references, organisational, structural and contractual constraints) but also of a more mobile nucleus that defines its openness towards the exterior, and its ability to be non self-referential.

Thinking of schools as systems we could say, with Maturana and Varela (1987), that openness is what allows an institution to stay alive. Closure, or immobility and self-referentialism, determine its death. Therefore dialogues, relations, and the dialectic between parts are vital in order for change (which derives from a constant attitude of research and valuing every protagonist's subjectivity) not to be an element causing lack of cohesion, but instead one that qualifies every part of the system. And here the *pedagogista* has an important role and responsibility.

Conclusions

Reciprocal *formazione*, the title of this chapter, has taken us into areas that the reader may not have expected to be invited to explore. Journeying through differences, across multiple contexts, we have tried to argue reciprocal *formazione* as a characteristic of the city of Reggio Emilia's whole educational system, a strategic function of *pedagogistas* and the *équipe pedagogica* in the network

52 Reciprocal *formazione* in Reggio Emilia

of relations and dialectical encounters that construct this experience. In the following chapters, the concepts, tools, professional roles, and forms of organisation we have outlined here will be the subject of deeper theoretical exploration, situated for the most part in real contexts, in which they acquire shape and substance.

Notes

1 To obtain parity, and receive an annual contribution towards their upkeep, non-State schools, including those run by municipalities, must show that they comply with a series of parameters listed in article 4 of law 62/2000.
2 The Teachers' Board consists of the headmaster and all the teachers in service at the school. It is the body responsible for planning, organising, checking, controlling, and evaluating the teaching and educational life of the school.
3 An I.C.I. is a state school complex within which schools of different order and grade co-exist: nursery, primary, and secondary schools, preferably close to each other in the territory. Accommodating children from 3 to 14 years of age under one presidency, one school board, one teaching board, I.C.'s offer a Plan of Formative Offer (P.O.F.) of continuity.
4 The Educational Offer Plan (P.O.F.) is the school's identity card: it sets out the school's distinctive lines, the cultural-pedagogical inspiration that drives it, the curricular, extracurricular, educational, and organisational planning of its activities. (Source: https://archivio.pubblica.istruzione.it/argomenti/autonomia/pof/default.shtml)
5 At a national level, *scuole dell'infanzia* for children aged 3–6 years are distinguished from "educational services" which welcome children aged 0–3. However, in Reggio Emilia, when referring to "educational services", we intend 0–6 settings, including both *nidi* and *scuole dell'infanzia*.
6 Conventions are administrative acts that can be of two kinds. The first is related to contracts drawn up with subjects who have participated in public exams or competitions or in tenders, and having arrived in first place owing to the quality of their educational project or the economic conditions they propose, obtain management of a structure that is the property of the municipality (management tender). These educational services (schools) are called "indirectly managed municipal educational services". These services are among those subject to protocols of understanding. The second kind of Convention, directly related to Protocols of understanding, is an act that commits the municipality to provide a contribution to private providers who, in premises of their own property, contribute to offering the city's families places in a *nido* or *scuola dell'infanzia*.
7 In the national context – albeit with local differences – the term "auxiliary staff" refers to those who, within educational services and *scuole dell'infanzia*, enact roles of care for the environment, tidying, cleaning, supporting children's meal times, and "door service". For further information on the role of auxiliary staff in Reggio Emilia, please refer to footnote n.21.
8 In 1951, a Psycho-pedagogical Medical Centre was also opened in Reggio Emilia with the contribution of Loris Malaguzzi who worked there until its closure in the early 1970s.
9 The MCE or Movimento di Cooperazione Educativa (Educational cooperation movement) was founded in Italy in 1951 inspired by the pedagogical and social thinking of Célestin and Elise Freinet. Freinet himself participated in the movement's first conference of 1952 in Rimini.

10 The C.E.I.S. or Centro Educativo Italo Svizzero (Italo-Swiss Educational Centre) is an educational village for children aged 2–11 years, founded in Rimini, Italy, on 1 May 1946 by Margherita Zoebeli, following international solidarity action on the part of the Swiss Workers' Relief.
11 Gianni Rodari (1920–1980) was an Italian writer, pedagogist, journalist, poet, and partisan. He wrote *The Grammar of Fantasy* and was a great innovator of children's literature. He founded the *Coordinamento Genitori Democratici*, an association for promotion of sociality.
12 Ada Gobetti (1902–1968) was an Italian journalist, translator, and partisan. She edited the journal *Educazione Democratica* (*Democratic Education*) and was part of the editorial board of *Riforma della Scuola* (*School Reform*). She founded and edited the magazine *Il Giornale dei Genitori* (*The Parents' Newspaper*).
13 The *Gruppo Nazioneale Permanente del Lavoro e dello Studio sugli Asili Nido* (Permanent National Work and study Group on the *Asili Nido)* later took the name of *Gruppo Nazionale Nidi e Infanzia* (National Group on *Nidi* and childhood) and is still active today. It was founded in Reggio Emilia in 1980, on the initiative of Loris Malaguzzi who was President until his death in 1994. Refer to: http://www.grupponidiinfanzia.it/
14 Anna Bondioli teaches General Pedagogy and Experimental Pedagogy at the University of Pavia. She has published several books on the *nido* and has always been involved in the *formazione* of educators.
15 Maura Forni is the Head of Coordination Services for social and socio-educational policy, planning, and development of the system of services in the Emilia Romagna region.
16 Viviana Tanzi is a *pedagogista*, and head of the public education sector in the municipality of Cavriago (RE), a tutor to several provincial and territorial pedagogical coordinations, and city officer for educational policy in the municipality of Sant'Ilario d'Enza (RE).
17 Regional law No. 11 of 15.7.2016: *Legislative changes in the area of social and housing policy for the younger generations, and early childhood education services, resulting from the reform of the local and regional government system.*
18 Law 107/2015: *Reform of the national education and formazione system with delegation for the reorganisation of existing legislative provisions* delegates the government with deliberating acts for instituting an integrated system of education and *formazione* from birth to six years.
19 The Consulta meets at least quarterly and is composed of:
   • the city officer for Schools and Social Services in a coordinating role
   • five representatives of City Council (three from the majority, and two from the minority, appointed by City Council, and serving terms of two years)
   • three representatives of the trade union confederations
   • two representatives of Women's Movements
   • a representative of the city's state education department
   • one representative from each *nido* and *scuola dell'infanzia* School and City Committee
   • one representative from each Neighbourhood Council
   • the *équipe pedagogico didattica* of the *nidi* and *scuole dell'infanzia*

20 In Reggio Emilia's municipal *nidi* and *scuole dell'infanzia*, the number of auxiliary staff varies in relation to the number of classrooms. Auxiliary staff are part of the working group, thus participating in all activities related to *formazione* and participation of families. Auxiliaries care for spaces and environments by tidying them and keeping them clean, assist the cook in preparing meals, support the class they are assigned to in daily life when required, maintain relations with families, and enrich

children's learning in aspects related to their own work, involving them in setting table, caring for plants, preparing spaces and materials, etc.

21 "Class meetings are the priority context for constructing the identity and the sense of belonging of a group of children, educators, and parents. The class meetings, by means of diversified strategies, times, and methods (for example, individual meetings, group meetings, and assemblies) have the aim to promote sociality, to share educational projects and proposals, and to construct exchange and dialogue around the different ideas about children, school, and learning. The class meetings are a constituent part of the progettazione of the educational and participation aspects of the preschool and infant-toddler centre. They are convened periodically by the classroom teachers over the arc of the year according to the needs and opportunities, which may also be indicated by the parents and by the City Childhood Council (Preschools and Infant-toddler Centres - Istituzione of the Municipality of Reggio Emilia, 2010, p. 16).

22 *Interconsiglio Cittadino* [City Intercouncil] is the name given in the 2009 version of the *Regolamento* [Rulebook] to what was previously known as *Consulta cittadina*.

References

Bondioli, A. (2001). Commento ai Lavori. Il coordinatore pedagogico per l'infanzia nei servizi pubblici e privati dell'Emilia-Romagna, Reggio Emilia.

Cagliari, P., Castagnetti, M., Giudici, C., Rinaldi, C., Vecchi, V., & Moss, P. (Eds.). (2016). *Loris Malaguzzi and the schools of Reggio Emilia: A selection of his writings and speeches, 1945–1993.* Routledge.

Campioni, L. (2003). I coordinamenti pedagogici in cifre. Il coordinatore pedagogico per l'infanzia nei servizi pubblici e privati dell'Emilia Romagna, primo seminario regionale.

Cavallini, I., Baldini, R., & Vecchi, V. (Eds.). (2010). *One city, many children: Reggio Emilia, a history of the present.* Reggio Children.

Cipollone, L. (1984). L'aggiornamento e il coordinamento pedagogico. Convegno del Gruppo Nazionale permanente di lavoro e di studio sugli asili nido, Venezia.

Crispiani, P. (2017). La pedagogia come scienza del pedagogista professionista [pedagogy as a science of professional pedagogist]. *Rivista SIPED, XV*(2), 121–144.

European Commission (2018). *The European Qualifications Framework: Supporting learning, work, and cross-border mobility.*

Faure, E., Herrera, F., Kaddoura, A.-R., Lopes, H., Petrovsky, A., Rahnema, M., & Champion Ward, F. (1972). *Learning to be: The world of education today and tomorrow.* UNESCO. https://unesdoc.unesco.org/ark:/48223/pf0000001801

Forni, M. (2001). L'intreccio socio-educativo nei servizi 0-18 anni: Il ruolo del coordinatore pedagogico tra cura e educazione. Il coordinatore pedagogico per l'infanzia nei servizi pubblici e privati dell'Emilia-Romagna, Reggio Emilia.

Gandini, L. (2017). Il ruolo del pedagogista: Intervista a Simona Bonilauri e Tiziana Filippini. In C. Edwards, L. Gandini, & G. Forman (Eds.), *I cento linguaggi dei bambini: L'approccio di Reggio Emilia all'educazione dell'infanzia* (pp. 193–201). Edizioni Junior/Spaggiari.

Gruppo di lavoro per la Convenzione sui diritti dell'Infanzia e dell'Adolescenza. (2020). *I diritti dell'Infanzia e dell'Adolescenza in Italia. 11 Rapporto di aggiornamento sul monitoraggio della Convenzione sui diritti dell'Infanzia e dell'Adolescenza in Italia.* https://gruppocrc.net/documento/11-rapporto-crc/

Malaguzzi, L. (2021). *Participation and social management: Either we do education together, or there is no education*. Reggio Children.

Maturana, H., & Varela, F. (1987). *L'albero della conoscenza*. Garzanti.

Municipio di Reggio nell'Emilia Assessorato Scuole e Servizi Sociali (1972). *Regolamento delle scuole comunali dell'infanzia*. Reggio Emilia: Municipio di Reggio nell'Emilia.

Musatti, T., & Mayer, S. (2003). *Il coordinamento dei servizi educativi per l'infanzia. Una funzione emergente in Italia e in Europa*. Edizioni Junior.

Pesci, G., & Bruni, S. (2006). *Il pedagogista: Innovazione e rivalutazione di un ruole*. Armando Editore.

Preschools and Infant-toddler Centres - Istituzione of the Municipality of Reggio Emilia (2003). *Charter of the City and Childhood Councils*. Reggio Children.

Preschools and Infant-toddler Centres - Istituzione of the Municipality of Reggio Emilia (2010). *Indications preschools and infant-toddler centres of the Municipality of Reggio Emilia*. Reggio Children.

Scuole e Nidi d'Infanzia Istituzione del Comune di Reggio Emilia. (2009). *Regolamento scuole e nidi d'Infanzia del Comune di Reggio Emilia [Indications preschools and infant-toddler centres of the Municipality of Reggio Emilia]*. Author.

Tanzi, V. (2001). Il ruolo e le funzioni del coordinatore pedagogico: quali scenari per il futuro? Il coordinatore pedagogico per l'infanzia nei servizi pubblici e privati dell'Emilia-Romagna, Reggio Emilia.

Urban, M. (2010). Rethinking professionalism in early childhood: Untested feasibilities and critical ecologies. *Contemporary Issues in Early Childhood*, *11*(1), 1–7. https://doi.org/10.2304/ciec.2010.11.1.1

Urban, M., Vandenbroeck, M., Van Laere, K., Lazzari, A., & Peeters, J. (2012). Toward competent systems in early childhood education and care. Implications of policy and practice. *European Journal of Education*, *47*(4), 508–526.

3

THE VALUE OF RELATIONALITY AND AN ETHIC OF DIALECTICS

Stefania Giamminuti

Introduction

In this chapter, we story the "value of relationality" and an "ethic of dialectics" in Reggio Emilia, and we invite an obligation to affect, solidarity, and participation elsewhere. A particular focus is on the entanglements of relations that characterise the system in Reggio Emilia, or what is known as *sistema pedagogico diffuso*. This diffused pedagogical system is characterised by its "dimension of strong collegiality and *confronto*" and "horizontal" relationships, and it affords "those conditions for acting in dialogue, in reciprocity, within an equality of roles that historically led us to not have positions of coordinators internal to the *scuole dell'infanzia*, such as occurs in other organisational systems in Italy and worldwide" (Claudia Giudici, President, Preschools and Infant-toddler Centres – Istituzione of the Municipality of Reggio Emilia, interview with Stefania Giamminuti, Reggio Emilia). In illustrating this reciprocity, we engage with daily praxis and collective research in Reggio Emilia and we draw connections with the thinking of varied and entangled fields of knowledge: affect theory (Manning, 2010; Massumi, 2015; Seigworth & Gregg, 2010); research-creation (Springgay, 2016); perspectives on care (Puig de la Bellacasa, 2017; van Dooren, 2014); posthuman knowledge (Braidotti, 2019); multispecies feminist theory (Haraway, 2016); anthropology (Ingold, 2013, 2021a); critical pedagogy and cultural studies (Giroux, 2016); and the environmental humanities (Bird Rose, 2004).

We begin by qualifying "relationality", acknowledging the connections to Malaguzzi's concept of a "pedagogy of relations" (Cagliari et al., 2016, p. 180), whilst wishing to disrupt conventional notions of what might constitute "relations" in early childhood settings. We then illuminate how the value of relationality is embedded and embodied (Braidotti, 2019) in ways of

DOI: 10.4324/9781003181026-3

The value of relationality and an ethic of dialectics **57**

thinking and doing that activate affect and reciprocity. We go on to propose that, in Reggio Emilia, "the emphasis on affectivity and relationality is an alternative to individualist autonomy" (Braidotti, 2019, p. 12), and we open a space for thinking with concepts such as care and solidarity. Finally, we engage with the concept of dialectics to illuminate the Italian experience of *confronto*. In so doing, we problematise the notion of participation, a concept that is fundamentally embedded within the Reggio Emilia epistemology and is often reduced to conventional practices and encounters elsewhere.

Our aspiration for the ideas and practices shared in this chapter is that they may suggest possibilities for how we can "labour together to construct affirmative ethical and political practices" (Braidotti, 2019, p. 19) in early childhood education and care internationally. For, whilst we acknowledge the many challenges the field faces, we also concur with Braidotti (2019) when she speculates that "despair it not a project; affirmation is" (pp. 3–4). We hope therefore that our musings may propel pedagogical, cultural, and organisational transformations; that they may stimulate new ways of thinking, acting, and researching in education and care; and that they may generate collective responses premised on relationality, affect, care, solidarity, dialectics, and participation.

The value of relationality

The well-known "pedagogy of relationships and listening", as theorised by Rinaldi (2006), "originates precisely from the idea that children are the most avid seekers of meaning and significance, and that they produce interpretive theories" (p. 113). This focus on theory making and broad connections has, in our view, often been overlooked in the many subsequent interpretations of this philosophical standpoint, which despite its pervasiveness in early childhood curriculum policy and discourse internationally, often lacks deep theoretical and conceptual examination in practice.

In a 1975 newspaper article, where he argues for greater participation and social management in *scuole dell'infanzia*, Malaguzzi emphasises the need for "open dialogue about all themes (without exception) pertinent to children's education" (Malaguzzi, in Cagliari et al., 2016, p. 208). This focus on "dialogue" suggests a far broader understanding of the ethical and political responsibilities of schools than the narrower approach of "listening to children" or following the "dogma of children's interests" (Giamminuti et al., 2022) within curriculum planning might imply, and it also extends the obligation to listen to all those who participate in the project of education. In the 1980s, when speaking to staff on the topic of "adapting methodology and educational practice in schools", Malaguzzi reiterates a need for "basing each element in the whole of the educational experience – professional, *progettazione*-connected, technical and relational – on a foundation of dialogue and participation"

(Malaguzzi, in Cagliari et al., 2016, p. 354). In contrast, in international educational policy and regulatory frameworks, "relationships" are often reduced to observable standards and teaching-learning exchanges that can be measured against normative and generalised categories representing conventional understandings of what it means to be in a "quality" relationship. In practice in fact, such considerations are far more complex and slippery, impossible to pin down and qualify according to linear, rational, and universal criteria. Teachers and children are often expected to conform to normative expectations, as opposed to considering cultural, contextual, and theoretical variations on the concept and experience of relationship itself. Such conventional approaches generally privilege dominant western views, silencing "other" perspectives on what might be considered a "good" relationship.

It is evident that we have no desire to dispense with relationships, rather we recognise that "one finds one's own self in responding to others, and so both self and other become entangled in ethical relationships" (Bird Rose, 2004, p. 13). Hence, we draw both on encounters within our research project and on the provocations to our thinking that come to us from many fields of knowledge, to disrupt normative views and entrenched positions. We prefer for this purpose the term "relationality" to "relationships" or "relations" because, while it conjures some familiarity, it also evokes something new. Furthermore, the term "relationality" in posthuman knowledge (Braidotti, 2019) implies an embedded action and as such creates an obligation, or "response-ability inside ongoing trouble" (Haraway, 2016, p. 16). We consider relationality as a "thinking as well as making" (Haraway, 2016, p. 14) practice, an essential value to inform praxis-theory-research in early childhood education and care settings. Fundamentally, "relationality extends through the multiple ecologies that constitute us" (Braidotti, 2019, p. 47). As such, it expands the field from the individual to the collective; it involves attentiveness to the human and non-human; and it engenders ethicality.

The value of relationality: affect and reciprocity

The present is held aloft by affect.

(Massumi, 2015, p. 61)

In the early stages of writing this book, we wondered whether theories of affect could assist us to conceptualise and describe what occurs in the relational encounters between *pedagogistas, atelieristas,* and teachers (and others, human and non-human) in Reggio Emilia. The tentativeness in the use of this term came primarily from the Italian-speaking authors, who wondered whether the translation of affect into the Italian noun *affetto* – a term far more in common use than the English *affect* – might conjure up ambiguity in imagining working lives driven by *affection* (the most accurate translation of *affetto*). Specifically, the translation of affect into *affetto* evokes memories of Reggio Emilia educators' early activist efforts to distance themselves from the prevalent term *scuola materna* (motherly school), proposing instead the term *scuola dell'infanzia*. This revolutionary choice was premised on the urgent need to contest the dominant view of early years settings as substituting for mothers and therefore intent primarily on care and safekeeping of young children, staffed by educators with limited *formazione*, and informed by a pedagogy which assumed that all young children required was having their needs met and receiving affection. Given that such assumptions around the role of early childhood settings in society are still prevalent many decades later, we certainly do not wish to buy into this discourse, rather we believe that drawing on contemporary theories of affect can help us to better convey the ethical and political obligations that drove the Reggio Emilia innovations in the first place. All of us agreed that the focus on individual emotions that the term affection implies was fundamentally reductive and possibly dangerous. In fact, as noted by Braidotti (2019):

> The capacity to affect and be affected is not to be confused with individualized emotions […] Affect needs to be de-psychologized, and to be de-linked from individualism in order to match the complexity of our human and non-human relational universe. This relational process supports a thick and dynamic web of interconnections by removing the obstacles of individualism. (p. 45)

As further evidenced by Massumi (2015), affect is a far more complex and multi-layered concept than affection; it is a verb more than a noun, a concept which brings us closer to aesthetic, philosophical, ethical, and political concerns. In our view there are two key aspects, rendered very effectively by Massumi (2015), which align the concept of affect to the experience of Reggio Emilia: firstly, the focus on the capacity to affect *and* be affected illuminates the reciprocity of relationality in the *pedagogista*-teacher-*atelierista* encounter; secondly, the attention to the middle, to what happens in between, is closely aligned to the notion of *sistema pedagogico diffuso*.

> The concept of affect that I find most useful is Spinoza's well-known definition. Very simply, he says that affect is "the capacity to affect or be affected". This is deceptively simple. First, it is directly relational, because it places affect in the space of relations: between an affecting and a being affected. It focuses on the middle, directly on what happens *between*. More than that, it forbids separating passivity from activity. The definition considers "to be affected" a *capacity*.
>
> *(Massumi, 2015, pp. 91–92)*

60 The value of relationality and an ethic of dialectics

In relation to the capacity to affect and be affected, it is important to note that in the initial stages our research was premised on the reductive assumption that *pedagogistas* were the ones sustaining teachers' professional learning. This belief was swiftly disrupted after witnessing many encounters in Reggio Emilia, or *aggiornamenti*, where what came to the fore was a mutual capacity to affect and be affected. This particularly occurs in the presence of the non-human actant pedagogical documentation (Giamminuti et al., 2021), which of course in turn assumes the presence of children and materials in the affective relationship. Thus, the intimate knowledge that teachers possess of everyday classroom events is metaphorically and literally brought to the table to affect all those present and invite change (Figures 3.1-3.4). Paola Strozzi emphasises the agency and potential of documentation, a contributor to relationality:

> Without documentation it would not be possible to enact this role. It would not be possible to speak about children simply in abstract, to speak about teaching and learning in abstract. We need fragments of evidence. Of course, artefacts are evidence, but if I don't have next to the artefact the process through which it was created, I don't savour it, I don't appreciate it. And to rely only on teachers' memories, it's not enough. So, we [*pedagogistas*] are with children through documentation. We are with teachers through documentation.
>
> *(Paola Strozzi*, pedagogista, *interview with Stefania Giamminuti, Reggio Emilia)*

FIGURE 3.1   *Pedagogista* Paola Strozzi and teacher Annalisa Rainieri viewing children's mark-making artefacts and documentation during an *aggiornamento* at *Scuola dell'infanzia* La Villetta.

The value of relationality and an ethic of dialectics 61

FIGURE 3.2   Aggiornamento at *Scuola dell'infanzia* La Villetta: teachers Ethel Carnevali and Annalisa Rainieri and *pedagogista* Paola Strozzi being with children through documentation.

FIGURE 3.3   *Pedagogista* Paola Strozzi and teacher Ethel Carnevali [re]viewing a classroom documentation panel, *Scuola dell'infanzia* La Villetta.

FIGURE 3.4   Aggiornamento at *Scuola dell'infanzia* La Villetta: teachers Ethel Carnevali and Annalisa Rainieri and *pedagogista* Paola Strozzi engaging in *confronto*.

Affect invites "other" points of view and disrupts hierarchical authority, as evidenced by *pedagogista* Simona Bonilauri: "between the professionalism of the *pedagogista* and the professionalism of the teacher there is a relationship of reciprocity. It is not a relationship of authority" (interview with Stefania Giamminuti, Reggio Emilia). Loredana Garofalo also highlights this relationship of reciprocity:

> To have the supervision of a *pedagogista* can often mean receiving constant feedback. But this is not born of control, rather it is born of collaboration and exchange: I have something to offer as a teacher, and thus I enter into an exchange with the *pedagogista*. This [exchange] affords me the possibility of connecting things and events to each other; it stimulates me at a theoretical level; it affords new keys for interpretation which weave in beautifully with everyday lived experience and daily work with the children; and it invites direct experimentation. Experimentation that connects deeply with more theoretical work, which in turn is nurtured by my own work; this generates true *progettazione*.
> *(Loredana Garofalo, teacher, interview with Stefania Giamminuti, Reggio Emilia)*

Loredana offers a keen image of the essential connection between affecting and being affected, as she illustrates the circularity of encounter between teacher and *pedagogista*, and between theory and lived experience. This encounter is both created by and generates relationality, and it occurs in the in-between, blurred, space of "collective experimentation" (Manning, 2015) created by documentation and *progettazione*, rather than within the strictures and separations of methodological programming and/or quantitative accountabilities. This is a space where the values of collegiality, co-responsibility and co-protagonism are propelled forward thanks to an epistemology of participation, whereby all professional roles feel legitimated and motivated to add value to the system. Psychologist Ivana Soncini also highlights the circularity that Loredana alludes to, and the necessity of taking responsibility for others' interpretations:

> We can't do without knowing the point of view of those who work directly with children, because we can't do without their interpretations. I take responsibility for how they see children and how they work with children, because obviously there is a circularity in this. For me their point of view is fundamentally interesting.
> *(Ivana Soncini, pyschologist and member of the pedagogical coordination, interview with Stefania Giamminuti, Reggio Emilia)*

This context where authoritarian hierarchy is disrupted and where different points of view are rendered fundamentally interesting characterises not only the relationality of teachers and *pedagogistas*, but also that of all other members of working groups in the *nidi* and *scuole dell'infanzia*, such as cooks and auxiliary staff (as illustrated in Figure 3.5).

FIGURE 3.5   Working group *aggiornamento* at *Nido-Scuola dell'infanzia* Nilde Iotti / Agorà: cook Rosanna Fadda, *pedagogista* Daniela Lanzi, and teachers Federica Barbiero, Barbara Camorani, Giulia Ovi, and Tiziana Palmisano.

64 The value of relationality and an ethic of dialectics

In Reggio Emilia, a key practice that is born of the value of relationality lies in the provision of, and co-responsibility towards, time for collaboration, *formazione*, and dialogue between all staff. This consideration of time as a right is informed by a systemic vision that does not consider organisational matters to be subordinate to pedagogical matters (Cagliari et al., 2016). In fact, *pedagogista* Paola Strozzi highlights how subordination is eschewed through a distinctive structuring of opportunities for *formazione:*

> Often *formazione* is interpreted primarily as *formazione* of teachers, while it is assumed that with other staff you speak only of organisational matters. Which is not the case, given that we have a significant number of hours dedicated to *formazione*, to *progettazione*, and to participation for all professional profiles; these occur as weekly or fortnightly opportunities for encounter and exchange between the different professional roles.
>
> *(Paola Strozzi, pedagogista, interview with*
> *Stefania Giamminuti, Reggio Emilia)*

It can be said therefore that affect drives both pedagogical encounters and organisational concerns. This has the potential to elevate affect to a quality of the system, as evidenced in the words of experienced *atelierista* Mirella Ruozzi (Figures 3.6 and 3.7), currently a teacher educator, for whom the capacity to affect and be affected is a vital part of daily work:

> My role is not to replace the *pedagogista*, nor to replace the teacher, but rather to maintain connections. And to sustain the desire of *nidi* and *scuole dell'infanzia* to work as a group, to not work alone. You might say "well, they don't work alone, there's a working group, there's a *pedagogista*". But if you are working deep into a project and you are part of a project group that meets regularly, when you attend these meetings in my role you can't just go to the *nido* or *scuola dell'infanzia* to collect material and bring it to the meeting. Instead, you need someone who helps you create a synthesis, an interpretation [...] So, together with the *pedagogista*, the teachers, the *atelierista*, we work on a first selection of documentation. Therefore, you arrive at these meetings with materials that in some way already define the choices made by that *nido* or *scuola*. This is an approach that I have taken with all *nidi* and *scuole dell'infanzia* involved in a project, which means that they felt less alone in their choices, but also that I can share with them what is happening in another school. There's this way of keeping the group connected, even when the group isn't coming together.
>
> *(Mirella Ruozzi, atelierista, interview with*
> *Stefania Giamminuti, Reggio Emilia)*

Mirella's words illuminate how in Reggio Emilia the capacity to affect and be affected is at the same time an individual responsibility, qualifying a

The value of relationality and an ethic of dialectics **65**

FIGURE 3.6 *Aggiornamento* at *Scuola dell'infanzia* XXV Aprile: *Atelierista* Mirella Ruozzi and *pedagogista* Paola Strozzi viewing documentation together with teacher Annetta Squarza (in the background) and *atelierista* Alessandro Mainini.

FIGURE 3.7 *Aggiornamento* at *Scuola dell'infanzia* XXV Aprile: *Atelierista* Mirella Ruozzi and *pedagogista* Paola Strozzi viewing documentation and reading children's words together with teacher Annetta Squarza.

66 The value of relationality and an ethic of dialectics

particular professional role within the system that is "materially embedded and embodied, differential, affective and relational" (Braidotti, 2019, p. 11), and also a collective, "differential attunement":

> Affect is a *differential attunement* between two bodies in a joint activity of becoming. What I mean by differential attunement is that the bodies in encounter are both completely absorbed in the felt transition, but they are differently absorbed coming at it asymmetrically, from different angles, living a different complexion of affecting-being affected, transitioning through the encounter to different outcomes, perhaps structured into different roles. But all of these differences are actively, dynamically co-implicated in the event.
>
> *(Massumi, 2015, p. 95)*

This image that Massumi (2015) conveys about bodies coming to an event asymmetrically, bringing their differences to bear and to be co-implicated, renders effectively the experience of the *sistema pedagogico diffuso* in Reggio Emilia, which relies for its very existence on the different professional roles "affecting-being affected" (p. 95). Furthermore, in the history of the educational project of Reggio Emilia there are many examples of the ways in which differences are actively co-implicated in what Massumi calls "events"; events can be many things, and from the point of view of Manning and Massumi (2014), these are creatively and ethically generated. For our purposes, an "event" can be seen as the coming together of *progettazione* and documentation.[1] This is made particularly visible through the system-wide research projects and thoughtful exhibitions hosted in the Loris Malaguzzi International Centre in Reggio Emilia, of which "Border-crossings" (Vecchi et al., 2019) is a prime recent example. Events, however, are not limited to such grand and rigorous exhibitions; the everyday fragments of documentation that are born of collective becomings are events in their own right.

This concern with collectivity, or with the system, brings us to qualify the other aspect which aligns the concept of affect to the experience of Reggio Emilia: the notion that "it focuses on the middle, directly on what happens *between*" (Massumi, 2015, p. 91). The term currently used to qualify the system of working relationships in Reggio Emilia – diffused pedagogical system – emphasises this space of in-betweenness.

> This idea of *sistema pedagogico diffuso*, both as a practice that has always existed and as a concept that has been created, is that we are formed together. Therefore, the pedagogical coordination has a responsibility towards *formazione*, but it does not detain the knowledge within *formazione*; the *pedagogista* forms herself together with teachers. The primary idea of *sistema pedagogico diffuso* is therefore this capacity for

each working group to generate *formazione* within themselves, and to welcome the new.

(Paola Cagliari, Director, Preschools and Infant-toddler Centres -
Istituzione of the Municipality of Reggio Emilia, interview
with Stefania Giamminuti, Reggio Emilia)

The concept of a diffused pedagogical system illuminates the fact that "affect arises in the midst of *in-between-ness*: in the capacities to act and be acted upon" (Seigworth & Gregg, 2010, p. 1); in the experience of Reggio Emilia, this means generating *formazione* from within, while welcoming the new. The concept of affect, aligned here to *formazione,* qualifies the value of relationality as something that is generated within the collectivity: "for the concept of affect to take on its full force and furthest implications, it is necessary to think of it as involving a multiplicity" (Massumi, 2015, p. 95). Such "multi-body situations" (Massumi, 2015, p. 95) are enabled by valuing relationality both in pedagogical practice-research-theory and in broad organisational concerns, or rather in recognising the fundamental interconnection between pedagogy and organisation, so that relationality and affect underlie all aspects of early childhood education and care systems. It is possible that, in contexts where both pedagogy and organisation (often known as "management" or "leadership") are informed by neoliberal values of rationality and individuality, affect may seem an unreachable utopia, or it may be actively avoided and perceived as dangerous for its potential to activate collectivities that tend towards creativity (Manning, 2010).

Neoliberalism elevates individual autonomy whilst mistrusting both creativity and collectivity, in so far as they do not act in service of the marketplace and in the pursuit of individual interests. Perhaps this is why, in many contexts where neoliberal values pervade educational policy and practice, the experience of Reggio Emilia may be viewed with fundamental mistrust and is often undermined by the misinformed as an "anything goes" pedagogy. Such constricting contexts frequently thrive on teachers' isolation, misconstrued as autonomy. Instead, as Massumi (2015) notes, "it's not just about us, in isolation. In affect, we are never alone" (p. 6). In Reggio Emilia, where teachers, *atelieristas,* and *pedagogistas* explicitly state that they never feel lonely, affect is at its greatest potential when group subjectivities are open to change and creativity, where all are recognised as "relational beings, defined by the capacity to affect and be affected" (Braidotti, 2019, p. 45). *Pedagogista* Elena Giacopini highlights how in this educational project collectivities are always in the making:

We have always worked with the intention that the experience of one *nido* or one *scuola dell'infanzia* would not belong solely to that centre or school, but rather that it participates in a collective municipal project, as *formazione* for that school and *formazione* for the system. We were creating a legacy for the system.

(Elena Giacopini, pedagogista, *interview with*
Stefania Giamminuti, Reggio Emilia)

68 The value of relationality and an ethic of dialectics

These words echo the belief that "the collective is never a thing in itself. It is a project for becoming" (Manning, 2010, p. 123), and furthermore that "what moves the collective is the affective tonality of a project in the making, a project always framed by the force of becoming" (Manning, 2010, p. 124). A *sistema pedagogico diffuso* is a project in the making, framed by the force of becoming, it is not just a thing in itself. The experience of Reggio Emilia does not stand still, but rather it is animated by the utopia of an educational project. Further, the notions of "a legacy for the system" and of "a collective municipal project" bring to the fore what Massumi (2015) terms "politics beyond the self-interest" which is "the foundation for practices of direct democracy, lived democracy, democracy as essentially participatory and irreducibly relational" (Massumi, 2015, pp. 97–98). The *nidi* and *scuole dell'infanzia* of Reggio Emilia practice "a democracy whose base concept is not the supposed freedom of the individual from the collectivity, but the freedom *of* the collectivity, *for* its becoming" (Massumi, 2015, pp. 97–98). This commitment to democracy as participatory and relational, premised on the becoming and freedom of the collectivity, relies on the value of relationality, affect, and reciprocity in pedagogy and organisation. Such possibilities are enhanced in contexts such as Reggio Emilia where different professional roles are "activated by relational ethics" (Braidotti, 2019, p. 46).

We recognise with Erin Manning (2010) that "affect moves being, dephasing being with respect to its individuality, causing it to overspill [...] It is transformative, and it is collective" (p. 122). Thus, in Reggio Emilia, affect has moved the being of teachers, *atelieristas, pedagogistas,* and others, causing individuality to overspill and the collective to emerge as a considerable force. In returning to our initial caution in regards to *affetto* or *affection,* we now invite others to recognise that "without the collective at the core of becoming, the power of affect is reduced to emotion and becoming devolves into personhood" (Manning, 2010, p. 123). It is the collective that moves us from *affection* to *affect* and as such, in contexts other than Reggio Emilia, any consideration of affect must be premised on welcoming collectivity as a value. We now turn to illustrating how the dedication to care and solidarity that distances the educational project from "individualist autonomy" (Braidotti, 2019, p. 12) further animates the value of relationality.

The value of relationality: worlds seen through care

Worlds seen through care accentuate a sense of interdependency and involvement.

(Puig de la Bellacasa, 2017, p. 17)

Similarly to affect, care "is not to be confused with individualized emotions" (Braidotti, 2019, p. 45), but rather "care joins together an affective state, a material vital doing, and an ethico-political obligation" (Puig de la Bellacasa,

The value of relationality and an ethic of dialectics **69**

2017, p. 42). Having delineated reciprocity and affect as fundamentally collectivist principles, we acknowledge furthermore that "the living web of care is not maintained by individuals giving and receiving back again but by a collective disseminated force" (Puig de la Bellacasa, 2017, p. 20). Care therefore can also be found in the in-between, rather than being an individual emotion and/or action. We might thus qualify the *sistema pedagogico diffuso* as a caring system, as a "collective disseminated force" which operates as a "thick mesh of relational obligation" (Puig de la Bellacasa, 2017, p. 20). This image is reflected in the words of *pedagogista* Paola Strozzi:

> I truly feel I have so much to learn from my colleagues and from the teachers. *Pedagogistas* should be grateful to teachers because they bring us the best of their experience, an experience that is also made of much physical toil. They share with us the best of the words of the children, the words of parents, children's artefacts – all this has meant much movement, physical movement as well, coming and going, collecting and placing, inviting children's attention. Therefore, we *pedagogistas* also need to offer gifts to teachers through our capacity to bring theoretical and practical references, so that the work inside the *nidi* and *scuole dell'infanzia*, and with the city and families, may be enriched by a deeper, broader gaze.
>
> *(Paola Strozzi,* pedagogista, *interview with*
> *Stefania Giamminuti, Reggio Emilia)*

The teachers, the *pedagogistas*, the toil, the movement, the words, the children, the families, the artefacts, the references, the *scuole* and *nidi*, the city; all are implicated in a mesh of relational obligation. In mentioning the physical toil of teachers, and the need for a relational obligation in response to this gift, Paola raises two key aspects of care: it is not always pretty, and it involves a different kind of temporality. As Puig de la Bellacasa (2017) notes, the "messy worldliness" of care can be easily neglected;

> Anybody who has been involved in caring for children, pets, elderly kin, an allotment, cells in a petri dish, knows that the work of care takes time and involves making time of an unexceptional particular kind. It requires having to deal with necessary material doings of maintenance that absorb time but ground the everyday possibility of living as well as possible – cleaning up vomit or digging ditches. Affectively, this aspect of care time can be enjoyable but also very tiresome, involving a lot of hovering and adjusting to the temporal exigencies of the cared for. Ethically and politically this work remains neglected, receiving among the lowest wages, even within sociotechnical regimes that put carers under high moral pressure because of the economic importance of their work.
>
> *(Puig de la Bellacasa, 2017, p. 206)*

70 The value of relationality and an ethic of dialectics

In the field of early childhood education and *care*, this no doubt resonates whilst raising the concerns of an underappreciated workforce. We speculate that valuing relationality, the affective, the in-between may enable a paradigmatic shift in such tensions of neglect while acknowledging fully that the "material doings" of the work are unlikely to disappear. To illustrate this potential for care and relationality to elevate and transform the daily toil, we share the words of Francesca Forenzi, teacher of infants and toddlers:

> I believe that there is a risk, particularly in the *nido*, at a human level, to be overcome by the toil, to be overcome by physical exhaustion. This exhaustion risks dulling our attitude of curiosity, our *pensiero progettuale*. It is in these moments in particular that we need to be reminded that there is more to our work, that our desire to research with children, to work together as a group, to engage in *confronto*, to support participation, needs to be nourished. The role of the *pedagogista* should also be that of continuing to nurture our fire. As a way of being together without standing above us, to be alongside us, to be available. And, primarily, to lift us up from some of the more mundane aspects of daily life. There are in fact situations, particularly in the *nido*, of strong everyday-ness in which we must dwell for extended periods of time. For example, mealtimes are very important moments, in which together with the children we need to celebrate great achievements, great transformations. And we could risk falling back on those which many years ago we used to call "routines" – you know, doing the same things in always the same way [...] There are all of these efforts, that a *pedagogista* should support, that make our work a practice of research. For families, the experience is transformed into participation and learning. And for the *nido*, I believe, it enables it to become even more a place of shared culture.
>
> *(Francesca Forenzi, teacher, interview with*
> *Stefania Giamminuti, Reggio Emilia)*

Francesca illuminates how the many daily practices of "adjusting to the temporal exigencies of the cared for" (Puig de la Bellacasa, 2017, p. 206), whilst potentially very draining both physically and intellectually, can also be rich in possibilities and full of daily moments of beauty. Her nod to routine[2] will no doubt resonate deeply with many teachers of young children, and perhaps may activate an awareness of how conventional notions of care can lead to elevating routine to an unavoidable practice, where there can be no alternatives to doing the same things in always the same ways. Thinking care differently, we propose, invites alternatives. In illustrating the potential of welcoming different ways of thinking and doing, Francesca suggests that this different gaze becomes a practice for caring, and at the same time caring becomes a way of producing knowledge. In the words of Puig de la Bellacasa (2017): "caring in this context is both a doing and ethico-political commitment that affects the way we produce

The value of relationality and an ethic of dialectics **71**

knowledge about things. It goes beyond a moral disposition or wishful thinking to transform how we experience and perceive the things we study" (p. 66).

Care is not a moral disposition or an individual emotion; rather, collective care transforms knowledge of children and others, for children and others. As evidenced in the words of both Paola and Francesca, this means transforming knowledge from within, rather than in a hierarchical sense whereby the *pedagogista* or educational leader might be viewed as holding the "higher" knowledge and thus demanding pedagogical changes that teachers will enact. As in the notion of reciprocal *formazione*, "care is not one way; the cared for conforms the carer too" (Puig de la Bellacasa, 2017, p. 219). Francesca's words emphasise for *pedagogistas* a responsibility towards teachers that is reminiscent of Puig de la Bellacasa's (2017) invitation towards caring for "things": "we must take care of things in order to remain responsible for their becomings" (p. 43). This means that we are all fundamentally implicated in each other's becoming through care. It is, once again, a space of the in-between: teachers, *atelieristas,* and *pedagogistas* caring for each other so that they remain responsible for their becomings, and in so doing caring for children, families, places, materials, living things, and the city, all enmeshed in a relational correspondence. We are compelled to think of *sistema pedagogico diffuso* as "melodies in counterpoint" (Ingold, 2021b, p. 107).

We further speculate that *progettazione* is a practice of care, not a moral practice but rather a politics of care that "involves affective, ethical, and hands-on agencies of practical and material consequence" (Puig de la Bellacasa, 2017, p. 4). Mirella Ruozzi speaks thus of *progettazione* and documentation, implying its ethical, practical, and caring potentialities:

> To observe and document, to re-elaborate that which you have observed and documented in order to think about how to go forward – this is very hard. And I have seen how important it is to do this together, not in solitude, but together. Because *progettazione* requires group work, multiple heads, multiple ideas, multiple thoughts; it is not something that can be done on your own. I don't believe anyone can engage in a research project, a project with children, by defining it alone. *Progettazione* as a way of being closer to children, being with them, accompanying them in their knowledge; but also *progettazione* as a way of working together. This for me is fundamental: working together, welcoming the error, the mistake, making it become a resource.
>
> *(Mirella Ruozzi,* atelierista, *interview with Stefania Giamminuti, Reggio Emilia)*

Mirella speaks here of how the relationality of *progettazione* and documentation, activated by care as an ethical and political concern, enables new and unexpected becomings. This contrasts with traditional strategies of observation

72 The value of relationality and an ethic of dialectics

and assessment in early childhood, which elevate individuality by being focused on one child and created mostly in isolation by one teacher. Such conventional practices generally respond to normative concerns and address preconceived outcomes rather than activating political and ethical matters or matters of care. Documentation and *progettazione* instead are a fundamental part of that "thick mesh of relational obligation" (Puig de la Bellacasa, 2017, p. 20) we referred to earlier, a place where, as evidenced by Mirella's focus on relationality and possibility/error, "subjectivity is thus both post-personal and pre-individual, relational and hence in constant negotiation with multiple others and immersed in the conditions that it is trying to understand and modify, if not overturn" (Braidotti, 2019, p. 42). As acknowledged by Rinaldi (2006), documentation is a subjective act, but in this constant negotiation with multiple others it becomes post-personal, pre-individual, and relational; thus it overturns the conventional by virtue of its situatedeness. Documentation is not abstract; it is a caring event.

Previously, we conceptualised documentation and *progettazione* as an "event"; Mirella's words emphasise the politics of care within such "events", likening such practices to what Massumi (2015) calls "event-care". In documentation, which brings people together and connects them to each other, there is "a kind of collective tending […] in the sense of attending to how an event is capable of producing mutually imbricated modes of existence or modes of living" (p. 169). We do not suggest that simply adopting practices of *progettazione* and documentation will lead to such collective tending elsewhere; instead, we continue to remain speculative and propositional, inviting others, in places other than Reggio Emilia, to "think about how things could be different if they generated care" (Puig de la Bellacasa, 2017, p. 60) whilst recognising that "what care can mean in each situation cannot be resolved by ready-made formulas" (Puig de la Bellacasa, 2017, p. 60). Once again, we eschew ready-made solutions whilst inviting an obligation to think differently and to act with care, for with relationality comes responsibility; in responding to one another we are also all responsible (Ingold, 2021a).

The value of relationality: solidarity, freedom, and democracy

While suggesting that we must all carry the burden of responsibility, we also acknowledge that such burdens are alleviated by solidarity. It is particularly hopeful for those who look to creating new projects of education to be reminded that from the beginnings of the educational project of Reggio Emilia through its many trials over the decades since, "the values of anti-fascist resistance persisted: solidarity, social justice, peace, democracy" (Moss, in Cagliari et al., 2016, p. 3). In creating something new, and in keeping it lively, solidarity is a fundamental matter, as acknowledged by Malaguzzi:

> We can all sense that something new is being born, and that past experiences we have lived through are being asked to come to terms with new

The value of relationality and an ethic of dialectics **73**

things, to be lived and expressed in more stimulating ways, with open exchange and broader solidarity.

(Malaguzzi, 1970, in Cagliari et al., 2016, p. 159)

Manuela Pederzoli, a teacher at *Nido d'infanzia* Panda since it opened in 1979, recalls how solidarity sustained responsibility:

I was very young, but from the beginning I shared this sense of solidarity, this sense of belonging, this desire for things to work well, because education is a common good.

(Manuela Pederzoli, teacher, interview with Stefania Giamminuti, Reggio Emilia)

This reminder of education as a common good positions solidarity as a practice of democracy. Indeed, in the experience of Reggio Emilia and in the words of Malaguzzi and many others, solidarity is always linked to a broader dedication to democracy itself and to life as citizens of a city and a region that is enduringly committed to democratic and participatory values, as evidenced by the words of *pedagogistas* Daniela Lanzi and Simona Bonilauri:

The values of solidarity, of cooperation, these do not belong exclusively to education, they belong to the region of Emilia Romagna.

(Daniela Lanzi, pedagogista, interview with Stefania Giamminuti, Reggio Emilia)

This aspect of collegiality is fundamentally an expression of the democratic fabric of the city. It is this democratic fabric that the pedagogical coordination pursues as its goal, because *nidi* and *scuole dell'infanzia* are places of democracy.

(Simona Bonilauri, pedagogista, interview with Stefania Giamminuti, Reggio Emilia)

This democratic stance means that solidarity, within the value of relationality, is a practice for disrupting conventional hierarchies in educational systems. In Reggio Emilia, power is not an extrinsic relation, of which Massumi (2015) highlights the implications: "if power just came at us from outside, if it was just an extrinsic relation, it would be simple. You'd just run away" (p. 19). Of the teachers, *atelieristas*, and *pedagogistas* interviewed for this project, many have belonged to the Reggio Emilia educational project for decades, including Loredana Garofalo who recalls her intentional decision to work in the *nidi* and *scuole dell'infanzia*:

Malaguzzi contended that children are not the only protagonists, we are all protagonists together. For me the *pedagogista* has always been such a precious resource. I believe in group work. I made the decision to work here, because I can find myself, my desires as a person, my values: culture, solidarity, social transformation.

(Loredana Garofalo, teacher, interview with Stefania Giamminuti)

Loredana's thoughts echo the words of Malaguzzi in a speech to staff in the 1980s, where he stated that "the educational hypothesis in our *scuola dell'infanzia* is a hypothesis of participatory education. In the sense that it recognises and enacts the needs and rights of children, families, teachers and school workers, actively to feel part of a solidarity of practices and ideals" (Malaguzzi, in Cagliari et al., 2016, p. 353). In contrast, Cameron and Moss (2020) bemoan what they term the "democratic deficit" (p. 3), referring to early childhood education and care in England but with a tone that strikes parallels with other contexts such as the systems in the USA and Australia that are similarly driven by neoliberal marketplace values. They go on to qualify this as "a system that fails the workforce as much as it does children and their families" (Cameron & Moss, 2020, p. 3), where retention and high turnover of staff are key challenges. They do not, however, present a doomsday scenario, but rather suggest hopefully that it is possible to re-imagine the role of the educator, to privilege beauty and generosity of indoor and outdoor spaces, to recognise children as citizens with rights, and to thoughtfully remunerate an educated workforce (Cameron & Moss, 2020).

As highlighted in the momentous choice made by Loredana and many others in Reggio Emilia to enduringly belong to this system and thrive within it, we propose with pragmatic hopefulness that such situations are indeed possible when relationality and solidarity are valued and integral to lives, thinking, and practices. The view of the *pedagogista* as a "precious resource" for enabling such thriving conditions is shared by others, quoted below: Manuela Pederzoli, a teacher, speaks of her *pedagogista* as being (metaphorically and physically) always by her side and as having the humility to *mettersi in gioco*[3]; Annalisa Rabotti, a *pedagogista*, recognises the need to co-participate with teachers; and Elena Giacopini, also a *pedagogista* with many decades of experience, speaks of the need to be in solidarity with teachers.

My *pedagogista* Paola Strozzi is an extremely courteous person. She came into the *nido* tiptoeing, like a teacher-colleague, saying: "I'm here to learn, because I don't know the *nido* as well as the *scuola dell'infanzia*". And so, she often stayed beside us in *aggiornamenti*, particularly in the early days, being humble and responsive to *mettersi in gioco* as a person, even in relation to the most minute aspects of our daily work in the *nido*. And she is always available, even for just a phone call.

(Manuela Pederzoli, teacher, interview with Stefania Giamminuti, Reggio Emilia)

[For all *pedagogistas*] to feel co-responsible and to co-participate in the care of these relationships is a fundamental prerequisite to support and sustain teachers' work. Their work is significantly complex. Teachers are the primary interlocuters of the contemporary.

(Annalisa Rabotti, pedagogista, *interview with Stefania Giamminuti, Reggio Emilia)*

To have worked as a teacher, I believe, was fundamental and foundational for how I later interpreted my role as a *pedagogista*. I felt more in solidarity, but at the same time when some things were presented to you as impossible you could also question that view, because you knew that in fact such things could be possible.

(Elena Giacopini, pedagogista, *interview with Stefania Giamminuti, Reggio Emilia)*

These perspectives highlight the role of the *pedagogista* as an amateur intellectual, working at the boundaries of the possible while being co-responsible, open to *mettersi in gioco*, and close to the teachers, in solidarity. Having noted above how *progettazione* and documentation are active participants in relationality, affect and care, we suggest here that these practices are also key in activating solidarity. As experienced teacher Simona Marani recognises:

Pensiero progettuale is after all an attitude, it is the way in which each day as a person, as a teacher, but also together with the group which whom you work, you open yourself to enter the *scuola dell'infanzia*. It is a way of thinking in solidarity. For me, to be in solidarity means to be on the side of children and families every day. This is the way in which, I believe, we should try to enter the *scuola dell'infanzia*. It is a way of thinking that is not still, it is dynamic thinking, in movement. It is a subjective way of thinking, but it is also the thinking of a group that creates itself.

(Simona Marani, teacher, *interview with Stefania Giamminuti, Reggio Emilia)*

This "thinking in solidarity" feels close to what Massumi (2015) calls "enthusiasm", or "the feeling of vitality that belongs to the relational field" (p. 141). Solidarity is not therefore, once again, an individual capacity but a relational one. We have conceived of the *sistema pedagogico diffuso* as a system of affect and care; it is also a system of solidarity. In thinking back to all the thoughts shared in this chapter from teachers, *pedagogistas*, and *atelieristas*, we can sense a sort of "relational freedom" that is activated through affect, care, and solidarity: "it is through relation that we derive greater potential, intensify our powers of existence. Freedom is never individual. It is by nature relational" (Massumi, 2015, pp. 202–203). Freedom in the context

76 The value of relationality and an ethic of dialectics

of education is the capacity to envisage alternatives to the way things have always been done, understanding that larger, democratic transformations can occur through situated ethics of caring and practices of solidarity. We now turn to considering how such freedoms might be activated through *confronto* and an ethic of dialectics, recognising that to be in solidarity does not mean that you have to always be in agreement; in fact, much the contrary, an invitation to disagreement is vital. Teacher Manuela Pederzoli illustrates this beautifully, providing a thoughtful segue into our musing on dialectics, *confronto,* and participation:

> I have always felt very gratified for the thoughts I have contributed with my colleagues, divergent ones too, in the sense that we don't always have to agree. I believe it is very important to have a constructive *confronto* on nearly everything. Discord is also important at times, to feel legitimated to express different points of view. In my opinion, this promotes the capacity to *mettersi in gioco.*
>
> *(Manuela Pederzoli, teacher, interview with*
> *Stefania Giamminuti, Reggio Emilia)*

An ethic of dialectics: *confronto* and participation

Of the very many terms we have found ourselves at a loss as to how to accurately translate into English without launching into a verbose discussion of the Italian linguistic and social heritage and Reggian contextual educational understandings, *confronto* is one of the most baffling. Interpreters familiar with the experience of the municipal *nidi* and *scuole dell'infanzia* translate *confronto* variously as: confrontation; exchange; dialogue, discussion; meeting – none of which are wrong in principle, but all of which fail to accurately convey its vitality and contextuality. In his writing on the topic, Moss (2018) participates in this unwillingness to translate:

> Important in this process is a readiness for "confrontation" [confronto], a willingness and capacity to question the interpretations and perspectives of others and to offer your own for similar challenge in frank but respectful exchange without degenerating into hostility and antagonism.
>
> *(Moss, 2018, p. 83)*

Pedagogista Simona Bonilauri quips, at the beginning of an *aggiornamento* held at the end of the school year at the *Scuola dell'infanzia* Bruno Munari: "there are many things I don't agree with here". Barbara Beltrami and Anna Tamburini, teachers from the 3-year-old class, joined by *atelierista* Barbara Quinti and by teacher educator Laura Rubizzi, are presenting their proposals for documentation detailing a project on time, to be offered to

The value of relationality and an ethic of dialectics 77

FIGURE 3.8 Aggiornamento at *Scuola dell'infanzia* Bruno Munari. Clockwise from left: *pedagogista* Simona Bonilauri; teacher educator Laura Rubizzi; teachers Anna Tamburini and Barbara Beltrami; and *atelierista* Barbara Quinti).

families at the end of the school year as a parting gift.[4] This *aggiornamento* (Figure 3.8) was rich in *confronto*, whereby theoretical perspectives on the notion of time, and varied understandings of children's competencies and how they might be documented, were debated thoughtfully and deeply.[5] The frank exchange resulted in formal changes in the phrasing of research questions informing the project, and in the layout of the documentation, but fundamentally all those participating in this event emerged with new pedagogical understandings that were generated through offering one's own perspectives and questioning the interpretations of others. While Simona's initial statement was frank and almost unforgiving, and at times the teachers might have been at a loss as to how to respond, the "confrontational" nature of the event was expected and even welcomed as an essential ethical stance, in order to give back to children and families something of value, capable of reflecting children's theories and capabilities.

We illuminate *confronto* here and we engage the notion in a somewhat original way, drawing from the concept of dialectics and proposing that an ethic of dialectics activates responses that are relational and participatory. Those who have found their own ideas and experiences to resonate with our above discussions on relationality may be surprised to find that this is followed by elevating dialectics to such as fundamental place in the experience of Reggio Emilia. In fact, conceptual leanings such as feminist new materialisms and

78 The value of relationality and an ethic of dialectics

posthuman thought generally eschew the dyadic and oppositional standpoint implied in traditional views of dialectics. Braidotti (2019) for example contrasts dialectics to what she terms "collective practice", as she notes that "the negative logic of dialectics is of no help in bringing about intensive, qualitative shifts in what a society or a community is capable of becoming" (p. 66). The Reggio Emilia experience embodies the features of posthuman knowledge that Braidotti (2019) emphasises: collective practice that combines critique with creation; privileging affirmative ethics as a praxis, being always in tension towards becoming, and welcoming creativity as a transversal force. It would appear therefore that dialectics may not be a useful concept for us to pursue. However, as Giroux (2016, p. 160) contends, "the meaning of the dialectic has an elusive quality" and we find that the concept of an ethic of dialectics illustrates how the *sistema pedagogico diffuso* privileges "a critical mode of reasoning and behavior" (Giroux, 2016, pp. 160–161). An ethic of dialectics engages with both reciprocity and *formazione,* as evidenced below in the words of Paola Cagliari:

> *Formazione* is never unidirectional, it is reciprocal. We view the teacher as a researcher, as a producer of knowledge, as a creator of processes and documents that are formational in nature and that enter into relationship with the *pedagogista* – a relationship that is dialectical and reciprocal. Because as a *pedagogista* you come with your own *formazione,* with your own knowledge that you offer, but in truth you are formed in your own profession by virtue of your relationship with the *nidi* and *scuole dell'infanzia.*
>
> *(Paola Cagliari, Director, Preschools and Infant-toddler Centres -*
> *Istituzione of the Municipality of Reggio Emilia, interview*
> *with Stefania Giamminuti, Reggio Emilia)*

Such critical mode of reasoning in Reggio Emilia is always a collective, affirmative, transformative, and creative practice, as opposed to a reductive oppositional stance. In fact, Simona Bonilauri's statement "I don't agree" (above) is not about creating opposition, but rather about propelling knowledge and creation. In the following excerpt from a letter to parents titled *The Profession of Parents,* Loris Malaguzzi brings together the notion of a "dialectical perspective" and "inseparable relations between living things and their environment", exemplifying the sort of argument we wish to convey:

> Pedagogy and psychology have helped us to react against an education that is too philosophical, too abstract, too authoritarian, idealistic or patronising, now working with the child-as-myth, now with the "subversive" "rebel" child only using adult schema, now with a child to be jealously protected, a small, defenceless, absorptive, passive creature. It is universally recognised today that to understand children, they must be studied as an

The value of relationality and an ethic of dialectics **79**

organic-psychic whole, and in relation to their parents. These relations can only be understood in a dialectical perspective of reciprocal, inseparable relations between living things and their environment.

(Malaguzzi, 1957, in Cagliari et al., 2016, p. 53)

In our view, it is this dialectical perspective that elevates *confronto* to a necessary everyday praxis. The following excerpts from interviews with teachers in Reggio Emilia illuminate this notion of an everyday dialectics as enriching thinking, research, and practice:

It's a continuous *confronto*. You have your own ideas, but you invite *confronto* daily, with your colleagues. *Formazione* is a daily praxis – to give ourselves time for *confronto*. For example, we are all now researching on nature and digital, the topic might appear the same, but the facets are all different. This, I believe, is authentic *formazione*.

(Annalisa Rainieri, teacher, interview with Stefania Giamminuti, Reggio Emilia)

Before I came to teach in Reggio's municipal *scuole dell'infanzia*, I was working in another context, where I had only one class. I worked with another colleague, and we had a *pedagogista* to refer to, but we worked primarily as a dyad […] In Reggio Emilia, I found myself in a *collettivo* with many professional roles, many different competencies, where we worked in collaboration with the kitchen as well. It was a significant change, but working with a group of people possessing so many different competencies has revealed itself to be a precious resource. It's not always easy, because *confronto* requires a certain wisdom of thought, but at the same time it affords intellectual liveliness. And, importantly, *confronto* supports you when there are moments of tiredness, when as a teacher you become aware of your own limits.

(Giulia Ovi, teacher, interview with Stefania Giamminuti, Reggio Emilia)

The *pedagogista* poses those uncomfortable questions, those questions which you had not considered, perhaps because you were deeply within the experience, or because you don't have her knowledge or because you aren't a *pedagogista*. These questions can shift your thinking, or propel your research forward.

(Ethel Carnevali, teacher, interview with Stefania Giamminuti, Reggio Emilia)

To share with someone else your observations, the children's drawings, your approach to creating a piece of documentation to display on your walls, or documentation that you wish to offer to families, I think this is always useful.

Because while you explain it and you narrate it to the *pedagogista*, you try to create an intelligent synthesis of what you wish to convey to families.

(Francesca Forenzi, teacher, interview with Stefania Giamminuti, Reggio Emilia)

A *pedagogista* who is within your *nido* or your *scuola dell'infanzia*, and other *nidi* and *scuole*, who is within the system, who participates, has a different lens to your own. Different lenses are necessary for us all to strive for the same goal which is to assist children to grow and to find their own paths, to show them the possible, and to reveal to them what they are capable of.

(Marika Lorenzani, teacher, interview with Stefania Giamminuti, Reggio Emilia)

These teachers align *confronto* with *formazione*, making dialectical relationality an essential part of their daily praxis and research (Figures 3.9 and 3.10). They also thoughtfully convey the necessity of multiple points of view, and they welcome sensations of discomfort to propel their work forward. Importantly, the teachers express a desire for the intellectual liveliness that *confronto* enables. As Giroux (2016) notes in relation to the dialectic, "we must consider new forms of discourse and practice in order to maintain the field's critical posture as well as its ability for self-renewal" (p. 160). Similarly, the teachers quoted above invite into their daily lives a critical posture and a self-renewal – of self and of knowledge – that keeps their work alive. Importantly, they imply that an ethic of dialectics

FIGURE 3.9   *Confronto* during an *aggiornamento* at *Scuola dell'infanzia* La Villetta: teachers Ethel Carnevali and Annalisa Rainieri and *pedagogista* Paola Strozzi.

FIGURE 3.10   *Aggiornamento* in the three-year-old classroom at *Scuola dell'infanzia* La Villetta, looking out towards the school park.

can create the conditions for eschewing solitude – professional, personal, and intellectual. This is close to Giroux's (2016) insight that "at the core of the dialectic is the notion that underlying the mediations that form the intersubjective space in which we live, work, study, and dream are social relationships" (p. 165). We foregrounded experiences of solitude in Chapter 1, when we discussed some of the organisational choices that have been made in Reggio Emilia to elevate the collective and safeguard the system. We return to solitude now, with a particular lens on how an ethic of dialectics, rather than creating opposing camps and being premised on negativity, can instead stimulate collective thinking and doing, as Malaguzzi aspired to when contemplating professional roles and systemic organisation in Reggio Emilia:

> Taking teachers from the deforming solitude old pedagogy gave us (and continues to give us) and situating them in shared constructions, work that calls for exchange, confrontation, updating, that constantly brings into play both personal and private experience; and through this reciprocal dialogue growth and enrichment, brings them to a human and professional awareness of the group.
>
> *(Malaguzzi, 1970, in Cagliari et al., 2016, p. 171)*

In a similarly critical vein to Malaguzzi, Giroux (2013) laments "neoliberalism's war against teachers in dark times", emphasising how contemporary educational policies and contexts act to isolate teachers, preventing them from critical thought and repressing active resistance. By stating that "we need a

82 The value of relationality and an ethic of dialectics

critical pedagogy that links pedagogical processes to radical modes of reasoning", Giroux (2016, p. 170) suggests that the dialectic may be essential to avoid surrendering to ideological and material forces. In the words of teachers and *pedagogistas* in Reggio Emilia, this connection between dialectics and collective thought and praxis shines through, banishing isolation:

> I believe that the dimension of *équipe* in the pedagogical coordination is very important. It has a component of *formazione* for it allows you to engage with different generations, and with those with more or less experience professionally – this is very positive. Your thinking is never alone, it is always in *confronto*.
> *(Daniela Lanzi,* pedagogista, *interview with Stefania Giamminuti, Reggio Emilia)*

> This continuous *confronto*, of always having access to someone else's gaze - this is so important in working with children. To not feel alone, to know that you can really rely on the listening of other competent people who are asking themselves questions together with you, in that moment.
> *(Marina Castagnetti, teacher, interview with Stefania Giamminuti, Reggio Emilia)*

> I have to emphasise how great is this responsibility of working alongside children. On the other hand, there is also this pleasure, this feeling of not being alone because we are on a shared path with children, families, and colleagues. We follow children's learning processes, but truthfully at the same time we are constantly revisiting our own processes, reviewing our own knowledge. And this is possible only, I believe, in *confronto* with others, with colleagues, with families. Otherwise, it is very difficult indeed to be so good as to reflect on oneself, in solitude.
> *(Simona Marani, teacher, interview with Stefania Giamminuti, Reggio Emilia)*

> The peculiarity of this *confronto* is to not be alone.
> *(Annalisa Rainieri, teacher, interview with Stefania Giamminuti, Reggio Emilia)*

Teachers who are not alone, who like Manuela (above), feel "gratified" for the thoughts they contribute through *confronto*, experience "openness", which means "to hold one's self available to others" (Bird Rose, 2004, p. 22). In so doing, "one takes risks and becomes vulnerable. But this is also a fertile stance: one's own ground can become destabilised. In open dialogue one holds one's self available to be surprised, to be challenged, and to be changed" (Bird Rose, 2004, p. 22). Holding oneself open to surprise, challenge and change is evident in the stance of all the teachers and *pedagogistas* interviewed for this

The value of relationality and an ethic of dialectics **83**

project. This embodies the dialectic through *confronto*: to be comfortable with risk, to be welcoming of difference and transformation, and to engage in a dialogue that is always situated, where "the outcome is not known in advance" (Bird Rose, 2004, p. 21) but the goal is always that of collective knowledge building and research.

In contrast, a preoccupation with known, expected, and generalised outcomes, which is prevalent in many educational contexts, is likely to lead to active avoidance of any opportunity for *confronto*, particularly when considering the dialectic's potential for emancipation (Giroux, 2016). The dialectic serves to uncover traces of the world in order to activate a collective emancipatory response that is facilitated through documentation. *Pedagogista* Elena Giacopini emphasises how the practice of organising *intercollettivi*[6] was born because staff "wished to have places for *confronto*, where they could debate documentation together, where they could generate ideas". She goes on to note that, to these *intercollettivi*, "the *scuola dell'infanzia* would bring the documentation, rather than the *pedagogista*. This practice supports a strong protagonism for teachers and for the *scuole*, which is very important, because it needs to become their own knowledge" (interview with Stefania Giamminuti, Reggio Emilia). This is an example of how organisational choices can support professional emancipation. Giroux (2016) contends that "any emancipatory notion of the dialectic has to be grounded in the process of critique and praxis" (p. 163); in Reggio Emilia dialectics is not an abstract construct but a lived experience, where critique and praxis, in the form of *confronto*, are indissoluble and actively sought.

In conclusion, we briefly turn to participation,[7] a well-known principle of the Reggio Emilia experience that is an essential aspect of both dialectics and relationality. Participation as "an intrinsic mode of being" and "vital lived relation" (Springgay, 2016, p. 71) has shone through all the interview excerpts shared above. In Reggio Emilia, participation is not "something to opt into or out of" (Springgay, 2016, p. 71), such as in conventional settings where families might choose to contribute to or avoid school and community events, but rather it is embedded and embodied in the fabric of everyday experience and relationality. In Reggio Emilia, participation is viewed as "vital and as inescapable" (Springgay, 2016, p. 73), and as "a politics of relation" (Springgay, 2016, p. 76). In the words of Malaguzzi:

> By making it participatory in this way, we give the work of education the meaning of a genuine practice of solidarity, of intersubjective proposals and research, of effectively checking our own personal action, and of a project turned to social ends.
>
> *(Malaguzzi, in Cagliari et al., 2016, p. 354)*

This image of education as a social project of solidarity is very different to neo-liberal views of schools as places where "participation is rewarded and

84 The value of relationality and an ethic of dialectics

deemed valuable" (Springgay, 2016, p. 73). Considered instead through the lens of relationality and dialectics, participation can be complexified as "vital, agentic, and in movement" (Springgay, 2016, p. 73); it is "a priori" for any kind of gesture of resistance (Massumi, 2015).

Conclusion

In this chapter, we have borrowed concepts familiar to the early childhood field – such as relationships, care, participation – and others relatively unfamiliar – such as affect, solidarity, *confronto*, and dialectics – and we have conveyed them in new ways by illuminating the experience of Reggio Emilia's *sistema pedagogico diffuso*. In conclusion, we continue to invite speculation for the possible, alongside a "response-ability" (Haraway, 2016) towards sowing seeds elsewhere. This is not an invitation to dispense with the existing worlds of early childhood education and care, a preposterous suggestion at best, but rather our hope is that we may together engage in what Puig de la Bellacasa (2017) calls "a politics of speculative thinking", which is also "a commitment to seek what other worlds could be in the making through caring while staying with the trouble of our own complicities and implications" (p. 204). The notion of "what other worlds might be in the making" excites us deeply. The next chapter brings to the fore complicities and implications within daily life in Reggio Emilia, highlighting how relational and dialectic encounters might generate situated thinking, new practice, and transformative everyday research.

Notes

1 This notion of *progettazione* and documentation as an "event" will be expanded on in Chapter 5.
2 We will return to the notion of routines in Chapters 5 and 6.
3 The practice of *mettersi in gioco* is discussed in Chapter 1.
4 We return to discussing this *aggiornamento* in Chapter 7.
5 We return to this in more detail in Chapter 7.
6 *Intercollettivi* are scheduled encounters between working groups of different *nidi* and *scuole dell'infanzia*.
7 We will return to participation in Chapters 8 and 9.

References

Bird Rose, D. (2004). *Reports from a wild country: Ethics for decolonisation*. University of New South Wales Press.
Braidotti, R. (2019). *Posthuman knowledge*. Polity Press.
Cagliari, P., Castagnetti, M., Giudici, C., Rinaldi, C., Vecchi, V., & Moss, P. (Eds.). (2016). *Loris Malaguzzi and the schools of Reggio Emilia: A selection of his writings and speeches, 1945–1993*. Routledge.
Cameron, C., & Moss, P. (Eds.). (2020). *Transforming early childhood in England: Towards a democratic education*. UCL Press.

Giamminuti, S., Merewether, J., & Blaise, M. (2021). Aesthetic-ethical-political movements in professional learning: Encounters with feminist new materialisms and Reggio Emilia in early childhood research. *Professional Development in Education*, *7*(2–3), 436–448. https://doi.org/10.1080/19415257.2020.1862277

Giamminuti, S., Merewether, J., & Blaise, M. (2022). Pedagogical documentation and the refusal of method: Troubling dogmas and inviting collective obligations. *European Early Childhood Education Research Journal*, 1–14. https://doi.org/10.1080/1350293X.2022.2046834

Giroux, H. (2013). Neoliberalism's war against teachers in dark times. *Cultural Studies - Critical Methodologies*, *13*, 458–468. https://doi.org/10.1177/1532708613503769

Giroux, H. (2016). Dialectics and the development of curriculum theory. *Counterpoints*, *491*(Curriculum: DECANONIZING THE FIELD), 159–176.

Haraway, D. (2016). *Staying with the trouble: Making kin in the Chthulucene*. Duke University Press.

Ingold, T. (2013). *Making: Anthropology, archaeology, art and architecture*. Routledge.

Ingold, T. (2021a). *Correspondences*. Polity Press.

Ingold, T. (2021b). In praise of amateurs. *Ethnos: Journal of Anthropology*, *86*(1), 153–172. https://doi.org/10.1080/00141844.2020.1830824

Manning, E. (2010). Always more than one: The collectivity of a life. *Body & Society*, *16*(1), 117–127. https://doi.org/10.1177/1357034X09354128

Manning, E. (2015). Against method. In P. Vannini (Ed.), *Non-representational methodologies: Re-envisioning research* (pp. 52–71). Routledge.

Manning, E., & Massumi, B. (2014). *Thought in the act: Passages in the ecology of experience*. University of Minnesota Press.

Massumi, B. (2015). *Politics of affect*. Polity Press.

Moss, P. (2018). What might Loris Malaguzzi have to say? *European Journal of Education*, *53*(1), 82–85. https://doi.org/10.1111/ejed.12256

Puig de la Bellacasa, M. (2017). *Matters of care: Speculative ethics in more than human worlds*. University of Minnesota Press.

Rinaldi, C. (2006). *In dialogue with Reggio Emilia: Listening, researching and learning*. Routledge.

Seigworth, G. J., & Gregg, M. (2010). An inventory of shimmers. In M. Gregg, & G. J. Seigworth (Eds.), *The affect theory reader* (pp. 1–25). Duke University Press.

Springgay, S. (2016). Towards a rhythmic account of working together and taking part. *Research in Education*, *96*(1), 71–77. https://doi.org/10.1177/0034523716664603

van Dooren, T. (2014). Care: Living lexicon for the environmental humanities. *Environmental Humanities*, *5*, 291–294.

Vecchi, V., Bonilauri, S., Meninno, I., & Tedeschi, M. (Eds.). (2019). *Bordercrossings: Encounters with living things, digital landscapes*. Reggio Children.

4

DIALECTICAL ENCOUNTERS IN REGGIO EMILIA

Paola Strozzi

Translated by Jane McCall

Introduction

The previous chapter highlighted how the dimension of relations constitutes an epistemological aspect that informs everyday practice and collective research in Reggio Emilia. In this chapter, following a short analysis of the concept of dialectics from this perspective, we will introduce the voices of some protagonists in a dialectical dimension, mainly adults but also children, using two fragments from different experiences to show how the ethic of dialectics is not only limited to the "big" choices that translate into *progettazione* notes. In fact, dialectical encounters do not only take place in the weekly *aggiornamento* included in the working contract but are, rather, a metaphor for ways of being related in our daily work, of knowing that we can count on each other, and of being reciprocally accountable for ideas, choices, and responsibilities. This cultural climate is made up of words, but also of gestures, documents and the listening and attention that is constructed and shared in school by both adults and children. It cannot be taken for granted that adults or children express evaluations, accept the expression of evaluations by others, or know how to contribute when opinions contrast. The more we can sense respect and reciprocal gain, the more these things can happen. In the words of Loris Malaguzzi (in Gandini, 2017):

> We need to know that, though naturally willing, children do not refine the art of becoming each others' friends and teachers by plucking models out of thin air or from manuals. They pluck and interpret their models from adults and teachers, the more that these are capable of working, being, discussing, thinking and researching together.
>
> (*p. 79, translated by Jane McCall*)

DOI: 10.4324/9781003181026-4

Similarly, it is not enough to introduce an organisational change (a weekly meeting for example) or to provide an additional professional role (such as the *atelierista*) to guarantee an ethic of dialectics; we also have to manage the complexities, inter-relations, and coherencies between values, practices, and reciprocal *formazione* in every moment of doing school and this is where we can see a particular, although not exclusive, responsibility of the *pedagogista*.

The first fragment of dialectical encounters we present touches on a fundamental experience of the *nido* and *scuola dell'infanzia*: the *accoglienza* or *the welcome* of new children and families at the beginning of the new school year. This is a special time with its own particular nature, made up of a myriad of tiny and often fragmented but fundamental details that require the intelligence, knowledge, and care of the working group. It is a time in which children, spaces, ideas, and clues (that we collect, expect, or perhaps only suppose) are all dialectical interlocutors. A second fragment will show, once again through working group voices, how dialectical exchange or *confronto* makes use of different points of view and of the critical but always in-solidarity gaze of colleagues. The situation we will see is very common: faced with children's representations of flowers in drawings, the knowledge of adults each with their own experience and role, helps us all to construct a gaze that is capable of challenging the ever-present risk of stereotypes, so far removed from the values of subjectivity, relations, and education.

Dialectics in daily contexts in Reggio Emilia's municipal *nidi* and *scuole dell'infanzia*

Returning to Giroux's (2016) affirmation, cited in Chapter 3, that "the meaning of the dialectic has an elusive quality" (p. 106), we will try to highlight how, in the daily contexts of Reggio Emilia's municipal *nidi* and *scuole dell'infanzia*, the dialectic becomes an ethic that we engage both in reciprocity and in *formazione*, and how, as noted in Chapter 3, it is experienced as collective, affirmative, transformative and creative practice. Why juxtapose the concept of dialectics alongside an ethic of collective practice? In an educational project with an intrinsically systemic nature, dialectical processes are, in essence, processes of creating meaning. The choice of having professional roles in the schools, each with different educational and cultural backgrounds, each with specific responsibilities but always existing in dialoguing, non-hierarchical relations, and the choice of making time for *progettazione*, documentation, and *confronto*, does not simply correspond to defining how a school is organised but to the intention of generating a continuous and retrospective "organisational process", in which shake-ups and negotiations can lead to reconsidering the meaning of experiences to which perhaps we had previously given a different interpretation.

88 Dialectical encounters in Reggio Emilia

For this reason, it is essential to look back at the definition of hierarchical relations examined in Chapter 2: a functional hierarchy exists in the educational system, but always in-dialogue, above all in the daily meaning-making and formative processes that are mediated and supported by documentation. In relation to the role of the *pedagogista*, rather than thinking only in terms of hierarchy, we need to think in terms of an authoritativeness that emerges in the quality of the arguments the *pedagogistas* are capable of bringing to the conversation. This authoritativeness is determined by the kind of dialectic they contribute to constructing, and for whose final synthesis they take responsibility. An authoritativeness that is not only given by a position or role, and which does not derive from displays of erudition but from relevance and depth in relation to the issues being examined, the significance of the synthesis offered, and the consideration that is given to different positions and points of view that have emerged.

Teachers too must construct their own authoritativeness with the working group and with families, and the documentation they work with and on helps with this construction. In this sense, there are obvious ties between dialectics and *pensiero progettuale*.[1] The dynamic nature of dialectics, by being premised not on the transferral of knowledge but rather on shared and transformational constructions of the meaning of educating, includes and makes use of practices that are apparently de-stabilising, such as openly expressed doubt, dissent, cognitive conflict, and negotiation. Searching for meanings, assigning meanings, communicating and clarifying meanings that are sometimes partial and always subjective, sometimes intentional and often implied, is the spirit that informs dialectical *confronto* in the schools.

Critical dialectical sharing of meaning in everyday contexts in *nidi* and *scuole dell'infanzia* informs our reciprocal *formazione* and reflection on practices, which are never seen as routine even when they constantly recur, but are instead considered as moments of care and learning: moments of possible creativity and transformability. Multiple perspectives and different interpretations amplify our possibility of understanding and assigning things with different meanings: they expand our trust in children, in families, and in colleagues. Multiple perspectives emerge as part of dialogue, but participants also understand and agree that in real dialogue which is not simply formal, not all perspectives are always equally relevant and shared. For example, if a choice based on values that are counter to the essence of Reggio Emilia's educational project should emerge in the dialectics (such as proposing de-contextualised reiterations of gestures on the grounds that it's always been done this way) it is maintained as part of the dialogue, but there is an obligation to make explicit the meanings that underlie this kind of affirmation and of which we are often unaware, as part of a perspective of *formazione* and of making choices coherent with the values framework. Our common streamed of culture is the tension or pull of research towards deeper and broader knowledge of children, and not the reiteration of teaching models. The dialectic we are speaking about therefore is framed by common

Dialectical encounters in Reggio Emilia **89**

values and premises, which are not optional and are only negotiable up to a point. Again, the nature of such negotiation is not formal but contextual, mediated by and based on documentation, and upon references that are not simply methodological but cultural, and which are continuously renewed.

Protagonists in this dialectic know that the common objective is not to come to a mannered and formal equilibrium, or indeed to assent to everyone's opinions, but rather for all of us to be oriented towards a purpose that has the children, and their wellbeing and knowledge, at its centre. This orientation towards contextual choices that are coherent with shared values also pre-supposes a final positioning that is not, however, all in the *pedagogista*'s head. The *pedagogista* is responsible for the synthesis that is produced after evaluating the different positions that have emerged, accepting them or confuting them, but behind everything there is a common framework and shared premises of values. There is no place in dialectics for uncritical acceptance of "just any opinion"; rather, confutative argumentation is part of the formative process. A general frame for this way of interpreting dialectical process can be found in the value given to each and every person's research and participation in a deeper broader knowledge of children, of how they learn and of how adults can participate in children's learning processes in "non-directive" ways. Relations between people, ideas, and environments are multiple and intense, so as not to run the risk of avoiding complexity, or reducing it to something simpler, but instead of trying to explore it and govern it. Complexity then is interpreted as a constituent part of the very concept of human and non-human relations, and therefore as a value.

If we think of the *nidi* and *scuole dell'infanzia* as ecological landscapes of wellbeing and learning for children and adults, then there is no point in separating didactics that reference specific disciplines (so-called activities) from lunch and nap time, play, assemblies, and expressive activities. There are no moments of "transition", which are often situations in which adults and children invest a great deal of "preparatory" effort. In Reggio Emilia, we do not use the term "transition" because every moment of life and school is an experience that generates learning for every child, in different ways, on emotional, social, and cognitive levels. We do not separate those necessarily recursive times of day such as lunch, sleep, and bathroom visits from play and learning. Nor do we much appreciate the undifferentiated term "activity" used for defining experiential contexts in schools, almost as if to demarcate children's passivity and activation as pre-established by adults. The entire day in the *nido* or *scuola*, although held in the rhythm of necessary times of arrival, lunch, and sleep, unfolds in a fluid time, the time of life in which many relations and multiple learnings flow.

How we create favourable conditions for these learnings, how we observe them, accompany them, give them more potential and document them, constitutes the heart of our research in daily contexts. For this to be true research, and not simply a series of reiterated settings, we need to have collaboration,

90 Dialectical encounters in Reggio Emilia

confronto, and negotiation. In the words of Paola Cagliari, "we must value and keep warm the capacity within each working group for generating *formazione* and bringing in [...] the new" (Paola Cagliari, Director, Preschools and Infant-toddler Centres - Istituzione of the Municipality of Reggio Emilia, interview with Stefania Giamminuti, Reggio Emilia). For example, the places in which *pedagogistas* draw on and promote research are not only the *nidi* and *scuole dell'infanzia* which they coordinate themselves directly, but also the pedagogical coordination, understood as a collegial place that is itself shaped together and that together gives shape to the system's directions for *progettazione*. The plurality and interweaving of places in which we do education and discuss education interprets the plurality of perspectives in the collective intelligence, collegiality, and *confronto* that nourish the system's educational culture.

Fragment 1: the classroom door of the new three-year-old children

We believe this experience, of relatively short duration and whose content was not apparently of great significance, can tell the story of how different professionalisms within a school encounter and collaborate with each other, creating a collegiality that is understood as a dynamic of thinking, of points of view, and of negotiation and construction of meanings. This fragment is an example of recurring *progettazione* because each year the working group, and in particular the two teachers welcoming new three-year-olds, meet with the *pedagogista* and *atelierista* to redefine several aspects related to the arrival of new children and families in school.

Before we narrate the experience, however, we need to underline how choosing a word to define these first days in school for three-year-olds is not something irrelevant. Ludwig Wittgenstein (2009) states that "the limits of my language signify the limits of my world" (p. 88, [translated by Jane McCall]). Language therefore defines our world and what is contained within it. Hence, to call a thing using one term rather than another means to create – or to situate ourselves within – spaces of meaning that are different. Over the years in Reggio Emilia, in considering how contemporary pedagogical culture has evolved, and in discussing this with staff and families, we have in turn called the initial period of school *inserimento* (to "insert", or "introduce into"), then *ambientamento* (to "acclimatize" or "settle in"), and more recently *accoglienza* (to "take to oneself" or to "welcome"). Etymologically *inserimento* derives from *in-serere* meaning to include something or someone in an already complete whole. *Ambientamento* derives from *ambire*, to surround, to become accustomed to an environment and to the life taking place within it. *Accoglienza* instead derives from *accolligere* and has a meaning of acceptance and hospitality. It presupposes openness to others, with their different ways of being and presenting themselves. In the field of pedagogy, it refers to a relationship of reciprocity: schools predispose themselves towards *accoglienza* or *the welcome*, children and families bring their own expectations, and the encounter between them generates new environments and new possibilities.

The fragment we have chosen is related to the concept of *the welcome* understood as an invitation to the new arrivals, and the intent of stimulating a desire to remain with the school and to experiment its possibility of creating wonder, almost seducing the children and adults. *The welcome* generates a desire to enter and become part of the school because in it we might encounter something that is unexpected and capable of making us curious. The environment thus is not a place already complete into which we can simply be "inserted", rather it waits for children's gestures and points of view and it anticipates their curiosity and *progettazione* in both material and immaterial aspects. Children bring with them qualities that are often difficult to decipher because they have indirect ways of communicating, and because their young age requires adults to be cautious, to offer themselves – and things – in less direct and impulsive ways. This adult caution is not only a way of taking time with things and for ourselves, but of cultivating and provoking curiosity, of offering clues to children and searching for clues from children. It is not customary to think or practice in terms of environments waiting for children and their gestures, where the child is perceived as a "communicating other" capable of shaping the actions we will carry out as adults and our choices of *progettazione*. In welcoming new children and families, schools more usually act with a mindset of detachment anxiety, of reassurance and continuity, but we believe school should be offered with greater courage and the ambition to dare, offering a welcome or *accoglienza* that is just the opposite of "inserting" someone into a place with fixed rules, predictable situations, and confirmed fears.

The "detail" we will be considering here is the door to the classroom of the new three-year-olds at the *Scuola dell'infanzia* Diana before the children have begun school, and how its design became the subject of analysis and debate between the two class teachers, the *atelierista*, and the *pedagogista*, and in the end involved the school's whole working group. Firstly, we must concur that in referring to "a detail" we do not do so in the general sense of "insignificant particular", rather that we consider a "detail" to be a kind of fractal: the small, minute, geometric entities that have the property of being able to reproduce on any scale. This concept, translated from geometry to education, conveys the systemic significance that a part has for the whole, and vice-versa, while simultaneously maintaining, as mathematician Benoit Mandelbrot (cited in Gallio & Masciarelli, 2013) suggests, an aura of both mystery and familiarity:

> It is held that in some way fractals have a correspondence with the structure of the human mind, that this is why people find them so familiar. This familiarity is still a mystery and the deeper we go into the topic the greater the mystery.

(p. 153, [translated by Jane McCall])

FIGURE 4.1   *Scuola dell'infanzia* Diana, *aggiornamento* in the atelier at the beginning of the school year.

A group – made up of teacher Laura Rubizzi (LR) and *pedagogista* Simona Bonilauri (SB), both with 30 years of experience, teacher Cinzia Incerti (CI) and *atelierista* Simona Spaggiari (SS) who have been with the *Scuola dell'infanzia* Diana for three and two years, respectively – is discussing the meanings and gestures of "the welcome" before new children start school. We share below an excerpt of the recording of this meeting, which the *pedagogista* opens by reminding everyone of the meaning of "the welcome", because there are different levels of awareness within the group.

SB: The welcome isn't a suspended time that starts on 1 September and finishes on 31 October. You all know how many connections the welcome has with the time before children start school and the time that follows […] It is certainly a special time though that we might define as a "genesis of geneses" because many threads for *progettazione* begin to emerge during this period.

LR: We could say that it's a time full of happenings, that requires a capacity for interpretation, and at the same time it offers us all many clues […] and each of us can try and make those clues visible so that they become a legacy of our collegiality, for the whole school.

SB: Exactly! The challenge is to construct a web of dialogue that can count on the power of different points of view and on the emotions each of you brings into play. It's a time that is rich with changes and it requires a lot of sensibility and flexibility.

SS: So if I understand properly (and I say this as a mother who recently experienced her child starting the *nido*) the particular quality of the time of the welcome is that it is not characterised by big projects and events but rather by multiple, minute and partial experiences, for both children and adults.

LR: Yes, it is actually a ferment, that is research for a right relationship.

CI: I don't know if I will be capable of picking up on so many things!

SB: No, look Cinzia, everyone approaches the situation with the knowledge they possess, and with their past experiences. And children are protagonists of their own ways of encountering the new environment; they *mettersi in gioco* (put themselves into play) in the encounter with others in the new environment.

It is not possible for us to share the full back and forth of the dialogue that took place in this initial meeting, however the working group, together with the *pedagogista*, agreed that, given the different degrees of professional experience within the group, in order to re-define the welcome for the new school year they would try and "distance" the concept of welcome by making slightly strange an experience that had become all-too-familiar for the school – welcoming new children – rather than simply passing information from the "experts" to the "novices" on how to prepare classrooms and initial proposals for play. At a later date, the working group meets to review their documentation of the first months of school in order to create a presentation for a *formazione* event with colleagues in other *scuole* and *nidi*. In referring to the intents they shared in their initial meeting, the *pedagogista* adds:

SB: We could include this tension of making something familiar strange in what Jerome Bruner suggests about the human attempt at escaping boredom. In fact, he states that "convention and canonicity are prodigious sources of boredom [...] Some even argue that it is the effort to overcome boredom that creates the "literary impulse", that the function of literary language itself is to make the all-too-familiar strange again" (Bruner, 1996, p. 139).

We believe that trying to look at consolidated things with curious new eyes, with a tension towards seeking something unexpected, is a powerful antidote to boredom. It's a fact that we can sometimes experience boredom together with children; in the long term though this is dangerous for education and together with other causes it may contribute to burnout. This tension towards conceptualising the many aspects of daily experience, inviting the working group to reconsider practices from the point of view of coherency with values and research, characterises the *pedagogista*'s work. This emerges clearly in the interviews conducted by Stefania Giamminuti as part of this research project. For example, as previously noted in Chapter 3, Ivana Soncini specifies that "we can't do without knowing the point of view of those who work directly

94 Dialectical encounters in Reggio Emilia

with children, because we can't do without their interpretations. […] there is a circularity in this" (Ivana Soncini, pyschologist and member of the pedagogical coordination, interview with Stefania Giamminuti, Reggio Emilia).

The declaration of intents of the *Scuola dell'infanzia* Diana in that particular year clearly states the intention of including the theme of welcoming in an extended journey of research, continuing well past children's first weeks of attendance, together with the intent of collecting and sharing as many clues as possible for greater focus in encounters with children and families. In Reggio Emilia, all the school spaces are prepared anew, following evaluations made in June, at the end of the previous school year.[2] In preparing the new environments, the working group is aware and concurs on the fact that every element in an environment communicates, and that care with detail makes a difference to quality of life for those who live in it. In relation to the concept of welcome, during the *aggiornamento* mentioned above, *pedagogista* Simona Bonilauri adds:

SB: We have to learn not to use descriptive thinking and language, not to stick to things too closely, constrained by conformist thinking. Not only must we not stick too closely, we have to counter this risk. I'm setting myself the challenge of having a more conceptual approach. Because I like learning with you!

Among several choices that will give form and concreteness to the concept of welcome this year in the *Scuola dell'infanzia* Diana, the decision is made to re-design the three-year-old classroom door, an important threshold that marks the entrance into a space previously unknown to the children. This is the *pedagogista's* invitation:

SB: First and foremost we need to consider the door as a metaphor. A threshold with two faces: entrance and exit. We mustn't dwell on the literal meanings of words, but rather we should cultivate the ambivalences that are intrinsic in metaphorical meanings, which are always open to things that haven't been thought of, or glimpsed, or experimented with before. Our question is: "Therefore, what is a door for a school"?

Laura Rubizzi, the most experienced teacher, reminds every one of the meanings that, for years, have been assigned to classroom doors:

LR: Like all the architecture in our *nidi* and *scuole dell'infanzia,* for many years our doors have been thought of as spaces that communicate, not anonymous places but rather places defined by the identity of their inhabitants and by "invitations" offered to children and adults.

In one example of a door, leading into the four-year-old classroom, we can see the names of children and teachers, a greeting, *ciao*, that is aesthetically

FIGURE 4.2 Detail of the five-year-old classroom mini-atelier door with warning signs: "halt, stop here, do not knock", "stop", "private".

pleasingly and unusually outlined with flowers and grasses, and there is a play of mirrors so that as the door opens the first thing you see is your own reflection and then gradually the room's inhabitants. This is not a model to be repeated every year but rather it remains an intentional space of *progettazione*, where we can find children acting as co-authors in the experimentation, as evident in Figure 4.2.

Doors transform during the year depending on what projects and events are underway (Figures 4.3 and 4.4).

FIGURE 4.3 Detail of the five-year-old classroom door with images of children's claywork and invitation to a school party.

96 Dialectical encounters in Reggio Emilia

FIGURE 4.4   Detail of the four-year-old classroom door with clues to a project underway on the theme of transformation.

The *atelierista* certainly has many ideas about designing a door, but perhaps less command of the pedagogical meaning and educational intent we might assign to a three-year-old classroom door during the welcome. In fact, in reflecting on the situation at a later date, *atelierista* Simona Spaggiari says:

> Frankly, I always keep doors open at home so I really had to collect my thoughts, and I remember making an effort and thinking "Ok then let's do this door" but I wasn't completely convinced, it didn't seem like the most urgent thing to be doing in that moment, it didn't seem a priority to me during the week in which we were preparing the whole school.
>
> *(Simona Spaggiari,* atelierista, *interview with Paola Strozzi, Reggio Emilia)*

This comment was made after the event, and with an awareness that wasn't there in the first meetings. In fact Simona's perplexities do not emerge in the *progettazione* conversation, instead she silently credits the more expert teacher. Obviously this is not always the case. During the original *aggiornamento* in which the door was being designed, teacher Laura Rubizzi summarises the evident intents:

LR: First of all, faced with the door the children have to be able to make sense of it, they should recognise something *simpatico* and captivating. They have to encounter traces of themselves and not anonymity, because it is the first thing they encounter of their classroom. And they need to feel an atmosphere of welcome.

The *pedagogista* reinforces this intent underlining that:

SB: The door must somehow be a synthesis and distillation of a thought that goes beyond. The intent for *progettazione* should find in the door itself an initial clue on which to work.

In order to continue thinking and reasoning the group moves over to their research zone – the door – and because at the end of the previous school year the pedagogical coordination had begun focusing on the subject of welcome, proposing it in *formazione* meetings with working groups, they ask a teacher from another class to photograph and document their group *confronto* (Figure 4.5).

As they stand by the door, Laura, the teacher, continues:

LR: Usually the names of the inhabitants are written on the classroom door but three-year-olds don't recognise their names yet, and sometimes the names are so high they can't see them.

There is a short on-site brainstorming to share feasible ideas and hypotheses. The *atelierista* asks for time to "visualise" (make visual) the ideas that are

FIGURE 4.5   *Confronto* by the classroom door.

98 Dialectical encounters in Reggio Emilia

emerging. Simona's background is in video-making, and on the basis of on her own design strategies she says:

> SS: I need to construct, and try things out by constructing, or move things around. I need to encounter things ... subjects (including children!) and elements, some here, some there, and start making hypotheses for connections, for reasoning, between elements ... and I think about them and talk to them without needing to write things down. I imagine. I imagine and then I begin constructing *possibles;* because, given that I have constructed myself through doing, in my creative process to construct means to get things into focus and to discover them. I have the spark of an idea or a possibility, but I need to practice in order to get it into focus and understand it better. When I design, I have to construct first, I need to "make" and understand with my hands, as well as my eyes or with my writing as you do Laura.

This exchange is significant in relation to the concept of dialectics: in fact, if everyone in an educational context has a similar background and *formazione*, or a similar way of thinking, then opportunities for exchange, creativity, negotiating ideas, and *confronto* are much reduced.

In a subsequent meeting, where the intent is to create a documentary synthesis of the year's "project of welcome" for children, Simona comments on her work as an *atelierista*: "the dialogue with matter and material is important to me, with a tool that goes beyond you and invites you into a dialogue that generates possible advances in your initial thinking. And here I did the same thing" (Simona Spaggiari, *atelierista,* interview with Paola Strozzi, Reggio Emilia).

This important reflection evokes a concept discussed in Chapter 3, where we argued that dialectics is not only expressed through humans, and human voices, but is also a conversation dialoguing through other identities, materials, and languages. In fact, Simona later added:

> It was precisely because the door didn't interest me much that I needed to make it visible even more, I needed to fall in love with it so that something creative would ignite between me and the door. I needed even more to make things visible and to play at constructing images of the possible.
>
> *(Simona Spaggiari,* atelierista, *interview*
> *with Paola Strozzi, Reggio Emilia)*

Simona makes some renderings of the door, and while showing them to the group she shares the various hypotheses they have produced.

> SS: Here (in Figure 4.6) the children's names can be seen by adults but lower down they can also be seen by children so they have a possibility of

Dialectical encounters in Reggio Emilia **99**

FIGURE 4.6   Rendering of the door to the three-year-old classroom, displaying names of children and teachers and drawings of zebras.

gradually finding their own names and starting to read them. The zebra is the symbol of the *Scuola* Diana, but the drawings are by five-year-olds in past years and testify to the value of different subjectivities, and of memory.

Teacher Cinzia agrees and adds:

CI: It's not just about expectations of what will happen, it is about valuing a legacy of what has been and what could be.
SB: Because these drawings are beautiful and beauty testifies to care and invitation.

We will return to the connection between aesthetics and care at the end of this fragment, by citing excerpts from a conversation with Vea Vecchi, the first *atelierista* of *Scuola dell'infanzia* Diana, with whom I had the opportunity to revisit this experience. In fact, this possibility of revisiting a project or part of a project at different times, through a multiplicity (an infinitude) of voices, underscores the notion of "diffused research data" which remains available to give more potential to *formazione*.

The group turns to discussing how a door might somehow become a "non-door" or a "non-closure", where closure is understood as separation. This idea of non-closure is fascinating, both for the *atelierista* and *pedagogista*! *Atelieristas*

100 Dialectical encounters in Reggio Emilia

try to "make the possible visible", as made evident by the title of the first exhibition narrating the experience of the municipal *nidi* and *scuole dell'infanzia* of Reggio Emilia "If the eye leaps over the wall. A narrative of the possible". This is often a very striking image for those who interrogate different professional roles in Reggio Emilia and the ways in which they interweave. In fact, our co-author Stefania Giamminuti commented thus when reading a first draft of this chapter: "This makes me reflect on how the *atelierista*'s work is about 'making the possible visible' whilst others might be engaged in 'thinking the possible' (*pedagogistas*) and 'doing the possible' (teachers). Obviously they all weave together and their competencies aren't so separate, but the point is that in an educational context that is considered dialectic, dialogic and enriched by different competencies, the possible is thought, made visible, and enacted in the collective".

The *atelierista* Simona goes on to say:

SS: Here (Figure 4.7) I've created an image, with real-life perspective, of what you could see just beyond the door. An invisible door, created by photographing it from the same perspective you might have just beyond the door.

CI: It's beautiful! It could turn into a game of surprise and would be a little disorientating for the children, like you said Simona (speaking to the *pedagogista*)!

FIGURE 4.7 Rendering of the door to the three-year-old classroom, as if it were transparent.

Dialectical encounters in Reggio Emilia 101

FIGURE 4.8   Rendering of the door to the three-year-old classroom, with an image of a grassy meadow and the names of children and teachers.

It is evident here how the power of images can clarify meanings and evoke prefigurations.

SS: This door (Figure 4.8) is just the opposite, and it's a game too. The first door splits reality, so that children can see exactly what they would have encountered when opening the door. This one instead turns things round completely. Will they encounter something they know inside the door, like a lawn? Or grass, and everything their senses can imagine in a grass meadow? But the grass is being offered to them in a way they've never encountered before: on the door, vertical, giant grass, macro-micro …

But Cinzia expresses a doubt:

CI: Mightn't it be too disorientating? What if we simply put some plant life and not a lawn?

The *pedagogista* once again invites the teachers not to rush straight to the object.

SB: Let's dwell on the idea of the metaphor-door, of a beyond. What is real, what is fake, this is already thinking of a beyond. Just as the use of the digital which Simona (*atelierista*) is proposing now is already a way of dwelling in the beyond.

FIGURE 4.9 Rendering of the door to the three-year-old classroom, with an image of a long branch with green leaves and the names of children and teachers.

This is an important contribution offered by the *pedagogista,* and by the ethic of *confronto* more generally. To avoid rushing always and immediately to define the act, but instead giving it time, and giving ourselves time to reflect on concepts we consider important to explore as adults, on the meanings we intend to propose with children. This is where the heart of research lies. Only by clarifying these aspects can we access and ignite the idea of research in daily contexts.

SS: This door (Figure 4.9) is a proposal of a more delicate idea that communicates an image of multitude and rhythm. The idea is that of a group, with little leaves that appear to be holding hands. There is an idea of expansion, of plants that from the door can go beyond, flowing into the environment.

SB: Yes, but let's remember the importance of communicating marvel, of seducing children a little too.

As we anticipated above, in revisiting these alternative proposals at a later date, Vea Vecchi, the first *atelierista* at the *Scuola* Diana commented:

> Generally speaking the doors are beautiful, because we always consider it very important to have an approach to beauty. Beauty belongs to children,

they notice it, and desire it. This is care for the concept of welcome, and at the same time it is aesthetic care. Aesthetics requires and promotes care and vice-versa. Beauty is a door open to others. It isn't something each person holds on to for themselves, it's a sharing.

(Vea Vecchi, atelierista, interview with Paola Strozzi, Reggio Emilia)

Reading Vea's comments, we might highlight the extent to which beauty and care here seem to be interlocutors in the dialectic, as if our decision-making takes into account not only colleagues but also the non-human. Vea Vecchi continues:

I was reading an article by Michele Serra[3] in *la Repubblica* newspaper after Gino Strada[4] recently passed away, and he tells us how Strada had asked Renzo Piano[5] to design a children's hospital for Emergency in Uganda,[6] not just any hospital but a "scandalously beautiful" one, because there is a sort of symbology. A *scuola dell'infanzia* that takes care to give beauty, in the sense of sharing of spaces and relations, is important. And even when we work in extremely urgent situations the supposed excess given by beauty can do us good.

(Vea Vecchi, atelierista, interview with Paola Strozzi, Reggio Emilia)

In the aggiornamento at *Scuola* Diana the working group continues their *confronto*:

LR: I like this idea (Figure 4.10); even though it's more classical it's certainly more feasible in the short term! There are hands at the top trying to touch each other, which is what we would like to happen here soon. The image isn't in colour anymore and the plant has become a climbing plant, the photo is in black and white. You did it to try another step between a subject and its representation didn't you Simona?

SS: Yes, but I'm not convinced. Of course the little hands meeting conveys a much more welcoming idea, softer and more familiar, but it might be a bit too reminiscent of advertising images. It's pretty, and sober, and a bit moral.

The *pedagogista* seems to agree that the image is more commonplace:

SB: It looks very well-mannered but at the same time with the play between image and concrete element, the children's names and the children's hands, it could offer a metaphor for the possibility of going on to explore other meanings.

104 Dialectical encounters in Reggio Emilia

FIGURE 4.10 Rendering of the door to the three-year-old classroom, with images of leaves and children's hands, and the names of children and teachers.

They then proceed to try out a series of photographs of real leaves: a game of real and pretend that convinces the teachers:

LR: Oh I can see the possibility here of picking up on games of real and pretend with the children, that are so important on the levels of emotion, expression, and cognition. On other and different occasions obviously!

Laura and Cinzia work with this idea of the door, adding in some real leaves (Figure 4.11). In the end, this is the door that was chosen for the first part of the school year. However, as a demonstration of how educational choices can change in the light of new sensibilities and values, when Laura (teacher) and Simona (*atelierista*) revisit this experience later on they comment: "Perhaps it (using real leaves) wouldn't happen today! We wouldn't be as interested now in bringing leaves inside that were picked outdoors. What persuaded us then was the idea of offering children a double representation, the leaf and an image of the leaf".

At the time of creating the door, the group's discussion does not stop with identifying the most seductive door but extends to sighting possible landscapes of *progettazione*.

SB: This year for our *progettazione* we will be continuing (among other things) to think about the concept of digital, physical reality and virtual reality, but we are far from wanting to construct outdated, unsuitable,

FIGURE 4.11 Real leaves have been added to the rendering depicted in Figure 4.10.

and failed dichotomies. We will need to think together with families too: what is "natural" and what is "digital"? How do children learn? How can we design interdisciplinary environments that make it possible for children to learn through researching?

SS: Three-year-old children live in this image culture too. What is an image for them? When is experience tied to something living and real or something simulating a tangible reality?

SB: We will need to explore the concept of simulation, of the artificial, further. What do we mean by artifice? What do we mean by natural? We are just beginning to discuss these large concepts.

LR: I remember we asked the five-year-olds a direct question last year: "In your opinion, when can we say something is living?" In the end their answer was: "We don't know! Anything's possible".

SS: Perhaps children think like the geneticist Edoardo Boncinelli who suggests that "the thing is alive when it moves ... The thing is alive when it transforms!"

This area of "the living" is particularly relevant today, as various contemporary studies on the concept of "liveliness" confirm. Jane Merewether (2019), for example, offers the concept of "enchanted animism" that "kindles children's sensitivity to Earthly processes, enabling them to listen to the Earth more attentively, with the awareness and responsiveness that a planetary crisis demands" (p. 233).

106 Dialectical encounters in Reggio Emilia

FIGURE 4.12   Tiny plants made by *atelierista* Simona and placed in a terracotta pot with other plants.

Meanwhile, the *atelierista*, coherently with her way of designing by doing, continues to play with simulations of the living, and with what she calls "a gap", which could be interpreted as a small distancing or cognitive leap to offer children. Later on Simona told us: "it was a gap the children had to guess about in order to understand whether a little plant that seemed to be living, was in fact living or not" (Simona Spaggiari, *atelierista*, interview with Paola Strozzi, Reggio Emilia). The working group found interesting clues for their work in the poetics of Sarah Sze, a North American artist who has represented the United States twice at the Venice Biennale and who creates installations from natural elements and a multitude of other materials: everyday objects, sculptures, and architectures that allow her to explore meaning and relations in the spaces and things that surround us.

Over the following few days, Simona (the *atelierista*) interprets suggestions from Sze, using paper, scissors, glue, needle and thread, and other materials to construct small plants that she inserts into a pot with other plants situated nearby the three-year-old classroom (Figure 4.12). In proposing this "installation" to her colleagues she says:

SS: I'm trying to make small fake plants, perfectly exact copies, so I've made tiny cuts in them to give the idea they have had a few accidents in life. I've put some in this pot and some in the grouting of the tiles at the entrance. They're little things in little corners, useless to all appearances. I want to try out installations where the plant subject isn't real but as well as beauty it has this fragility that generates empathy and the desire to care.

Other ideas were added to Simona's, such as projecting outdoor contexts in nature onto indoor surfaces like walls and large lengths of fabric (Figure 4.13).

Dialectical encounters in Reggio Emilia **107**

FIGURE 4.13   Projection of the image of a grassy meadow onto white fabric.

Later on, teacher Laura comments on trying out tools, materials, and spaces with her co-teacher and the *atelierista*:

Each proposal we choose already has the seeds of possible relaunching, so in those years the idea of real and pretend was slowly transforming into an intent of offering children contexts in which, increasingly, different possible representations of the real were made visible. Different, novel possible points of view can become interesting immersive simulations. Like the time we filmed the grass of the large mound at the back of the school, making it into a sort of grass mass indoors, where children could continue their play in the winter, and make believe in real time by pretending to go into the grass, building imaginaries. It wasn't the grass of the mound in the garden but it was something that looked like it and that you could create stories and simulations with.

(Laura Rubizzi, teacher, interview with
Paola Strozzi, Reggio Emilia)

Atelierista Simona adds:

At the same time we were trying to understand how children engage with representation. Multiple realities exist and the important thing is to manage to find a way, to find your own guiding map in this complexity of multiple representations of the real, in school and out.

(Simona Spaggiari, atelierista, interview with
Paola Strozzi, Reggio Emilia)

Progressing from thinking about a value or "content" such as welcome to identifying a gesture like designing a door (that is practical but leads to a consideration of contemporary ethical themes like the relation between reality and

108 Dialectical encounters in Reggio Emilia

simulation) testifies, we believe, to the way dialectical encounter in *scuole* and *nidi dell'infanzia* doesn't take place simply between people who work there together but considers objects (a door) and places (a classroom) as interlocutors too. Together with these dialectical encounters, our encounters with contemporary cultures and sensibilities[7] also nourish our tension towards research.

Fragment 2: a portrait of yellow daisies

We now turn to another example of a meeting between teachers Marina Mori (MM) and Paola Strozzi (PS), *atelierista* Vea Vecchi (VV), and *pedagogista* Tiziana Filippini (TF), who discuss the work produced by children in the course of a project. The focus here, perhaps in more obvious ways than the previous example, is on knowledge processes, primarily children's but also those of adults in their sensibility and competence for analysing and supporting the most suitable learning contexts. We believe the example will illustrate clearly how *confronto*, and approaches to organisation that are coherent with the value of *confronto*, inform constant self-*formazione* and reciprocal *formazione*. The concept of taking care of common experiences – children's, the school's or of the educational project as a whole – necessarily also includes processes of evaluation and self-evaluation as a significant part of professional relations and reciprocal professional growth.

Careful structuring of our 36-hours per week working contract makes it possible to have the extended and simultaneous presence in school of more than one professional competency, each with its own roles and responsibilities. While this has given us favourable conditions for daring to interpret, it also requires the reciprocal generosity of offering each other the points of view that are intrinsic to each individual's subjective culture. To enable an ethic of dialectics, the fact that each person dares to interpret must be valued without diminishing the quality and depth of thinking. This means being aware that the dynamic of our communication has to be attentively monitored so that we all know we are counting on everyone listening and expressing themselves, and that this requires rigour and commitment, so that we must not be discouraged and offended, or withdraw. It takes courage and rigour but the gains are constant, and the feeling of being part of a construction that goes beyond our own individual contributions is inestimable. In reality, although everyone is involved, what we might call a "culture of dialectics" requires special responsibility on the part of the *pedagogista*s who, with their professional background, and the variety of cultural, social, and organisational contexts they work in, can more easily find operative resources and references.

This example of a portrait of yellow daisies highlights a situation in the course of a proposal to children in which doubt generates critical dialogue between teachers, *atelierista*, and *pedagogista* resulting in a change in adult strategies and relations with the children involved. This situation, in which

Dialectical encounters in Reggio Emilia **109**

a working group reads or analyses children's drawings, interprets them, and identifies possible relaunches, in this case also critically analysing the teachers' role, is frequent in our *nidi* and *scuole dell'infanzia*. We share here the analysis of drawings by four children, two girls and two boys, and the initial part only of a broader project, seeking primarily to highlight the dimension of dialectics and *confronto* between adults.

It is a Monday morning in early October in the five-year-old classroom of the *Scuola dell'infanzia* Diana. Gabriele has brought in some large yellow daisy flowers (topinambur) gathered in the countryside with his parents, and placed in a vase on a classroom cupboard. A conversation begins in the large class group on the theme of Sunday outings to the countryside with parents, but few children mention any of the typical flowers or plants that inhabit the countryside. Few seem to have noticed them, or have any memory of them.

No one mentions the yellow daisies, not even the child who has brought them to school. This surprises us slightly, because large clusters of these tall daisies brighten things up with their yellow colour in the countryside and city outskirts for the whole month of October, marking the time between the end

FIGURE 4.14 The yellow daisies of the topinambur plant in Reggio Emilia's outskirts.

110 Dialectical encounters in Reggio Emilia

FIGURE 4.15 Initial drawings by Giulia and Martina.

of summer and autumn's advance. We do not insist too much during the conversation, but we propose that the whole class draw these well-known flowers, using the daisies on the classroom cupboard as a reference point. The whole class of children draws, dividing into groups autonomously among the classroom tables. First we will consider the drawings and words of two girls, Giulia and Martina, then two boys, Eduardo and Riccardo.

Giulia and Martina are aged about five-and-a-half. They both love drawing and are great friends. As often happens the two girls sit close to each other, with other classmates nearby. As Giulia is drawing, she says: *Daisies are too easy. You only need to do the stem, the leaves, a circle and they're done*! Martina adds: *I often draw flowers, I know how to do... roses a lot!*

Marina (teacher) and I (Paola) make a note of this quick definition of drawing flowers. Giulia and Martina seem to be referring to a mental schema for the shape of flowers more than the memory of a real encounter. We communicate our shared fears in a rapid exchange of looks and words: perhaps there is a risk the girls are thinking in stereotypes, and not only of gender: "we're girls, we love flowers, flowers can be drawn quickly using this schema". An analysis of the boys' flowers seems to confirm our suspicions. We decide therefore to ask the *atelierista* and *pedagogista* for a meeting to talk about our observations and interpretations, and perhaps identify a direction for our work.

As with the fragment examined previously in this chapter, where we were reminded through the *pedagogista*'s words of the need to pause within *confronto* and not rush into interpretations, here again what is highlighted is the way dialectics is an essential part of meaning-making. It is only one month since the start of the school year and clues like the ones above, that tell us about how children are reading and representing their knowledge and experience, are particularly precious.

VV: Even though the girls seem to describe the daisies in a simple way on a verbal level, almost with a daisy stereotype in mind – "You just have to do a stem, and leaves and a circle and it's done" – in reality their drawings aren't at all stereotypical. You can see these girls are used to drawing, they love drawing and experiment with it.

PS: (smiling) You seem very well disposed today Vea! Don't you find the stems a bit rigid, the leaves all the same, positioned too symmetrically? And the time it took them to do the drawings was rather quick, almost as if they had in mind a ready-made drawing schema rather than remembering or imagining real flowers.

VV: No, I wouldn't say that. First of all Giulia's daisies are bowing down a little, and they're different from each other, to the point that a bud is already present. The flowers haven't been drawn with a simple "circle" the way she says. We could define Martina's drawing as slightly more recurrent but, for example, the liberty she has taken in making the leaves blue is not insignificant! I have seen much more stereotyped representations of flowers at this age!

MM: Giulia and Martina were sitting close to each other and although we don't have detailed notes, it seemed to us that there was a lot of looking, especially on Martina's part, making us think she was maybe using the strategy of copying her friend's drawing.

VV: Of course we can see common elements between the two girls, like the shape of the leaves attached tightly to the stems, but as always it isn't a question of "simple copying". To copy something, you have to be able to read it. If Eduardo and Riccardo had been sitting next to Giulia too, they probably wouldn't have known how to vary the shape of their leaves much.

TF: Copying is a positive strategy when you are capable of taking elements from someone else and giving them your own personal interpretation, when you are able to take something, what you are ready to grasp with your own perceptions and personally transfer into the lines of your drawing. Even when you copy there are still things you have to invent, because there is always a movement from a subject (in this case it's two-dimensional) to something equally symbolic, of which you are the creator. This cognitive and perceptual shift is made up of both mental and motor neurological maturation.

112 Dialectical encounters in Reggio Emilia

There is an implicit element in this conversation connected with the meaning of the act of "copying" that it is opportune to clarify. The working group is well aware of the difference between a request to copy a model as faithfully as possible, and the copying children do when they choose a companion they consider likely to be more capable than them of creating something they are trying to create too. Together with the arguments put forward in the conversation above, we can say that copying can be viewed as a conversation in which children borrow each other's ideas and each child evolves them in their own language.

VV: Of course! Drawing is an extraordinary language, and I don't understand why adults in schools are still in so much of a hurry to give children solutions so that you do a flower like this, and instead you do a tree like this …

TF: An important relationship exists between the drawing schemas children learn and our more general cultural schemas: it's one we could explore further, and discuss with families too.

MM: Yes, yes, we do that! The three-year-old parents tell us the children often ask them to draw things for them. It is a way of being together, playing, and responding to your child's request in a pleasant way. But parents, so they tell us, also know they can't draw and even when they don't intend to, they end up proposing very stereotyped figures with their children, of rigid daisies and little houses with pointy roofs.

PS: They might be sensitive, cultured parents who understand immediately that we don't just have so-called primary colours in the *scuola dell'infanzia* or even at the *nido*, but rather a range of shades of felt pens and paints. So they buy boxes of felt pens at home as well, they tell us, with at least two or three yellows and blues. What else can we say about their interactions when drawing with their children?

TF: These are certainly important discussions for us to have and to share with parents. A drawing schema can also be an act of intelligence, until it becomes a prison and stereotype that means we see uniquely what we already know and expect. We're all aware of the extent to which we only see what we know, as Maturana and Varela contend. And it is a pity to have barriers towards possible encounters.

PS: And another thing! We suggest that with their children, like we do at school, the parents might argue from the start for the possibility of not drawing a "subject" but rather a "subject in relation" and we explain the reasons for this. For example, this request children frequently have towards parents to make a drawing of "a child", which often responds to the urgency parents feel for their children to be able to draw the human form. We suggest that parents ask them if they want "a child running", or "riding a bicycle", or "sitting at the table eating", and so on. Then, even though the parent's drawing might end up stereotyped in some way, it

Dialectical encounters in Reggio Emilia **113**

conveys to the child that there isn't only one way to draw the subject, that subjects are always related to their context, and at least the result will be more fun, and open to children's comments, than simple stereotypes of the human figure like the ones on signs.

VV: Yes, and you could also give them another piece of advice. Because satisfying children's legitimate request to have something drawn quickly in a stereotyped way can turn into a trap. Even unconsciously you are still offering your child a single simplified model. So another thing we could do is to highlight the strategy of drawing as opposed to giving them a schema. For example, faced with a request to draw a subject there in front of us, like some grapes that have been placed on the table for a snack, we can say: "wait a minute I'm not quite sure, I'll try and draw this big grape first and then I'll put this one that looks a bit less purple next to it … I can't see the stalk … I'll have a proper look now … ah it's all twisted here on top so I'll draw that …", and so on, so that the child can understand that it is important to look, that there isn't only certainty in drawing, that you can choose different ways, and there is uncertainty, and comments and so on. And then we can propose variations, like, "do you know what we can do? Grapes aren't always purple. What if we make them blue? What taste would they have then? Where would they grow? Would you like to pass me colours to draw grapes with?" and so a child can understand that it isn't only the subject of a drawing that isn't simple and banal, but rather the act of drawing itself, and though it might be pleasurable it's also complex and personal. I have a memory I've already told you about, something that really struck me. A little girl asked me: *Can I make a zebra blue?* And I replied: "Naturally. Of course. You can draw the way you want!" and she said: *Yes, I understand! Because drawing is like a dream, you can do what you want!* I've used the sentence often with children after that episode, to underline the freedom of being able to change reality as they draw.

PS: But it isn't always like that Vea, because, for example, if you want to convey the idea of that tree (pointing to a tree visible from the classroom window) you can only distort it up to a point.

VV: I don't agree! If I like the tree a lot and it somehow becomes a blue tree because I put my love of blue into the tree, and give it to the tree as a gift as I'm drawing. The tree's identity comes from this encounter between me and the tree: the encounter between my wishes and the tree's.

PS: I understand. It's like seeing. A drawing is never just a reproduction, it's always an interpretation.

VV: Yes, it is the outcome of an encounter.

MM: Paola, it's like saying when I look at your drawing of the tree, I'm not only looking with the intention of seeing the tree, the way I do with

114 Dialectical encounters in Reggio Emilia

a photograph (though I know taking a photo of a tree is a process of interpretation too of course) but the intention of seeing a dual identity, the tree's and yours, a piece of your identity at the time of the encounter.

VV: Or the intention of appreciating a different way of seeing the tree from your own. All art is like that! In any case, we need to try and avoid schemas as much as possible in the language of mark-making and drawing because a drawing is not only a formal structure but an intellectual structure too. We risk offering an eye through which reality is seen as partial, simplified, and univocal. Obviously children like stereotyped drawings and they feel they can recognise them straight away, but just as they invent personal ways of playing and constructing and so on, they can invent personal ways of drawing too, and try out lots of marks. And they can discover it a bit at a time. There is no discovery in quickly reproducing a stereotype!

PS: Yes, children's inventive creativity and liberty were clearer to me in abstract drawings. I remember with some three-year-olds we proposed they draw "a mark running" or "a mark jumping", "a sad drawing", or "a merry drawing" and so on. But come on now, what do you both say about the boys' drawings? Listen to what they said while they were drawing!

We have intentionally included the full transcript of the above conversation, to give an account of how dialectics between people of different professional backgrounds united in a common mission requires this complex exercise, in which each person has opportunities for expressing their point of view and questioning the connections between theory, practice, and research. It is a conversation that testifies to the value of complexity and the ethic of dialectics: dialectics between colleagues, dialectics with trees, dialectics with flowers, and the dialectics with different disciplines.

Gender differences are always interesting to consider as part of the broader landscape of subjective differences, and for an understanding of the ways children interpret and resolve school proposals. Eduardo and Riccardo offer us interesting clues through their drawings (Figure 4.16) and comments: Eduardo says *I'm used to drawing trucks* and Riccardo says *cars and spaceships are easier!*

VV: (laughing) Riccardo seems to be saying it's easier to draw something you like, and that you have certainly repeated more often than drawing daisies.

MM: Riccardo's structure is really a bit reminiscent of a spaceship. The structure is mechanical more than floral, although then he puts it in a plant context by drawing grass at its feet.

VV: But he has captured the vertical aspect of a yellow daisy, which is usually much taller than other plants, and he's made it quite robust as well!

Dialectical encounters in Reggio Emilia 115

FIGURE 4.16 Initial drawings by Eduardo and Riccardo.

>
> Eduardo seems to have drawn a slightly mechanical form in red too. The daisies are represented in a radial form and the leaves are very rigid. The elements are scattered. He has sectioned pieces as if he was thinking of truck components, but it's his own personal, intelligent strategy.

PS: Excuse me Vea, in your opinion, when children draw do they all need to go through this phase of composing various elements of a complex subject into a whole, like a bunch of flowers? We know that our eyes move backwards and forwards over the whole, noting details and pausing over them for different amounts of time, and that this varies from child to child. And we know that simply looking is active time, a "creative" process, if you like.

TF: Yes because, as were saying, our brains don't register everything they perceive!! They have to identify, select, and recognise. Our cultural foundations, interests, and expectations lead us to a selective perception of reality, as if we can only see what we're ready to see and want to see.

PS: Yes, but what I want to understand (because although we've been working together for a while this has to do in particular with the language of mark-making and drawing) is if the capacity for composing several elements into one single drawing always comes after the elements have been drawn singly, or does it happen often that children have tangles of sensory data in their head and try to detail it in a drawing?

VV: Yes, first you get a perception of the whole and then you extract detail from it, but really it depends very much on the individual child. I still perceive the whole first for example, and then I draw the whole too, perhaps because I'm interested in the atmosphere or because I capture its perfume … but Tullio my husband (who is an architect) joins together details and the whole straight away.

PS: And that's not easy!

VV: No, it's not easy! In fact I continue to be amazed at how often we take going from three-dimensional reality to two-dimensional drawing for granted. I need to represent such a complex reality with my marks, a reality that is not only made of form, but of density, perfume, a setting, a story and so on. And I'm using marks I'm not familiar with yet and have to invent because the language of marks and drawing is symbology. It's the way children learn to talk, and to walk … it's all a personal invention.

MM: Vea, you're saying it's like verbal language and it's true, words are invention and not just repetition, but even before children are born, they are immersed in words, and as soon as they're born, they're exposed to the request, the necessity almost, and pleasure of talking. But that doesn't happen with drawing, which we propose much later with children, and with a fraction of the frequency of talking.

This conversation occurred only a month after the start of the school year, but working groups often start with clues and doubts like these to construct their initial *progettazione* journeys, reasoning together on the meanings of their choices well before they begin organising specific didactics. Elements of research and *progettazione* emerge from *confronto* and exchange, not as certainties, but rather as possibilities. Before we turn to a subsequent situation of adults analysing the second drawings made by the same children, we share an excerpt from the school's declaration of intents in that year:

There is much talk today of ecology, and rightly so, but in Italy at least there is very little truly ecological education. Children like adults know many things virtually (from the names of prehistoric animals to the names of galaxies) but perhaps they have few emotional and physical ties to natural environments very close by. We believe that the first elementary but essential ecological attitude is that of considering things other than Self, plants for example, as living organisms. Until this sentiment becomes more widespread, the predatory attitude that unfortunately is characteristic of too many people will always have the upper hand. Plants at most will be considered decorative objects for the home, fenced in by gardens, and not subjects. The aim we are setting ourselves at school is for children to see and encounter things through establishing dialogue with them: yellow daisies, trees, but also theatres, city streets, and so on. All things that leave too many people indifferent. Instead our wish is for children to know how to look at them and listen with curiosity, and participation, asking lots of whys, and with feelings of love, care, and responsibility towards them[8] [...] Can deeper knowledge of living subjects, like flowers living around the school, spark a gaze that is more curious and investigative? Yellow daisies are one of many elements we could begin with, open to transforming into subject-friends and subjective identities if we get closer with a desire to really see, to understand and to feel. We believe it is possible to encounter the extraordinarily meaningful even in this extraordinarily ordinary subject

(Declaration of Intents, five-year-old class,
Scuola dell'infanzia Diana).

After the meeting, and after writing our declaration of intents, we decide to go on an outing with the children to a field of yellow daisies, to document their encounter, and then perhaps to ask children to make a second drawing of daisies in order to understand if and how their drawings undergo change and contribute to changing a knowledge relationship under construction. We now turn to excerpts from a subsequent meeting between the teachers and *atelierista*, where they are commenting on drawings by Eduardo, Riccardo, and Giulia, followed by a phone call with the *pedagogista* who had received images of the children's drawings by email.

MM: As well as the daisy's star structure, Eduardo has caught the activity of the inhabited meadow in his second drawing (Figure 4.17), in fact

FIGURE 4.17   First and second drawings by Eduardo.

his comment about bees was *I've always done bees like this* [tummy up] *because I don't know how to turn them round the other way!*

VV: Mamma mia! Do you see how Eduardo is putting different parts together here? He's using a radial structure again to represent daisy petals, it looked more like a sun before, but here he's doing it while he changes the size and colour of the flowers. In the orange daisy here on the right the direction of the petals, they're bending right down. So he has caught lots of differences and found lots of solutions for representing them in his drawing. The bees are marvellous because they are also telling a story of the vital living relations daisies have, and that the child has understood. It's a very important detail.

PS: Look! There are some bees on the flower. Some are flying here and there, and two are on the flower. Even though Eduardo didn't tell us, or we weren't capable of picking it up from him, he has probably understood the very important relation of sucking the nectar.

VV: From a truck to this piece of a meadow of yellow daisies and bees, there's been a huge change! I suspect you teachers have been soliciting children's memories and observations frequently, but in diversified and intelligent ways. You're probably soliciting the right way because the results aren't stereotyped.

MM: The differences between Giulia's first and second drawings are even greater (Figure 4.18).

TF: Yes, there are big differences, but as well as the fact that Giulia is very good at drawing, we can almost see a study of different plants and stems intertwining.

FIGURE 4.18 First and second drawing by Giulia.

FIGURE 4.19   First and second drawing by Riccardo.

MM: To tell the truth we did get the children to think about branches and stems intertwining quite a lot, underscoring it with movements of our arms and body, almost the way stems dance and intertwine. We tried to accompany them a lot while they were observing, but not so much in the moment of drawing.

VV: Yes. You might have intervened too much, although you've done it well. That is to say without giving them banal schemas, or producing stereotypes. I've always told you that on average the children who come out of your class draw better, but you really must be careful to intervene in very diversified ways, in zones the child is already researching.

PS: Riccardo seems to have made extraordinary changes (Figure 4.19). The difference in these slim stems is really obvious, the corollas with yellow and orange petals and sepals, and perhaps there are even veins on the petals, or pollen from the pistils, done with darker dots.

VV: What did Riccardo say about this change of his?

MM: He was very satisfied, but we haven't transcribed the recordings yet.

VV: The leaves are still attached in a way that looks a bit structural but to make up for it we can see this important attempt at representing roots underground. It's very important for us to get his comments, you can even ask him now, after the event, because we need to know the kind of traces a sudden large change leaves, on a verbal level too. You're sure you didn't intervene too much?

MM: Riccardo was a great explorer out in the fields. He invited his companions – we have our notes here and he says – *Shall we go into the daisies' house, right into the middle of them?* And I say, *From a distance the daisies looked all the same but when you see them close up you realise they have different faces*! I wanted to underline the differences between daisies by talking about "faces" not just shapes, and I wanted to offer it as a personal note, not something prescriptive children have to stick to.

VV: Very good! But while they were drawing what did you say?

MM: Well, on the table they had pictures of daisies that we had taken in the field and various bunches of flowers with daisies and other flowers and grasses we had picked. We added in yellow highlighters too and other felt pens to their materials. We were close to the children at different times, inviting them to observe all the many differences between the flowers, in terms of shape of course, but because the shape comes from different phases of its growth.

VV: I find just a slight dissonance in the speed with which the children's drawings have changed. I'd like to understand more about how you intervene when they're drawing and I'll tell you why. Such a sudden change in all the children doesn't correspond with individual rhythms and explorations capable of igniting motivation, and motivation doesn't spark for everyone at the same time or from the same element of an experience. A second, more critical, evaluation of the conditions you have constructed is that when children are drawing, we must be very cautious about calling attention to daisies present on the table, the buds, the tree-like structure of the plant, the presence of young and old flowers together on one branch, different yellows and so on. What made me think about this is the picture you took during the work with the children (Figure 4.20). Do you see?

VV: "Look at this", "Look at that", "This looks like", "You could add something here". Sometimes we risk referring to too many things. Saying "look" is something I risk doing myself sometimes, but what does it mean? There is a risk of "look" turning into an empty word. Why look? What is the motivation? If children aren't ready to see then it's an empty word for them. Photographs and real flowers present on the table simultaneously are powerful go-betweens and usually give

FIGURE 4.20   The teacher intervening during the second drawing.

Dialectical encounters in Reggio Emilia **121**

rise to significant results on the level of the final products. But if children don't also have time to look, to be aware, and go deeper with joy and pleasure, then we risk cacophony.

TF: I agree with Vea. There's a risk of a "dictation" on the level of observing – what to be careful of, how to resolve an issue on the technical level – but what implications does this have for children's subjectivity? Underlining aspects that are "missing" from their work rather than the original communicative elements in what they are drawing. We need to be careful to let each child have time to notice elements, choose them, find ways of representing them, and evaluate their own work.

MM: The children's knowledge suggests how we can intervene differently with each one of them, for example with shyer children I was careful to praise what they had already drawn first. With children who rush through things I underlined the importance of being more careful with detail.

VV: Yes, ok then. Let's say it is always fundamental to intervene by starting with where the children are in a given moment, and support observations that are close to what these particular children find interesting. It was useful that first of all you asked the children for a drawing with no intervention, for a good understanding of where the children were in terms of interests, competences, difficulties with drawing, and so on.

MM: The aim of my intervention (Figure 4.20) was to help the children connect that bunch of daisies on the table with the whole experience of exploring the meadow.

TF: But can memory only be supported by verbally proposing that children remember details, and not in other ways instead? When you two teachers go from child to child are you capable of identifying which memory is useful to each one? Don't you risk intervening in a way that is just a little too homogeneous and undifferentiated? Does everyone need the same intervention in order to remember?

VV: Who decides the relevance and importance of the elements to be observed and drawn? Doing a portrait in drawing is different from doing it with a camera or another medium. And moreover, a child might wish to highlight a detail but not know how to do it on a technical level yet; how to exert pressure on paper with a felt pen to get a more intense colour, for example, or how to define a space before proceeding to colour it in.

MM: But, again, my intervention takes into account the possibility of explaining technical elements.

TF: Another important element we mustn't risk is that of children not trusting their own evaluations of their work because really, it's all in the teacher's hands. Children understand this from the tones we use, our gestures and expressions, the number of times we get up close to them and so on. I think after you have transcribed some of the recordings it would be interesting to understand the group dynamic.

122 Dialectical encounters in Reggio Emilia

VV: That is just the doubt I had looking at Leonardo's expression (the child standing). Whether there isn't a risk of children only trusting your judgement, and not counting on the potential of reciprocal comments from each other.

PS: But they need to be accompanied in an appropriate way because often, partly because their vocabulary is incomplete, they quickly give out biting judgements, and these start off emotional conflicts that risk making group work heavier going for no reason.

TF: Well, then perhaps we ought to challenge them with the collective endeavour of a portrait of daisies, rather than only an individual task.

VV: For children who are a bit insecure the presence of an adult confirming their choices step by step is important. Their questions show this: "Teacher is it ok like this?", and "Do you like it?". When we hear children asking too many questions like these it's a good idea to wonder: Will the child feel capable of daring without the adult as a reference point? I'm speaking a bit generally, now really, because it's always a good idea to be alert, myself more than anyone! Anyway, there can be no doubt you have both been careful to support the children's observations and made it possible for them to have differentiated models and not banal conformist ones. The risk we always have to keep in mind, especially with children who aren't very confident or autonomous yet, is of them not being able, or daring, to go without adult indications. A second doubt I have is, to what extent can teachers always intervene in light, not too intrusive ways? How much can children conserve of what they succeed in doing without the presence of a *brava*[9] [good] teacher?

PS: You're right, in fact, I remember something I read recently about intercultural didactics in maths which more or less said that the habit of not taking personal initiative, of not trusting in your own capacities, can easily become a mental habit that is difficult to shake off, and I remember the author gave the example of "photocopy dependency" which was crystal clear, where children learn to colour the same drawing and have the same reading of reality.

We believe this kind of meeting, which we often call *confronto* in Italian, clearly illustrates how each person in the group feels legitimised to express doubts and opinions, raise issues and invite responses. Each person finds a space for expressing their own argumentations, sometimes on the basis of specific knowledge and competencies. For example, the *pedagogista* urges the teachers to "be careful to let each child have the time to notice elements, choose them, [...] and evaluate their own work", while the *atelierista* expresses a doubt about the teachers' intervention, saying, "that is just the doubt I had looking at Leonardo's expression". Instead, the teacher gives her reason for the choice, maintaining that children "need to be accompanied in an appropriate way". Each person however is also willing to revise their convictions in the light of new information rather than relying uncritically on colleagues' proposals. In short, this daily dialectic is made up of opinions that dialogue together rather than one prevailing over the other.

With the above reflections as a starting point, the group identified successive relaunchings that would challenge everyone: children to encounter the daisies, teachers to re-read their verbal interventions, and the *atelierista* and *pedagogista* to identify different concurrent opportunities for children to carry out research in as autonomous a way as possible. One proposal we worked with among many possible others was that rather than observing and drawing several aspects of the daisy's life with only one mixed vase of flowers as a reference, we chose to delimit the field by putting several vases on the table, each with daisies in a different phase of life: one was filled with daisy buds; one with open flowers; one with fading flowers; and one with completely wilted daisies. This was a way of continuing to respect the idea of identity and portraits of a complex life, while offering children the opportunity to focus on important details, all on one table to maintain an idea of unity. The separation of life phases was only provisional and momentary in order to better grasp their singularities, and so that children could dedicate more time to finding strategies to represent a particular moment in the life of the yellow daisies. Moreover, each child knew that as well as being able to draw a phase of the daisy's life they could also make other portraits, unhurriedly, with longer, more diversified times. Or they could reason about the representations made by others, which is a way of organising our viewing and observation as we work.

Here we can see a detail from Giulia's third drawing (Figure 4.21). Giulia comments: *the ones full of yellow are the young daisies, they're nice and open to make the yellow shinier. They were golden where the light was! Then, some others are darker because they've been open longer and absorbed much more sun!*

FIGURE 4.21 A detail of Giulia's third drawing.

124 Dialectical encounters in Reggio Emilia

FIGURE 4.22   First drawing by Riccardo.

In Riccardo's third drawing (Figure 4.23), he returns to the schema of his first drawing (Figure 4.22) but brightens it with light. Riccardo says: *the daisies are bright because they are wet and the light is striking them!*

VV: This is a kind of drawing that teachers (not you two) often consider unsuccessful because it is too far from reality in their opinion. Drawings are

FIGURE 4.23   Third drawing by Riccardo.

always an interpretation of reality and a good representation is one that succeeds in giving us a personal interpretation of the subject. For example, in this drawing the daisy transforms into a sort of lighted torch and has an almost mystical aspect. It is an excellent drawing in my opinion, and conveys much about the identity of these yellow daisies. Look how Riccardo has gone back to his first schema, and this tells us how his research is a deeply personal interpretation. I am struck by his words too, when he says, *the daisies are bright because they are wet and the light is striking them!* and I feel there is an assonance with Giulia when she says, *the ones full of yellow are the young daisies, they're nice and open to make the yellow shinier. They were golden where the light was!* Riccardo probably heard Giulia's words, and also, children in the group are beginning to share meanings and strong imaginaries related to the light, colour, and the life of daisies. Here there are really "good" teachers and a rich vital context.

Concluding notes: dialectics and *progettualità*

We have intentionally highlighted the dialectical aspect of relations between certain professional roles in Reggio Emilia's education system as part of the landscape introduced in Chapter 3, however we must remember the extent to which *confronto* is woven into many other aspects of being and doing school. *Progettazione,* which will be examined more closely in Chapters 5 and 6, is rooted in dialectics. A dialectic of doing and making, that is creative and designerly, not interpreted only as an exercise in transferring culture from one professional profile to another, but rather viewed as the shared tension towards understanding and researching the best learning contexts for children and adults themselves.

The decisive role of documentation is made evident in this chapter and in the following ones. In fact, we have seen how our protagonists' comments become more relevant and knowledgeable the more they are based on the evidence of images of children, the evidence of their products and the evidence of their words. We have also seen how the comments are more uncertain when elements of documentation are missing. Something is obviously always missing, but in this case again what is missing becomes the clue for a next step, or invites greater attention in other contexts.

Although the affirmative tones of contributions by the *pedagogista* and *atelierista* might seem more evident to the reader, it should not escape us how much the heart of the issues examined here lies with children's own points of view, their gestures, their possibilities of discovering, engaging, and communicating. In the example of the classroom door, the children's point of view is hypothesised, anticipated, and desired. In the example of the yellow daisies the children's point of view, expressed in drawings, surprises us (with stereotypes),

126 Dialectical encounters in Reggio Emilia

alarms us somewhat (by having no references to the daisy's life context), disconfirms (the adult's ways of accompanying children to observe details) and makes us change a proposed context (by accentuating different phases of a daisy's life). No adult is the guarantor of what must happen; all the adults, with their own culture and experience, converge, with the non-human of nature, aesthetics and communication, in hypothesising contexts for and with children. All of them, enthusiastically, surprisingly, continue to learn about children's learning.

Notes

1 To be explored in greater detail in Chapters 5 & 6.
2 In Reggio Emilia's municipal *nidi* and *scuole dell'infanzia*, the school year begins for children on September 1 and ends on June 30, with the possibility of applying for attendance in July in schools managed by educational cooperatives that are part of the public integrated system. All staff in *nidi* and *scuole dell'infanzia* directly managed by the Reggio Emilia municipality remain present at work during the first week of July and the return to work during the last week of August to prepare and re-organise the school spaces, work on documentation and attend meetings to greet and welcome children and families.
3 Italian journalist, humourist, writer, and television author.
4 Italian war surgeon, human rights activist, peace activist, and co-founder with Teresa Sarti of Emergency, an international non-governmental organisation.
5 Italian architect and Senator for Life in the Italian Senate.
6 http://www.rpbw.com/project/emergency-childrens-surgery-center
https://www.archdaily.com/965709/childrens-surgical-hospital-renzo-piano-building-workshop-plus-studio-tamassociati
7 As explored in Chapter 7.
8 We can see here a strong connection with the concepts of "lively ethography" and "response-ability" discussed in the Prologue and Chapter 1.
9 In this discursive and dialogic context, the term *brava* (good) refers to an attitude of attentiveness towards children on the part of the teacher, coupled with competency and sensibility in supporting them.

References

Bruner, J. S. (1996). *The culture of education*. Harvard University Press.
Gallio, F., & Masciarelli, A. (2013). *Il principio di significatività: Una visione 2.0 della realtà*. Youcanprint.
Gandini, L. (2017). La storia, le idee, la cultura: la voce e il pensiero di Loris Malaguzzi. Interviste a cura di Lella Gandini. In C. Edwards, L. Gandini, & G. Forman (Eds.), *I cento linguaggi dei bambini: L'approccio di Reggio Emilia all'educazione dell'infanzia* (pp. 55–111). Edizioni Junior/Spaggiari.
Giroux, H. (2016). Dialectics and the development of curriculum theory. *Counterpoints, 491*(Curriculum: DECANONIZING THE FIELD), 159–176.
Merewether, J. (2019). Listening with young children: Enchanted animism of trees, rocks, clouds (and other things). *Pedagogy, Culture & Society, 27*(2), 233–250. https://doi.org/10.1080/14681366.2018.1460617
Wittgenstein, L. (2009). *Tractatus logico-philosophicus*. Einaudi.

5

THE VALUE OF ARTFULNESS AND AN ETHIC OF MAKING

Stefania Giamminuti

[In Reggio Emilia] we are all somewhat artists by disposition.
(Simona Bonilauri, *pedagogista*, interview with
Stefania Giamminuti, Reggio Emilia)

Introduction

In this chapter, we render the inextricable connection between theory-practice-research that enlivens daily life in the municipal *nidi* and *scuole dell'infanzia*, framing *pensiero progettuale* as both an "artful" (Manning, 2016) collective project, and as a praxis of "making" (Ingold, 2013). We begin by speculating around the elusiveness of the term *progettazione*, engaging with the tensions that relate to both the linguistic hurdles (it can be a hard work to pronounce) imposed by the purists (such as us) on those who speak all languages other than Italian, and the conceptual challenges that the notion of *progettazione* engenders in those for whom daily pedagogical work is often governed by more predictable approaches, tools, and affinities. By grounding our deliberations in praxis, we wish to imply that despite its elusiveness *progettazione* is possible anywhere.

We then offer a historical perspective on *progettazione*, tracing through the memories and experiences of key protagonists the collective search for a way of working that would distance the experience of Reggio Emilia from the practices of *programmazione* (programming) which prevailed elsewhere, towards the invention of a way of thinking and acting in solidarity with the social, political, and educational utopias on which the educational project was founded. We also foreground the fundamental contemporary shift in

DOI: 10.4324/9781003181026-5

128 The value of artfulness and an ethic of making

terminology, with a more frequent use of the term *pensiero progettuale* being deeply intentional.

We lean on disciplines beyond pedagogy, such as architecture, philosophy, the arts, and anthropology to illustrate how and why *pensiero progettuale* pushes the boundaries and invents new ways of thinking and doing not just pedagogically. In essence, it is not possible to describe or explain the meaning and experience of *progettazione* without drawing heavily from other fields of knowledge; those who try to grasp this concept by reducing it to the realm of educational theory and practice will inevitably fail. In our encounter with the arts and philosophy, we draw on Erin Manning's (2016) notion of "artfulness" to illuminate *pensiero progettuale* not only as an artful endeavour, but as collective practice that is "palpably transindividual" (Manning, 2016, p. 58). The concept of artfulness helps us because it elevates our thoughts around *progettazione,* which in manifestly individual societies might be easily interpreted as simply a personal quality a creative educator might aspire to. Rather, we illuminate the transindividual nature of *pensiero progettuale* through the words of teachers, *atelieristas* and *pedagogistas* to render the ways in which in Reggio Emilia *progettazione* permeates the system. We also take inspiration from the thinking of master architects to further expand the possibilities of working artfully in pedagogical contexts.

Finally, we dwell on the fact that a life of *pensiero progettuale* is tangible. In a turn from our initial musings around its elusiveness, we conclude this chapter by speculating about the ways in which *progettazione* is a process of craftsmanship and "making" (Ingold, 2013), one that is hardly linear but that nonetheless belongs in the realm of the real and the possible.

Progettazione as an elusive concept

Progettazione is perhaps the term that most activates the protective instincts of protagonists of the Reggio Emilia experience and the translators who work with them, while embodying the occasional frustrations of international audiences. These frustrations are often the expression of what Gunilla Dahlberg and Peter Moss (2005) have termed "totalitarianism of the same" or a desire to make the Other into the Same. St. Pierre (2021a), writing about post qualitative inquiry, a "new" and relatively unknown approach to scholarly research in the social sciences, purports that:

> The Other, Difference, is neither recognizable nor welcome. To keep its dominant structure intact, the social sciences are expected to repeat themselves, to be the same and recognizable – what everybody knows. The new is suspect because it might well erode that structure, especially if it refuses its precious, pernicious methodologies and enables different, unrecognizable, approaches to inquiry. (p. 488)

The value of artfulness and an ethic of making **129**

Progettazione, in the eyes of those who cling to conventional pedagogies and predictable approaches in educational settings, is suspect. We know that there are also many educators who encounter Reggio Emilia and welcome the ambivalence, difference, and originality of this term; it may be that these are the same people who are increasingly disenchanted by the totalitarianism of neoliberal influences on pedagogy. In fact, the determination of the "purists" to hold onto this novel term is a practice of resistance and an invitation to welcome otherness, rather than an act of righteousness or elitism as is often implied by those who prefer more familiar terms in educational discourse. Robert-Holmes and Moss (2021, p. 1) lament the "technical, instrumental and economistic terms" such as "quality", "early intervention", "best practice", "investment", "outcomes", and "readiness" with which we seemingly unproblematically talk about early childhood education and care today, as if we have no other words to understand each other. They go on to suggest that "the way we talk so often today about young children and services for them is the language of neoliberalism" (Robert-Holmes & Moss, 2021, p. 1). Maintaining the term *progettazione* introduces a stutter in the power that neoliberal language exerts over early childhood pedagogy; far from being elitist, it is a choice of democracy and respect for the complex and unique experience the term represents. As Claudia Giudici emphasises, it is an invitation to dialogue:

> When we began using the term *progettazione,* it was not utilised in educational settings, therefore we borrowed it from other disciplines. Specifically, from architecture and design, as a kind of higher and more attuned form of thought, with more affinity towards the ways in which we were interpreting the learning processes of children and adults. And so, meanings stratified. Therefore, for us to maintain this term introduces also an estrangement, a specificity which renders the term unique and therefore tries to convey this complexity [...] a word like "design" in English can only ever be partial. I'm not saying it isn't correct, but it conveys in a very partial way one of the many meanings we assign to that one word, and even more so *pensiero progettuale.* It is a way of signalling an originality, illuminating a specificity with which to dialogue.
>
> *(Claudia Giudici, President, Preschools and Infant-toddler Centres - Istituzione of the Municipality of Reggio Emilia, interview with Stefania Giamminuti, Reggio Emilia)*

Originality is a powerful instrument of renewal and resistance. We concur with Robert-Holmes and Moss (2021) when they state that neoliberalism is "resistible" and "resisted" (p. 2). We view the tenacity with which educators in Reggio Emilia have held onto the term *progettazione,* despite the difficulties they have encountered in making themselves understood, as a practice of resistance that should be valued and sustained. However, once the Italian word is attempted or mastered, we empathise deeply with those who are using this terminology in dialogue with other educators, leaders, and policy makers in their own contexts for whom this term will be unfamiliar and may cause irritation and dismissiveness of the experience of Reggio Emilia as foreign, elite, and indeed suspect. We have all encountered this resistance, and we firmly believe that we should not be discouraged by such displays of totalitarianism, but rather we should continue to pursue and elevate alternatives to the attention of those who persist with imprisoning early childhood pedagogy within technical and economistic terms. It is not necessary nor desirable to be what everybody knows, to be recognisable and the same.

If we are to look for a definition of *progettazione,* together with documentation (for as we argue in this chapter the two are inseparable), it lies in the relationality of theory-practice-research as a quotidian way of thinking, acting, and being which informs all organisational, theoretical, cultural, pedagogical, and political practices in Reggio Emilia. Being a *pedagogista,* and being a teacher or an *atelierista,* are all acts of *progettazione. Formazione* itself is a practice of *progettazione.* This is fundamentally why the concept is so deeply elusive; in Reggio Emilia it permeates all, and if those who encounter the experience attempt to reduce *progettazione* to the design of learning experiences, they are likely to miss its far-reaching possibilities for transformation. As noted by *pedagogista* Elena Maccaferri, "*pensiero progettuale* is not limited to teaching and learning processes, rather it is an attitude of constant reflection in order to think of the new" (interview with Stefania Giamminuti, Reggio Emilia). This does not mean that *progettazione* is unreachable, rather that it requires welcoming conceptual discomfort and an openness to uncertainty and experimentation.

Progettazione, pensiero progettuale and documentation

Loris Malaguzzi (1982, in Cagliari et al., 2016) was at pains to emphasise that the *nidi* and *scuole dell'infanzia* "never created a programme" (p. 295). A perusal of the historical archives of the Documentation and Educational Research Centre in Reggio Emilia would reveal a plethora of what over the years have been alternatively termed: "work plans" (*piani di lavoro*); "work projects" (*progetti di lavoro*); "processes of knowledge appropriation" (*processi di appropriazione conoscitiva*); and declarations of intent *(dichiarazioni di intenti*). The timeline is not so important, nor is the specific terminology; what is fundamental to understand is that, within a broader disciplinary context that celebrated programming and used the conventional language of planning, the experience of Reggio Emilia was always pushing boundaries and searching for the new.

The value of artfulness and an ethic of making **131**

Teachers, *atelieristas,* and *pedagogistas* may have used familiar terms such as "programme", "programming", or "plan" in their daily interactions in the past, but in fact they were always tending towards something different, yet unknown and unnamed, whereby children's ideas were always listened to, teachers' inventiveness was encouraged, research was a value, and changes in direction were welcomed and sought after. In addition, such evolving documents were always accompanied by teachers' own reflective diaries, with interpretation emerging as a necessary value, *confronto* with others being deemed essential to the evaluation of learning contexts, and transformation and experimentation being welcomed. Such efforts were also always informed by a collective tension towards participation, with conventional programming approaches proving ineffectual in sharing with families the evolution of ongoing projects; hence a firm desire to keep families "within" the educational project led to an openness towards the ways of documentation, which was incompatible with the conventionality of programming. At this time, all were engaged in seeking an alternative lexicon.

Greater collective awareness around consolidating the term *progettazione* emerged in the early 1980s, when Malaguzzi spoke often in meetings with staff about practices and ways of thinking that were in fact being invented within the *nidi* and *scuole dell'infanzia.* We trace below, through the voices of key protagonists in published writings and interviews for this research project, how the growing resistance towards *programmazione* ("programming" – no hesitation here in translation) and the invention of *progettazione* was born of welcoming systemic theory and values of complexity and participation. In narrating and conceptualising this experience, we also draw on connections with post qualitative inquiry (St. Pierre, 2021a, 2021b) and the influence of method (Manning, 2015) on research and pedagogy.

We then turn to emphasising the fundamental interrelationship between *progettazione* and documentation. We lament the fact that in many international contexts the practice of documentation has been unthinkingly adopted by educators and/or demanded of them by policy directives, and is thus generally and swiftly superimposed onto existing pedagogies and practices and utilised simply as "evidence" of events that have occurred, often adding substantially to teachers' workloads without in fact contributing to their knowledge and *formazione,* and definitely not enabling democratic processes of research dissemination and dialogue around education. We do not despair however, for we know of many settings that boldly work with documentation in affinity with the knowledge shared by colleagues in Reggio Emilia, and we acknowledge that such places recognise documentation and *progettazione* as inextricably related. Fundamentally, you can't do one without the other; possibly, they are one and can only be really understood together. Finally, we share the meaning and experience of *pensiero progettuale* in the words of teachers, *pedagogistas,* and *atelieristas,* foregrounding further thinking around artfulness that follows in the chapter.

132 The value of artfulness and an ethic of making

From *programmazione* to *progettazione*: welcoming complexity and participation

The emergence of *progettazione,* in language, thought, and action, occurred in Reggio Emilia many decades ago and was the fruit of encounters with a myriad of disciplines beyond the field of pedagogy, driven by Malaguzzi's voracious reading in disparate fields of knowledge, but also by the innovative daily research conducted within the *nidi* and *scuole dell'infanzia* by children and adults alike. In 1988, at an event of *formazione* for staff in the municipal *nidi* and *scuole dell'infanzia*, Malaguzzi embraces systemic theory, citing many thinkers sympathetic to complexity, and proposes this way of encountering the world as a significant influence on the daily work of the *nidi* and *scuole dell'infanzia* (Malaguzzi, 2021). This event was specifically focused on *progettazione*, and within his talk Malaguzzi frequently juxtaposes the infinite possibilities of *progettazione* with the prescriptiveness of *programmazione*:

> Programme is an idea that already contains a certainty of prescription and that predicts the moment of actuation, so that procedural schedules are already inscribed in this ante-thinking, this premeditated thinking, and through these procedures and a series of coherent contingencies, programme comes to achieve its objectives.
>
> *(Malaguzzi, 2021, p. 41)*

Programming thrives on predictability and simplicity, as suggested convincingly and succinctly by teacher Francesca Forenzi: "programming is the easiest tool to simplify the thoughts of adults who are afraid to dare with children" (interview with Stefania Giamminuti, Reggio Emilia). Premeditated thinking, the purview of programming, is the anthesis of daring and eschews complexity. Even though in contemporary pedagogical thinking and practice programming has been widely discredited for being too prescriptive and lacking in boldness, it is still alive and thriving (despairingly, perhaps it endures because of these qualities). By virtue of its simplicity and predictability, programming lends itself to more effective surveillance and can also appear to respond far better to accountability concerns that are rife in educational systems across the world.

Simplicity, predictability, surveillance, and accountability are all privileged in neoliberal discourses, perpetuating neoliberal values of conventionality and linearity in educational contexts. As Giamminuti and Merewether (2022) argue: "conventional pedagogies, that yearn for the predictability of recipes by the minute and elevate neoliberalism's longing for linearity, are devoid of aesthetics and experimentation and leave little space for imagining any sort of correspondence or alliance between things" (p. 18). *Progettazione* instead is born of alliances and relations: "to think in the way of *progettazione* is to think relationally" (Simona Bonilauri, *pedagogista*, interview with Stefania

Giamminuti, Reggio Emilia). This tension towards systemic thinking and complexity of thought and action is evident also in the words of Ivana Soncini:

> The epistemology behind the concept of complexity was not simply a reference point for the Reggio Emilia Approach, but also for the evolution of many other disciplines in the humanities and sciences. The cultural sensibility of those times led to questioning, in many fields of knowledge, of linear and dichotomic thought, caged within dominant and preconceived theories, which pedagogy often relies upon. Therefore, the role of the *pedagogista* felt supported and legitimated in constructing a "bridge" towards other knowledges, other horizons for research, integrating these within concrete experiences with children, for a progressive and innovative school. *Progettazione*, within *formazione* for teachers and *pedagogistas*, must give shape to this "bridge" and never take it for granted.
>
> *(Ivana Soncini, psychologist and member of the pedagogical coordination, interview with Stefania Giamminuti, Reggio Emilia)*

Progettazione is a collective act of resistance against linearity and a gesture of hope for the future, "for the problem with the straight line is simply this: once it has reached its end, what then?" (Ingold, 2013, p. 139). Fundamentally, the passage from *programmazione* to *progettazione* relates to a desire to refute conventional, positivistic, linear approaches to pedagogy that were pervasive in Italy and internationally at the time of the birth of the educational project of Reggio Emilia, and which continue to be highly influential in other educational contexts today, where the straight line and an orderly end is exalted. It is important to emphasise that this engagement with systemic thinking can be maintained only when pedagogy opens up to other fields of knowledge, distancing itself from the primacy of educational theory and practice to embrace a more open understanding of what might constitute professional knowledge in the field, as noted on several occasions by members of the pedagogical coordinating team in Reggio Emilia:

> The curiosity and pleasure of broadening pedagogy's cultural context, which we considered too constricting and suffocating, has always brought us to privilege an interdisciplinary approach, assisting us in elaborating thinking in connection with the emerging cultures of other fields of knowledge such as cybernetics, biology, physics, neuroscience, architecture …
>
> *(Filippini, 2000, pp. 2–3[our translation])*

A pedagogy that would make treasure of many other disciplines in the humanities and sciences.

> *(Ivana Soncini, psychologist and member of the pedagogical coordination, interview with Stefania Giamminuti, Reggio Emilia)*

134 The value of artfulness and an ethic of making

Our professionalism is interdisciplinary.

(Simona Bonilauri, pedagogista, *interview with Stefania Giamminuti, Reggio Emilia)*

Pensiero progettuale is ecological and systemic (not positivistic) thought. It crosses the boundaries of pedagogy, engaging with emerging cultures in other fields of knowledge.

(Pedagogical Coordination of the Municipality of Reggio Emilia, 2014, p. 72)

Atelierista Mirella Ruozzi recalls how important openness to fields of knowledge was in early research projects such as *The City and the Rain* from the early 1980s, where Malaguzzi invited the adults to "search for clues", thus contesting linearity while at the same time emphasising the importance of *formazione* and the value of culture[1]:

At the time of the project *The City and the Rain* we were really at the crossroads between programming and *progettazione,* and Malaguzzi had led many symposiums on this passage. The fact of going into the city and collecting the photos was also about collecting clues [...] So *progettazione* was beginning to be defined also as a journey you undertake which, to some extent, you can prefigure as an adult, because you engage in *formazione* on that topic, be it "the city and the rain" or the trees, or the gardens ... We refer to these as teachers' cultural premises.

(Mirella Ruozzi, atelierista, interview with Stefania Giamminuti, Reggio Emilia)

On the topic of searching for clues, a criticism that is often levelled at the experience of Reggio Emilia, and specifically to *progettazione*, is that it lacks direction and rigour. In contrast, programming, where clues and discoveries are eschewed in favour of certainties, is celebrated as possessing rigour. This misplaced criticism belies a lack of understanding of *progettazione*, and an assumption that rigour and prescription are one and the same. This assumption is not the purview of pedagogy; it also lies at the heart of contemporary debates on research in the social sciences and is contested by researchers such as Elizabeth Adams St. Pierre, who writes compellingly about post qualitative inquiry.[2] Specifically, Malaguzzi's 1988 musings around *programmazione* cited above echo St. Pierre's contemporary scathing critique of methodology in social sciences research:

Prescribing "what to do" in advance – the purview of methodology – always limits the new, by assuming there is a subject who exists prior to thought; by retaining the theory/practice binary; by assuming thinking and doing

The value of artfulness and an ethic of making **135**

are in opposition; by assuming thinking is not doing; and, in the social sciences, by privileging the doing, always the doing, always practices, always application. What do I do and do next? What do I do if someone hasn't told me what to do? How can I be scientific if I don't know what to do, if I'm lost? Oh, pray, what to do without methodology!

(St. Pierre, 2021a, p. 482)

Programming tames teachers into relying on "what do I do and do next", while *progettazione* celebrates the right to be lost and the possibilities of being uncertain. *Programmazione* as outlined by Malaguzzi, and methodology as viewed by St. Pierre thus have much in common: prescriptiveness; "ante-thinking"; "premeditated thinking"; and "procedures" to name a few. The full purpose of ubiquitous planning templates in educational settings is to "limit the new", to govern practice and to pit thinking and doing in opposition to each other, creating a chasm separating theory and practice, limiting research to that which is done "on" schools by "expert researchers" located in universities. St. Pierre (2021a) expresses the hope that "deconstructing pre-existing methodologies should give way—sooner rather than later—to overturning methodology altogether so that something different could be thought" (p. 486). *Progettazione* is "something different", and thus it has the potential to overturn dominant pedagogical methodology when in alliance with documentation. Methods and programmes instead risk leading to what Malaguzzi, in a speech delivered in Reggio Emilia in 1982 at a meeting with the School Management Councils called "caged-in experience":

Permanent *progettualità* is the primary value in our contents. If someone asks us for a programme we say we don't have one. Notice that this is no coincidence: in twenty years we have never created a programme, even though we have always worked with work plans and with work projects. But we have always refused to make a programme, because the risk of a caged-in programme is that in some way it generates caged-in experience. But this originality [in our work] is formed through a very long process, which is the process of research, the process of curriculum project and planning, the process of controlled execution, of evaluative analysis of the results, and the process of decisions.

(Malaguzzi, 1982, in Cagliari et al., 2016, pp. 295–296)

Similarly, Manning (2016) refers to method in research as "an apparatus of capture" (p. 32). In delineating the refusal to programme and be caged in or captured, Malaguzzi is compelled to emphasise rigour in originality while eschewing conventionality and banality. This argument for rigour is familiar to researchers in post qualitative inquiry, who are often called to defend their research against conventional criteria that celebrate certainty and aim for generalisable

136 The value of artfulness and an ethic of making

results, when in fact "given that every post qualitative study is different, generalities about its goodness are not possible" (St. Pierre, 2021b, p. 7). In the 1988 speech on *progettazione* cited above, Malaguzzi contends that "certainly programme is necessary for constructing and hypothesising an event and the future in some way, but it rests on a theory of certainty that we do not share" (Malaguzzi, 2021, p. 43). Embracing uncertainty is a key aspect of *progettazione*, which "accepts doubt, uncertainty and error as resources, and is capable of being modified in relation to the evolution of the contexts" (Preschools and Infant-toddler Centres - Istituzione of the Municipality of Reggio Emilia, 2010, p. 12). In post qualitative inquiry this capacity to modify is what Lather (2013) calls "getting lost", which she suggests "might exactly be about an accountability to complexity and the political value of not being so sure" (p. 642). Loredana Garofalo recalls how when she first began working in the *scuole dell'infanzia* in the early 1980s teachers would create documents that were called "programmes" and which made them feel "apparently more certain", whilst in their daily work they constantly maintained a tension towards the unexpected:

> At that time, programming apparently made us feel more certain, but it was misleading. Because then we didn't know where to fit in the unexpected in our writings. So, we brought the unexpected into the class meetings, we narrated it. We didn't write it down; we told the story. Therefore, it would somehow be lost in the telling and in the lived experience, becoming personal knowledge. *Progettazione* instead is something that you can consolidate as *formazione*; it is not left to the wind, it is not static, but rather it moves.
>
> *(Loredana Garofalo, teacher, interview with*
> *Stefania Giamminuti, Reggio Emilia)*

Loredana's metaphor of *formazione* as being in movement aligns *progettazione* with the qualities of non-linearity, unpredictability, and collectivity that are celebrated in movement ontologies (Truman & Springgay, 2015). In *progettazione,* spaces are created for "the incalculable, the messy, not knowing" (Lather, 2013, p. 642), elevating to collective knowledge those stories that Loredana suggests were otherwise lost in experience and consigned to individual memory when programming. Importantly, as Loredana notes, these spaces for "not knowing" are collective spaces of knowledge building and *formazione*. Differently from conventional programming, which in its certainty is essentially an individual and exclusive practice, *progettazione* is relational and participatory. In his 1988 speech, Malaguzzi (2021) refers to *progettazione* as "a process for knowing which does not follow the old paths, but verifies a very different [kind of] conjecture, in which knowledge draws its permanent and continuous nourishment from a circular kind of co-participation, between ourselves, objects, feelings, people, things and living beings etc." (p. 33). This echoes Lather's (2013) contemporary thoughts on the contributions of post

The value of artfulness and an ethic of making **137**

qualitative inquiry, which she calls "a counter science on our own terms" that "can be community based, community sustaining, and community serving in ways that might help alter the structures of institutions in more expansive democratizing ways" (p. 642).

In conclusion, the passage from *programmazione* to *progettazione* signalled in the experience of Reggio Emilia welcoming of complexity, resistance against linearity and the strictures of method, and an openness to participatory practices tending towards democracy. It continues to create a stutter in conventional pedagogical approaches elsewhere, appealing to those for whom the predictable and banal holds no seduction. Its otherness remains necessary.

Progettazione and documentation: Theory-practice-research

> Our experience is constructed on and lives through a strong connection between theory and practice. Therefore, our efforts to live *progettazione* and to elaborate its relationship to programming, then the emergence of *pensiero progettuale* as an attitude better able to keep connected what we do amongst ourselves, with children, with families, with the broader context, all rely on a constant exercise of opening up the mind, revisiting theory in deep connection to practice.
>
> *(Filippini, 2000, p. 3 [our translation])*

Following the publication of the seminal Harvard Project Zero and Reggio Children research project *Making Learning Visible* (Giudici et al., 2001), documentation[3] garnered significant, and justified, attention worldwide. In the decades that followed, documentation is firmly established internationally in theory, policy, and practice; it is widely published about, and there are many educational contexts that work thoughtfully with documentation in attunement and dialogue with the experience of Reggio Emilia. However, documentation is also widely misunderstood, maligned, and frequently misused.[4] Gunilla Dahlberg (2012) refers to pedagogical documentation as a "dangerous enterprise" that "always has social and political implications and consequences" (p. 229) and that can easily lead to children and teachers being governed and tamed by instrumental policy concerns and neoliberal values. We wish to note the necessity, for all settings attuned to the experience of Reggio Emilia, to recognise that documentation and *progettazione*, are interdependent and inseparable. It is not possible to enact *progettazione* without documentation, and without *progettazione* documentation remains a record of what happened. As *pedagogista* Elena Giacopini matter-of-factly states:

> If you create documentation at the end of a journey, notwithstanding the good intention of producing a chronological narrative, you risk offering settled

138 The value of artfulness and an ethic of making

evidence that does not solicit new questions. Provocatively, I could say that it loses value, or perhaps it is indeed useless from a stance of *pensiero progettuale.*

(Elena Giacopini, pedagogista, interview with
Stefania Giamminuti, Reggio Emilia)

Malaguzzi emphasised this connection in his 1988 speech on *formazione,* where he conceives of *progettazione* as "strategies" free from the restrictions of programming, a "possibility" rather than a rulebook, that however requires documentation to lean on:

We feel the necessity and urgency – not only professional but human – to face up to problems, events and situations in ways that are free of programmed restriction, and trust in a sort of strategic capacity, in strategies for intervening. These strategies should not be considered so much an ABC, a complete and defined alphabet, but instead as a possibility which, in order to be realised, requires having processes of experience, of competences, and of acquiring a capacity for conjecture and openness to discussion, supported as much as possible by documents [documentation] we can lean on.

(Malaguzzi, 2021, p. 34)

This need for *progettazione* to lean on documentation is expressed by *pedagogista* Paola Strozzi, who at the time of Malaguzzi's 1988 speech was a teacher at the *Scuola dell'infanzia* Diana engaged in those very conjectures Malaguzzi refers to:

An educational project with such breadth as ours could have only chosen a strategy such as *progettazione,* to sustain this idea of work that is done together between adults and children, of thought that constantly renews itself beginning from clues, from traces, from suggestions that emerge from the context, from the environment, from relationships. This is a work of constant reflexivity that needs to rely on writings, because they allow you to focus, to keep a memory, to leave traces – and so the role of documentation, it's all interconnected.

(Paola Strozzi, pedagogista, interview with
Stefania Giamminuti, Reggio Emilia)

Marina Castagnetti was also a teacher in the *Scuola* Diana at the time of Malaguzzi's speech, and she recalls these frequent occasions of collective *confronto* and *aggiornamento,* where all staff together with Malaguzzi would lean on documentation, bringing together theory and practice, knowledge building, and the imagining of infinite possibilities:

It was all part of this larger nurturing circle, of the work with children, the *confronto* with Malaguzzi, working on brief projects and long ones,

The value of artfulness and an ethic of making **139**

bringing forth new ideas. Because Malaguzzi listened to you and absolutely wanted to hear from the teachers what their prefigurations were, he wanted to know what type of hypotheses we had in relation to our *progettazione*. He listened with great curiosity and would truly give legs to what you were doing. So, we when talk about *progettazione*, we refer to a way of working that keeps practice and theory connected.

(Marina Castagnetti, teacher, interview with
Stefania Giamminuti, Reggio Emilia)

Marina highlights how *progettazione* brings together theory and practice, but she also acknowledges how documentation is a "crossing" between being a teacher who conforms and a teacher as researcher who "designs" and transforms with *pensiero progettuale*:

Documentation for me is a crossing between being a teacher who conforms to what is required of her, and a teacher as researcher who designs learning contexts, who engages in *progettazione,* who focuses on the quality of learning contexts, on the quality of materials, on the quality of ideas. In your role as a teacher and in *confronto* with others, you create conditions that are extremely creative and transformative, nurtured by the transformations you experience with children. You also always maintain a conceptual stance, focusing on concepts, translating them into contexts, and elaborating them through documentation.

(Marina Castagnetti, teacher, interview with
Stefania Giamminuti, Reggio Emilia)

The focus Marina places on a "conceptual stance" is important; concepts, often those that derive from beyond the boundaries of pedagogy, matter. Daniela Lanzi illustrates the role of the *pedagogista* in these encounters, emphasising both the importance of being "within" the experience, and the potential of documentation to concretely draw in those who have not witnessed the events firsthand (as evidenced in Figures 5.1, 5.2 and 5.3):

In our daily work, *pensiero progettuale* is difficult. It's difficult because it requires immediate and ongoing steps and evaluations; you need to understand if you have understood, and you need to consider if you have understood what the children have understood. I enjoy most, and would never give up, the meetings where together with teachers you dwell on the documentation, you try to understand what has happened, and you think of what to do. You consider the documents you have, the materials you have, the documentation you have collected, and you start from there. You read the notes, you look at the images you have chosen, you try to decide if the words you have chosen are relevant and coherent, you consider whether

140 The value of artfulness and an ethic of making

FIGURE 5.1 *Aggiornamento, Scuola dell'infanzia* Diana: *pedagogista* Simona Bonilauri dwelling on documentation and children's artefacts with *atelierista* Federica Castrico and teachers Cinzia Incerti, Giuseppina Ronchelli, and Mariagrazia Romanazzo.

FIGURE 5.2 *Aggiornamento, Scuola dell'infanzia* Diana: *pedagogista* Simona Bonilauri reading documentation.

The value of artfulness and an ethic of making **141**

FIGURE 5.3   *Aggiornamento, Scuola dell'infanzia* Diana: teacher Giuseppina Ronchelli sharing documentation and children's artefacts in clay.

you should use others … I believe that teachers' writings are fundamental to *pensiero progettuale*, because when you write you are already trying to create a synthesis. *Pedagogistas* should never be external to these situations, they are never outsiders in the process of interpretation, they are within.

(Daniela Lanzi, pedagogista, *interview with Stefania Giamminuti, Reggio Emilia)*

To be within the process of interpretation is a key responsibility for *pedagogistas* and is the focus of significant *formazione*. Teacher Loredana Garofalo emphasises how these interpretative encounters, which lean on documentation, are terrain of exchange for teachers and *pedagogistas*, what she calls work that is truly *progettuale*:

Pedagogistas offer constant feedback. But this is not a strategy of control, rather it's a collaboration, an exchange; I have something to offer you as a teacher, and this opens an exchange. The *pedagogista* affords me the

142 The value of artfulness and an ethic of making

opportunity to create connections between things, she gifts me provocations also on a theoretical level, she offers me keys for interpretation that weave beautifully into everyday life, connecting with our frontline work with children, and supporting our own individual tension towards experimentation. A more theoretical approach, which in turn is nurtured by my own work, can't help but lead towards work that is truly *progettuale*.

(Loredana Garofalo, teacher, interview with
Stefania Giamminuti, Reggio Emilia)

This interconnection between theory-practice-research is brought to life in the events and dialectical exchanges narrated in Chapter 6, where the "documents" on which teachers, *atelieristas* and *pedagogistas* lean on are framed within a constant "capacity for conjecture and openness to discussion" (Malaguzzi, 2021, p. 34), within the ecological system that is created in the encounter between *progettazione* and documentation. In Chapter 6, clues, traces, and hypotheses are illuminated in the narrative of daily life, and thus *pensiero progettuale* and documentation appear inseparable.

Pensiero progettuale in daily life

For several years now, *progettuale* [designerly] thought and action, as a theory-practice structure sustaining the values and possible meanings of our educational project, have framed our *formazione* projects.

(Filippini, 2000, p. 2 [our translation])

Recently in Reggio Emilia, the term *pensiero progettuale* is used more frequently and in preference to *progettazione*. There are many reasons why the choice has been made to privilege this term, with one being the emphasis on "the project" that the use of the term *progettazione* unintentionally brought about in international contexts. The various translations of *progettazione* into "project work", "project approach", or similar, and the seductive projects that have been shared over the years in publications, presentations, and exhibitions, have frequently resulted in the misplaced assumption that to engage in *progettazione* is to devise and enact a project, and thus that *progettazione* begins and ends with the life of a project. We trust that our above deliberations on the pervasiveness of *progettazione* in organisational, cultural, social, and pedagogical realms in Reggio Emilia might help assuage such misunderstandings. Teacher Marika Lorenzani, who echoes the words shared by many other teachers and *pedagogistas* in interviews for this research, believes that daily life is a project:

I deliberately speak of daily life, and not of projects, because for us daily life is a project. Daily life needs to have its own *progettuale* [designerly] lens because it all belongs to a design of the quotidian, meaning that there is thought behind it. It means that people have come together and have asked each other questions about, for example: "in your view, if the child eats in this way rather than another"? To give value to all that children encounter within our *nidi* and *scuole*.

*(Marika Lorenzani, teacher, interview with
Stefania Giamminuti, Reggio Emilia)*

Behind these words lies a deeply rooted belief, brought about by decades of collective thinking and research in Reggio Emilia, that, particularly in the *nido*, daily life should never be reduced to routine. In many other contexts of early childhood education and care, "daily routines" have been elevated to a pedagogical necessity and a cultural expectation, with predictability celebrated in the name of young children's perceived needs for both learning and survival. In these contexts, reliance on routine often drives and consequently limits every aspect of pedagogical decision-making and relating for both children and adults. In Marika's words instead, we can glimpse an overlooked "routine" – mealtimes – reframed as a possibility for research, valued as an opportunity for asking each other questions as opposed to being governed by answers and instrumentalised by reductive decision-making. Rather than being defined once for all and repeated the same day after day, mealtimes become occasions for recognising and attending to young children's infinite individual capabilities and communicative capacities, viewed as opportunities for co-construction of learning, and valued as events of reciprocal care and wellbeing for children and adults. Within routine-governed pedagogies, minds and bodies are often separated in the name of young children's urgent and unequivocable needs. Instead, by perceiving daily life as a project, minds and bodies, thinking and doing, learning and acting, are all seen as inextricably related and engendering of infinite curiosity, leading to possibilities for research and innovation.[5] Teachers, *atelieristas* and *pedagogistas* convey how the use of the term *pensiero progettuale* shifts attention from the realm of the project to the quotidian, engendering a focus on complexity, non-linearity, and relations with humans, places, and materials. For example:

Our work, our being together with children, our way of educating, from gestures to thoughts, to all that we live each day […] this effort to be visible to the city, to the world. All this is *pensiero progettuale. Pensiero progettuale* is to give meaning to what you do every day, not just in relation to a project, for example on drawing and mark-making or other topics. Everything is *pensiero progettuale*, from how I welcome the children in the morning to how I say goodbye in the afternoon.

*(Manuela Pederzoli, teacher, interview with
Stefania Giamminuti, Reggio Emilia)*

144 The value of artfulness and an ethic of making

We can somehow define *progettazione* as the strategy that we have chosen to do school, to sustain processes of relations, of research, and of knowledge construction for children and adults. In truth all other projects make sense if they graft onto the larger project that is daily life [...] You enter the same place each day and it is never the same. *Progettazione* is when each day, through the good and the bad, within situations that can be very complex, you are still able to find the extraordinary in the ordinary.

(Simona Marani, teacher, interview with
Stefania Giamminuti, Reggio Emilia)

Pensiero progettuale is sort of an attitude that accompanies us each day in living our quotidian. Not simply when we might begin a project with children, but rather when we welcome families in August and September, when we prepare the environment, when we design contexts. It is an attitude that must embrace the entirety of everyday life, and the whole system. Because pedagogical *progettazione* exists only within a broader *progettazione,* in relation to the system.

(Giulia Ovi, teacher, interview with
Stefania Giamminuti, Reggio Emilia)

The teachers' words convey an image of *pensiero progettuale* as essential to daily life. More than an attitude, more than a praxis, more than individual; it is a collective way of being and doing. As Manuela suggests, "everything" is *pensiero progettuale*, from the morning when you welcome the children to the ongoing responsibility of being visible to the city and the world. For Simona, as for the others, daily life is an extraordinary project that takes meaning from relations. Giulia traces these relations: children; families; environments; materials; and finally, the system. In fact, design thinking, as *pedagogista* Daniela Lanzi and teacher Loredana Garofalo suggest, is a way of living the educational project itself:

Pensiero progettuale was chosen because it is a thought characterised by connections. Therefore, I believe that teachers should understand *pensiero progettuale* not simply as a pedagogical choice, but as a choice about how to live school. So *progettazione* relates to educational *progettazione, progettazione* in relation to how you live and interpret the contexts you design and create, and to the way of working with families. I feel that *pensiero progettuale* should be interpreted by teachers and *pedagogistas* as a strategy of mind that relates to how you live the entire educational project.

(Daniela Lanzi, pedagogista, *interview with*
Stefania Giamminuti, Reggio Emilia)

Pensiero progettuale is nothing less than the soul of these schools. It's very difficult to channel it into a definition because it is what you live as a teacher, and even as a parent. A parent here is not called upon simply as parent of

The value of artfulness and an ethic of making **145**

their own child, in a restricted and narrow *confronto* between school and family. No. We constantly invite others to be within a group, to turn their glance towards the other.

(Loredana Garofalo, teacher, interview with
Stefania Giamminuti, Reggio Emilia)

Daniela and Loredana highlight that *pensiero progettuale* does not belong only to teachers who live the quotidian with children, but rather, as a quality permeating the system, it is essential to welcoming families, and to the daily work of *pedagogistas* themselves:

Pensiero progettuale is an attitude that traverses your whole way of being a *pedagogista*, your way of being a teacher. It becomes a fundamental concern for the everyday, not simply for projects. Specific projects require probes, tenacity, deepening knowledge, a particular kind of returning, specific timing. But *pensiero progettuale* is an attitude that gives form to your full way of being a *pedagogista*.

(Paola Strozzi, pedagogista, interview with
Stefania Giamminuti, Reggio Emilia)

Paola goes on to emphasise the need for flexibility, listening, and openness to change:

Pensiero progettuale is a very flexible way of thinking. It is a way of thinking that listens, is propositional, passionate, because you must contribute to it; it must be responsive and flexible because it is open to change, rather than simply tending towards what might be considered the attainment of a "best".

(Paola Strozzi, pedagogista, interview with
Stefania Giamminuti, Reggio Emilia)

The qualities of *pensiero progettuale* delineated above – change-oriented, propositional, passionate, relational, non-linear, welcoming of the unexpected, mired in uncertainty, always in movement, participatory, creative, open to conjecture, complex, experimental, dedicated to originality – render this term unfamiliar to conventional pedagogy and bring it closer to the disciplines of the arts. We opened this chapter with the words of *pedagogista* Simona Bonilauri, who contends that there is something of the artist in all those who work within the educational project of Reggio Emilia. Vea Vecchi, *atelierista* of the *Scuola Diana*, recalls in disgusted delight:

Another comment from people visiting our schools, typical especially of people coming from the pedagogical field, is: "You are very good, but there is an excess of aesthetic care in your work". An excess of aesthetic care!

(Vecchi, 2010, p. 82)

146 The value of artfulness and an ethic of making

In contrast to such reductive criticisms which perceive the *nidi* and *scuole dell'infanzia* of Reggio Emilia as conveying an excess of aesthetic care, we contend that the revolutionary invention of the atelier, which brought educational experience forcefully into dialogue with the arts, was a choice that led to transformation of the pedagogical quotidian, bringing "a new way of seeing into schools and into the process of learning compared with customary views and pedagogical tradition" (Vecchi, 2010, p. 12). Such aesthetic care is not limited to the atelier, but rather the presence of the atelier itself generates ongoing dialogue with the arts, engendering a collective responsibility and curiosity on the part of teachers, *atelieristas* and *pedagogistas* alike to embrace the visionary stance and complex relational thinking that arts-based practice demands. As noted by Malaguzzi:

> The *atelier* has always repaid us. It has, as desired, proved to be subversive- generating complexity and new tools for thought […] the *atelier* has protected us not only from the long-winded speeches and didactic theories of our time (just about the only preparation received by young teachers!) but also from behaviourist beliefs of the surrounding culture, reducing the human mind to some kind of "container" to be filled.
> *(Malaguzzi, in Gandini, 2012, pp. 49–50)*

Giamminuti and Merewether (2022) argue that "the atelier, as a subversive place, makes pedagogical alternatives possible" (p. 19). We now turn to considering such pedagogical alternatives, illuminating how *pensiero progettuale*, conceptualised as "artfulness" (Manning, 2016), tends towards participatory subversiveness and innovation in practice.

The value of *artfulness* in Reggio Emilia

> Artfulness, the aesthetic yield, is about how a set of conditions coalesce to favor the opening of a process to its inherent collectivity, to the more-than of its potential. The art of participation is the capacity, in the event, to activate its artfulness, to tap into its yield. Artfulness is the force of a becoming that is singularly attendant to an ecology in the making, an ecology that can never be subsumed to the artist or to the individual participant. Artfulness: the momentary capture of an aesthetic yield in an evolving ecology.
> *(Manning, 2016, p. 58)*

The term "artfulness" (Manning, 2016), which we have chosen here to convey a more nuanced understanding of *pensiero progettuale*, emphasises collectivity and process in arts creation, hence it was compelling to us as concept to think with. There were other terms we grappled with, in response to the research data, to convey the key value that underlies working with *pensiero progettuale*; but none of them seemed able to capture the meanings we intended. We considered *the value of design* but were wary of its limitations and of the risk of taming the term into educational discourse ("curriculum design" comes to mind). We favoured *the value of artistry* but worried about its connotations of individuality, with the risk of artistry being associated with a virtuoso artist working on her own towards a celebrated creation. We did not wish to perpetuate the misunderstanding of "the project" being the celebrated outcome of *progettazione*, but rather we considered it necessary to emphasise everyday practice and collective process. Artfulness pushes the boundaries of artistry by engaging with what Manning (2016) calls "the manner of practice and not the end result" (p. 46).

We speculate that in settings such as the municipal *nidi* and *scuole dell'infanzia* of Reggio Emilia, where the value of artfulness is lived across all aspects of daily life through *pensiero progettuale*, it becomes possible to resist the instrumental practices that govern educational settings while remaining open to dialogue with differences and knowledges from other disciplines. The concept of artfulness brings educational settings closer to the inventiveness of the arts, thus inviting practices of originality and "collective experimentation" (Manning, 2015) within a relational ecology of becoming. We unapologetically aspire to "an aesthetic yield" in the "evolving ecology" (Manning, 2016, p. 58) of educational settings. In other words, we hope to see early childhood education and care not as something that sits still and repeats itself through prescriptive and governing practices, privileging isolation, but rather as something that is constantly in becoming, artful in its core being, and openly democratic. It is the question of what we wish school to be, as Manuela Pederzoli contends:

> What does it mean to do school together in this way? It means that all has not been prescribed or pre-defined, but rather it is always in becoming, and shared with others.
>
> *(Manuela Pederzoli, teacher, interview with*
> *Stefania Giamminuti, Reggio Emilia)*

This also means that we dissent with those who suggest that aesthetic care is superfluous in early childhood settings. The aesthetic dimension, which Vecchi (2010) defines as "an attitude of care and attention for the things we do, a desire for meaning; it is the opposite of indifference and carelessness, of conformity, of absence of participation and feeling" (p. 5), is indispensable. Care, attention, desire for meaning, participation, and feeling are all mistrusted within instrumental practices such as programming, and studiously avoided in conventional assessment strategies in early childhood education and care. *Pensiero progettuale* instead, in its artfulness, welcomes the

148 The value of artfulness and an ethic of making

aesthetic dimension, affording rigour, originality and experimentation to the design of teaching and learning experiences, assessment practices, the choices relevant to environments and materials, dialogue with families, encounters between working groups, and broader relationships within the local community and far beyond. As Malaguzzi (in Gandini, 2012) noted, the atelier, with its artful practice, "protected" the Reggio Emilia experience from the pressures of reductive behaviourist thought and the power of conventional, linear pedagogies.

One key aspect on which conventional and artful pedagogical approaches differ is in their interpretation of what might constitute effective assessment and evaluation. It is beyond the scope of our contribution to offer an extended critique of conventional evaluative approaches and to concretely propose alternatives; however, we wish to emphasise that an artful stance extends also to practices of assessment and evaluation, specifically in the potential created through *progettazione* and documentation to do far more than measure the performance and achievement of individual children against standardised criteria and predetermined outcomes. In the words of experienced teacher Simona Marani as she describes *progettazione*:

> You must be predisposed to observe and document what is occurring. You must foresee moments where together with your colleagues you pause, to see, to consider the thoughts, the materials you have collected, and to review with someone the thoughts you have written down or the ones in your mind. These elaborations allow you then to also evaluate how the children have been within that context you offered; this is one of the greatest differences between *progettazione* and programming. Because when you evaluate you do so by considering the contexts you were able to propose and, importantly, how you as an adult were within that context and what you offered, or did not offer, to children.
>
> *(Simona Marani, teacher, interview with*
> *Stefania Giamminuti, Reggio Emilia)*

Evaluation here is not intended as a narrow, linear practice of applying pre-determined criteria to measure individual progression and performance. Rather, it is welcomed as collective opportunity to embrace thoughtful design of participatory contexts and to constantly evaluate their potential for individual and group learning. In Reggio Emilia, individual children's learning remains a focus of care and attention for all, with competencies assessed in relation to a broad range of capabilities in dialogue with current national policy documents and evolving professional knowledge and research; however, this evaluative stance always considers the potential of the contexts offered and the responses of adults within these. It is also informed by an empathetic and valuing glance towards all children and each child, with teachers encountering children within processes of knowledge construction and relationality and offering opportunities for evolution of knowledge and competencies.[6] In fact, the participatory, reflexive, transformative, process-oriented, and practice-based focus that Simona alludes to affords evaluation the qualities of artfulness. Furthermore, teacher Loredana Garofalo emphasises the potential of *progettazione* to generate questions and its openness to infinite possibilities, both qualities necessary to artfulness as participatory:

> What is *progettazione* if not this context that you create where there are no preconceived objectives, where you close nothing but open everything, where you do not have answers but instead you seek questions. It is quotidian, because every time you propose something to children you need to appreciate that anything can happen.
>
> *(Loredana Garofalo, teacher, interview with*
> *Stefania Giamminuti, Reggio Emilia)*

Manning (2016) similarly contends that "art, as *a way* of learning, acts as a bridge towards new processes, new pathways" (p. 47). We speculate that *pensiero progettuale*, not settled on a final product and focused on collective becoming, is "still on its way" (Manning, 2016, p. 47). To value artfulness and to strive towards "a certain attunement of world and expression" (Manning, 2016, p. 47) in all aspects of working with young children was a revolutionary choice in the early decades of the educational project of Reggio Emilia. Teacher Manuela Pederzoli recalls how the inauguration of *Nido d'infanzia* Panda in 1979 featured exhibitions of paintings and other artwork by local artists, initiated by the *pedagogista* at the time, noting that: "to welcome this idea of the arts, of beauty, from the very first months of life, was an important wager" (interview with Stefania Giamminuti, Reggio Emilia). It was a wager, but it became a way of life, permeating all aspects of the experience into the future and becoming essential to all.

We now turn to tracing connections between *progettazione* and the discipline of architecture, referring to the work of master architects to speculate the possibilities generated by thinking pedagogy differently. We also dwell on the key notion of "constraints", demystifying the pervasive assumption that in Reggio Emilia there are no constraints and that it might therefore be this apparently unbridled freedom of thought and action that compels originality and artful experimentation. This assumption has generated significant mistrust in the experience of Reggio Emilia, which is frequently dismissed as lacking rigour and being out of touch with the "reality" and demands of educational practice, hence we feel a responsibility to convey the fundamental importance that constraints have on both artful practice and freedom itself.

Pedagogy, architecture, and the potential of constraints

As conveyed above by Claudia Giudici, in Reggio Emilia the term *progettazione* was borrowed from other disciplines: "specifically from architecture and design, as a kind of higher and more attuned form of thought" (interview with Stefania Giamminuti, Reggio Emilia). But there are as many ways of doing architecture as there are of practising pedagogy. Our purpose here is to pursue possible ways of conceptualising the relationship between architecture and pedagogy; our musings are relatively brief and hence possibly reductive, but we wish to indicate a particular connection with the kind of architecture that generates emotions, pushes boundaries, and has the capacity to move us.

Wiggins and McTighe (2012) have used an analogy with architecture to speculate on educational matters, specifically the introduction of Common Core Standards in the USA and their relationship to curriculum. In so doing, the authors have embraced dominant terms in both educational and architectural discourse:

> So, what is the proper relationship between the Standards and curriculum? Consider another analogy with home building and renovation: The standards are like the building code. Architects and builders must attend to them but they are *not* the purpose of the design. The house to be built or renovated is designed to meet the needs of the client in a functional and pleasing manner – while also meeting the building code along the way.
>
> *(McTighe & Wiggins, 2012, pp. 26–27)*

To unpack this citation, first of all from the point of view of education, it is of note that Robert-Holmes and Moss (2021) cite the Common Core Standards in their scathing critique of neoliberal education reforms, suggesting that "these 'high stakes' tests link evaluation of teachers to pupils' test scores and penalise public schools that are persistently unable to meet the progress targets" (p. 35). Further, Sahlberg (2011) notes that such global educational reforms "search for safe and low-risk ways to reach learning goals. This minimizes experimentation, reduces the use of alternative pedagogical approaches, and limits risk-taking in schools and classrooms" (p. 178). Our expansive conceptualisation of *pensiero progettuale* as experimental and welcoming of risk would suggest a fundamental distance from such instrumental goals. Furthermore, a concerning consequence of such reforms is what Ball (2003) hauntingly refer to as the "terrors of performativity", whereby "performativity and accountability agendas are radically undermining the professionalism of teachers in the hunt for measures, targets, benchmarks, tests, tables, audits to feed the system in the name of improvement" (p. 1046). This leads to what Malaguzzi called a "prophetic pedagogy" which:

> knows everything beforehand, knows everything that will happen, knows everything, does not have one uncertainty, is absolutely imperturbable.

The value of artfulness and an ethic of making **151**

It contemplates everything and prophesies everything, sees everything, sees everything to the point that it is capable of giving you recipes for little bits of action, minute by minute, hour by hour, objective by objective, five minutes by five minutes. This is something so coarse, so cowardly, so humiliating of teachers' ingenuity, a complete humiliation for children's ingenuity and potential.

(Malaguzzi, in Cagliari et al., 2016, p. xvii)

Ball (2003), in describing the "terrors of performativity", shares stories of teachers who have experienced such humiliation at the hands of neoliberal educational reform. *Pensiero progettuale* instead elevates collective competencies and distances itself from initiatives that seek to govern teacher professionalism. This premise would certainly suggest that we refute the above citation by McTighe and Wiggins altogether, but it is not simply the reference to educational standards that makes us uncomfortable. The analogy with home building can have some appeal, but as it is phrased it reflects a very reductive view of the possibilities of architecture. To suggest that the purpose of architecture might be to meet client needs in a "functional and pleasing manner" (McTighe & Wiggins, 2012, p. 27) would cause many intelligent architects to shudder. At a basic level, building codes generally have sections titled something like "alternative solutions", which recognise that deviations from the standard are necessary and allow for research, artfulness, and the unexpected. At a more inspiring level, architecture should transcend the established, as RCR Arquitectes stated in their acceptance speech for the 2017 Pritzker Architecture Prize[7]:

For us, architecture is the art of materializing dreams throughout a long journey [...] We must admit that it may not be easy, but our commitment is to awaken emotions in the people who live in the spaces we create. To become conscious of their experience, to comprehend the true nature of things and to transcend the established, to arrive at new and unexpected results. Architecture is like music, but less ephemeral. It is like poetry, but more prosaic. All this is because we want to feel and make others feel.

(Aranda et al., 2017)

We prefer to think of *progettazione* in pedagogical settings in these terms: "the art of materializing dreams"; "like music but less ephemeral"; "like poetry but more prosaic"; capable of transcending the established; desirous of arriving at new and unexpected results; and always concerned with feeling (Aranda et al., 2017). The difference thus between building that meets the standards and architecture is akin to the difference between programming and *progettazione:* one seeking standardisation, measurement, objectivity, and predictability; the other relishing artfulness, inventiveness, feeling, and complexity. One is the expected, it is foregone. The other is a provocation, it is research,

152 The value of artfulness and an ethic of making

it is a promise of beauty and a question for others to pursue, creating opportunities for movement and transformation:

> *Pensiero progettuale* is not something that you as a teacher consume, rather it is a privilege that you have, to create dynamic learning contexts where you search for the question, the unexpected, even the discomfort and embarrassment that can arise in response to children's questions. These are all opportunities: for growth, for movement, for transformation. This for us is research.
>
> *(Loredana Garofalo, teacher, interview with*
> *Stefania Giamminuti, Reggio Emilia)*

Loredana's words echo those of master architect Peter Zumthor, whereby the "teacher" Zumthor refers to could be an adult (teacher, *pedagogista, atelierista*) or child alike:

> Practicing architecture is asking oneself questions, finding one's own answers with the help of the teacher, whittling down, finding solutions. Over and over again. The strength of a good design lies in ourselves and in our ability to perceive the world with both emotion and reason. A good architectural design is sensuous. A good architectural design is intelligent.
>
> *(Zumthor, 2006, p. 65)*

We speculate that "good" *progettazione* should also be sensuous and intelligent, and furthermore that by "materializing dreams" (Aranda et al., 2017) through emotion and reason, *progettazione* in both pedagogy and architecture is not reduced to a utopian practice, but rather relies on creative freedom and systematic, collaborative thinking and doing. In fact, Zumthor (2006) states that his favourite definition of design is "associative, wild, free, ordered, and systematic thinking in images, in architectural, spatial, colorful, and sensuous pictures" (p. 69). Architecture that has the capacity to move us is generated through the encounter between dreams and experience with the world, or in the words of master architect Louis Kahn, between the measurable and the unmeasurable:

> A great building, in my opinion, must begin with the unmeasurable, go through measurable means when it is being designed, and in the end must be unmeasurable.
>
> *(Kahn, cited in Green, 1961, p. 3)*

Progettazione and documentation exist in the realm of the unmeasurable, thus they have the capacity to move us. A culture that speaks only in measurables has nothing moving to say, it becomes entirely predictable and governable. Measurable means such as pedagogical knowledge, local policy documents, national testing requirements, contextual and broader constraints

The value of artfulness and an ethic of making **153**

and expectations, should not govern us; we master them, we use them, we re-imagine them, and we contest them as our means to reach for the unmeasurable. Measurable means should not be our starting point nor our ending point; they sit in our pocket as tools, they do not colonise our imaginations nor do they imprison our professional inventiveness. In fact, *pedagogista* Paola Strozzi acknowledges that within an expansive definition of *progettazione* as life also lies the practical need to devise and execute plans:

> I believe that *progettazione* is coherent with an idea of education that is close to life. However, within *progettazione*, within thoughtful practice, there are also programming elements because at some point you must decide what materials to use and when to offer them to the children. Many things need to be programmed, meetings with families need to be set in a calendar … You must also carefully consider the offerings to children, because if we believe that children have a hundred languages, then they must be afforded the opportunity to speak.
>
> *(Paola Strozzi,* pedagogista, *interview with Stefania Giamminuti)*

In fact, in defining *progettazione* during the 1988 speech cited earlier, Malaguzzi (2021) would contend that it is close to what he terms "strategy", and in turn "the important quality of strategy – and to me it seems an art – can also be found where, for the sake of opportunism etcetera, we give space to programmes" (p. 46). But the unmeasurable beginnings and endings, and the openness to changes in direction, are what make it an art. As Green (1961) notes about Louis Kahn, "his work was always distinguished by an obvious refutation of a superficial, momentarily effective solution" and "the need to question again was stronger than the desire to resolve" (p. 3).

As we have delineated above, such qualities of complexity, non-linearity, and constant questioning belong also to *pensiero progettuale* in Reggio Emilia, and they bring us to the final point we wish to make in illustrating possible connections between pedagogy and architecture: the notion of external constraints. Some such constraints fall under the definition of what we might consider "measurables", or aspects that might be associated with programming, but there are many other constraints that define, regulate, and shape pedagogical practice; these can be situational, cultural, political, or organisational. Our concern is the misplaced assumption that the work of the *nidi* and *scuole dell'infanzia* of Reggio Emilia, with its focus on dreams and utopias and the infinite possibilities derived from artful practice, is free from constraints. This assumption belies limited knowledge of local and contextual conditions[8] and also reflects a lack of understanding of architectural design and *progettazione*, which in fact thrives and relies on constraints:

> Design process evolves most decidedly by integrating external constraints, converting them into internal growth factors: folding them into its

154 The value of artfulness and an ethic of making

self-generative activity [...] Welcoming of intrusion from outside, such a process is "pliant". Which is not the same as "compliant". It does not conform to external constraints. It folds them in – to its own unfolding. It uses them to vary its results, to creatively diverge [...] The "in-folding" approach invites the desires and values of others, among other alien "constraints", to feature as positive occasions for growth. This is a welcoming approach to design, constitutionally accepting of what lies outside its control, tending from the very beginning towards productive engagement. "Folding-in" architecture is as directly an ethics as a design endeavour: an ethics of engagement.

(Massumi, 2013, pp. 51–52)

An ethics of engagement, and a tension towards creatively diverging, most certainly inform *pensiero progettuale* in Reggio Emilia, within education and care contexts that face numerous constraints every day. Rather than being beholden to external constraints though, the experience of *progettazione* in Reggio Emilia is one of "folding-in" (Massumi, 2013). Further, Reggio Emilia dialogues with a myriad of local, national, and international interlocuters and frequently such interlocuters bring divergent views and propositions; *pensiero progettuale,* as a permeating quality of life, enables educators to view the desires and values of others, though they may occasionally be perceived as alien constraints, as positive occasions for growth. Thus, *progettazione* in Reggio Emilia can be considered a "welcoming approach to design" (Massumi, 2013) that imbues pedagogical, cultural, organisational, and political matters.

Furthermore, under the impression that the complex and beautiful work of *progettazione* is only possible because the context is one of unbounded freedom, many dismiss *pensiero progettuale* as impossible elsewhere. Such critiques arise not only out of a misunderstanding of local conditions and a dismissiveness of *progettazione,* but they also reflect a misconception of what constitutes freedom itself. As Massumi (2015) notes: "freedom is not about breaking or escaping constraints. It's about flipping them over into degrees of freedom. You really can't escape the constraints" (p. 17). Massumi (2015) theorises freedom as a "creative conversion" of constraint, but he notes that this occurs in situations of connectedness: "autonomy is always connective, it's not being apart, it's being in, being in a situation of belonging that gives you certain degrees of freedom, or powers of becoming, powers of emergence" (Massumi, 2015, pp. 39–40). *Progettazione,* artful and collective, affords the possibility of flipping constraints over into degrees of freedom, helping you feel enriched and alive:

I feel enriched and also alive, because each project has this open gaze. This sits well with my own history, my own curiosity in always looking forward, pushing ahead despite any obstacles.

(Marika Lorenzani, teacher, interview with
Stefania Giamminuti, Reggio Emilia)

The value of artfulness and an ethic of making **155**

As Massumi (2015) notes, this "sense of vitality or vivacity, a sense of being more alive [is] a lot more compelling than coming to 'correct' conclusions or assessing outcomes […] it might force you to find a margin, a manoeuvre you didn't know you had, and couldn't have just thought your way into. It can change you, expand you. That's what being alive is all about" (pp. 10–11). This emphasis on change and on vitality, we believe, sums up many of our musings on *pensiero progettuale*, and the focus on finding a manoeuvre and being drawn into situations leads us towards our concluding thoughts on "an ethic of making".

An ethic of making: craftsmanship and the real

While we have reiterated throughout this chapter that *pensiero progettuale* is premised on interconnectedness between theory-practice-research, the lofty artful ideals we have espoused in the latter part of our discussion might place us at the mercy of those who contend that concrete pedagogical practice in such arguments is frequently dismissed as lesser. Chapter 6 which follows will hopefully dispel such critiques, but before we turn to the stories of daily contexts narrated there, we wish to illuminate what we have termed an "ethic of making", thinking with anthropologist Tim Ingold (2013). Thus, in conclusion to this chapter, we turn our attention back to the necessity always of doing, alongside thinking and researching; or in other words the aspiration of being grounded in the real.

Teacher Marika Lorenzani reminds us that the pedagogical coordination, which might be reductively perceived by others as simply providing outside theoretical support to educators who concretely live the daily events, instead affords "a great richness of people who come from the *scuole dell'infanzia* and from the *nidi* and who together reason about real things, not about arbitrary theories that are not connected to everyday life, but rather about things that actually happen" (interview with Stefania Giamminuti, Reggio Emilia). In the citation below, as Ingold (2013) muses on the relationship between dreams and the real, he refers to artists, architects, composers, and writers – we might extend this to teachers, *pedagogistas* and *atelieristas* engaged in *pensiero progettuale*:

> Artists, architects, composers and writers are likewise bent upon capturing the insights of an imagination always inclined to shoot off into the distance, and on bringing them back into the immediacy of material engagement. *Like hunters, they too are dream catchers.* Human endeavours, it seems, are forever poised between catching dreams and coaxing materials. In this tension, between the pull of hopes and dreams and the drag of material constraint, and not in any opposition between cognitive intellection and mechanical execution, lies the relation between design and making. It is

156 The value of artfulness and an ethic of making

precisely where the reach of the imagination meets the friction of materials, or where the forces of ambition rub up against the rough edges of the world, that human life is lived.

(Ingold, 2013, p. 73)

The notion of *pensiero progettuale* as quotidian, as the place where the real world and ambitions meet, illuminates everyday tensions "between the pull of hopes and dreams and the drag of material constraint" (Ingold, 2013, p. 73). In Reggio Emilia theory and practice (or design and making) are not pitted against each other, one mistrusting the other as so often occurs in other contexts, but rather they are inextricably connected through *pensiero progettuale* and documentation, and thus daily life is lived. Ingold's (2013) concept of "making" is inherently compelling to us because it recognises that successful design relies on "the immediacy of material engagement" (p. 73). Teacher Marina Castagnetti emphasises this need to "do", or to continually "make things" as a process of *formazione* and as a way of *mettersi in gioco*[9]:

This quotidian *formazione*, this openness to *mettersi in gioco* because things need to get done. And the doing is very much an adventure, it's a constant challenge that is lived everyday.

(Marina Castagnetti, teacher, interview with
Stefania Giamminuti, Reggio Emilia)

What appears essential to an ethic of making in Reggio Emilia is this capacity to *mettersi in gioco*, this adventure and challenge that Marina refers to, or what we might conceptualise, in tune with Ingold's (2013) anthropological writings, as "learning to learn":

Learning to learn, for [anthropologists] as for the practitioners of any other discipline, means shaking off, instead of applying, the preconceptions that might otherwise give premature shape to their observations. It is to convert every certainty into a question, whose answer is to be found by attending to what lies before us, in the world, not by looking it up at the back of the book. In thus feeling forward rather than casting our eyes rearwards, in anticipation rather than retrospection, lies the path of discovery.

(Ingold, 2013, p. 2)

This echoes the fundamental difference we have outlined above between programming, which is governed by certainty and by discipline-specific preconceptions, and *pensiero progettuale* which welcomes questions, uncertainty, and experimentation. Teacher Giulia Ovi emphasises the importance in *progettazione* of converting certainties into questions through the practice of adults

The value of artfulness and an ethic of making **157**

who are capable of *mettersi in gioco* before offering experiences to children, to create anticipation and lean into discovery:

> The fact of *mettersi in gioco* ourselves before proposing something to children helps us to construct imaginaries, to foresee possibilities in terms of how the children might encounter this context, what they might do. Another very important aspect relates to the questions we adults pose to ourselves, before beginning a project. Questions for us are like maps of thought and reflection.
> *(Giulia Ovi, teacher, interview with Stefania Giamminuti, Reggio Emilia)*

This is what Ingold (2013) might call "the way of the craftsman", which "is to allow knowledge to grow from the crucible of our practical and observational engagements with the beings and things around us" (p. 6). Teachers as craftsmen engage in *progettazione* that always strives to be in tune with the world, with the contemporary, and with the questions that matter to children and adults. Manuela Pederzoli reiterates Giulia Ovi's thoughts on the need for adults themselves to engage with experiences and tools that might be offered to children:

> It's important for us adults to *mettersi in gioco*. For example, once in an *aggiornamento* we experimented with setting up a webcam so that it could project the image of an object onto several different classroom surfaces. Prior to proposing this context to the children, we played with it as adults. We believe it is important to construct some knowledge around the possibilities that different tools afford before you propose them to the children. Then the children will explore the objects in their own ways, and they will ask themselves questions. It's important to have this attitude of curiosity, to try and know things. We feel that as adults we are capable of *mettersi in gioco*, always trying to understand. And so, to *mettersi in gioco* means to take risks, to *mettere le mani in pasta* [literally, to "put your hands in the dough" – figuratively, to use your hands to experiment, to "do"]. It is in this welcoming of risk that we often identify possible relaunches. Because ideas come in the making.
> *(Manuela Pederzoli, teacher, interview with Stefania Giamminuti, Reggio Emilia)*

Ideas come in the making, as you touch the world with your hands. Manuela emphasises the necessary humility and curiosity of making, the importance of being open to new knowledge and unexpected encounters. The way in which adults' knowledge grows through these practical and observational engagements is carefully rendered by *pedagogista* Elena Giacopini:

> Teachers and *pedagogistas* recognise themselves as holders of knowledges, who regenerate their knowledge in response to how children interpret their own knowledge. We are fortunate to be working

158 The value of artfulness and an ethic of making

not on finite knowledge, but rather on how that knowledge is being processed. Such processes are not always evident; at times we intuit and perceive clues, and other times they elude us. Documentation, or noticing, allows us to revisit those situations that we were able to intercept, those which manifest themselves, and on which we can dwell on together with children. Thus, we can relaunch questions and proposals and we can activate other contexts of play and experience, coherently with the aspiration of not superimposing our choices on the children's choices. This means increasing the potential to promote other dialogues, imagining human relationships but also environmental relationships. By this I intend that we might reconsider our choice of certain materials over others, or we might offer them in a particular setting in the classroom or another. This means to share with children queries to investigate, which might be new pathways or perhaps only questions that have been reformulated. The processes of listening and observation carry on, and modifications can be introduced in response to how the children position themselves and interpret those changes. To solicit the desire to know and to explore relationships with possible, provisional, meanings. The adults' responsibility to choose, however, remains.

(Elena Giacopini, pedagogista, *interview with Stefania Giamminuti, Reggio Emilia)*

Teachers and *pedagogistas* as "craftsmen" (Ingold, 2013) or "activators of contexts", whose knowledge grows from engagement with questions, materials, environments, relations, meanings. Teachers who, in the words of Manuela Pederzoli, never believe they have arrived but always wish to generate new thoughts and create enticing contexts:

To be a teacher who never thinks she knows all, who never thinks she has arrived, but rather to be a person who generates different thinking and strives always to create interesting contexts. This is how *pensiero progettuale* proceeds. A teacher that is open, attuned, passionate.

(Manuela Pederzoli, teacher, interview with Stefania Giamminuti, Reggio Emilia)

As Annalisa Rainieri suggests, this openness to knowledge also requires a curiosity towards contemporary life, and a need to be in tune with the constant political and social transformations of the place in which one lives and works:

We must constantly adapt to transformations in society, accommodating political and social changes. So, it's a constant becoming, a continuous obligation to *mettersi in gioco.* If you wish to continue in this path,

The value of artfulness and an ethic of making **159**

you must have a predisposition to be in constant *formazione*, to grow and to study.

(Annalisa Rainieri, teacher, interview with Stefania Giamminuti, Reggio Emilia)

Ingold (2013) notes that "we are accustomed to think of making as a project" (p. 20) that culminates in the production of an artefact. This reflects the misunderstandings, foregrounded above, which reduce *progettazione* in Reggio Emilia to "the project" published in books or showcased in travelling exhibitions. Ingold (2013) goes on to propose his own concept of making as "a process of growth", whereby the maker is "a participant in amongst a world of active materials" (p. 21). Furthermore, "in the process of making [the maker] 'joins forces' with [the materials], bringing them together or splitting them apart, synthesising and distilling, in anticipation of what might emerge" (Ingold, 2013, p. 21). *Pedagogista* Elena Giacopini suggests this process of growth, where to "reason on experience" means to join forces with humans and materials such as documentation, to be open to what might emerge, creating possibilities for further experimentation (*mettersi in gioco*):

Doing is fundamentally important, but also to be able to re-visit, to re-listen, to re-think, to return to a context that is similar but also different, affording the opportunity to revisit queries. This possibility, or rather this need, is recognised for children and their teachers, because reasoning together generates new considerations and enables appreciation of the taste of the experience, whilst soliciting a way of thinking that is divergent, creative, critical and collaborative, and fundamentally non-judgemental. Children thus learn to know themselves as they encounter and engage with the outside world. For adults, to experience is to be able to return to reflect with colleagues, children, and families on what has been done, to be able to reason about it again, to be able to interpret it, considering how to *mettersi in gioco* once again. Dewey highlighted the importance of the philosophy of experience, of going well beyond the practice of activities delineated within specific times, which conclude with a tidy up, thus erasing traces of the experience itself.

(Elena Giacopini, pedagogista, *interview with Stefania Giamminuti, Reggio Emilia)*

It is important to emphasise here is that it is in fact documentation which places *pensiero progettuale* firmly in the realm of the real: fundamentally, the interconnectedness between *progettazione* and documentation enables an ethic of making. Documentation is "an active player" (Giamminuti et al., 2021, p. 446) with which one joins forces to artfully tend towards the new. Thus, in aspiring to understand the experience of *pensiero progettuale,* one must turn to considering the relations and encounters that occur in the process and praxis of documentation. As Ingold (2013) reminds us, "even if the maker has a form in mind, it is not this form that creates the work. It is the engagement with materials. And it is therefore to this engagement that we must attend if we are to understand how things are made" (p. 22). To focus simply on the outcome of a "project" in the hope of reproducing it, without delving deeply into the ways in which it came to be through documentation, is to miss *pensiero progettuale*'s value of artfulness and ethic of making. This engagement around documentation will be rendered in detail in Chapter 6, but we foreground its possibilities here, in the words of Francesca Forenzi:

> The *pedagogista*, who is external to the event but knows you well, sees what you have created, keeps the threads of what you are doing with your group of children and families, can understand the directions in which you are heading, and can support you with relaunches. It can be as simple as offering advice "perhaps you could try this", or it could be a question "why didn't you try this other thing?" In sharing observations and discussing them, relaunches and insights emerge which you can then follow through with her support, her gaze.
>
> *(Francesca Forenzi, teacher, interview with Stefania Giamminuti, Reggio Emilia)*

FIGURE 5.4   *Pedagogista* Paola Strozzi and teacher Ethel Carnevali considering the communicative value of images and writings on a documentation panel in the three-year-old classroom, *Scuola dell'infanzia* La Villetta.

The value of artfulness and an ethic of making **161**

Loredana Garofalo further emphasises how this encounter with *pedagogistas* around documentation is enriching for all because it creates a terrain of exchange where theory and practice come together in respect of reciprocal knowledge and experience:

Documentation is that common object around which we all gather, each in our own roles. I have felt encouraged, I have grown, I have welcomed insights, I have accepted criticisms, because the context is always one of exchange. We can enrich each other, also recognising that as a teacher I am starting from something I believe to be "good"; because we bring lived experiences, we are in tune with the classroom group, we know the children, we know the families. As a *pedagogista* you must acknowledge this, even if your own thinking might take you somewhere else. Together, considering what the children have brought and the stories I have told, we can then speculate how to create conditions where I can listen to children better, I can be more attuned to possible relaunches. It's beautiful to hypothesise possible relaunches with the *pedagogistas,* and their theoretical contribution is very precious.

(Loredana Garofalo, teacher, interview with
Stefania Giamminuti, Reggio Emilia)

"Relaunches"[10][*rilanci*], cited by Manuela, Elena, Francesca, and Loredana, are a key aspect of *progettazione,* emerging from the encounters and exchanges that occur with documentation, which itself is an active player in suggesting possible relaunches. Relaunches are also significant moments in the process of making, or what Ingold (2013) defines as a "procession":

The process of making is not so much an *assembly* as a *procession*, not a building *up* from discrete parts into a hierarchically organised totality but a carrying *on* – a passage along a path in which every step grows from the one before into the one following, on an itinerary that always overshoots its destinations. (p. 45)

Relaunches thus are steps that grow from the steps that were taken before, they are not an assembly of preconceived and planned discrete activities offered to children with the aim of "building up" to a final predetermined outcome. In fact, the hope is always that the itinerary of *progettazione* will always overshoot its destinations. To further speculate with Ingold (2013), we suggest that ideas for relaunches emerge out of the process of "co-operating with one's work" (p. 128). *Pensiero progettuale*, as an ethic of making, "is strung out in the lines of practice" (Ingold, 2013, p. 128). In fact, Ingold's (2013) image of thinking and imagining going on "as much in the hands and fingers as in the head" (p. 128) is extraordinarily compelling and accurately conveys what occurs in the many *aggiornamenti* that were witnessed for this research project, where

162 The value of artfulness and an ethic of making

FIGURE 5.5   *Aggiornamento, Scuola dell'infanzia* Diana. *Pedagogista* Simona Bonilauri, *atelierista* Federica Castrico and teachers Cinzia Incerti, Giuseppina Ronchelli, and Mariagrazia Romanazzo co-operating with one another's work.

FIGURE 5.6   *Aggiornamento, Scuola dell'infanzia* Diana. *Pedagogista* Simona Bonilauri and teacher Mariagrazia Romanazzo viewing documentation and engaging in *confronto*.

The value of artfulness and an ethic of making **163**

teachers, *atelieristas* and *pedagogistas* gathered around documentation, co-operating with one another's work (Figures 5.5 and 5.6). The metaphor of thinking not happening simply in the head also conveys the deep interconnections between theory-practice-research that are essential to an ethic of making, and it reflects the reciprocal relationship between different professional roles in Reggio Emilia.

Conclusion

In this chapter we have framed *pensiero progettuale* as both an "artful" (Manning, 2016) collective project, and as a praxis of "making" (Ingold, 2013) that is possible anywhere educators are prepared to resist the prescriptiveness, predictability and linearity that dominate pedagogical contexts. We contend that *pensiero progettuale* is a practice of collective resistance and participation which is in tune with many disciplines beyond pedagogy, always tending towards the new, the unmeasurable, and frequently overshooting its destinations.

Pensiero progettuale is creatively diverging, non-compliant, welcoming of constraints, and in tune with the world and its "becomings-with" (Haraway, 2016). It is also fundamentally non-linear: "[the designer's] path, like that of the mythical Daedalus, is always labyrinthine, never straight" (Ingold, 2013, p. 63). This labyrinthine path of theory-practice-research will be brought to life in detail in Chapter 6, which opens with a beloved quote by Malaguzzi, who contends that "destinations are important and will not be lost from sight, but more important is how and why we reach them" (cited in Filippini, 2006). This powerful metaphor, in which teachers are rendered as explorers, is echoed by anthropologist Tim Ingold (2013) in his thoughts around design and making:

> "If the mind wants to be involved in the process of making", writes design theorist Lars Spuybroek (2011: 160), "it must not only be open but forward-looking, in the direction of as-yet-unknown creation". This is a matter of not predetermining the final forms of things and all the steps needed to get there, but of opening up a path and improvising a passage. To foresee, in this sense, is to see *into* the future, not to project a future state of affairs in the present: it is to look where you are going, not to fix an end point. Such foresight is about prophecy, not prediction. And it is precisely what enables practitioners to carry on. (p. 69)

While our artful turn in this chapter might risk generating the assumption that in the practice of the *nidi* and *scuole dell'infanzia* of Reggio Emilia destinations may be disregarded in favour of creative freedom and constant changes in direction, such is not our intent at all. In fact, Chapter 6 will illuminate the many ways in which destinations are always kept in sight by adults and children alike, whilst Chapter 7 will discuss an ethic of research, the importance of being driven by questions, and the key role of foresight in

164 The value of artfulness and an ethic of making

enabling practitioners to carry on innovating. As both Malaguzzi and Ingold contend, to see into the future and imagine possible destinations is fundamental to *progettazione* and "making". However, such destinations, differently to the minute and linear objectives that govern conventional pedagogies, are always aspirational, tending towards unmeasurables, open to transformation, and welcoming of non-linear approaches. These destinations are not fixed end points, but rather they are ideas to dialogue with through a participatory and artful stance. Our concluding invitation therefore is to open up paths and improvise passages, to foresee destinations but not to fix an end point, and thus to carry on collectively in the daily artful work of *pensiero progettuale*.

Notes

1 The value of culture is discussed in depth in Chapter 7.
2 We cited Elizabeth Adams St. Pierre's work extensively in Chapter 1, and we return to it here to speculate about post qualitative inquiry's affinity with *progettazione*.
3 Variously known as "pedagogical documentation" and/or "educational documentation", but here we prefer to use the shortened term "documentation" which is most frequently used in Italian – *documentazione* – in daily conversation in Reggio Emilia.
4 In Chapter 9, we discuss how neoliberal marketplace values have hijacked documentation and transformed it into a tool for accountability, control, and surveillance, dismissing its core ethic of democracy and research and its purpose of contributing to the common good. In Chapters 6 and 7, we illustrate the ways in which documentation enables and sustains a lively daily culture of research in *nidi* and *scuole dell'infanzia*.
5 This tension towards daily life as a project, which respects some measure of predictability in valued daily events and relationships whilst always being open to transformations and questioning, will be explored in detail in Chapter 6, where *pensiero progettuale* brings to a daily "routine" the qualities of research involving five-year-old children and the working group of the *Scuola dell'infanzia* Diana.
6 This will become evident in the thoughtful documentation shared in Chapter 6.
7 The Pritzker Prize is "granted annually and is often referred to as 'architecture's Nobel' and 'the profession's highest honor'" (https://www.pritzkerprize.com/about).
8 Many of these constraints and conditions, including the existence of a national pedagogical framework, are delineated in Chapter 2.
9 We defined this concept in detail in Chapter 1.
10 Chapter 6 will offer further thoughts and concrete examples of relaunches.

References

Aranda, R., Pigem, C., & Vilalta, R. (2017). *RCR Arquitectes' Pritzker Prize Acceptance Speech*. ArchDaily. Retrieved 30 August 2022 from https://www.archdaily.com/871902/rcr-arquitectes-rafael-aranda-carme-pigem-ramon-vilalta-pritzker-prize-acceptance-speech#:~:text=Emotions%2C%20happiness%2C%20pride%2C%20humility,of%20gratitude%3A%20To%20the%20Pritzker
Ball, S. (2003). The teacher's soul and the terrors of performativity. *Journal of Education Policy, 18*(2), 215–228. https://doi.org/10.1080/0268093022000043065

Cagliari, P., Castagnetti, M., Giudici, C., Rinaldi, C., Vecchi, V., & Moss, P. (Eds.). (2016). *Loris Malaguzzi and the schools of Reggio Emilia: A selection of his writings and speeches, 1945–1993*. Routledge.

Dahlberg, G. (2012). Pedagogical documentation: A practice for negotiation and democracy. In C. Edwards, L. Gandini, & G. Forman (Eds.), *The hundred languages of children: The Reggio Emilia experience in transformation* (pp. 225–231). Praeger.

Dahlberg, G., & Moss, P. (2005). *Ethics and politics in early childhood education*. Routledge.

Filippini, T. (2000, June). *Il pensare e l'agire progettuale* Come si costruisce un'ipotesi progettuale: Relazioni introduttive alle giornate di studio sul percorso di formazione, Villa Levi.

Filippini, T. (2006, January). *Observation, interpretation, and documentation* winter institute. Italy: Reggio Emilia.

Gandini, L. (2012). History, ideas and basic principles: An interview with Loris Malaguzzi. In C. Edwards, L. Gandini, & G. Forman (Eds.), *The hundred languages of children: The Reggio Emilia experience in transformation* (pp. 27–71). Praeger.

Giamminuti, S., & Merewether, J. (2022). The Reggio Emilia atelier as a place of disruption: Remaking pedagogical alliances through aesthetics and experimentation. *Pedagogies: An International Journal*, 1–21. https://doi.org/10.1080/1554480X.2022.2106233

Giamminuti, S., Merewether, J., & Blaise, M. (2021). Aesthetic-ethical-political movements in professional learning: Encounters with feminist new materialisms and Reggio Emilia in early childhood research. *Professional Development in Education*, 7(2–3), 436–448. https://doi.org/10.1080/19415257.2020.1862277

Giudici, C., Rinaldi, C., & Krechevsky, M. (2001). *Making learning visible: Children as individual and group learners*. Reggio Children.

Green, W. (1961). Louis I. Kahn, architect: Alfred Newton Richards medical research building. University of Pennsylvania, Philadelphia, 1958–1960. *The Bulletin of the Museum of Modern Art*, 28(1), 2–23.

Haraway, D. (2016). *Staying with the trouble: Making kin in the Chthulucene*. Duke University Press.

Ingold, T. (2013). *Making: Anthropology, archeology, art and architecture*. Routledge.

Lather, P. (2013). Methodology-21: What do we do in the afterward? *International Journal of Qualitative Studies in Education*, 26(6), 634–645. https://doi.org/10.1080/09518398.2013.788753

Malaguzzi, L. (2021). *Design/Progettazione in infant-toddler centres and preschools: Research open to wonder, between the possible, probable, and unpredictable*. Reggio Children.

Manning, E. (2015). Against method. In P. Vannini (Ed.), *Non-representational methodologies: Re-envisioning research* (pp. 52–71). Routledge.

Manning, E. (2016). *The minor gesture*. Duke University Press.

Massumi, B. (2013). Becoming architectural: Affirmative critique, creative incompletion. *Architectural Design*, 83(1), 50–55. https://doi.org/10.1002/ad.1524

Massumi, B. (2015). *Politics of affect*. Polity Press.

McTighe, J., & Wiggins, G. (2012). From Common Core Standards to curriculum: Five big ideas. *The New Hampshire Journal of Education*, 25–31.

Pedagogical Coordination of the Municipality of Reggio Emilia (2014). Quasi una conclusione. *Bambini*, XXX(3), 72–73.

Preschools and Infant-Toddler Centres - Istituzione of the Municipality of Reggio Emilia (2010). *Indications preschools and infant-toddler centres of the Municipality of Reggio Emilia*. Reggio Children.

Robert-Holmes, G., & Moss, P. (2021). *Neoliberalism and early childhood education: Markets, imaginaries and governance*. Routledge.

Sahlberg, P. (2011). The fourth way of Finland. *Journal of Educational Change, 12*(2), 173–185. https://doi.org/0.1007/s10833-011-9157-y

St. Pierre, E. A. (2021a). The lure of the new and the hold of the dogmatic. *Qualitative Inquiry, 27*(5), 480–590. https://doi.org/10.1177/1077800420939133

St. Pierre, E. A. (2021b). Post qualitative inquiry, the refusal of method, and the risk of the new. *Qualitative Inquiry, 27*(1), 3–9. https://doi.org/10.1177/1077800419863005

Truman, S. E., & Springgay, S. (2015). The primacy of movement in research-creation: New materialist approaches to art research and pedagogy. In T. E. Lewis, & M. J. Laverty (Eds.), *Art's teachings, teaching's art: Philosophical, critical and educational musings* (pp. 151–162). Springer.

Vecchi, V. (2010). *Art and creativity in Reggio Emilia: Exploring the role and potential of ateliers in early childhood education*. Routledge.

Zumthor, P. (2006). *Thinking architecture* (2nd ed.). Birkhauser.

6

PENSIERO PROGETTUALE AND EDUCATIONAL RESEARCH IN EVERYDAY CONTEXTS IN THE *NIDI* AND *SCUOLE DELL'INFANZIA* OF REGGIO EMILIA

Paola Strozzi

Translated by Jane McCall

Introduction

This chapter argues the important connection between *pensiero progettuale* and research, considered as foundational values of educational experience in Reggio Emilia's municipal *nidi* and *scuole dell'infanzia*, emphasising the ties between research and everyday contexts. In doing so, it proposes an interpretation of the concept of "daily routines" in an approach to setting the table with five-year-old children, an event that is routine in its timing, but *progettuale* in the way it takes place. Through the voices and workings of a group of three five-year-old children, we will see how an everyday context such as setting the table, and the intent of communicating to younger children how this is done, using different languages of expression (verbal, graphic, alphabetical, photographic), warms the children's interest and generates organisational, collaborative and evaluative competences. Instead, for the adults, it will be emphasised how the process of preparing, interpreting, and relaunching warm and challenging contexts unfolds in a strategy of *progettazione* and research, as Loris Malaguzzi's metaphor of teachers as explorers suggests:

> Teachers are like explorers using maps and compasses. They know the directions, but they know that every year the terrain, the climate, the seasons and the children add new ones, and that the order of times and problems can change. Destinations are important and will not be lost from sight, but more important is how and why we reach them.
>
> *(Loris Malaguzzi, cited in Filippini, 2006)*

DOI: 10.4324/9781003181026-6

168 *Pensiero progettuale* and educational research

In this chapter we revisit the dynamic of relationality between different professional roles in the working group, highlighting in particular the issue of deep knowledge of the disciplines (mathematical and others), and of relaunching, or evolving contexts in response to clues that are collected during the course of an experience.

Pensiero progettuale and research in everyday contexts

> Our schools have not had, nor do they have, a planned curriculum with units and subunits (lesson plans), as the behaviourists would like. These would push our schools towards teaching without learning; we would humiliate the schools and the children by entrusting them to forms, dittos, and handbooks of which publishers are generous distributors.
>
> *(Loris Malaguzzi, in Gandini, 2012, p. 62)*

The cognitive sciences, in positing children's learning and the learning of human beings in general as a process of construction that is subjective and intersubjective in nature, certainly influenced Reggio Emilia's tension towards design thinking in its educational experience. Within this vision of human beings, *pensiero progettuale* enables us and facilitates us to engage in research in everyday contexts in *nidi* and *scuole dell'infanzia*, because it is only by promoting the action of research that we feel we are promoting situations of real learning.

The *nidi* and *scuole dell'infanzia* are educational places, therefore their purpose, through a holistic attitude of care and well-being, is to privilege socialisation and learning in children and adults: "fellow travellers in a shared journey through knowledges" (Cappelletti, 2000, p. 43), while also acknowledging the distinctive qualities of each protagonist and the specificity of roles. This metaphor of learning as a journey, much like the metaphor of teachers as explorers, offers us interesting suggestions for interpreting educational dynamics. On one hand are children, "native builders" of hypotheses and meanings in their relations and encounters with the world, avid researchers and negotiators of the meanings assigned by others to the world; on the other are adults who, freed from the preoccupation of imparting content, build their profession on research. Children research their learning and adults participate with loans of knowledge to support them in overcoming obstacles that in that moment in time they cannot overcome alone, at the same time researching how children learn individually and in groups, and what conditions are favourable to learning. *Pensiero progettuale* cannot rely on manuals, nor can it be improvised, as Loris Malaguzzi reminds us:

> It is true that we do not have planning and curricula. But we search for them and that is why they become something else. It is not true that

we rely on improvisation, which is an enviable skill. We do not rely on chance either, because we are convinced that what we do not yet know can to some extent be anticipated. What we do know is that to be with children is to work one-third with certainty and two-thirds with uncertainty and the new.

(Gandini, 2017, p. 100, [translated by Jane McCall])[1]

Design thinking has to hold in mind and weave together several threads: sometimes the threads are obvious ones like spaces and materials; other times they are silent but operative, such as adult knowledge of the children themselves and of the subject or object being researched; sometimes the threads are intentions, involving organisational aspects, and time for *confronto* and exchange; and at times the threads are implicit but decisive, such as ways of communicating. *Pensiero progettuale* evolves research that is ecological, because it holds together several inter-related and contextual variables, but the research is also pragmatic because it is useful to those particular children, and to that particular working group, and because it respects and values the different subjectivities involved. The literature is very useful to us because it is not sufficient to experience events, we must interpret them, but without constraining experiences within arid and predictive taxonomies and currents of thinking. Not all experiences and projects developed with a design approach are broadly innovative: often they represent advancements only for a particular school or class, but because *progettazione* relies upon annotation and argumentation it offers real and useful suggestions for further research in broader contexts of *formazione*.

Design thinking regards learning as always being an opportunity for and the practice of research, for children and adults, which occurs not only in the unfolding of new projects or within specific deeper investigations, but above all in the unfolding of everyday events. Thinking in a design way means actualising values not simply in the substantial choices, such as those relating to the architecture of a school, or organising the times of the day, or the configuring and re-configuring of staff roles, but by thinking about the significance of the most minute details of everyday contexts: how to welcome children and families in the morning; how to conduct a conversation with children in a large group; how to document lunchtime at school; how to open a meeting with families. This "how" implies that we also share the "why", that we convey the meanings of each context, thus originating and producing evaluation and *formazione*. This is a special responsibility of the *pedagogista* and the pedagogical coordination, although pedagogical care is a responsibility shared in different ways by all the educators and the whole working group in the *nido* or *scuola dell'infanzia*. This approach, in thinking of the *nido* and *scuola dell'infanzia* and experiencing them each day, is made up of professional *formazione* and reciprocal *formazione* as continuous and never-completed processes, but above all as motivating processes, because all of the

170 *Pensiero progettuale* and educational research

adults, including parents, each within their own role, are together the primary researchers and interpreters of how children can be educated.

For everyday life to become an area of research not only does it need to be observed by the *pedagogista* and recounted by its protagonists, it also needs to be re-read and documented as part of *progettazione*. It is necessary to select out certain parts from the daily flow, to gather evidence, to play it back in slow motion, to discuss it from different points of view, to identify its limits and potentials, to introduce changes and evaluate the results.

Everyday contexts and routines

Those familiar with the experience of Reggio Emilia know how rarely we use the term *routine* because of the way it is often interpreted in 0–6 years educational contexts in Italy and elsewhere. For many decades in Italy the uninformed practice of poorly trained and poorly paid staff, in services considered more child minding than education, was based on routines. Automatic routines marked the timed situations of children's "arrival", "nappy changing", "free play", "roll call", "little activities", "mealtimes", "sleep", moulding children into conformity and acquiescence. In contrast, it is particularly important to emphasise the special responsibilities, of educators in general but above all of *pedagogistas,* in monitoring the quality of recurring contexts in the everyday life of children: quality intended here as significance, meaningfulness, beauty, pleasurableness, care, and culture – especially in 0–6 services.

Clearly children need to be able to identify and experience repetitive elements and strategies: environments, people, situations and ways of relating all mark time in the *nido* and *scuola dell'infanzia*. In order to know, and to feel safe, well, and capable, children need to be able to anticipate events and gestures, to build and share, through a sense of stability, common vocabularies and scripts. However, a watchful eye is needed to ensure this necessary repetition does not degenerate into boredom, or stability into mechanical and automatic reiteration. Something that has always helped us avoid this risk is to maintain our gaze on self-assessment and researching together. Research, therefore, that does not gaze only towards the unknown, or apply itself simply to new subjects and topics, but rather consciously desires re-readings of things that appear consolidated, as generators of new possibilities and new meanings.

The example of setting the table

The fragment of experience we have selected clearly highlights the dialogue and contributions of different professional roles, showing specifically how *pensiero progettuale* requires a complex but flexible structure. It is based not only on encounters between the different professional roles but on the following:

FIGURE 6.1 Table set for a springtime lunch at *Nido d'infanzia* Gianni Rodari, Reggio Emilia.[2]

writings and design tools; documentation composed of different forms of note-taking and various steps of interpretation; the ability to structure experiential knowledge in formal ways; and a collective professionalism that is permanently under construction, relying on competencies that are not only performative but interpretative and discursive.

The daily context of setting tables for lunch is inscribed in Reggio Emilia's organisational value and choice of maintaining a kitchen and dedicated staff in every municipal *nido* and *scuola dell'infanzia*.

> In the Infant-toddler Centres and Preschools of Reggio Emilia, the kitchen has always been an important element of quality in the identity of the services, conveying values and choices [...] Each day, our kitchens affirm the possibility to create shared culture as a space of negotiation and exchange among adults, between adults and children, and among children, starting from food as an essential condition of life.
>
> *(Tedeschi, 2008, p. 14 and 16)*

Furthermore, "the presence of the cook and auxiliary personnel in the on-site kitchen at each preschool and infant-toddler centre is an indispensable condition for the educational quality of the service. It is an added value that fosters an openness to listening, information, and relations with the families around the issues of diet, health, and well-being" (Preschools and Infant-toddler Centres - Istituzione of the Municipality of Reggio Emilia, 2010, p. 18). As well as being an activity all the children particularly enjoy and representing a valuable opportunity for developing and consolidating motor, social, and organisational autonomies, and growing a sense of responsibility towards a group of friends for the completion of a task, setting the table also includes

172 *Pensiero progettuale* and educational research

elements of learning in the field of maths, and zones of research for teachers on how children process this learning.

Each day in fact, in different ways within the *nido* and different classes of the *scuola dell'infanzia* taking into account the age of the children and the structure of each *nido* or *scuola*, the class groups carry out a quick and often playful check of who is present and who is absent. In conversation together we design the several experiences that will follow in the day and share out various tasks: going to the kitchen to fetch fruit for the 9 o'clock snack; telling the cook how many children will be present for lunch, and how many will remain for the afternoon snack after rest time[3]; requesting the day's menu and sharing it with classmates; distributing fruit and napkins; preparing materials for the day's experiences together with the teacher; accompanying auxiliary staff in activities such as watering plants, tidying the pantry, and arranging paper towels in the toilets. Of all these daily "tasks" perhaps the most coveted is that of being "waiters" in groups of two or three, which is why the children often create a special calendar so they can confirm whose turn it is to take on this role. Again, this calendar is not a tool the teacher delivers and that children simply fill in, but is often constructed in interesting ways by the children themselves, with all the associated challenges of interpreting and using codes (alphabetical for names, and numerical for days) and symbols (to mark turns). Once the children have decided who is in charge of setting the table on a particular day, the waiters go into the kitchen at about 11.45 to fetch a trolley the cook has prepared with everything required for the task, they move it into the dining area and, depending on their age, under the watchful eye of an auxiliary staff member they set the tables with a tablecloth and napkins, flat plates and pasta bowls, glasses and cutlery.

In narrating this event, I will draw from internal documentation of the *Scuola dell'infanzia* Diana, class C (children aged from five to six years). The teachers are Lorenza Bianchi (LB) and Marina Mori (MM), the teacher educator is Paola Strozzi (PS), the *pedagogista* is Tiziana Filippini (TF), and the *atelierista* Isabella Meninno (IM). The auxiliary member of staff paired with the class[4] is Simonetta Cattozzo (SC). I will also draw on notes from the various kinds of formal and informal meetings and exchanges through which the experience took shape. In this way, it will, I hope, become evident how design thinking is nourished by a dialectical attitude that, although making use of formal and scheduled meeting times and documents, plays out in our everyday relations.

In introducing the *Scuola dell'infanzia* Diana's Declaration of Intents, it might be useful to clarify some theoretical and value-based references that had been discussed and shared at the system level on different occasions, and which the *Scuola* Diana specifically revisited that year with the expressed aim of building shared culture within a group of professionals possessing different degrees of experience, and deepening it in the construction of daily contexts.

Pensiero progettuale and educational research **173**

The role of the *pedagogista* is situated very clearly in this zone, but always within an ethic of dialectics and research. In re-visiting values and references, we turned to diverse sources in the literature of various disciplines, to psychology, and to both local and international experiences.

Collective aggiornamento[5] *(the whole school working group and the* pedagogista): *writing the school's declaration of intents*

Pensiero progettuale requires a focus and preparedness on diverse reference sources, which is often curated by the *pedagogistas* prior to meeting with the working group in the *aggiornamento*. It is the pedagogista's responsibility to bring knowledge (from her own readings, or system knowledge constructed within the educational system) to meetings with teachers. However, they are not the only ones to do this. On the contrary, as illustrated in Chapter 4, the *atelieristas* and teachers also bring significant understandings, but it is the *pedagogista's* responsibility to collate, discuss, and synthesise re-elaborations of the group's knowledge. Daily research in the *nidi* and *scuole dell'infanzia* is therefore based on this practice of bringing things into clearer focus during *aggiornamento* meetings, where thinking and doing act in concert.

During this particular year I had been included in the Diana working group as a teacher educator[6] by the pedagogical coordination, and given the task of accompanying *progettazione* and documentation in the various classes in the area of maths. The school's *pedagogista* and I, both together and separately, prepared for the first *aggiornamento* which would focus on experiences in the area of maths with five-year-olds, by bringing texts and multiple sources. In the first working group *aggiornamento* dedicated to this theme, as well as our theoretical knowledge about maths, we revisit fundamental aspects related to the values of educational *progettazione*. Coherently with an educational approach that speaks of languages and research projects, rather than disciplines and activities, our reference is an idea of maths as a means for observing, interpreting and representing reality, constructed in exciting, dense, and meaningful experiences that are capable of developing strong mathematical thinking and rendering it explicit.[7]

The *Indicazioni nazionali per il curricolo della scuola dell'infanzia e del primo ciclo di istruzione* [National Indications for *scuola dell'infanzia* and primary education curriculum] (Ministero dell'Istruzione dell'Università e della Ricerca, 2012), the national pedagogical framework currently in use in Italian schools for ages 3–11 years, poses as a primary objective on completion of primary school (6–11 years) the development of "a positive attitude towards mathematics, due also to multiple experiences of meaningful contexts that let children sense how the mathematical tools they have learned are useful in real life operations" (Ministero dell'Istruzione dell'Università e della Ricerca, 2012, p. 97, [translated by Jane McCall]). In the aggiornamento,

174 *Pensiero progettuale* and educational research

the pedagogista and I revisit and discuss this source, and other theoretical and values-based references in an evident effort to clarify and connect (by not dealing with them separately) three essential aspects of *progettazione* knowledge:

- The epistemological aspect, which relates to defining the field of knowledge, in this case the meaning of cardinal numbers, counting, and operations.
- The cognitive aspect, related to how children encounter, interpret, and work with numbers at this age.
- The didactic aspect, related in a more specific way to the pre-figuration of the most pertinent learning contexts for that particular group of children.

It is important to be reminded of these highly inter-connected components, which can only be examined separately for the purpose of analysis, in documents that specifically reference them, and situations of formazione and argumentation that take place at different times. During the *aggiornamento* I relay fragments of my discussions with colleagues in other schools, to remind the working group that it is neither useful nor coherent with children's ways of learning to work with mathematical themes by "starting with simple proposals of rhythm" or "starting with nursery rhymes that contain numbers". Together with the *pedagogista,* we initiate a discussion on the connections between knowledge and children's transversal ways of learning. What does it mean when we use the expression "to start with", or "a simple proposal"[8] in the field of maths?

PS: Just as in the area of language where no one would consider developing children's competences in the pre-school age through activities that are purely grammatical, so it is with mathematics which is present in the most varied situations both as a tool and as a language, organising reality. Here too references to the discipline are essential – not for them to be immediately translated into activities, or prerequisites, but so that we can come to understand the epistemological nature of the meanings that the children will encounter.

The *pedagogista* confirms this:

TF: Children gradually discover that symbols and mathematical procedures are not objects of reality but cultural objects, modalities elaborated by the human mind for relating to reality. The different symbolic systems such as numbers, geometry, and schemas are interwoven. At this age children are questioning and discovering the dual nature of numbers: tools for conceptualising and communicating situations (how many

Pensiero progettuale and educational research **175**

elements are present), and objects on which to reflect (different functions in different contexts: quantity, order, identity codes).

PS: In this sense the performative aspects and the language aspects interweave to advantage. Language takes on a fundamental role, because it is a fixing element of a perceptive nature and it determines reference schemes with an evocative value, because the exchange between language schemata that have already been constituted and new experience determines processes of reorganisation, and finally, because the expression of language goes beyond the function of "inner language", "for oneself", and becomes the means of inter-personal communication (Cannizzaro et al., 2000).

TF: In our common understanding, there is a more obvious construction of a signifier, such as recognising or writing a number, as opposed to the construction of its meaning, thus confusing knowledge of numbers with their symbolic representation in base ten.

PS: Moreover, in traditional didactics there is a risk of segmenting maths into general abilities (classification, sorting, logic and so on) and isolating them from the general context, relying on the instructional power of activities that are supported by highly-structured materials, and believing competences acquired in one context can simply and easily be transferred to another.

Following this initial collective *aggiornamento* each class goes on to write a declaration of intent. The following excerpt is from the declaration of the five-year-old classroom:

> For the past two years these children have participated in the daily experience of setting the table. We know that all the children can set the table correctly, and functionally, for the number of diners, but we wonder whether, and to what extent, this daily experience, because of its frequency, risks becoming ritualised, thus losing opportunities for learning and evolution.
>
> We believe it is opportune, during these first months of school, to gather observations on the knowledge and skills all the children have, while they set the tables, and to involve Simonetta, the auxiliary colleague paired with our class, so that we can then move forward with more precise and differentiated ways of organising this event. At the same time we are trying to understand more about children's awareness of the operation of setting the table, by asking them and ourselves certain questions:

1 Performative aspects aside, how well do children also know how to verbally describe setting the table?
2 Can the children find other symbolic systems besides verbal communication to explain or describe setting the table?

176 *Pensiero progettuale* and educational research

3 How can reasoning about representations of complex operations, with elements of quantity, shape, correspondence and temporal sequence, be useful for children to explore thinking strategies that can be generalised to other contexts?

4 In seeking out representations (visualisations) of procedure, to what extent does a group of children make use of individual contributions and vice-versa?

Class aggiornamento *(class C teachers, auxiliary colleague, teacher educator,* pedagogista): *writing the class declaration of intents*

School and class declarations of intent are shared and discussed – with verbal and written comments and suggestions for additions and deletions – by the teachers, teacher educator, and *pedagogista*, and are also the focus of *aggiornamenti* meetings. These are an opportunity to reason more fully on suitable ways of organising learning contexts that have been identified, beyond what is written in the *progettazione* intents.[9] In this specific case, the *pedagogista* re-affirmed the significance of setting tables at school, directly involving the auxiliary colleague paired with the class:

TF: It is our habit to propose setting tables with chairs arranged around them, explaining to the children that one plate, one glass, and a set of cutlery should be placed in front of each chair, and correcting any errors as we go along. We know our adult intents are always attuned and in-solidarity with children, but this approach, especially with five-year-olds, almost risks distorting the potential of setting the table, turning it into a routine that is hardly productive in advancing mathematical reasoning. The less we artificialise a real situation, instead maintaining natural variations and stumbling blocks, the more we can support children's capacity for analysis and conceptualisation.

I (PS) confirm the need and opportunity for gathering more precise elements that might enable us to design a context of setting the table based on questions that have been expressed in the bi-monthly class *aggiornamento*. In this initial situation, we therefore agree to:

• Gather rapid but wide-ranging observations of how children set the table and avoid orienting the children by putting out the correct number of chairs.

• Conduct and transcribe small-group conversations on the theme of setting the table, in order to better understand how children explain their experience verbally. The conversations will be initiated with the question: "You have been setting the table for a long time now, but would you also be able to recount how to set the table?"

Collective aggiornamento: confronto *with initial documentation*

The agenda for this meeting is based on *confronto* between all three classes on work they have been doing in connection to the theoretical and values-based references that were previously shared, the school's declaration of intents, and the *progettazione* notes of each class. From observations which have also been carried out by our auxiliary colleagues, it emerges that almost all the five-year-olds are confident in setting the table. The children make agreements about dividing up tasks – some set plates, some set glasses and so on – organising whose turn it is and choosing which tables to set. They arrange the tableware in a complete and correct manner. A particularly interesting issue is raised in relation to how the children choose and lay the tablecloths, which come in different shapes and sizes.[10]

PS: It isn't only a matter of matching the shapes of table and tablecloth, which is interesting in itself because it gives children an opportunity to reason about elements for recognition and location of geometrical shapes, but rather that this problem specifically raises the (underestimated) issue of laying the tablecloths correctly on the corresponding tables.

MM: Perhaps we have always anticipated this problem-opportunity and resolved it mainly through adult help, with either ourselves or auxiliary colleagues assisting the children when they're setting the table, because we always considered that the difficulty was simply a question of manual dexterity and not very significant for children's learning.

We decide to examine the conversations and then return to the theme of tablecloths. A transcript is reproduced below of a conversation with Cristian (C), Francesco (F), and Lorenzo (L), on the subject of how to explain setting the table to children in the four-year-old class; my notes and those of the teachers and *pedagogista* appear in a column on the right in blue, as per the original format. This practice of organising notes into columns, often drawn onto simple notepaper whilst jotting down dialogues between and with children, allows teachers, and all others involved in a project, to reflect more deeply on children's thinking and language, and to consider the role of adult interventions. Although it retains all the speed and dexterity of notetaking, this practice accustoms us to thinking interpretatively, making it easier to identify and offer possible points of view and relaunches to colleagues.

In this specific instance, the content of the columns is not derived from notes, but from the transcription of a recorded conversation which, with notes (interpretations) added on one side becomes even more valuable for *confronto* with colleagues and *pedagogista*, whether together in a meeting or reflecting and adding notes when alone. This practice is of vital importance in the *formazione* of young teachers who sometimes risk underestimating how very acute children are at sensing and interpreting adult expectations and adapting

178 *Pensiero progettuale* and educational research

to them, or who perhaps do not yet have enough experience in spotting possible areas for relaunching.[11] In our regular meetings with families, these notes help to reconstruct children's understandings, assisting us in highlighting how children make meaning in a given experience, as opposed to offering a simple account of the subjects we have worked with. We now turn to an excerpt from the first conversation on the topic of how to set the table:

MM: You know how to set the table don't you?[12]

L: *Of course we do! We've always been waiters! Well, not always!*

C: *When we were three we set the table in the large refectory, even at three years old, but not so much at four.*

MM: The importance of the recursive nature of daily life and of memory

L: *But lots at five, because ... we're big now!*

C: *We're big and we can manage it!*

MM: Well seeing as you've become very good at it ... would you like to tell me how to do it?

C: *First you put the tablecloth on*

PS: First, after: the ordinal nature of gestures

L: *Tablecloths*

F: *But first you have to see their shapes [of the tables]*

TF: Seeing = considering

L: *It's true, if it's square you need a square tablecloth*

LB: Form, shapes, square = important geometric definitions

F: *If we put the smallest tablecloth on the biggest table, and then we put the big tablecloth on the small table ... that's no good!*

PS: If, then = logical connectives

C: *That's true because the children would be treading on the big tablecloth!*

L: *And how would we be able to eat on that big table? With the small tablecloth you can't!*

TF: Irony and real problems in a play of possibilities

F: *After that you put the plates and you have to be careful not to let them fall because they can break!*
C: *Then the other plate*

F: *The big one for pasta*
C: *Then the cutlery ...*
L: *The forks, the knives that we only use with meat though; spoons, then glasses and the bottles of water then we're finished! Actually then we go and get the food with the trolley and we give it to the children.*

PS: After, then = connectors of time that order the sequence of setting the table

In our *confronto* over this first conversation we note that the children are also verbally confirming the confidence they have acquired in setting the table, as previously observed by teachers and auxiliary staff.

PS: They seem so confident that most of the conversation revolves around two particular points: their memories of setting the table in past years, and what is perhaps the most pressing problem this year: correctly matching the different shapes of tablecloths with the corresponding tables. The children use some terms that are geometrical in nature like "shapes" and "square", they rely on pertinent reference systems such as "if (the table) is square you need a square tablecloth", and they express hypothetical evaluations like "if we put the smallest tablecloth on the biggest table, and then we put the big tablecloth on the small table ... that's no good".

We[13] also discuss the mathematical significance of handling "discrete" operations, such as counting and positioning plates and glasses in correspondence with the number of diners, and "continuous" operations such as evaluating if a tablecloth is correctly placed on the table without hanging down at the side in unexpected or inappropriate ways. What takes place on the cognitive level?

PS: A discrete activity, such as setting dishes, glasses, and cutlery (related to numbers, not spatial arrangement) is easier to remember and monitor because it involves segmenting an overall operation and anticipating each single sequence; furthermore, verification is possible at the end of each sequence. A continuous activity instead, such as laying out a tablecloth, relies more on experience, because controlling the way it

180 *Pensiero progettuale* and educational research

falls on four sides of the table cannot be done only at the end, but has to be done whilst positioning it. The question of evaluating geometrical forms (the shape of a tablecloth) and measuring them in terms of their congruency with another form (the shape of the table) is considerably complex in itself. Therefore, the children cannot rely on precise rules like the progression of natural numbers (which they have yet to consolidate) and have to proceed, individually or in pairs, through the means of small adjustments and continuous evaluations.

What emerges in the *aggiornamento* discussion is the importance of letting children deal with challenges offered by geometrical aspects: form and size, and strategies of progressive adjustment.

T.F.: Like learning to walk, and spatial orientation, these complex challenges and learnings that geometrical concepts such as length, width, depth, and direction are firmly anchored in, require a long apprenticeship of performing and communicating before they can be represented symbolically in words, marks, or alphabetical and numerical codes.

As usual in reporting our shared analyses and comments, I have highlighted the passages that seem most promising, that point us in the direction of possible relaunches. The term "relaunch" defines an idea or proposal arising from a context that has been experienced by (or with) children, but introducing something new, either into the context itself, or by creating a new context, perhaps only very slightly different, always careful to verify if we have succeeded in moving children's proximal, potential, zones of development, and with the aim of offering new conditions for them to advance and go deeper. The concept of relaunching was introduced by Loris Malaguzzi (1991) during an *aggiornamento*, when he used the metaphor of a game of ping-pong to describe the teacher-pupil relationship:

And what does it mean to play ping-pong? First of all, it means having the reciprocal intention of playing the same game, that is, of accepting the common ground, which is no small thing; secondly, it means taking on certain rules, the ball has to pass across, the ball has to be thrown back, the ball has to be able to pass over the net again and be thrown back again, and so on. If you, as teachers, situate yourselves here on one side and the children on the other, then perhaps you will realise that what you are having is truly, and not only symbolically, a game of ping pong, and that you have it every day, every minute [...] and here we need to understand what it means to respond with a forehand, or a backhand, what it means to respond in a way that facilitates the other person responding back, it means understanding what strategies are developed over the course of the challenge, over the course of the game, what it means to disorientate or make it difficult to answer, or make it easy, or pretend that I always position my ball there, and then suddenly - tac! - throw it in another direction [...]. The important thing is to understand that adults cannot play ping-pong with children if the adults impose their laws, their strengths, their norms, their experiences. If they want to continue their discourse with children, that is, to play the ball back and forth with children, it is clear they have to adopt a strategy [...] Children will play if they find the terms of a viable logic.

(Malaguzzi, 1991, [translated by Jane McCall])

Relaunching calls for an acute capacity for observation because it does not simply involve the adding on or juxtaposition of proposals. A relaunch is not prescribed from the outset, based on the supposed teaching order of contents; instead, it is oriented by an explicit objective that is often stated in *progettazione* notes, in what we call our *progettazione* intents. Relaunches can also be inspired by past experiences or curricular references but must always be pertinent to the children and the content. They call for inventiveness and creativity in order to feed curiosity and motivation. Something changes in a relaunch, and not always in the same zone. It could be the question that changes, or the way of formulating a proposal, or the spaces, the materials, the tools, the groups of children, or teachers. Those relaunches that engage with the same content but through different expressive languages are particularly interesting and productive, for example exploring the concept of rhythm through body language, sound language, or the graphic language. However we wish define the relaunch, it is always situated in a dimension of inventiveness, as opposed to mechanics.

PS: In relation to the issues of geometry, and evaluating continuous quantities ... besides giving children time to arrange the tablecloths, reasoning with them about the best strategies, we could also propose some games with folding and cutting, not only enabling the children to revisit the question of the main plane shapes like squares, rectangles, circles and triangles, but also to experiment with changing shapes and creating symmetries depending on the folds and cuts they make (with paper serviettes and napkins for example).

MM: Instead, in relation to counting crockery and setting it on the tables, where most of the children are clearly quite confident in their actions but others have obvious insecurities, we could problematise it by proposing a variation on the situation, for example by preparing tables with materials for drawing or constructing in clay for groups of four or six children.

182 *Pensiero progettuale* and educational research

LB: Or, in pairs they could prepare the trays of fruit in the kitchen with Nadia (cook), or the lunch trays!

PS: Or we could involve them in setting out materials "for sale" on the shelves of the shop in the play area and invite them to keep a track of the number of products they want to display.

In terms of *pensiero progettuale*, we can ask ourselves if these ideas are relaunches, or germinations of problems that are capable of activating new design paths and design contexts for that class, affording new knowledge and strategies to the pathway that is being observed, in this case, the experience of setting the table. Design thinking is a complex and non-linear weave, in which it is up to the teacher to see and propose possible connections. Children make connections, but it is the teacher's task to make them visible and give them value. In this case, we worked with all these different pathways, individually and in pairs, in everyday contexts. Our account here follows the journey of setting the table, with one group of children, but all the paths were simultaneously active in the class. During the *confronto* a new hypothesis (or what we would call a relaunch) emerged for confirming and reinforcing the children's sense and strategy of counting:

PS: What if we propose that the children not only set the table but that they autonomously prepare the trolley with all the required materials, selecting them from the kitchen cupboards? To date, the children have set the tables by taking dishes from a trolley prepared by our auxiliary colleagues who organise them into sorted piles of plates, glasses, cutlery, and so on, in the exact numbers required. What would happen if the children had to prepare the trolley themselves, taking the dishes from a cupboard containing a very large amount of crockery? It's not just a numerical complication, it's a spatial one too!

MM: Oh yes! And not only would the children have to consider what objects to select and how many to choose, from within the large numerical and qualitative variety available, they would also have to arrange the necessary elements on the limited space of the trolley (it has two shelves): it's a numerical and spatial context!

LB: And certainly the group would have to engage in different agreements and division of tasks!

PS: In regards to documentation I think it would be a good idea for us to record[14] the children's conversation as they are carrying out the operation, and then later on transcribe the verbal interactions in such a way as to note the alternating voices.

TF: Good, good! I won't be here at the time, and this structure of documentation will allow me to understand more easily both the individual

	utterances and the communicative rhythm of the group, and I can offer you some feedback!
MM:	Shall we take some photographs too? I think the teacher following the group will be enough, what do you think?
PS:	Well actually, when you're in the pantry with the trolley you could ask Nadia (cook) or Simonetta (auxilliary) to take some pictures, with you suggesting which moments to capture of course! Afterwards we'll add the pictures of the children preparing the trolley to the other documentation, in order to keep trace of any further elements related to individual strategies, or strategies enacted in pairs and groups.

We organise the documentation of the conversation into a structure that retains the diachronic dimension (each child's words transcribed in sequence in one column) and the synchronic dimension (the various columns reconstruct the sequence of the conversation). Later we add photographs taken by the teacher, and notes to help us reason together on the children's words and gestures and continue our *progettazione*. The photographs were selected by the teachers in order to document, in a concise and incisive manner, the children's counting strategies while they organised the trolley. This kind of in-process documentation is sometimes generated by an individual teacher, sometimes by a pair of adults, at times by considering the advice of a colleague, often the *atelierista*. In this case, to support the teachers in selecting their photographs, I offered them references related to the importance of reading gestures when observing elaborations of the concept of number and numerical operations (Wagner Alibali & DiRusso, 1999). In fact, the function of gesture in keeping track as they count seems to gradually become clearer to the children themselves. For example, Andrea (another child from class C) says: *Let's count again and you tell me when we get to 22 … 18, 19, 20 … and hold up your fingers or I won't be able to remember.* Research – confirmed by the branch of neuroscience that studies so-called "embodied knowledge" – indicates that mind is not only connected to body, but the body influences mind, although the idea may appear counter-intuitive (Lakoff & Nunez, 2000).[15]

Class aggiornamento: *analysis of ongoing documentation*

The material collected during observations was presented by the teachers and discussed with the *atelierista* and the *pedagogista*. It would be interesting, but too extensive, to recount in full the *aggiornamento* during which we analysed all the documentation we had collected. In essence, the documentation highlighted that in preparing the trolley the children were generally confident when counting up to a quantity of 10, and also that most children can navigate

184 *Pensiero progettuale* and educational research

their way up to a quantity of 20, and that after 20 greater difficulties emerge. Compared with the situation of setting the table, the number of counts for "checking" purposes strategically increased when children were preparing the trolley. There are also a greater number of opportunities for evaluating quantity along imaginary number lines. Giacomo (another child from Class C) for example says: *There are 25 of us and 23 plates ... so only ... 24, and 25, are missing.*

MM: So, what do you think? Can we move on from this operational level of setting the table to a more representational level, as we hypothesised in questions 2, 3, and 4 of our declaration of intents[16]?

IM: Up to now I have only been listening because as an atelierista I don't feel very knowledgeable in the field of maths, but I think it is important to propose that the children hypothesise other languages as well as the verbal, to communicate or "teach" the other children the procedure of setting the table!

TF: Even though we foresaw this passage, I think it is important to explore the theoretical implications of this possible choice, with the intent, again, of constructing and reinforcing an explicitly shared culture in the working group, in which, as Isabella has just reminded us, there are different levels of knowledge and professional experience. So, I'd like to ask Paola (Strozzi) to bring some references to our next meeting, so that she can help us construct some arguments, as she has done from the beginning of the experience.

Tiziana's words highlight the *pedagogista*'s responsibility, her care towards the *formazione* of the whole working group, and how, to achieve this, we start with situations enacted locally, whilst constantly searching for a broader range of references and resources. This knowledge is built during *progettazione* of an experience, and not at the end, through reflection and shared debate. By not reasoning in abstract ways but connecting documentation of a context with theoretical references, and by offering our contribution in a dialogical way and requesting that of others, we can all feel part of a larger educational project, united in our commitment to the work we are doing together. This sentiment counters the mindset of specialised roles, and the indifference and mistrust that at times consequently emerges. Although we each have our different competences, what emerges is a feeling of sharing and of co-responsibility. It is evident in this encounter that there is no hurry to immediately identify actions to propose with the children, but instead a tension towards nurturing possible interpretations and ideas emerging within the group.

Pensiero progettuale and educational research **185**

Collective _aggiornamento_: from setting the table to representations of setting the table

The next collective _aggiornamento_ begins with reasoning on the "knowledge at play" and the learning we intend to promote by proposing further experiences with the children (the intentionality of a relaunch).

_TF:_   I'd like to emphasise the importance, on the level of learning, of the complexity of these operations the children are carrying out: they are commenting on their gestures and the gestures of others, they are making connections, and enacting inferences between gestures and memory.

_PS:_   The children's obvious willingness to be explicit about the operations involved in preparing the trolley, even the problematic passages, is something we mustn't take for granted, to the point that our national pedagogical framework for the _scuola dell'infanzia_ indicates amongst the general objectives of educational processes that it is essential for children to learn to negotiate with others, identify the most pertinent explanations, remember and reconstruct what has been done through documentation, and discover that memories and reconstructions can differ.

_IM:_   Well then, it will certainly be useful to propose to the children that they make a representation of setting a table. We know how important the medium or language we use is for communicating the content in our minds to others, for producing an external representation of an internal representation, and we don't take this choice for granted. Each medium, whether verbal language, drawing, symbols, simultaneously requires and promotes technical, emotional, and cognitive competence!

_PS:_   And different media have different kinds of descriptive power and pertinence, therefore making it possible to re-represent the content or concept itself at the same time. Annette Karmiloff-Smith (1995) calls this "representational redescription", the continuous mental process by which our brain processes the information gathered. I'll read you a passage I find particularly interesting and pertinent:

> The RR [representational re-description] model is fundamentally a hypothesis about the specifically human capacity to enrich itself from within by exploiting knowledge it has already stored, not by just exploiting the environment. Intra-domain and inter-domain representational relations are the hallmark of a flexible and creative cognitive system. The pervasiveness of representational re-description in human cognition is, I maintain, what makes human cognition specifically human.
>
> _(Karmiloff-Smith, 1995, p. 192)_

186 *Pensiero progettuale* and educational research

In fact, by visualising our thinking strategy to ourselves as well as to others, or following its tracks where it weaves with the thoughts of those we are carrying out an action/reasoning with, we modify mental representation itself, producing an advance.

IM: Also, in order to represent, children must gradually construct a spatial and psychological distancing from the situation they intend to represent. We can see a clear example of this in mark-making and drawing when, in order to represent a person in profile, children find it very difficult to renounce drawing both eyes, because although they can only see one in the moment of drawing, they know that really there are two.

PS: I suggest we do not choose the representation medium straight away but simply propose to the children, in small groups, the challenge of explaining to their younger friends how to set the table. We could ask them this question: "Children, you are very good at setting the table, so would you be able to teach the four-year-olds how to set the table too"? Then we can see whether they immediately go to drawing or choose another medium!

IM: I think they'll propose making a video! These are today's children!

MM: It will depend on the group. I bet they all choose different ways but still, the challenge of coming to an agreement will be interesting.

PS: I agree with you Marina, and that will complicate the documentation a little, but it will be interesting to try and document the different strategies children find for communicating the procedure to others, and then perhaps we can see whether, and to what extent, these affect their competence in setting the table.

The transcript below is drawn from a conversation with Cristian, Francesco, and Lorenzo on the subject of explaining how to set the table to children in the four-year-old class. The teachers' notes are on a column on the right in blue.

MM: Children, you who all know how to set the table really well, would you also know how to teach the four-year-old children how to set the table? They might not know how but next year when they're eating in the big dining room, they'll have to do it!

L: *Of course! I can do that straight away …*	LB: Optimism is one of Lorenzo's characteristics
F: *Even though it's a bit complicated …*	MM: Francesco is more realistic and therefore more prudent

Pensiero progettuale and educational research **187**

C: *They're little and they can't understand very well ...*

MM: Cristian is an older brother and perhaps more used to his younger sister not understanding

F: *They might not understand the things they need to do to set the table straight away, you might have to tell them lots of times!*

PS: Repetition as teacher

L: *In the meantime, they have to stand there and listen, with no one walking around!*

MM: Listening as a learning strategy

C: *What if someone can't remember?*

PS: Concern about memory

F: *We can tell them every day.*

MM: Again, repetition as a strategy for memory and learning

L: *But when lots of days go by you forget things!*
C: *Well it's difficult then!*
L: *We could write a note so after if you get someone to read it then you remember.*

MM: Writing and reading as learning strategy.

MM: What can we write in the note?
L: *Learn how to set a table!*

LB: Urging

C: *Then, how you must set the table.*

TF: There is a "how" – a procedure can be taught.

F: *We'll write a letter to all the four-year-olds then they can take it home with them so they can read it and they won't forget*

PS: The "how" can be defined in something written on paper.
This useful strategy is born of children's familiarity with the transit of objects, ideas and memories between home and school and vice-versa, which in itself is not a casual choice but stems from a deep belief in strong relations.

L: *Or then we should make a drawing in pencil, draw a character or someone setting the table.*

IM: Or in drawn images

188 *Pensiero progettuale* and educational research

C: *Or we could do a table with cut-lery on it then they understand where to put things ...*
L: *Yes, but the tablecloths aren't on it ...*
F: *Well then we can write that you need a table, and a tablecloth.*

PS: The children seem to be posing the problem of the completeness of elements necessary for explaining

L: *Perhaps we could let them see us setting the table, then they watch us, and then they [will] have learned, but after we will be in elementary school and we can't come here and teach them about it, they won't allow us!*
C: *Or in the evening they could watch their parents setting the table when they're making dinner too ... it isn't exactly the same because there are small tables here and at home there are big tables.*

PS: Here the children are posing the issue of explanations or instructions that are independent of their own presence. The "node" or central issue is one of communicating across distances.

MM: Another possible "didactic element": examples at home and at school

MM: Well let's try and repeat all the beautiful ideas you've had up to now.
MM: You said we can tell the four-year-old children how to set the table if they stay still and pay attention listening to us, or that you can show them how to do it but only now, not next year when you will all be at elementary school. Then you thought you could make some notes and write how to do it and they could read these at home lots of times until they learn. Or also that you could make some drawings and some writing...
L: *In my opinion the first thing we need is [some paper for] a note and I would write on it:* "First of all put the tablecloth on". *Then we can write* "Put the plates out".

PS: It is important for the teacher to give back to the group a synthesis of their thinking so they can clarify and move forward

MM: Writing seems to be perceived as the most effective tool for explaining, the sequence is ordinal and defines the elements and gestures necessary for setting the table.

F: ... *Then the big plates*
L: ... *Then the forks, knives, spoons, and then the glasses. But we can do all these things in drawing, because they don't know how to read words.*
C: *I would draw all the things, but with an arrow that shows where you put them.*

IM: Cristian, who doesn't know how to write, proposed drawings again, but he adds the symbol of an arrow which he likes and has already used in other representations. He proposes using it as an indicator for spatial relations.

F: *But if you put the table all laid out then they won't understand what they have to put first and what they have to put after... I'm going to do a table first, then the plates a little bit separate, then the other plates a bit more separate, then even more separate the cutlery, then the glasses ... then stop.*
L: *But there's a problem! What if they lose the notes we make for them?!*
C: *Yeees, idea!! perhaps we can do it with video!*

MM: More "didactic" ideas (for possible relaunching): video and photographs

L: *Yes, we can do it on the television, so that they watch it every time and remember, or we could put a photograph and then we could put the children sitting there with a stick and teach them what they have to do* (show them by pointing at the photo)*!*
We'll prepare the photos; we could begin with today or with tomorrow.
C: *I would start with drawings*
L: *But to do something like that we oughtn't to use all the felt pens, we should just use one pencil, or one felt pen, then we should see something — like see something laid out.*

PS: The children know themselves how to search for tools suited to the representation: materials and models.[17]

IM: The children know how to make hypotheses about and search for the tools necessary to realise their projects, an operation that is by no means a given, absolutely intelligent, and supported in school from three years old (and before that in the infant-toddler centre).

F: Let's go and get the trolley!
(which is ready because it's nearly
time to eat)

Cristian and Francesco draw while
Lorenzo offers to be the guide,
setting the table and giving a com-
mentary. Actually, he goes through
it very quickly saying: *"Now I'm
putting on the tablecloth, now the
plates, now the glasses".*

Lorenzo, uninterrupted by the requests of his friends, who appear to be drawing from personal memory rather than using specific visual references, completes the task of setting the table and then rushes to draw. Something unexpected is happening, though not exceptional for those who are familiar with children! The group has fully understood the teacher's proposal and is enthusiastically adhering to it. The procedures of table-setting can be communicated to their younger companions in many different ways: verbally, in writing, through live performance (at school or at home), or through drawing, video, and photography. All of these are possible, as the adults had hypothesised in their *aggiornamento*, but without imposing the medium on the children in hierarchical or prescriptive ways. The times of *progettazione*, especially those directly involving the children, require teachers to make choices while in the context. Later these can be discussed, in a quick *confronto* with a class colleague, or the *atelierista*, or even on the phone with the *pedagogista*. If mistakes are made, changes of direction can follow.

The children's emotions and engagement are high, and even though it is lunchtime the teacher does not interrupt the work, but lets the children continue to experiment with their ideas. This continuation of experience beyond the foreseen times and modalities is a liberty and responsibility that design thinking requires and makes possible: it is constructed with the working group because it also requires other people at school to be flexible with times (the kitchen, auxiliary staff, and other colleagues), but it offers teachers the possibility of constantly making choices that take into account objectives, contextual events, organisational constraints (and if they are flexible or not!), interpretations of the events taking place, and children's intentions and expectations. The teacher's choice of not interrupting the experience to conform to timetable requirements could be read as an insignificant detail, but in reality it testifies to how an organisation centred on meaning, as opposed to routines and job descriptions, enables those small and unusual changes that, in the words of Malaguzzi (in Gandini, 2017) make "a school that is lovable (busy, inventive, liveable, documentable and communicable, a place of research, learning,

Pensiero progettuale and educational research **191**

re-cognition and reflection) where children, teachers and families feel well" (p. 74, [translated by Jane McCall]).[18]

As they are drawing the children comment specifically on the symbol of the arrow, to which they assign an ordinal function for the execution of the table-setting.

FIGURE 6.2 Drawing of a table-setting by Francesco.

FIGURE 6.3 Drawing of a table-setting by Lorenzo.

192 *Pensiero progettuale* and educational research

FIGURE 6.4   Drawing of a table-setting by Cristian.

C: (looking at Lorenzo and Francesco's drawings) *They all had my idea of the arrows!*
F: *No! Otherwise [if they don't have the arrows] they can't understand what goes first, what goes second, what goes third, what goes fourth and what goes fifth!*
C: *And sixth, seventh, eighth, and ninth ...*
C: *Oh, I forgot the dishes!!!*
(They laugh loudly)
L: *Dishes are important, if not are they going to eat off the tablecloth?*

In contexts such as these, error is often commented upon by children with joyful humour.

At this point the teacher proposes suspending the work, not just because it is past lunchtime, but also not to risk burning up the children's enthusiasm and her own and limiting possibilities for reflection. The following day the group returns to their project. The children are clear about their objectives and the work done the day before. The teachers agree they will start with a situation of evaluation and self-assessment, as is often the case when children are producing individual pieces of work but converging on a common purpose. The theme of evaluation and self-evaluation is vitally important in design thinking: an exercise that is often implicit but that becomes powerfully meta-cognitive when it is made explicit, shared, and argued in the group. Quickly consulting each other, the teachers make some final agreements before meeting with the children.

PS: Perhaps Marina, if Cristian, Francesco, and Lorenzo can't identify a drawing among those they have made that is useful to explain how to set the table, you could suggest they make a new one all together, the three of them. It would be much more difficult, but that way we would be able to see what elements they think are essential to communicate!

The following is the transcript of the conversation that took place:

MM: Children, you have made three different drawings, all three of them are very interesting, but how do we know which is most suited to explaining how to set the table?

MM: The issue of evaluation and self-evaluation is introduced in relation to specific objectives.

L: *Let's go to the four-year-old children and try and get them to guess.*
F: *But perhaps they won't be able to understand...*
L: *They might think it's a mess! And crumple it up!*

PS: Recipients as evaluators and the risks of non-competent evaluation.

MM: Perhaps we could try it out among ourselves first, to see if you can understand from each drawing how to set the table! Let's look together at Francesco's drawing (Figure 6.2) *and he can explain:*
F: *I've done arrows that show all the things you have to put [on the table] because ...*

PS: Francesco begins to recount his own drawing arguing for the significance of the arrows in relation to the ordinal nature of the gestures necessary for setting the table.

L: *Just on one table?*
F: *Yes, because first the tablecloth goes on, then the plate that goes underneath, then the plate that goes on top, then knife and fork and then the glass.*
C: *Isn't there something missing? I think there is, but it's something all of us forgot, it's the bottles.*

LB: Honest, mannered criticism.

F: *It's true!*
L: *And perhaps we need lots of glasses, lots of plates, and lots of knives and forks ... Sorry Francesco I'm not angry! Have I prepared just one place here or lots of places? I would say lots of places!*

PS: Cristian and Lorenzo search for the criteria used in their own drawings in Francesco's.

194 *Pensiero progettuale* and educational research

C: *But he has a lot of room there where he can put the other plates, the other glasses, and the bottles too.*

F: *I've left some room for the person setting the table!*

PS: Francesco who, objectively, has identified a structure that is more synthetic and evolved than those proposed by his companions, justifies what in their eyes is something missing from the drawing.

F: *I've done the tablecloth because it's the first thing and so I drew it here* (pointing to the lower part of his drawing paper)

L: *But you can't see the table legs!*

F: *They're underneath*

IM: Francesco is beginning to give up drawing what he knows in favour of what can be seen, a long and by no means simple process.

C: *You're looking from above, like if I see from above like this* (raising his hands above the table) *I can't see the legs ...*

MM: Competent criticism.

F: *Then the plates second and the other plates third, then the knives and forks fourth then the glasses fifth.*

MM: (turning the sheet of paper 180 degrees) What if a child reads it like this: first the glasses, then the knives and forks then the plates ... what would they be putting? What can we do [about this]?

MM: The teacher is posing the problem of a change in the order of actions depending on the reader changing viewpoint (relaunching in context).[19]

F: *We can write that you should start with the tablecloth ... We'll write: "You start with the tablecloth".*

PS: The children, particularly Francesco, know the meaning of alphanumeric codes and their uses.

Francesco can write some words autonomously but so as not to risk misunderstandings he asks the teacher to write the sentence on a piece of paper: "You start with the tablecloth". Then he immediately copies the sentence onto his drawing.

Pensiero progettuale and educational research **195**

Looking at Lorenzo's drawing
(Figure 6.3)

L: *Before anything else I made three circles*
F: *Which are the tables!*
L: *Yes, then after that I did the tablecloths and then the plates.*
C: *You can't really understand here what you did first, whether it was the plates or the tablecloths, you should say:* "I did this first; first this, or first that other!"

IM: Competencies in identifying possible ambiguities and reading the clarity of each other's communication in the structure of the drawings seems to be growing in the group together with a capacity for offering suggestions.

L: *I put the tablecloths in, and after that I began to do the plates, first the big plates, then the small plates, then I did the arrows.*
F: *Why did you do the arrows?*
L: *What! Sorry but because he [Cristian] said we definitely have to do them... then I drew arrows on the plates to attach them on the tables, then the glasses, then the forks... I made lots of arrows that go on the tablecloth, this goes like this, this one like this...*

IM: The children are coming up against the problem of copying the structure of each other's drawings without fully understanding them. However, Lorenzo entrusts the arrows with the meaning of a note indicating the direction.

F: *I can't really understand much because all the arrows joining up are a bit confused ...*

Looking at Cristian's drawing
(Figure 6.4)
C: *First there's a tablecloth that goes here, the arrow shows the square tablecloth that goes on the square table, then the fork goes here, then the spoon goes here too.*

PS: Cristian utilises the arrow symbol to highlight elements that have the same shape.

F: *I understand, it's all the things that go on the tables!*
L: *Now we have to show them to the others [and see] if they understand! I'll show Giacomo.*

MM: Lorenzo is remembering the situation they decided on for verifying earlier.
PS: We could define this as a contextual relaunching identified by the children themselves.

F: *I'll show Chiara*
C: *I'll show Andrea*

They proceed to call their three friends and show them the drawings all at the same time, generating a certain confusion.

MM: Perhaps a group of friends will show solidarity towards the attempts they have made!

F: *The tablecloths start for first.*

MM: It might be a good idea to explain to your friends what you have drawn and why.
F: *These drawings are to make you understand ... setting the table.*
L: *To make the four-year-olds understand what you have to do to set the table.*
C: *So, we have come to ask you if you can understand [from our drawing] what [things] you have to put out to set the table.*

PS: But it is difficult to find the words to ask for a judgment

Looking at Cristian's drawing:
Chiara: *I understand there's a fork and a spoon drawn here.*
Giacomo: *I understand the knife.*
Andrea: *I understand the tablecloth.*
Chiara: *But you can understand the things you need to set the table: if a person has to set the table, here's the fork, here's the knife and you need them to set the table ...*

Looking at Francesco's drawing:
Chiara: *You can understand here too because there's a tablecloth, plates, forks* [she points to the arrows].
F: *They're not forks, those are arrows ... because that way the four-year-old children understand what goes first, what goes second, what goes third, fourth and fifth.*

Pensiero progettuale and educational research **197**

Chiara: *First the tablecloth ...*
F: *Yes, because I wrote there: "Start with the tablecloth, then the plates second, the other plates third, and the cutlery fourth".*

Looking at Lorenzo's drawing:
Giacomo: *I don't think you can understand [this] very well!*
Chiara: *In my opinion you can understand Francesco's best because it shows everything, and you can see best how to set the table.*
C: *But there are spoons, plates, tablecloths, glasses here too [indicating his own drawing].*
L: *There is everything in mine too.*
Chiara: *But in Francesco's, everything is all lined up.*

PS: This context allows verification of the clarity of communication. For the children, the presence not only of "all", but of "all lined up", seems to be a convincing criterion.

F: *In this drawing of Lori's (Lorenzo) it's all disorder, in mine everything is lined up by the arrows.*

It is evident from these dialogues between children, and also in the conversations between adults that were shared in Chapter 4, how *confronto*, exchange, evaluation and self-evaluation do not come into play at specific scheduled moments, but rather represent the shared cultural climate of doing school. This relational culture of being and doing school meshes an ethical attitude of genuine interest and welcome for everyone's opinions (although these are open to counterarguments) with the cognitive gains this type of dialectics affords.

When children work alone, they do not generally negotiate or test their perspectives against the theories of others. Children in learning groups are more likely to perceive the temporariness of their theories because they experience knowledge as a constant process of negotiation and reflection [...] Children learn to see themselves as thinkers with different points of view. Children in learning groups accept one another's opinions and feelings and offer their own opinions and feelings, whether they are in agreement with or differ from their peers.

(Krechevsky, 2001, p. 260 and 263)

198 *Pensiero progettuale* and educational research

The group continues its work (Cristian, Francesco, and Lorenzo)

As hypothesised above, the teacher proposes with the children that they reason together on the drawings they have made and choose one, or perhaps make a new one that could be clearer for the four-year-olds. Perhaps Marina was not explicit enough, or more likely the children had a great desire to experiment with the other languages and expressive techniques they had previously discussed. The fact is that the children propose experimenting with other expressive media.

L: *Can we take photographs today like we said? We can do them one at a time.*
F: *We'll queue.*
L: *There are three of us so we can set three tables, but there should be four of us because …*
F: *One can take the photos and the other two can set the tables.*

PS: When the children are emotionally and cognitively involved in a project not only do they continue to recall the group intent, but they also look for forms of organisation that to their mind are effective for moving the project forward. In this case, the organisation they have identified is the "queue", a procedure they had already seen other children using while making the preparatory drawing for the "Beautiful Wall" (Vecchi, 2001).

MM: In your opinion, what should you photograph in order to teach people how to set a table?

MM: The teacher reminds them of the aims of the project so that they don't only focus on group agreements.

What is evident here is how the teacher does not lose sight of the objective, and how she makes choices in this regard, although elsewhere *progettazione* is often interpreted as "letting yourself be guided wherever the children take you".[20] Without prescriptive programmes to guide us it is not an easy balance to strike. Two elements come to our aid: the tension towards research that demands we do not rush towards the objective of transferring knowledge, and the strategy of documentation that makes it possible for us to critically reinterpret our gestures and language. New possibilities have emerged: will the children consider it appropriate to combine drawings and photographs to communicate with their four-year-old "colleagues"?

L: *When it's set … with the table all set!*
C: *Nooo! While we're setting the table!*
F: *When someone starts setting, we'll photograph them so that they can understand from the photos what goes first.*

MM: Francesco underlines his strategy of precisely identifying how the events follow one another, the before and after.

Pensiero progettuale and educational research   **199**

C: *Then when it's finished.*

MM: Cristian draws a logical conclusion: if before is important then the end is equally so.

F: *But you need the things in the middle too, the plates, the glasses ...*
L: *The bottle goes in the middle! But the first thing is the tablecloth.*

PS: Lorenzo completes his companions' explanation and reminds them of the necessary spatial arrangement. It is as if the children take turns in the group to define the overall thinking, but with each one underscoring their own personal thumbprint.

F: *Empty! And then the other photos with things we put on the tablecloth.*
L: *I think two of us could set the table and the other one can take photographs.*
C: *I don't know maybe we need three tables.*
L: *But can we choose two tables, or three, or one ... it's a problem!*
F: *What if we need four?*
L: *Well how many plates and things do we need?*
F: *Shall I go and count the chairs?*
L: *No, we have to find out from the class how many children there are, so then we know and we can set the table!*

TF: Agreements are important for proceeding as a group within a project, as are the questions that emerge and the attempts at answers. For the children, this ferment of ideas and questions drives their research.

They go into the classroom to ask about the number of children.
Cristian: *Twenty four of us!*

The number of children has only now emerged as a variable, and the "table-setters" have not considered it in their representations. The teacher does not refer to it because from the age of three, it is one of the situations of correspondence that is most experienced and consolidated: who is present, who is absent, places at the table, handing out sheets of paper for drawing, and so on. In this case, the discussion centres on the creation of a tool to communicate a strategy for setting the table, irrespective of the number of diners. The children run into the kitchen to ask Nadia (the cook) for a trolley, and they then begin transporting dishes onto the trolley in an enjoyable game of passing hand-to-hand and counting. Lorenzo takes the

200 *Pensiero progettuale* and educational research

FIGURE 6.5   Cristian places his hands on two piles of dishes laid out on the trolley in the kitchen.

plates one at a time, counting and singing *one, two, three* ... then he passes them to Francesco who puts them on the trolley. Cristian takes charge of the photography and immediately makes the others move the trolley to a more convenient position for photographing it empty. However, he loves counting so much that he constantly interrupts what he's doing to check his companions' sums, especially when it comes to the higher numbers. While preparing the trolley Cristian shows his friends an efficient way of checking total quantities "at a glance".

Placing his hands on two piles of dishes (Figure 6.5) Cristian says: *they're equal*. Thus, even before he can verbally explain the concept of equal, Cristian expresses it through the gesture of positioning his hands, and by a careful eye check. His body understands relations of size, number, and weight that cultural symbolic codes have systematised and that the children will have to master. Although Francesco and Lorenzo understand the meaning of counting and are familiar with some of the simpler procedures, they sometimes have difficulty with numbers over 20. When they have almost finished preparing the trolley, Cristian suggests they count two at a time: *it's always just one, one, one. It's going to take us three hours ... we're never going to finish. Let's do two, four, six ...* He thus demonstrates his advanced competence in counting strategies, perhaps in part still in the form of nursery rhymes based on even numbers, but effective nevertheless. At a future date we could ask Cristian to argue his proposal more effectively, but in the excitement of preparing the trolley, photo reporting, and the table setting

Pensiero progettuale and educational research **201**

FIGURES 6.6–6.15   Photo-report created by Cristian during the preparation of the trolley.

to come, this would be neither advisable nor interesting to the children themselves.

MM: Did you get everything you need?
Everyone: *Yeess!*
F: *Actually, we don't have any bottles.*
L: *We need four of them.*

202 *Pensiero progettuale* and educational research

They take the trolley into the space where the tables are and decide that Francesco will take photos while Cristian and Lorenzo set them.

Immediately Francesco positions himself close to the "little theatre", from where he photographs all the empty tables.
C: *You can place yourself in the middle!*

IM: The children suggest strategies to each other related to the medium being used.

Slowly Francesco moves to the centre of the dining area, in between the tables, a position from which he can photograph all the tables, simply by rotating his body as the children bring new objects to a table (from flat dishes, to pasta dishes, to glasses etc.).

PS: Francesco seems to be concentrating hard on his role as photographer, but perhaps he has also chosen a strategy already: to photograph each table in the moment each single operation ends, tablecloth, plates, glasses, etc.

Lorenzo and Cristian set the tables in silence, first tables with chairs, which they use as a reference for dining settings.
L. (referring to the rectangular table that has no chairs): *There are no chairs, perhaps it will take three!* (Then he arranges the eight plates he has left) *like this they seem good!* Francesco is taking photographs in silence, concentrating very hard, careful not to miss any of the changes taking place on each table.

At the end, they check if anything is missing.
L: *Francesco what have we been doing?*
F: *I was taking photographs and you two laid the tables.*
L: *But before that we prepared the trolley, it was the first time!*

Pensiero progettuale and educational research **203**

MM: Did you like that? Did you encounter any difficulties, any problems?

C. *Yes, we liked it, it was easy.*
F: *I liked the counting because it was easy.*

MM: Today you prepared the trolley too. In your opinion is this something we need to explain to the four-year-old children?
L: *Yes, because then they'll learn how to prepare the trolley too!*
So, after that we came here [dining area].
F: *We put the tablecloths on.*
L: *Francesco started taking photos of us and we started setting the tables, we've already done our work now.*
F: *Perhaps now we need get the photos to come out of the camera to carry on. Paola, show us the photos that were taken yesterday!*
L: *Perhaps Isabella could tell us too and when she's got them out of the disk* [digital camera with removable memory], *we have to explain them to the children.*

MM: Might there be some other ways of explaining to the four-year-olds how to prepare the trolley, instead of just the photos? (relaunching in context)

MM: This is an important question to ask children at the end of any experience. It invites them to rethink not only cognitive aspects (problems, solutions, etc.) but emotional ones too.

TF: The teacher is struck by the children's enthusiasm and wants to understand if new pathways will open up for communicating a performative strategy. However, she might be proposing too many things at once. We can always try, but it is important to proceed in relation to the children's responses without imposing or forcing things.

L: *Let's make a drawing.*
F: *I'd like to write.*

MM: The children remember the solutions identified for setting the table: drawings and writing.

C: *Me too.*
C: *We don't know how to write really well but we know how to copy.*
MM: Let's think about the important things, what's important for preparing the trolley.

204 *Pensiero progettuale* and educational research

L: *I'd like to write:* we prepare
the trolley.
C: *Yes, our title is: WE PREPARE
THE TROLLEY.*

We ask the children if everyone
wants to write the same thing, they
say *"yes"* and so we continue the
dictation, sentence by sentence.

PS: A bit rushed perhaps. The children could have been asked whether they wanted to construct the whole text first or dictate a bit at a time (self-evaluation)

Everyone begins to copy:

L. *I've written "pre-pa-ri-amo il
ca-rre-llo" [we pre-pare the tro-lley]*
(singing) *la-la-la - with everything
that goes on it ... la-la-la ...*
F. *Now we have to write the things that
go on it! First thing: the flat dishes.*
C. *First the plates, if you say "first"
it's quicker to tell them, so let's write,
FIRST THE PASTA DISHES.*

PS: First, second ... the return of the importance of defining the ordinal aspect of sequencing operations

F. *Mari* (teacher) *write the P first.*

TF: Children advising the teacher how to write a word isn't simply fun, but it reflects something of the atmosphere in a group that feels the teacher as a participant in thinking that circulates and is shared.

L: *Then the flat dishes, the second
thing is the flat dishes*
C. *Or you can say SECOND FLAT
DISHES*

PS: "Or you can say" – group communication requires propositional language.

[The children copy]

L. *After the flat dishes ...sssss we
have the glasses, let's write it like this!*
F. *We can write, THIRD THE
GLASSES.*

Lorenzo then writes FLAT (piani),
but it comes out FLAT.TH (piani.te)

Pensiero progettuale and educational research   **205**

Knowing Lorenzo's humorous side MM reads "piani.te", Lorenzo laughs out loud and decides to rub it out and begin again writing "third" (terzo).

F. [looking at the phrase he has just written] *It's one word made of two things ... flat + third.*

MM: The children are discovering the rules of written language (a zone for other possible relaunchings).

MM reads out all the text dictated by the children up to this point and asks them if she should add anything else.

C. *Fourth forks, spoons and knives.*
F. *We could say cutlery too,*
FOURTH CUTLERY.
L. *Yes because you need cutlery to eat with.*
C. *Like spoons and forks ...*
L. *It's too long to say them all, it's better to write just "fourth, cutlery".*

PS: Lorenzo is reasoning on an issue that is not banal: writing is demanding work so if we can replace several words with one indefinite adjective like "all" or a numeral like "fourth" it's worth doing!

L. *FIFTH THE TABLECLOTHS*
The children play with the sounds "*qua*" (kwa– near here) and "*qui*" (kwi – here)

MM: Playing and joking with word sounds and their written form is both a situation of fun and of learning.

F. *There's just one left, the bottles.*
L. *The last one.*
F. *SIXTH*
C. *AND THE BOTTLES LAST*

At the end Cristian sings "*yeah-yeah-yeah!*" and exclaims: "*Now what do we have to write?*"
Nothing!
L. *I can't read it though! I haven't learned to read yet!*

MM: Again, this is an important kind of awareness: it isn't enough to be able to draw a sign in order to decode it, however this can be learned.

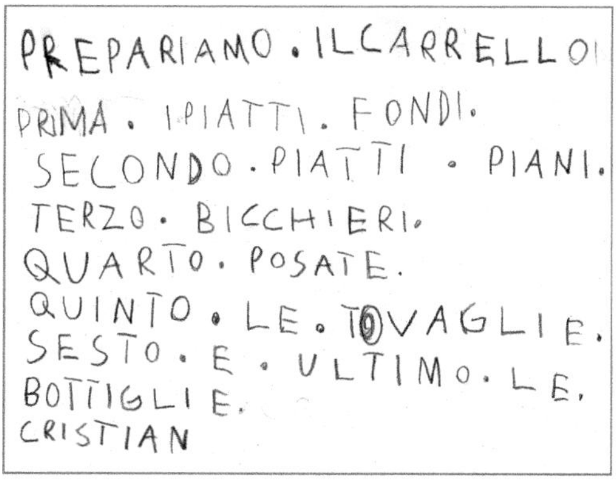

206 *Pensiero progettuale* and educational research

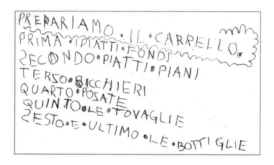

FIGURE 6.16 Instructions on how to set the table, written by Cristian.

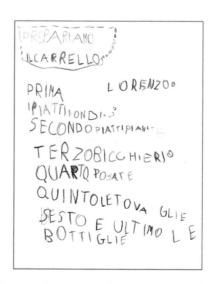

FIGURE 6.17 Instructions on how to set the table, written by Francesco.

FIGURE 6.18 Instructions on how to set the table, written by Lorenzo.

Pensiero progettuale and educational research **207**

The following day ...

Several photographs have been taken. The children seem fascinated by the possibility of printing, selecting. and reusing them. In a phone call about various matters we inform the *pedagogista* about this situation and Tiziana comments: "to me this possibility of taking pictures over time, selecting them, composing and re-composing them, sometimes with different purposes, seems very powerful, and we would do well to explore it with other children and in other situations". The children also ask if they can use the computer to look at the photographs Cristian took while they were preparing the trolley. They comment together on both photo reportages, first looking at them on the screen, and then on black and white printouts. They grow more ambitious: if they can make instructions for setting the table then they can also make some for preparing the trolley. I comment: "we could call this a relaunch that the children have identified themselves, a situation that always testifies to an experience's emotional and cognitive efficacy!"

The three children take turns to propose which pictures they think are most suited and clearest. Of the 39 photographs Francesco took, 13 are discussed and of these 9 are chosen to narrate how to set the table. All the photographs Cristian took are chosen for the narrative of how to prepare the trolley. We print them all up in a 10 cm × 15 cm format after the children have evaluated that they are sufficiently clear. This issue of evaluation and self-evaluation in learning processes is fundamentally important and can always be found in curriculum guidelines. In our example, we can see how the shared effort of a group of children to create a communication tool for other friends requires both individual work and the negotiation of shared tasks, and how these are always accompanied with autonomous comments to each other that are often humorous and self-deprecating. The teacher is not the final judge. We do not hear the children turning to the teacher to ask: "Is this OK teacher?"; "Teacher, do you like this?"; "Teacher, have I finished?". Their positive self-evaluations of the work they have done, together with their group strength and co-constructed journey, leads the children to identify further destinations themselves, such as using photographs to explain setting the table. Even the non-simple question of relaunching, an essential part of design thinking, can be considered not to be entirely in the hands of teachers, but the object of a negotiation between protagonists of the experience.

To make our communication more synthetic and effective, we have not included in this collection all 39 photographs taken by Francesco, but only those the children commented on, explicitly expressing the criteria for choosing or rejecting them, agreed upon by the group, for use in the "Instructions for setting table for four-year-olds". Some photographs were rejected without comment.

As in their initial conversation, while selecting photographs the children also seem aware of the difficulty of laying the tablecloths (Figures 6.19–6.21). The consolidated strategy of setting the table by using chairs as indicators for

208 *Pensiero progettuale* and educational research

FIGURE 6.19   *This one is good because you can see the side well.*

FIGURE 6.20   *No. This tablecloth is hanging crooked, and there's a lot of floor ... then they'll go and put things on the floor!!! Ha! Ha!*

FIGURE 6.21   *This one isn't useful because there is only a bit of tablecloth and all you can see is children setting the table.*

FIGURE 6.22   *This one is useful though, because they can understand how to put the plates next to the chairs.*

the position of plates has returned (Figure 6.22). It also seems the presence of people in the photo is quite a welcome element (Figure 6.23). This is something we have often witnessed, in different kinds of experiences; Malaguzzi said that children do not like anonymity. We notice that in cases where the children can't decide between two different pictures (Figures 6.26 and 6.27 for example) they use the conditional tense *we should decide!* rather than the

Pensiero progettuale and educational research **209**

FIGURE 6.23 *Hey! You (teachers) are in this one too! And we're in it too!*

FIGURE 6.24 *Too tilted!*

FIGURE 6.25 *No. Because the tablecloth hasn't been put on very well. It's not good!*

FIGURE 6.26 *We can keep this one because there aren't too many of the same kind of plate … there are six. So they can understand how many children there are on just one table!*

FIGURE 6.27 *We should decide between one of these two (6.26 and 6.27) because they have different tables in them.*

210 *Pensiero progettuale* and educational research

FIGURE 6.28   *Let's choose this one where the table's almost ready.*

FIGURE 6.29   *There are glasses on this one too, and that's good, but they are a bit too transparent (not very visible).*

FIGURE 6.30   *You can't see this one properly. It's blowy (blurred)!*

indicative "we decide" or imperative "decide!", demonstrating how aware children are of being part of a group experience rather than an individual one.

Class aggiornamento: evaluation of work in progress

In this class *aggiornamento*, we reason together about the potential, for both individual and group learning, of current contexts and possible ones. Here our comments centre above all on the evidence emerging from one group, composed by Cristian, Francesco, and Lorenzo, but obviously in this meeting we also considered all the other simultaneously active contexts with the five-year-olds, both in class and around the school.

> TF: To me it seems that the children are working on different kinds of agreements: sharing what the purpose of their project is, agreeing on what techniques to use, and dividing tasks up among themselves.

PS: This issue of dividing up tasks involves evaluative and self-evaluative skills, and the capacity to forecast and plan. Not only does it touch on fundamental emotional and social spheres, but also on cognitive aspects of absolute importance that merit a deeper analysis so that we can identify relaunches, for this group and for the class.

MM: They are focusing better on the communicative efficacy of the work they have produced, and therefore distancing themselves from the prevalent egocentric evaluations that characterise so many early childhood theories. For example, Lorenzo says: *I can't read it though! I haven't learned to read yet!*

LB: What is highlighted on the individual level is how all the children take great interest in working with numbers and initial forms of counting, especially Cristian.

SC: (laughing) Now when they come and collect the trays for their second course, they count the portions we have prepared!

IM: Lorenzo's light-hearted singing of syllables as he writes them, and his comments hypothesising that the four-year-olds might interpret one of the drawings as *eating from the floor* helps everyone to consider errors as something amusing, and therefore not emotionally frustrating.

TF: Francesco seems to pay a lot of attention to aspects of geometry: *But first you have to see the shapes of the tables*, and to spatio-temporal relations such as *before, after, in-between*. Obviously, he is still constructing these competencies, but they are very evident in his mark-making and drawing and in his verbal language where the words before, after, and in-between occur with a certain frequency. Basically, the whole proposal of making instructions for setting the table relies not only on recognising the necessary operations, but on a cognitive elaboration of their relations. How the children choose, agree on and complete tasks of a technical nature such as photography, on the subjective individual level and as a group, is worthy of more investigation, for us to understand more, if possible, about the connections between the different languages they use. For example, do Cristian's counting competences show a connection with his strategies when taking photographs, or in putting images together for communication purposes? As well as in his drawings, do Francesco's supposed competences with spatio-temporal relationships also return in his approach to the language of photography, and if so, how? Does Lorenzo's capacity for seeing the humorous side of situations help him to identify problems, and solve them?

PS: Ah yes Tiziana, all these questions generate ideas for preparing other contexts, as well as this current project, and other observational focuses related to daily situations that exist in class, not just for these children, but for the others too.

212 *Pensiero progettuale* and educational research

MM: In relation to writing, and in particular to copying words written by an adult (or a more competent friend in some cases), we proceeded well didn't we Tiziana?!

TF: The operation of dictation-writing-copying appeals to children because they feel they can use a complex code, of which they as yet have only mastered a few rules, and that they can produce very effective work because it is understandable for those who receive it. We just need to be very careful not to replace the children in elaborating the text, which they absolutely must feel they are the authors of, and the clarity of which they will be able to verify when recipients read it. In their effort to recognise and reproduce the shapes of letters and words, to understand their sounds, and decode the meaning of spaces in what is written on paper, each child in their own way is discovering the rules of grammar and syntax.

PS: I think we are doing ok because, if you look, in the case of Cristian and Francesco we can see how they chose to space out what for them are largely still groups of letters rather than actual words, by using dots, as well as maintaining the correct blanks spaces. Lorenzo and Francesco decided to highlight the title in a sort of cloud. Marina was willing to respond to the children's questions, but without being in a hurry to promote precocious learning, of a standard and formal nature.

MM: Look everyone, in this situation, I really felt like a researcher interested in understanding subjective and group ways of interrogating and testing these symbolic and cultural codes of writing, of reading and of calculating, that I know are absolutely complex!

All the notes that were shared in the aggiornamento refocused and re-oriented the bi-monthly class *progettazione* and the weekly *progettazione* that followed. In particular, we decided that the next meeting would open with all the materials the children have produced up to now laid out on the table, including our transcripts of their conversations.

The next appointment with the children

The teacher immediately realises that the group can remember every tiny detail of what has happened so far and does not consider it opportune to recap the project. Unanimously and enthusiastically, the children decide that having written down and taken photographs of the process of preparing the trolley, it is absolutely essential to now also write down the act of setting the table. Cristian, Francesco, and Lorenzo do not seem to ask themselves whether and how written notes will help their four-year-old friends to understand (or *learn* as they have defined it in their project) how to set a table. They seem to set aside the significant problem of the reading difficulties of the recipients of the message, although they know about this and highlighted it in their first conversation. They seem more concerned with maintaining a sort of criterion of "procedural equity": if there are written texts, drawings, and photos of the preparation of the trolley, then the same is due to the setting of the table. The question of how the material they produce will then be used seems to have been set aside for the time being.

The writing takes place with the same care and modalities discussed in the aggiornamento: the children dictate to Marina what they think should be written. The teacher writes in capital letters, spacing the words and composing lines that reconcile the sense of what the children say and the space on the paper. As they dictate, the children carefully mark the ordinality of their sentences, emphasising the numbers with their voice: **one** – *put on the tablecloth;* **two** – *set out the flat dishes* … and so on. The children copy what the teacher has written on a sheet of paper, consulting it individually and together, getting close up and commenting on parts that have been copied or are still to be copied. The teacher does not intervene during the work of copying. Due to a technical problem, we have unfortunately lost the sound recording of this situation, but from the photos and notes of the adults present (Marina and Paola) we can sense a general air of good humour, and of children commenting on different ways of organising their writing on the paper's space.

Francesco: *Why did you make the numbers small Lori?*
Lorenzo: *No, they are not all small, these ones are big* [pointing to 6 and 5].
Francesco: *First we need 1, then 2, then 3, then 4, then 5; and 6 is the last one!*
Lorenzo: *I'll put arrows on it then, so you can understand the numbers are one after the other!*
Cristian: *I've made the numbers big!*
Lorenzo: *Yes, and the words are big too … in my opinion yours is better Cristian!*

FIGURES 6.31 and 6.32 Lorenzo, Francesco, and Cristian writing and laughing together.

MM: All three of you have finished your writing children, but you know, don't you, that one will be enough to explain setting the table to the four-year-olds?

Francesco: *I agree with Lorenzo: Cristian's is good.*

The children are experimenting with the complexity of the inherent elements of written code. The adults decide not to intervene, considering the risk of immediately pointing the children towards a choice that would interrupt the project's fluidity and de-motivate them. The question of comprehensible writing can possibly be taken up when they make their choice of a final format for communicating with the four-year-olds.

MM: Well children, we have to stop again here for today because it's already 10 o'clock, and as you know we are expected at the theatre at 10:30. You have made drawings of setting the table, you have written how to prepare the trolley and how to set the table. Where shall we begin tomorrow?

Lorenzo: *The photos! We need the photos we decided on!*

Cristian: *But we haven't decided about the trolley photos!*

MM: Very well! Tomorrow we'll go back to the photographs together with all the rest of your work!

The following day ...

The photographs are fascinating. Both Cristian and Francesco enthusiastically declare their wish to work on their own photo reportages and so they all decide together that Cristian will be entrusted with *explaining the trolley with the photographs* and Francesco and Lorenzo with *explaining setting the table*. They decide to cut out their chosen photographs (printed on A4 paper in black and white) and then paste them onto a larger A3 sheet, chosen from the different sizes of paper and card available because *it is bigger and you can understand properly.*

FIGURE 6.33 Creating photo reportages.

Pensiero progettuale and educational research **215**

FIGURE 6.34   Cristian's reportage "Preparing the trolley".

The teachers then comment on the children's work:

MM: In the way Cristian has arranged the photographs, two strategies he used to draw setting the table return: the circular arrangement of elements, and the inclusion of arrows to show the direction of the process, which in this case is the loading of the trolley.

PS: Exactly! But in his drawing of setting the table the arrows specifically indicated a relation of analogous shape rather than of successive elements,[21] but now – probably convinced by the use of arrows that Francesco proposed – Cristian is using arrows to indicate successive gestures. It is really evident how in this group there are productive contagions from a cognitive point of view, as well as excellent social relations.

After reconsidering and confirming the five photographs selected from Francesco's photo reportage, Francesco and Lorenzo ask for them to be enlarged and printed in colour, in a 13 cm × 18 cm format. They cut them out and then line them up before pasting them to the lower part of a 70 cm × 100 cm sheet of white card. They explain their choice like this:

Francesco: *The photographs need to be big because then they look good on the poster and colour photos are more beautiful.*

Lorenzo: *And for a poster you really need a big sheet like this, nice and hard so they can put it on the dining room wall and they'll remember as they set the table.*

Francesco: *And then we'll put the words and drawings on it too!*

Lorenzo: *Of course, but shall we give them the other photos of Cristian's trolley too, so they can understand everything!*

216 *Pensiero progettuale* and educational research

Cristian concurs with his friends, probably satisfied that his most recent work is also required. The "billboard" will therefore consist of a row of photographs of setting the table, with the addition of arrows drawn in pencil above and below the pictures.

Lorenzo: *Come on, let's take it to the four-year-old class now!*
Francesco: *No! To our friends first!*

The differences in the protagonists' points of view helps us to suggest a pause to evaluate the work they have done together with Isabella and Tiziana. Tiziana couldn't be present, but we have notes from Marina, Paola, and Isabella:

MM: You can see how the children don't discard anything! They wanted to put their drawings and words about setting table on this panel. There were a lot of attempts but, in my opinion, these were more to figure out how they could fit everything on than to construct clear communication about the procedure for setting the table.
IM: More than an instruction booklet or leaflet, they are making an exhibition of their products!
MM: I tried to cast doubt on their work being comprehensible, but the children seemed impervious to criticism at the moment, and perhaps even a bit annoyed.
PS: However, they are continuing to reason about the symbol of the arrow and assign it with communicating the temporal sequence of gestures for setting the table. That is not trivial reasoning.
IM: Since other groups are also working on this question of how to make setting the table visible and communicable, as well as other things such as the game "free a friend",[22] I propose the group presents its work to friends in the class tomorrow.
PS: I think it would be more productive to have a discussion with an extended group of friends: 26 children is too many. It would be more confusing than helpful.

We decide that we will suggest the children go and verify their work with the same group of friends who have already commented on their drawings. Both the authors and the invited friends are enthusiastic about the proposal.

Andrea: *In my opinion, if they can't understand the photos very well, or the numbers, because they can't read, the teachers can read it to them, because they always read and children listen.*
Chiara: *You have to write the instructions, then they can listen and learn them!*

Pensiero progettuale and educational research   **217**

During the discussion, the choice of using Cristian's text is confirmed, as first suggested by Lorenzo and Francesco. In fact, in referring to Cristian's writing, Giacomo states: *everything is written properly here*. Giacomo's advice is readily accepted, and it is agreed to put Cristian's text in the large space above the images, enlarged to A3 size. The enlargement was suggested by the teachers to be consistent with the 70 cm × 100 cm format the children have chosen.

Francesco: But we need the numbers of the pictures here too! [pointing underneath each picture].
Cristian: *Yes, and the arrows* [pointing] *– first the tablecloth, – then the plates, – then the bowls, – then the glasses, – then the spoons, the forks, and the bottles.*

Therefore, at the conclusion of this meeting the numbers and arrows are added beneath the images.

In reality only five photographs were chosen, with corresponding numbers and arrows. However, neither the authors nor the recipients are concerned about this "minor" inconsistency. The teachers don't feel it is appropriate to point it out, faced with the children's pride on completing their large billboard for setting the table.

The following day, the five-year-olds share their billboard with the children in the four-year-old classroom during the assembly. From the teacher's notes, which were taken during the event and therefore certainly only partial, it seems the four-year-olds did not ask for much explanation of the drawn elements, and that thanks to the authors' explanations they approved the work, perhaps in part because they were used to setting the table from the previous year. It seems there was also some applause.

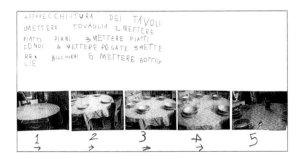

FIGURE 6.35   "Instructions for setting table for the four-year-olds". Setting table: (1) put the tablecloth on; (2) put the flat plates on; (3) put the pasta dishes on; (4) put the cutlery on; (5) put the glasses on; (6) put the bottles on.

218 *Pensiero progettuale* and educational research

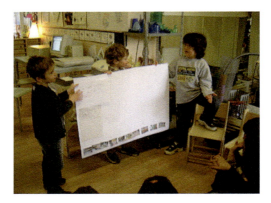

FIGURE 6.36   Presenting the billboard to the four-year-olds.

An unexpected relaunch

Some days later, while Lorenzo and Francesco were playing with Lego bricks and consulting an instruction leaflet to make a construction together, they raised the issue of the size of their own poster of instructions for setting the table and came up with the idea of making a more convenient instruction leaflet. In the children's words: *to photocopy, one for every child, to keep in their pockets and look at if they forget*. Of course, this opportunity was welcomed by the teachers. The idea led the authors to review and re-select their images, and to choose a vertical layout, from bottom to top, similar

FIGURE 6.37   Francesco and Lorenzo's "Instruction leaflet for table-setting from the five-year-old class" to be kept in your pocket.

Pensiero progettuale and educational research **219**

to the one Francesco identified for his drawing, and without further need for instructions, because the arrangement and images were unanimously declared to be clear enough.

Conclusion

The necessary synthesis of work carried out by different groups of children, constructed by teachers with the *atelierista* and *pedagogista* to identify re-launches, is not produced at the end of a project, but is a specifically designerly way of thinking supported by the many notes and documentary steps accompanying the experience as it unfolds. Other specific situations require a synthesis that must take account of different purposes and interlocutors. A synthesis presented to families for example is different from one intended to promote internal *formazione* in the working group of a school, and different again from one presented to colleagues in other *nidi* and *scuole dell'infanzia*. Having discussed the aspect of dialectics among adults in previous chapters, in this one we have tried to emphasise the different voices in a group of children, in a multiplicity of unfolding experiences which although related to reasoning shared among them on the theme of setting the table, activated different expressive languages in a designerly way.

Pensiero progettuale is always transformative, just as the nature of research in daily contexts is transformative, because it generates change in the context it is produced in and resonates throughout the entire system. This attitude of research, which influences the whole life of the school, also promotes changes in habits and routines, and these outcomes of reflection, matured in journeys of research, become new ways of inhabiting our everyday contexts in school. However we define it this is *composite* research [resulting from the addition of several elements], which will always be born from dialogue based on the documentary evidence we have collected. It is, therefore, research that is not produced without the kind of documentation that asks for, but also increases, our competencies of analysis and reflection. We practice problematic thinking which, though it is hard work in some respects, and certainly makes us responsible, does not paralyse or limit us but assigns great trust to every worker in the *scuole dell'infanzia*, and a large space of freedom for trying out, searching, expressing oneself, interpreting, negotiating, and arguing one's point. The gains are reciprocal.

In order to generate research and theories, everyday contexts must not be replicates or replicating, must not be modelled but co-evolutionary, that is to say ever-changing, because they are imbued with the subjectivity of those who dwell in them, the point in history in which they occur, the geography that they are a part of, and the culture they reference. Everyday contexts that inform theories of education and which are themselves informed by these theories continually evoke wonder, the ferment of ideas, and debate. We use theories not only to identify directions for our work, but to appreciate how children think and know the world. An epistemological choice we turn to in the next chapter on the value of culture and an ethic of research.

Notes

1 This reflection appears also in the English language edition of this volume; however, we have chosen to quote the Italian version because it is more comprehensive. Also refer to page 63 of the following: Gandini, L. (2012). History, ideas and basic principles: An interview with Loris Malaguzzi. In C. Edwards, L. Gandini, & G. Forman (Eds.), *The hundred languages of children: The Reggio Emilia experience in transformation* (pp. 27–71). Praeger.

2 For an in-depth look at dining and table setting see Cavallini, I., & Tedeschi, M. (Eds.). (2008). *The languages of food: Recipes, experiences, thoughts.* Reggio Children.

3 Parents can choose whether children end their school day at 1 p.m. after lunch, without their afternoon rest at school, or 4 p.m. after rest and a snack, or at 6.30 p.m.

4 As noted in Chapter 2, auxiliary staff are a constituent part of the school working group, responsible for care and cleanliness of the indoor and outdoor areas and, together with the cook, for preparing and distributing food. They work with all the children and staff in the school. At the beginning of the school year, decisions are made in an *aggiornamento* meting about pairing each auxiliary with a class in the school, paying special attention to ongoing projects and to meetings with families.

5 Times for *aggiornamento*, for the class and the whole school working group, are included in the working hours and are a compulsory part of the work although partly flexible in terms of times and organisations: They are always explicitly agreed among the working group and are given orientation in the annual system *formazione* project.

6 Refer to Chapter 2.

7 In an essay on the study of neural functioning in relation to mathematics (Dehaene, S. (2000). *Il pallino della matematica.* Mondadori), French neuroscientist Stanislas Dehaene writes: "there is no doubt that feelings should have their place in any theory of brain function, including our research into the neural basis of mathematics. A phobia of mathematics can paralyse children to such an extent that it prevents them from learning the simplest algorithms; conversely, a passion for calculation can turn a shepherd into an arithmetical prodigy" (p. 261).

8 The Italian term *proposta* [literal translation "proposal"] is used frequently in Reggio Emilia to indicate the offering of a learning experience (encompassing context, materials, events, ideas, etc) to children.

9 The written intentions of the organisational plan are not exclusively actionable, but include reasoning and choices on spaces, times, materials, instrumental and human resources, observational and documentary structures, hypotheses for subsequent meetings with colleagues and with families.

10 The five-year-old dining area has one round table with about 10 seats, 2 rectangular tables with 6 seats each and a square table for 4.

11 The concept of relaunching will be discussed later.

12 The question was not presented with exactly the same syntax we had agreed on but the meaning did not change. Depending on the group teachers can decide how to favour children's protagonism and the circulation of their thoughts.

13 In attendance the teachers of the C class (MM & LB), the teacher educator (PS), and the *pedagogista* (TF).

14 Since this proposal was made with all 26 children in the class divided into groups of three or four, we preferred to use an audio recorder and some photographs rather than video, in order to speed up the process of putting together the most significant parts.

Pensiero progettuale and educational research **221**

15 Lakoff & Nunez (2000) state that the mind is intrinsically embodied, thinking is mostly unconscious, and that concepts, including those of a mathematical nature, are largely metaphorical.
16 Refer to the *Scuola dell'infanzia* Diana declaration of intents cited above, and specifically to questions 2, 3, and 4.
17 This idea of children's capacity for looking for and finding materials, tools and references in order to achieve their objectives is particularly important for learning. It is something still rarely practised in schools and merits deeper research.
18 The notion of "amiable school" also appears in Gandini, L. (2012). History, ideas and basic principles: An interview with Loris Malaguzzi. In C. Edwards, L. Gandini, & G. Forman (Eds.), *The hundred languages of children: The Reggio Emilia experience in transformation* (pp. 27–71). Praeger. (pp. 41 and 43).
19 Contextual relaunching as an intervention the teacher had not foreseen in the design notes, but which she consciously chooses to do because it is suggested by the current situation. The relaunch can be verbal, gestural, tool-based or mixed, as in this case where the teacher poses the problem of the point of view of those who will be using the drawing by turning the paper round and asking the children a question. It is very useful for contextual relaunches to be noted in the observational documentation in order to evaluate their effectiveness and pertinence at a later date.
20 This is discussed in detail in Chapter 7.
21 Cristian comments on his drawing: *first there is a tablecloth which goes here, and the arrow shows the checked tablecloth that goes on the square table.*
22 A board game with board, characters and dice, similar to the Game of the goose, invented that school year by a different group of six children in the five-year-old class.

References

Cannizzaro, L. P., Crocini, P. P., & Mazzoli, P. (2000). *Numeri: Conoscenze e competenze. Un progetto tra scuola dell'infanzia e scuola di base.* Junior.
Cappelletti, A. M. (2000). *Didattica interculturale della matematica.* CEM.
Cavallini, I., & Tedeschi, M. (Eds.). (2008). *The languages of food: Recipes, experiences, thoughts.* Reggio Children.
Dehaene, S. (2000). *Il pallino della matematica.* Mondadori.
Filippini, T. (2006, January). *Observation, interpretation, and documentation.* Reggio Children International Winter Institute, Reggio Emilia.
Gandini, L. (2012). History, ideas and basic principles: An interview with Loris Malaguzzi. In C. Edwards, L. Gandini, & G. Forman (Eds.), *The hundred languages of children: The Reggio Emilia experience in transformation* (pp. 27–71). Praeger.
Gandini, L. (2017). La storia, le idee, La cultura: La voce e il pensiero di Loris Malaguzzi. Interviste a cura di Lella Gandini. In C. Edwards, L. Gandini, & G. Forman (Eds.), *I cento linguaggi dei bambini: L'approccio di Reggio Emilia all'educazione dell'infanzia* (pp. 55–111). Edizioni Junior/Spaggiari.
Karmiloff-Smith, A. (1995). *Beyond modularity: A developmental perspective on cognitive science.* The MIT Press.
Krechevsky, M. (2001). Form, function and understanding in learning groups: Propositions from the Reggio classrooms. In C. Giudici, C. Rinaldi, & M. Krechevsky (Eds.), *Making learning visible: Children as individual and group learners* (pp. 284–295). Reggio Children.
Lakoff, G., & Nunez, R. (2000). *Where mathematics comes from: How the embodied mind brings mathematics into being.* Basic Books.

222 *Pensiero progettuale* and educational research

Malaguzzi, L. (1991). *Aggiornamento sul tema della matematica* Reggio Emilia, Centro Documentazione e Ricerca Educativa. Reggio Emilia.

Ministero dell'Istruzione dell'Università e della Ricerca. (2012). *Indicazioni nazionali per il curricolo della scuola dell'infanzia e del primo ciclo d'istruzione.* Author.

Preschools and Infant-toddler Centres - Istituzione of the Municipality of Reggio Emilia (2010). *Indications preschools and infant-toddler centres of the Municipality of Reggio Emilia.* Reggio Children.

Tedeschi, M. (2008). A multisensory kitchen. In I. Cavallini & M. Tedeschi (Eds.), *The languages of food: Recipes, experiences, thoughts* (pp. 14–19). Reggio Children.

Vecchi, V. (2001). The curiosity to understand. In C. Giudici, C. Rinaldi, & M. Krechevsky (Eds.), *Making learning visible: Children as individual and group learners* (pp. 158–213). Reggio Children.

Wagner Alibali, M., & DiRusso, A. A. (1999). The function of gesture in learning to count: More than keeping track. *Cognitive Development, 14*(1), 37–56. https://doi.org/10.1016/S0885-2014(99)80017-3

7

THE VALUE OF CULTURE AND AN ETHIC OF RESEARCH

Stefania Giamminuti

Premise: the words we choose

The words we choose to delineate our value and ethic in this chapter – culture and research – are much used, misused, and instrumentalised. We are very much aware of the narratives of power and exclusion that they both conjure and also of the risks inherent in privileging such terms. However, much like Tim Ingold (in Angosto Ferrandez, 2013, p. 299), whilst compelled to consider alternatives, we really couldn't help but use these words, but in so doing we recognise that both culture and research are "the name of a question but [...] not the answer":

> I think we can hold onto the concept of culture as a question, the guiding question, the thing that underwrites our inquiries [...] when it comes to finding answers to the questions of culture, we have to go wherever we need to go. We might get into all sorts of interesting arguments about how people come to know what they do.
>
> *(Ingold, in Angosto Ferrandez, 2013, p. 299)*

The word "culture" emerged so forcefully from interviews for this research project that it was impossible to ignore; teachers, *pedagogistas,* and *atelieristas* all spoke of culture, but when they did so culture was not defined as a graspable state they aspire to emulate nor was it conceived as an elitist place they aim to reach in their daily work. Rather, culture was conceptualised as the question that brings them into dialogue with a world that is larger than themselves, a world which reaches far beyond the often stifling and isolating boundaries of pedagogy and which includes families, citizens, city, and children as valued interlocuters and co-producers of culture.

DOI: 10.4324/9781003181026-7

224 The value of culture and an ethic of research

In relation to the terms research and innovation which permeate "the field" (St. Pierre, 2018) of Reggio Emilia, we find ourselves experiencing an interesting conundrum. This chapter seeks to espouse a view of research that distances itself from the exclusive and elitist views perpetuated by the academy, where one of the authors of this book is firmly located. In addition, the educational project of Reggio Emilia has, albeit tentatively, always pursued dialogue with the academy, whilst successfully resisting the "strictures of methodological ordering" (Manning, 2015, p. 52) that a closer relationship or formal endorsement of the educational project by the universities might entail. In its relationships with the academy, the Reggio Emilia approach has both been rigorously lauded as producing legitimate theoretical knowledge, and reductively dismissed as simply an example of "good practice". This ambiguity reflects how contested is both the field of pedagogy and the discipline of educational research, and it is also an expression of broader mistrust towards progressive experimentation.

Professor Susanna Mantovani (2017) defends Reggio's "experimentation" and she defines it as "qualitative, difficult to measure, but genuine and creative experimentation because it is guided by questions, curiosities, and hypotheses on children and on the physical and social environment where each school is located" (p. 16 [our translation]). She goes on to argue that "definitely Reggio Emilia engages in cultural politics, culture of childhood, culture. And in research [...] Reggio Emilia's pedagogy is today at all effects scientific, founded on paradigms that must be recognised and defended, and which certainly do not belong to an academic pedagogy" (Mantovani, 2017, p. 16 [our translation]). We add our voices in defence of Reggio Emilia's inventiveness, for as Lather (2013) argues, "in inventing practices that do not yet exist, 'deep critical rumblings' abound" (p. 643). It is these deep critical rumblings in response to Reggio Emilia's inventiveness, and the ensuing constant risk of capure, that we aspire to defy with our choice of the words research and innovation in this chapter.

Introduction

Valuing culture in Reggio Emilia is an expression of what Malaguzzi (1975, in Cagliari et al., 2016) called "interested schools":

> This means offering an unambiguous design for interested schools, but also means offering schools divested of ideological and political bias because they are *interested* in their own construction through dialogue, exchange, debate, and through research into ethics and ideals that express their antagonistic and liberating concept of culture. (p. 233)

In illuminating what this "design for interested schools" and "liberating concept of culture" might look like in daily life through the words of the

The value of culture and an ethic of research **225**

protagonists of the Reggio Emilia experience, we draw on the thinking of philosopher Rosi Braidotti (2019) and anthropologist Tim Ingold (2017, 2021). Braidotti (2019) laments what she calls "theory fatigue", whereby neoliberal and right-wing ideologies and practices, specifically in Europe and the USA in the context of populist political movements, have increasingly led to explicit hostility towards the arts, culture, and the field of the Humanities in general. She expresses nostalgia for the times when intellectual disputes centred on defending "an anti-elitist conception of culture, cultural access and production, that favours cultural creativity as a collective activity and a form of democratic participation" (Braidotti, 2019, p. 27). This lament echoes words spoken by Malaguzzi in 1945 when he contended that "culture must become a common estate of all people, not of the select or privileged few" (in Cagliari et al., 2016, p. 38), a priority that has since informed the daily work, infinite choices, and multiple relations of the *nidi* and *scuole dell'infanzia*.

In choosing to elevate the value of culture to prominence in this chapter, we respond to this nostalgia whilst adding our own voices in "speaking truth to power" (Braidotti, 2019, p. 27), drawing hope from the determination of teachers, *pedagogistas,* and *atelieristas* to cross boundaries of knowledge in defiance of growing anti-intellectualism. This is what Braidotti (2019) terms "the posthuman convergence", a movement which "enacts a transversal embrace of conceptual diversity in scholarship" (p. 28) and, most importantly, "favours hybrid mixtures of practical and applied knowledge, and relies on the defamiliarization of our own institutionalized habits and thoughts" (pp. 28–29); this, in our view, is what the experience of Reggio Emilia intends when valuing culture. Thus, in this chapter, we illustrate ways of thinking, being, and doing which draw on culture as a tension towards conceptual diversity, a favouring of the interrelationship between theory, knowledge, and practice, and a resistance towards institutionalisation and conventionality.[1]

Ingold (2021) echoes the thoughts we have delineated above when he expresses his fear that "the imbalances of the world – of wealth, climate and education – will render thinking unsustainable, and jeopardize the life of the mind" (p. 2). He calls this "an epidemic of thoughtlessness" (p. 2) and contends that "if, today, our world is in crisis, it is because we have forgotten how to correspond" (p. 9). Ingold (2017) defines correspondence as "the process by which beings or things literally answer to one another over time" (p. 14). In speculating about what valuing culture might mean for the experience of Reggio Emilia, we welcome correspondence as a concept to think with, because its focus on complexity, process, open-endedness, dialogue, and the value of subjectivities is entirely coherent with what protagonists in Reggio Emilia convey about their experience of social life within educational services and in the city. To ask questions of culture therefore is to ask questions about how knowledge arises within dialogical engagements. Furthermore, our arguments in this chapter convey how for teachers, *atelieristas,* and *pedagogistas* to speak of culture and to value culture means to participate in a creative and collective practice of interdisciplinary thought-making, or in Ingold's (2021) words, to "be ever-present at the cusp where thinking is on the point of settling into the shapes of thought" (p. 11).

In this chapter, we also convey how an ethic of research permeates all aspects – pedagogical, organisational, cultural, social, political – of daily life in Reggio Emilia. In doing so, we embrace a view of research as "the only great freedom we are allowed, as a great possibility and resource" (Malaguzzi, 2021, pp. 27–28). To inform our speculations, we draw upon three key notions from contemporary theorists who question the methodologies and techniques on which the research academies rely in their powerful efforts to govern and promote research imperialism: research as movement (Springgay & Truman, 2018); post qualitative inquiry, experimentation, and "the creation of the new" (St. Pierre, 2021b, p. 6); and "thinking in the making" (Manning, 2015, p. 61).

Culture and the posthuman convergence

> We continued to believe that we could find in our city the conditions and the strength to be a different school, to be an important educational experience; a school that is free, secular, open and welcoming to all, to all cultures, to all social backgrounds, to all beliefs. Because children belong to everyone […] We have an obligation to defend this possibility of choosing a different kind of school.
>
> *(Manuela Pederzoli, teacher, interview with*
> *Stefania Giamminuti, Reggio Emilia)*

In this chapter we grapple with the key question of what constitutes ethical knowledge production within a discipline – education – that is notably constrained by instrumental, conventional, normative, and institutionalised perceptions around the knowledge that counts. We defend the right for schools to "to produce knowledge otherwise" (Braidotti, 2019, p. 91) and thus to be fundamentally different. In engaging with culture as a question, we also ask who might be conceptualised as a "knowing subject" (Braidotti, 2019, p. 101), illuminating how the Reggio Emilia experience has always recognised children, educators, families, citizens, and non-human others as valued knowledge co-producers. Dominant worldviews and practices would relegate schools, families, and teachers to the subservient role of users and reproducers of culture, extraneous to cultural production; instead in Reggio Emilia, thinking and knowing are recognised as taking place in the world (Braidotti, 2019), thus all human and non-human protagonists in the experience are legitimised as knowledge holders, producers, and contaminators.

Braidotti (2019) suggests that within what she calls "the posthuman convergence", knowledge is produced from a stance of complexity, not simply because of the complex social and technological aspects that govern its generation in contemporary times, but also because of the ways in which "complex transversal posthuman subjectivities" are constructed through the "multiple ecologies of becoming subjects" (p. 95). We dwell below on how such multiple ecologies have emerged in the many research projects that have been disseminated as travelling exhibitions from Reggio Emilia and/or Reggio Children publications. Further, we argue that such experiences are premised upon "generative forces and affirmative ethics" (Braidotti, 2019, p. 125), often leading to "conceptual and methodological transformations" (Braidotti, 2019, p. 77) for *nidi, scuole dell'infanzia,* and beyond. The collective and artful qualities of the educational project of Reggio Emilia, which have been extensively discussed in earlier chapters, are essential to generating such expansive transformations. Importantly, as will appear evident from the many fragments of interviews cited in this chapter, within this scenario the *pedagogista* acts as an essential activator of, and a key participant in, ethical knowledge production and conceptual creativity. This responsibility is exemplified in the interview excerpt cited below, where Manuela Pederzoli aligns a definition of culture to the commitment towards being of service to others, thinking collectively, and giving life to a different kind of school:

> To be men and women of culture, thinking educators, who offer in service to others their own talents, their own capabilities, their own ways of being […] The *équipe pedagogica* plays a significant role in coordinating all these thoughts, giving life to the projects and to the "ferment" of ideas that exist within the *nidi* and *scuole dell'infanzia,* and also by making the decisions that are necessary to realise them.
>
> *(Manuela Pederzoli, teacher, interview with*
> *Stefania Giamminuti, Reggio Emilia)*

Children as knowing subjects

> We adults need first and foremost to be convinced that children are not only holders of rights, but that they are holders of their own culture, they are holders of a capacity for developing more culture, and they are capable of building their own culture and contaminating our culture.
>
> *(Malaguzzi, 1993, in Cagliari et al., 2016, p. 423)*

During an *aggiornamento* held at the end of the school year at *Scuola dell'infanzia* Bruno Munari (Figure 7.1), teachers Anna Tamburini and Barbara Beltrami from the three-year-old class, joined by *pedagogista* Simona Bonilauri, *atelierista* Barbara Quinti, and teacher educator Laura Rubizzi, present their draft

FIGURE 7.1   Aggiornamento at *Scuola dell'infanzia* Bruno Munari. Clockwise from left: *pedagogista* Simona Bonilauri, teacher educator Laura Rubizzi, teachers Anna Tamburini and Barbara Beltrami, and *atelierista* Barbara Quinti.

documentation narrating a project on the concept of time.[2] In viewing the documentation, Simona lingers on the research questions that the teachers convey in the document. She dismisses the first question "How to respect the naturalness of children's time?" as conceptually misleading, because, she suggests, "there is already artifice in children from a very young age". Simona recommends removing this question from the document. Then she contends that the second question "How can we find ways of rendering the passage of time more comprehensible to children?" could be expressed more effectively, because its wording implies that the teachers are attempting to conventionalise the passage of time for children.

Atelierista Barbara joins in the discussion, suggesting that the question of how to "render time comprehensible to children" implies an instructional stance on the topic. Simona agrees, and argues that in fact "children construct their own time, there is no need for you to render it comprehensible". In an effort to invite the teachers to focus on what matters, Simona further states: "you can expound all you like on the concept of time. It is not indispensable. There are two questions only that are important: "What is time?" and "What idea of time do children have?" She thus invites all those present at the meeting, and those who will one day read this documentation, to recognise the children as knowing subjects. In fact, some weeks later, in an interview which also involves *pedagogista* Tiziana Filippini, Simona recalls the events of that afternoon at *Scuola* Munari:

Simona Bonilauri:	[speaking to Stefania] during last week's *aggiornamento* at *Scuola* Munari, perhaps you noticed how hard it was for the teachers to think relationally.
Stefania Giamminuti:	Yes, yes.
Tiziana Filippini:	This [capacity to think relationally] is exactly what we work on increasing through *formazione*.
Simona Bonilauri:	In fact, I relaunched the *aggiornamento* and I said to the teachers: "I will come back another time and you have to show me the children". Because they had lost the children completely [...] Somehow, we [*pedagogistas*] have insisted on what we call the adult's cultural premise in *progettazione*. Therefore, we have said to teachers "you must try to communicate your cultural premises", and in this case the topic was time, can you imagine where they've ended up, an incredibly difficult proposition. But we did ask them to consider the cultural premise, didn't we ...
Tiziana Filippini:	But that also means cultural premises in relation to the child, the image of the child that you must not lose sight of.
Simona Bonilauri:	Of course, but the cultural premise is relational. The problem is that they couldn't understand this.
Tiziana Filippini:	Because it's difficult.
Simona Bonilauri:	That's what I'm saying, it's difficult. They take it literally. And so, in this case on the topic of time, they launched into a premise where they said "well time, not time" ...
Tiziana Filippini:	Thousands of concepts about time and the child isn't there anymore.
	(Simona Bonilauri and Tiziana Filippini, pedagogistas, *interview with Stefania Giamminuti, Reggio Emilia)*

To outsiders, it may appear as though the *confronto* at *Scuola* Munari between teachers, *pedagogista* and *atelierista* is somewhat harsh and unforgiving. What is missed in this interpretation of the events is the fact that these exchanges occur in an ecology of ethical knowledge production, where all participants concur in the responsibility and right to "produce knowledge otherwise" (Braidotti, 2019, p. 91), and where all adults share a fundamental commitment to making visible to others the child as a knowing subject, in relational dialogue with other knowing subjects, humans, and non-humans.

230 The value of culture and an ethic of research

As teacher Marina Castagnetti emphasises below, it is within such episodes of *confronto*, where contexts are considered from a multiplicity of critical perspectives, that culture is generated:

> To observe and come to know a context from multiple perspectives, this is an exercise in democracy [...] Within the *confronto* that we nurture, everyone should become capable of recognising the qualities of the work being done, and by qualities I intend the different levels that give value to the work the children are doing and the thoughts the children are elaborating, in a synergistic way [...] It is also fundamental to have a relationship of reciprocal trust, where we are discussing this documentation, this project, and I know that you will contribute ... it is an intellectual expectation. If we talk about solidarity and giving value to children's processes of knowledge construction and ways of learning, giving value to their culture, then we all concur in this endeavour.
>
> *(Marina Castagnetti, teacher, interview with
> Stefania Giamminuti, Reggio Emilia)*

All concur in making children's culture visible, within a framework of intellectual ferment that values both the thinking of adults and the knowledge of children. Teacher Lucia Colla notes how important this stance is for the *nidi:* "I have always believed that the *nido*, which we view as an educational institution and as a place where an extraordinary culture of very young children is constructed, is otherwise undervalued and generates very little expectations in relation to its capabilities" (interview with Stefania Giamminuti, Reggio Emilia). *Atelierista* Mirella Ruozzi further emphasises the risks inherent in neglecting children's knowledge, and she identifies documentation as a key ally in cultural thought-making:

> An adult who studies and reads, and adult who interrogates herself on how to bring children closer [...] I document what are brief fragments of children's learning processes that give me a sense of where the children are, where I can be together with the children. They are there. You can support them to go further, but you have to know where they are. Otherwise, you risk offering experiences that are as old as anything, and the children have already been there.
>
> *(Mirella Ruozzi, atelierista, interview with
> Stefania Giamminuti, Reggio Emilia)*

A fundamental criticism that can be levelled at pre-packaged and linear educational programs and policies is that they dismiss the child as knowing subject, offering instead experiences that are repetitive and disconnected from the world. In response to such normative approaches, which act to silence culture and difference, it is essential to give voice to all knowing subjects, each one an expression of a subjective declination of culture as dynamic, situated, and in constant transformation. Further, in settler-colonial spaces, such reductive pedagogies risk silencing indigenous children through privileging "constructions of knowledge that assimilate and demand normative cultural responses" (Rigney & Kelly, 2021, p. 9). As Rigney and Kelly (2021) argue, indigenous children's learning and listening is constrained through the perpetuation and enduring power of such normative and blind pedagogies. However, in being responsive to a plurality of knowing subjects, it is possible to work towards ensuring "the visibility of First Nations epistemes in dialogue with western traditions and diasporic communities from around the world" (Rigney & Kelly, 2021, p. 2). A school that welcomes a plurality of knowing subjects, truly listening to all children and contesting the enduring power of hegemonical discourses and conventional hierarchical structures is a democratic school:

> The democratic school should not only be permanently open to its students' contextual reality in order to understand them better and to exercise its teaching activity better, but it should also be disposed to learn of its relationship with the concrete context. Thus, proclaiming itself democratic, it must be truly humble in order to be able to recognize itself, often learning from one who was never schooled. The democratic school that we need is not one in which only the teacher teaches, in which only the student learns, and in which the principal is the all-powerful commander.
>
> *(Freire, 2005, p. 133)*

In her argument for a posthuman convergence, Braidotti (2019) refers to what she terms "missing people": those who have been "eliminated, disqualified" from major and often minor science – such as indigenous people and "feminists, queers, otherwise enabled, non-humans or technologically mediated existences" (p. 162). While Braidotti herself does not mention young children, we believe that as a minority who depend entirely on adults for their visibility and are normalised within the dominant culture, young children also belong to a "missing people". For educators in Reggio Emilia and those who are internationally in dialogue with this experience, to value a culture of childhood is to enact a "radical politics of immanence" and to constitute children as "political subjects of knowledge" (Braidotti, 2019, p. 162). Teachers, *pedagogistas*, and *atelieristas* struggle together for children's visibility and emergence as knowing subjects and citizens. As Braidotti (2019) notes, such struggles require the formation of alliances[3]; in fact, the *confronto* that occurred in the *aggiornamento* at *Scuola* Munari recounted above is an event that relies on cultural alliances of solidarity between teachers, *atelieristas,* and *pedagogistas.*

232 The value of culture and an ethic of research

The following interview excerpts further exemplify the significance of such alliances for individuals and for the collective:

> I have known *pedagogistas* that are extremely cultured. This does not mean that they are erudite in every field of knowledge, but rather they are cultured in the sense of being able to locate research references to resolve a problem, even very concrete problems, not only theoretical ones.
>
> *(Ethel Carnevali, teacher, interview with Stefania Giamminuti, Reggio Emilia)*

> A different teacher, a teacher who seeks out different cultural opportunities and different spaces for *formazione*.
>
> *(Marina Castagnetti, teacher, interview with Stefania Giamminuti, Reggio Emilia)*

> We have to be capable of listening to the contemporary, and modifying our own role. We are very different from the teachers that opened the first *scuole dell'infanzia* in Reggio Emilia, and we will continue to be different in the future. We have to be open to transforming our professionalism in tune with the contemporary, in relation to a social, political and cultural context that is always evolving.
>
> *(Ethel Carnevali, teacher, interview with Stefania Giamminuti, Reggio Emilia)*

> I was a young teacher back then, and Prof. Malaguzzi intimidated me a little, but I also felt that his mind was open 360 degrees. He was a man of culture, who communicated to us from the very beginning how important it was to educate to beauty, to the arts, to participate in and know of the contemporary. He expected you, as a teacher, to be a person of culture, a passionate person.
>
> *(Manuela Pederzoli, teacher, interview with Stefania Giamminuti, Reggio Emilia)*

These excerpts highlight how teachers and *pedagogistas*, "in producing knowledge [...] are also producing their own selves as people who know" (Ingold, 2021, p. 10). This aspiration towards becoming a "different" teacher, a knowledgeable and passionate teacher in tune with the contemporary, who participates in the construction of a "different" school, is born of broader cultural, social, and political ferment. Such ferment was a defining feature of the key decades of the 60s, 70s, and 80s, as Ivana Soncini recalls:

> We were all heading in the same direction of cultural sensibility, and you were supported by the cultural and social ferment of the city. *Pedagogistas*

The value of culture and an ethic of research **233**

were facilitated within this climate to create links between a pedagogical approach that was dedicated to research – the progressive school, the school as laboratory – and a progressive cultural and social context.

> *(Ivana Soncini, psychologist and member of the*
> *pedagogical coordination, interview with*
> *Stefania Giamminuti, Reggio Emilia)*

The progressive political, social, and cultural context of the city of Reggio Emilia facilitated the emergence of a shared view of children as knowing subjects, however the pathway was not always strewn with success, as Tiziana Filippini recalls:

> The pedagogical coordination always had to strive for strategies that would make visible, communicable and debatable the idea of services for children, the idea of the city's investment […] in the 1970s we were in Via Toschi, under the offices of the PCI [Italian Communist Party], and we were striking and shouting because they wanted to cut, like they did in Modena, first the *atelierista* and then the internal kitchen.
>
> *(Tiziana Filippini*, pedagogista, *interview with*
> *Stefania Giamminuti, Reggio Emilia)*

Cultural alliances and political struggle go hand in hand in this experience, and furthermore the gains of history do not guarantee smooth sailing in the future, as Malaguzzi (2021) cautions us to remember that "the image of the child is a precarious image, an oscillating image that changes with history" (p. 47). As teacher Daniela Iotti emphasises, documentation is a key ally in communicating this image of the child as knowing subject and citizen:

> It is important to consider communication, privileging videos that convey concepts and that do not constitute, somehow, a pleasant culmination at the end of a discourse. We have video-recorded events in the city, making visible our experiences within the city and our relationships with the city. However, with our recordings we do not wish to convey simply the pleasantness of an event, rather we want to communicate to the city the importance of children's participation as citizens of the present.
>
> *(Daniela Iotti, teacher, interview with*
> *Stefania Giamminuti, Reggio Emilia)*

To make visible the child as knowing subject requires the creation of enduring alliances beyond the school environment, and well beyond the confines of educational forums. The primary responsibility of elaborating cultural syntheses and of maintaining dialogue with local politics falls to the *pedagogistas* who, in the words of Simona Bonilauri, act as "partisans[4]":

> The pedagogical coordination has a fundamental role of cultural synthesis and cultural elaboration. It is also an instrument of cohesion, and it is a political lever within the local municipal administration. Therefore, we *pedagogistas* are like partisans, and we believe we have had and continue to have a decisive role at the cultural and political levels. We have always carefully curated the idea of the culture that is created within educational services. The culture that services produce needs to be elaborated, nurtured, and sustained.
>
> *(Simona Bonilauri, pedagogista, interview with*
> *Stefania Giamminuti, Reggio Emilia)*

In their quotidian partisan efforts to elaborate and sustain the culture produced within the *nidi* and *scuole dell'infanzia*, teachers, *pedagogistas,* and *atelieristas* together "contribute to the collective construction of social horizons of hope" (Braidotti, 2019, p. 91) and they "re-ignite a democratic imaginary worthy of our times" (Braidotti, 2019, p. 94). More recently, as the city of Reggio Emilia emerges from the devastating years of the COVID-19 pandemic, where children "were often invisible in the public debate" (Mucchi et al., 2021), teacher Evelina Reverberi (2021) revisits with contemporary urgency a historical commitment to represent children as knowing subjects:

> The city and those who live in it have never needed children's thoughts as much as this moment in history, their traces accompanying us to regain a gaze curious and full of hope, capable of feeling wonder, a gaze going beyond the schematic where everything finds spaces of interconnection. All this lets us imagine a city that highlights children's thinking, so that everyone can feel their value, breathing life into a great network of thoughts between adults and children, migrating through the city, into homes, passing through visible and invisible boundaries to build a planetary dimension of relations [...] If school is not a place of indifference, but lives its context fully, then dialogue between school and city [...] will always help the community to grow. (p. 4)

Schools as interested places, where culture remains a question of care and solidarity. Further, for those living in settler-colonial spaces, we are compelled to recognise that "much has been silenced [...] history is contested [...] knowledge has been and continues to be manipulated" (Bird Rose, 2004, p. 11). Cultures emerge also in the silences and in the contested, liminal spaces where intellectual and physical oppression is a feature of the lives of many children and families. We now turn to illuminating the ways in which the democratic participation that the educational project of Reggio Emilia consistently aspires to extends to non-human others, creating "a becoming-world of knowledge practices" (Braidotti, 2019, p. 102) in which missing peoples (and non-peoples) correspond with each other.

Thinking that takes place in the world

> There is a qualitative difference between accepting the structural interdependence among species and actually treating the non-humans as knowledge collaborators.
>
> *(Braidotti, 2019, p. 77)*

We delineated above how we perceive of culture as a question about the knowledge that matters, and about whom we choose to elevate to the position of knowing subjects. We now turn to the question of culture as thinking, and specifically the question of where thinking takes places and who participates in it. Whilst we firmly concur in the project of making visible the young child as knowing and thinking subject, there are also risks in focusing *only* on the child, as *pedagogista* Elena Giacopini cautions: "perhaps for too many years we have contributed to generating a misunderstanding that continues to have currency today: that it is sufficient to listen to children. Listening seriously to children is certainly fundamental, but it is essential to premise and clarify the educational intentions that inform our listening" (interview with Stefania Giamminuti, Reggio Emilia).

In recognising that such intentions must encompass adults and non-humans as knowledge collaborators, we caution from a common misinterpretation of the Reggio Emilia pedagogy as pursuing "the dogma of children's interests" (Giamminuti et al., 2022). This dogma, fuelled by the misunderstandings that Elena refers to, is "premised on the assumption of human, and specifically child, centredness, which effectively places all others in subordinate roles, rotating around the centre in hierarchical levels of importance" (Giamminuti et al., 2022, p. 4). Hence, we are not proposing the child as the only knowing subject but rather, as Simona Bonilauri and Tiziana Filippini discuss in the interview excerpt cited above, we wish to emphasise that the cultural premise is always relational, dismissive of "narcissistic singularity" (Bird Rose, 2004, p. 21), and welcoming of complex dialogic circumstances. The experience of Reggio Emilia continually seeks dialogue with a conversing world composed of a multiplicity of "things" such as paper, thread, lines, words, stones, trees, snow (Ingold, 2021) and more.

> Nature is not silent. It may have nothing to say, and were our ears open only to facts and propositions *about* the world, as the protocols of science require, then indeed we would hear nothing. We would be deaf to the gale

236 The value of culture and an ethic of research

in the trees, the roar of the waterfall and the song of the birds. For these are propositions that stand only for themselves. They are *of* the world, and it behoves us to attend to them.

(Ingold, 2021, p. 122)

The *nidi* and *scuole dell'infanzia* have always been open to attending to and conversing with the world, consistently engaging in a tension towards connectivity that frees all – humans and non-humans – from "the bondage of monologue" (Bird Rose, 2004, p. 21). As *pedagogista* Paola Cagliari (2019) emphasises in relation to the system-wide research project on "encounters with living things and digital landscapes" (Vecchi et al., 2019), "we must let children discover that what we have with digital tools is a *dialogue*, in which it is necessary for the intelligence of human beings to meet the intelligence of devices" (p. 13). Furthermore, *atelierista* Filippo Chieli with *pedagogistas* Tiziana Filippini and Elena Maccaferri (2022), while discussing a recent project on "resonances between dance and music" (Anceschi & Maccaferri, 2022), highlight that the aim of *progettazione* is to "build contexts which allow the children to find themselves in situations which are significant for them, where the learning processes can take root in lived experiences" (p. 108).

Many historical projects from the *nidi* and *scuole dell'infanzia* disrupted the dominant and normative "monologue" – or scientific-factual approach to learning about the world – replacing it with "noisy and unruly processes capable of finding dialogue with other people and with the world itself" (Bird Rose, 2004, p. 21). Such experiences include: encounters between children and stone lions in the city's *Piazza San Prospero* (Reggio Children, 1996); enchantments with birds (Reggio Children, 1995) and fish (Cipolla & Reverberi, 1996); dialogues with columns (Filippini & Vecchi, 2011); encounters with light in the ateliers (Filippini & Vecchi, 2011); conversations with city parks (Reggio Children, 2008) and city spaces (Davoli & Ferri, 2000); and engagements with food, ecology, and art (Cavallini & Tedeschi, 2008). More recent examples include: resonances between children, dance, and music (Anceschi & Maccaferri, 2022); encounters with words, mark-making, and matter/materials (Vecchi & Ruozzi, 2015); and conversations with living things and digital landscapes (Vecchi et al., 2019). Importantly, this extensive but reductive list does not include the infinite gestures of daily attunement to the world that occur within the *nidi* and *scuole dell'infanzia*[5] and which may not make their way into large-scale exhibitions and publications, but are nevertheless treasured by children, teachers, and families as reminders of "modest protests and precarious pleasures" (Alaimo, 2016, p. 188).

This practice of "thinking as the stuff of the world" (Alaimo, 2016) requires the complicity of adults whose own thinking also takes place within the world.

The value of culture and an ethic of research **237**

FIGURE 7.2   *Pedagogista* Paola Strozzi, *atelierista* Paola Gallerani, and teacher Annalisa Rainieri critically considering an offering for the children in the three-year-old classroom at *Scuola dell'infanzia* La Villetta.

Teachers, *atelieristas,* and *pedagogistas* constantly pursue knowledge beyond the boundaries of pedagogy:

> I value the culture that we, as teachers, must have in order to engage in research with children. It is important for teachers to go beyond the boundaries of pedagogy, and to engage with other fields of knowledge.
> *(Giulia Ovi, teacher, interview with Stefania Giamminuti, Reggio Emilia)*

> We work assiduously on didactics, on environments, on layouts of space and materials, but this is a project that relates to people's lives, to children's lives. This idea that we propose of a different man and woman, for a new humanity, a new cosmogony, not just humans. I believe that a *pedagogista* within this educational project should be as cultured as possible, open to many fields of knowledge. Malaguzzi said so, Malaguzzi absolutely *was* so.
> *(Paola Strozzi,* pedagogista, *interview with Stefania Giamminuti, Reggio Emilia)*

Culture emerges here once again as a question of the knowledge and thinking that matters, highlighting the urgent need to disrupt the confines of educational discipline knowledge with its relentless pursuit of factual content

238 The value of culture and an ethic of research

knowledge. Braidotti (2019) identifies such disruption of "disciplinary purity" as a defining feature of the "PostHumanities", whose "strength is directly proportional to their relational ability to open up to each other and to the world" (p. 102). Thus, in recognising that the practice of conversing with the world is premised on "relational openness" (Braidotti, 2019), teachers, *pedagogistas,* and *atelieristas* constantly enact collaborative and democratic practices of knowledge production, and they disrupt conventionality of thought.

Affirmative ethics and conceptual creativity

> I could never see myself working in another kind of school, that would constrain me within a reductive role. Instead, I aspired to multifaceted work, where I could be a teacher with children but at the same time, I could be co-constructing things with parents, dialoguing, engaging in *progettazione* together, creating cultural contexts.
>
> *(Francesca Forenzi, teacher, interview with*
> *Stefania Giamminuti, Reggio Emilia)*

Several of the interview excerpts cited throughout this chapter have referred to the appeal of the *nidi* and *scuole dell'infanzia* in being different and offering broader scenarios for cultural connection. What is also unique about this difference, in relation to other known pedagogical experimentations, is that it is incredibly broad-reaching and enduring. Peter Moss (in Cagliari et al., 2016) defines the educational project of Reggio Emilia as "radical public education enacted on an unprecedented scale and sustained over an unparalleled period of time" (p. xiv). We wish to highlight here how this exuberance and liveliness is sustained by a stance of "affirmative ethics" (Braidotti, 2019) which embodies hope and a constant collective tension towards conceptual creativity.

Braidotti (2019) defines affirmative ethics as "a collective practice of constructing social horizons of hope, in response to the flagrant injustices, the perpetuation of old hierarchies and new forms of domination" (p. 156). This seems to us entirely in tune with the experience of Reggio Emilia from its beginnings arising out of the domination of fascism, to the present struggles and into the future. In fact, as the co-authors of this book discussed the concept of affirmative ethics in one of many editorial meetings, Paola Cagliari reflected upon how, when entering the *Scuola dell'infanzia Diana* as a teacher in the 1980s, she breathed affirmative ethics, encapsulated in the invitation to always maintain a valuing gaze on the other, and to embrace a critical stance towards habit, stereotype, and intellectual laziness. Affirmative ethics endures as a foundational stance of the Reggio Emilia ecological system, and as an obligation to the hopeful future of the experience and of its protagonists.

Conversely, conventional educational settings generally resist any invitation towards possibility; rather, it suits the hegemony to dampen any efforts at innovation through the pervasive narratives of negativity and habit: "it can't be done here" or "this is the way it has always been done". Such responses prize governability, ignore the value of culture, silence differences, eschew alternatives, and perpetuate injustices. Giroux (2021) paints a despairing picture of what he calls "pandemic pedagogy", or a contemporary time defined by: "teachers under siege"; "education in crisis"; a "fascist abyss"; the "plague of thoughtlessness"; "organized forgetting"; and "the plague of inequality". He further emphasises that pandemic pedagogy "produces an endless array of authoritarian pedagogical practices that serve to exploit, dominate, and depoliticize us" (Giroux, 2021, p. xiii). Much of this politics of domination is laid at the door of neoliberalism, which, as Braidotti (2019) laments, is "killing our freedom softly" (p. 94). To participate in this foreboding and negativity, however, would result in further subjugation, as Braidotti (2019) herself notes:

> Negativity expresses itself in a social and psychological dimming of a sense of possibility, which triggers a systemic fragmentation and a shattering of our relational capacity. This weaking of the desire to act often feeds an appeal to external powers to take over the task of organizing how to live our lives. (p. 179)

The deficit political and cultural discourses that surround teachers and educational contexts today serve the interests of those in power, who feel legitimated to produce ever-increasing instruments of surveillance and accountability. Braidotti (2019) proposes "affirmative ethics" as an alternative to negativity, as a praxis which "defends community-based experiments to transform the negative conditions and states into affirmative alternatives" (p. 175). At the core of affirmative ethics is the tension towards activating transformation, with collectives enacting a cooperative actualisation of possibilities and as yet unimagined interconnections (Braidotti, 2019). Essential to this is a culture of valuing unconventional knowledge production and promoting innovative collective thought and action. Braidotti (2019) emphasises that "affirmative ethics build on radical relationality, aiming at empowerment. This means increasing one's ability to relate to multiple others, in a productive and mutually enforcing manner, and creating a community that actualizes this ethical propensity" (p. 167). The cultural synergies and solidarities that characterise the relationships among teachers, *pedagogistas* and *atelieristas* in Reggio Emilia are premised on nurturing radical relationality and experimentation. This extends to the city and its citizens, including families, through the creation of multiple, tangible "affirmative alternatives" (Braidotti, 2019, p. 180).

For example, as the citizens of Reggio Emilia emerged from the COVID-19 pandemic emergency, an exhibition was held in the historical building

240 The value of culture and an ethic of research

Palazzo Magnani, titled *Somersaults of Thoughts*. This exhibition was one of many initiatives created during the pandemic, which were aimed at continuing to "guarantee children's right to social life, beauty, and culture" (Mucchi et al., 2021, p. 1) throughout unimaginable times, with the *nidi* and *scuole dell'infanzia* continuing to offer themselves as "a laboratory for learning and relations with children, families and communities" (Mucchi et al., 2021, p. 1). *Somersaults of Thoughts* was conceived as a dialogue with a retrospective exhibition of the work of illustrator Olimpia Zagnoli, and it proposed itself as a sort of "manifesto of children's and teachers' creativity, inviting the city and others to renew their thinking on childhood culture, keeping investment high in quality places of education for children from birth" (Mucchi et al., 2021, p. 2). This potential is acknowledged by parents, who upon visiting the exhibition commented thus:

> This city exhibition is an extraordinary event, that lets an infant-toddler centre leave the infant-toddler centre to inhabit a cultural place in the city with full entitlement and with such young children.
> *(Daniela, cited in Mucchi et al., 2021, p. 8)*

> The *Sommersaults of Thoughts* exhibition gives value to the culture of childhood, both through context and through content – that is to see the parallels between art and childhood.
> *(Benedetta, cited in Mucchi et al., 2021, p. 9)*

These affirmative words embody Giroux's (2021) more hopeful prediction that "the force of education operates in multiple social and public spheres and those spaces should be places where individuals can realize themselves as informed and critically engaged citizens" (p. xii). Thus, to conceive of the value of culture through the lens of affirmative ethics is to create the conditions for keeping democracy alive in times of crisis, in schools and beyond. Tangibly, this occurs by imagining and creating civic opportunities for recognising young children and their educators as knowledge producers. Such possibilities are at once locally conceived and globally significant, and they are within the reach of all of us, for once an ethics of affirmation is welcomed, then "it is logically and materially impossible to exhaust all possibilities" (Braidotti, 2019, p. 180). As Braidotti (2019) urges us, "the ethical implication is to get going [...] because of the abundance of the yet unfulfilled possibilities, much remains to be done [...] we need to start somewhere, however humbly" (p. 181).

It is important to note that a key quality of such ethical and affirmative initiatives is that they are not profit-oriented and opportunistic, but rather that they produce knowledge through collective practices. Essential to this is a shared stance of conceptual creativity and generosity of thought. Conceptual creativity relies on the capacity to build knowledge cooperatively, and thus to welcome collaborations with disparate disciplines and voices, and in particular with the arts. Examples of such collaborations abound in Reggio Emilia, with notable projects including the historical *Theater Curtain* (Vecchi, 2002) where the children of the *Scuola* Diana designed and created the actual curtain of the Ariosto Theatre in Reggio Emilia, and most recently *Resonances between Dance and Music* (Anceschi & Maccaferri, 2022) which saw children and adults converse with dancers and musicians and with the instruments of their arts. Notably, the publication that narrates the latter project includes a number of contributions from eminent voices pertaining to the fields of philosophy, ethnomusicology, neuroscience, and the arts. Seeking out these knowledgeable points of view and nurturing dialogue with known cultural figures in Italy and beyond has always been a responsibility of the *pedagogistas*. Braidotti (2019) notes that "critical thinkers need conceptual creativity as well as renewed trust in the cognitive and political importance of the imagination as a collectively shared resource" (p. 84); imagination is a collectively shared resource is the epistemological premise of *pensiero progettuale*.

Culture as correspondence

What is culture, and what does it mean to create culture? I believe culture is born of lively group work.

(Loredana Garofalo, teacher, interview with
Stefania Giamminuti, Reggio Emilia)

Professional relationships in Reggio Emilia are premised on relationality, reciprocity, solidarity, and care, and the question of culture is fundamentally inseparable from these collective and individual dispositions and practices. Thus the group work that Loredana refers to goes beyond a simple interaction amongst individuals with different professional roles, to become a "correspondence":

Correspondence is about the ways along which lives, in their perpetual unfolding or becoming, simultaneously join together and differentiate themselves, one from another. This shift from interaction to correspondence entails a fundamental reorientation, from the between-ness of beings and things to their *in-between-ness*.

(Ingold, 2021, p. 9)

In-between-ness implies collective care and shared obligations, to join in with each other, as Ingold (2021) clarifies: "interaction goes back and forth as agents, facing each other on opposite banks of the river, trade messages, missiles, and merchandise. But to correspond, in my terms, is to join with the swimmer in the midstream. It is a matter not of taking sides but of going

242 The value of culture and an ethic of research

along" (p. 18). This bears a close relationship to Malaguzzi's contention that "learning and teaching should not stand on opposite banks and just watch the river flow by" (in Gandini, 2012, p. 58). This practice of going along together, and its significance in both contributing to making visible a strong culture of childhood and in transforming pedagogy, is exemplified in the words of Simona Marani:

> To engage in *confronto* with *pedagogistas* is for us an opportunity for *formazione*, because they assist us in interpreting children's research through a more cultured lens, and they support us in knowing children's culture more deeply. Reflecting together helps us to transform teaching and learning contexts, and importantly it supports us in crafting relaunches, which are notably difficult for teachers.
>
> *(Simona Marani, teacher, interview with*
> *Stefania Giamminuti, Reggio Emilia)*

Pedagogista Paola Strozzi echoes these sentiments when she states that one of the most important attributes of *pedagogistas* is "to be capable of generating this capacity to make connections" (interview with Stefania Giamminuti, Reggio Emilia). This is a responsive approach to the collective work, where to correspond means to carry shared responsibility. As Ingold (2017) contends, "there cannot be one without the other: to be answerable, one has to be able to answer. And to be able to answer, one has to be present" (p. 20). This practice of answerability does not remain only within the *pedagogista*-teacher relationship, but rather it extends to broader cultural scenarios in which *pedagogistas* are fully present, as noted by those acting in different roles within the system:

> The pedagogical coordination has this particular filter or gaze, together with a constant and quotidian possibility of relations with the *nidi* and *scuole dell'infanzia*, that confers it the responsibility to maintain current knowledge and ongoing analysis of that which occurs within the *nidi* and *scuole dell'infanzia*, in relation to the city. When I say "city" it's a metaphor that relates to the social, political, cultural, or pedagogical questions and debates, alongside daily life in the schools.
>
> *(Claudia Giudici, President, Preschools and Infant-toddler*
> *Centres - Istituzione of the Municipality of Reggio Emilia,*
> *interview with Stefania Giamminuti, Reggio Emilia)*

> Our relationship with the pedagogical coordination also serves the purpose of keeping us connected to the cultural and political scenarios.
>
> *(Simona Marani, teacher, interview with*
> *Stefania Giamminuti, Reggio Emilia)*

The value of culture and an ethic of research **243**

> We *pedagogistas* have the gift of living of relations, of constantly listening. We have always emphasised this relationship, which is none other than understanding how things change in the city. We keep ourselves constantly informed of how things change within the municipal council, and within each working group in the *nidi* and *scuole dell'infanzia*.
>
> *(Tiziana Filippini,* pedagogista, *interview with Stefania Giamminuti, Reggio Emilia)*

The capacity to correspond is a fundamental quality of the role of the *pedagogista*. Furthermore, the points of view shared by Claudia, Simona, and Tiziana convey the social life of the *nidi* and *scuole dell'infanzia*, and of the city and its cultural and political scenarios, as "a long conversation, a toing and froing that carries on indefinitely" (Malinowski, n.d. cited in Ingold, 2021, p. 152). Ingold (2021) points out that these conversations extend beyond human beings and indeed beyond living things. This is acknowledged in Reggio Emilia where, for example, in the research project *Mosaic of Marks, Words, Material* (Vecchi & Ruozzi, 2015), marks, matter/materials, words and children were all conceived as conversing partners and generators of rich cognitive and expressive possibilities. Correspondence in social life in Reggio Emilia is a way of "living a life with others – humans and non-humans all – that is congizant of the past, finely attuned to the conditions of the present and speculatively open to the possibilities of the future" (Ingold, 2021, p. 200). This speculative openness turns culture into a question. Our concluding remarks on the value of culture relate to its significance for those who engage in their own toing and froing, beyond Reggio Emilia.

> This is what I have been calling *correspondence*, in the sense of not coming up with some exact match or simulacrum for what we find in the things and happenings going on around us, but of *answering* to them with interventions, questions and responses of our own. It is as though we were involved in an exchange of letters. "Let's meet the world" […] is an invitation – an exhortation or command even – to join in such a correspondence.
>
> *(Ingold, 2021, p. 200)*

Our invitation is to join in an exchange of letters, corresponding with and answering to Reggio Emilia with obligations of our own, understanding that the only way to move forward is to meet the world.

An ethic of research: the creation of the new

In Reggio Emilia, an ethic of research and a historical resistance towards the "dogmatic" (St. Pierre, 2021a) leads to an intellectual tension towards the "not yet" (Braidotti, 2019; St. Pierre, 2021a) and a collective obligation towards

244 The value of culture and an ethic of research

the creation of "the new" (Kuntz & St. Pierre, 2021; St. Pierre, 2021b), as rendered by *pedagogista* Elena Giacopini:

> We had to invent a way of working with children - not just relational care, not just dyadic relationship. Research as a daily attitude was enacted through observation and especially *confronto* between adults in relation to our interpretations, welcoming multiple theoretical references and connecting dialectics, theory, and practice [...] If we research, we must do so on something we do not know, or on something regarding which we have open questions, questions which may surprise us. That's why it's hard work, because generally habit, or the presumption that you already possess adequate knowledge, forcefully emerge. Often, researching with children gifts wonder and fun, and importantly it leads to discovery of new theories, verbal and visual metaphors, and displacements which surprise us and make us feel good [...] Perhaps this is what it means to research in school: to consider the implications in daily life, to adopt other organisations, to renew didactics, to value and legitimise the knowledge expressed by children, and to transform the quotidian, otherwise it isn't research. The most significant outcome of experiential and contextual research must be transformation of daily life, or it doesn't become something that is useful for the school.
>
> *(Elena Giacopini,* pedagogista, *interview with*
> *Stefania Giamminuti, Reggio Emilia)*

In interviews for this project, the "the not yet" and "the new" were often rendered with the term "innovation", not to be confused with the normative definitions of innovation that dominate conventional academic research. Innovation as transformation of the quotidian has been an epistemological premise of the educational project, and a key responsibility for the *pedagogistas*, from the time when Loris Malaguzzi, together with others such as Sergio Neri and Bruno Ciari, brought to this profession "a strong political stance, and their concern was innovation" (Paola Cagliari, Director, Preschools and Infant-toddler Centres - Istituzione of the Municipality of Reggio Emilia, interview with Stefania Giamminuti, Reggio Emilia). Thus emerged "a role of the *pedagogista* that is not crushed by managerial and administrative tasks, but rather is a role of constant research and *formazione*" (Claudia Giudici, President, Preschools and Infant-toddler Centres - Istituzione of the Municipality of Reggio Emilia, interview with Stefania Giamminuti, Reggio Emilia).

Paola Cagliari further qualifies that "it was Malaguzzi who decided that *pedagogistas* would not be directly engaged in administrative tasks. He acknowledged the necessity of administrative thought, but he did not believe in dedicating time to administrative action" (interview with Stefania Giamminuti, Reggio Emilia). The practical decision to liberate *pedagogistas* from routine administrative tasks freed up space for dedication to research and

The value of culture and an ethic of research **245**

innovation. Furthermore, the choice of creating a pedagogical coordination, differently to more conventional organisational leadership structures in Italy and elsewhere that rely on one internal coordinator/principal[6], elevated innovation from an individual interest to a collective obligation: "as a *pedagogista* you don't simply work with your own *nidi* and your own *scuole dell'infanzia*, rather you have a responsibility of research and innovation towards the system" (Claudia Giudici, President, Preschools and Infant-toddler Centres - Istituzione of the Municipality of Reggio Emilia, interview with Stefania Giamminuti, Reggio Emilia).

For the *nidi* and *scuole dell'infanzia* therefore, to participate in innovation means to create the conditions for "auto-generative change within each school, leading to research that generates elements of transformation and innovation, of new perspectives at the level of the system" (Paola Cagliari, Director, Preschools and Infant-toddler Centres - Istituzione of the Municipality of Reggio Emilia, Interview with Stefania Giamminuti, Reggio Emilia). As Ivana Soncini acknowledges, such a quality is unusual in pedagogical settings and relies on documentation:

> I would claim research and innovation as a merit. Perhaps in this we were the first ones to claim these terms from the sciences, to whom research and innovation are usually attributed. Because pedagogy has always been considered lesser. When I go elsewhere and claim that the privileged context for observation of a child with difficulties remains the school, there's immediately a resounding applause, because the school is always considered subordinate by those who believe that research and innovation are the purview of clinical contexts.
>
> *(Ivana Soncini, psychologist and member of the pedagogical coordination,*
> *interview with Stefania Giamminuti, Reggio Emilia)*

In the opening of this chapter, we briefly delineated how, despite being reductively dismissed by the academy as simply an example of "good practice", the experience of Reggio Emilia is in fact scientific. The *nidi* and *scuole dell'infanzia* generate theory and research, though this might not be apparent when judging the experience from the perspective of conventional methodological approaches that dominate research in the social sciences and humanities more broadly, and education specifically. As Manning (2015) notes in relation to "research-creation" (which we will explore below), the research that Reggio Emilia engages in and conveys to the broader field of pedagogy "proposes new forms of knowledge, many of which are not intelligible within current understandings of what knowledge might look like" (Manning, 2015, p. 53). When judged from the perspective of current understanding of what constitutes pedagogical knowledge, Reggio Emilia's tension towards the new and different is easily misunderstood. Further, as St. Pierre (2021b) argues, "so much effort in preexisting social science research methodologies focuses on how to represent the real, authentic lived experiences of human beings. Representation is not the goal of post qualitative inquiry. Its goal is, instead, experimentation and the creation of the new, which is very difficult" (p. 6). Representation is also privileged within traditional approaches to observation and planning in early childhood settings, which generally mistrust experimentation; the objective of *progettazione* and documentation instead is not to represent what happened, but rather to interpret, to cohesively connect theory and practice so that they nurture each other, constantly tending towards artful and unimagined possibilities.

The Reggio Emilia ethic of research, with its obligation towards the creation of the new, has much in common with research-creation and post qualitative inquiry, and particularly with what St. Pierre (2021a) calls "an invitation to work at and beyond that edge, where anything can happen and does; where the new beckons us to think and live differently; where the new, always unrecognizable, demands our best work" (p. 480). The research that occurs in Reggio Emilia, connecting pedagogical, cultural, social, and organisational thought and action, is not about reproducing known methods to arrive at recognisable results, rather it is a practice of working at the edge of the possible; "if the eye leaps over the wall" as the first title of *The Hundred Languages of Children* exhibition declared many decades ago. All participate in working at the edge of the possible, constructing research from the time at which it is first imagined, through its iteration and interpretations; throughout these events, there is no separation between observed and observer, or between "the researcher" and the "object of research". This collective practice of welcoming the new creates knowledge that is never generic, but rather it is contextualised and transferable to other contexts so that they too can become places of research, contributing to creating an extended community of researchers whose eyes leap over the walls (physical and virtual) that are constantly erected in educational settings, threatening their very existence.

Research as movement

You are aware of your own personal responsibilities, but you are also always in relationship with others, and you can always offer your own contribution to others. This is a constant of our work, which gives you strength to engage in ongoing transformation requiring openness of mind and capacity to welcome ... The world has changed, situations have changed, families have changed, and children have changed. It is essential to be always in movement, with your mind constantly open towards humanity. This means to not remain relegated within your own knowledge, closed within your profession, but instead to gaze towards humanity. It is necessary to be a person who attempts to understand the present, keeps a memory of and is grateful for the past, and appreciates those who contributed, before you, to make this experience possible.

(Manuela Pederzoli, teacher, interview with Stefania Giamminuti, Reggio Emilia)

Conventional research approaches – and conventional pedagogical practices – rely on methodology as a way of perpetuating the known and thus, in a way, they stay perpetually still. They claim to be innovative, but are mistrustful of difference and prize linear, organised thought and action. As St. Pierre (2021a) argues, within these dominant paradigms the role of research is reduced to finding out what already exists, preventing us "from attending to what is coming into being" (p. 481). Much like the obedient social science researchers, tamed teachers give in to pre-packaged curriculum in their teaching and end up discovering only what already exists, precluded from attending to the new by the forces of conventionality and governability. In Reggio Emilia, instead, teacher Manuela Pederzoli (above) illuminates the fundamental importance of eschewing what is already given and disrupting what lies within the bounds of your profession. She sees movement as a necessity, and she further highlights how this is possible when you avoid the strictures of pre-determined thought:

To do school together in this way is a project in perpetual becoming. This means that things are never pre-determined, but they are always in becoming, and you share this becoming with others, who always offer an enriching contribution. We always try to be intelligent teachers, who might understand children.

(Manuela Pederzoli, teacher, interview with Stefania Giamminuti, Reggio Emilia)

Pedagogista Annalisa Rabotti renders movement in her role as "positive incompleteness of things, this idea of always searching for something that is incomplete, because anyway you won't ever be able to close the circle" (interview with Stefania Giamminuti, Reggio Emilia). Manning and Massumi (2014) ask "What is it, in a work of dance, that gives it this capacity to linger, to reactivate itself, contagiously beyond its duration?" (p. 31); we can ask the same of the experience of Reggio Emilia, discovering parallels between this way of doing school together, this "project in perpetual becoming", this "positive incompleteness of things", and a work of dance that lingers contagiously. This way of doing school and research is a "milieu of mutual envelopment" (Manning & Massumi, 2014, p. 32) and it relies on individual and collective ability to be in constant movement, to not wish for pre-set beginnings and tidy endings but rather to dwell with curiosity in the "speculative middle" (Springgay & Truman, 2018), where "you are not there to report on what you find or what you seek, but to activate thought. To agitate it" (p. 206).

248 The value of culture and an ethic of research

The speculative middle, this difficult, uncertain, situated and responsive place to be, is the place of *progettazione* and documentation, whose ambition is not to report but rather to activate thought responsively within the situation, to be unconventional and to speculate about what is possible. We are compelled to reiterate that in Reggio Emilia this is not simply a quality of daily pedagogical practice or even reduced to isolated moments of observation and evaluation, rather it belongs to the system as a whole. The quality of research as movement in this experience is about a collective tension towards transformation, as *pedagogista* Annalisa Rabotti suggests:

> Another quality of the educational experience in general, but also local to individual *nidi* or *scuole* is this *progettuale* tension towards change. You change if you welcome this tension *progettuale*, if you can devise projects, if you see yourself into the future.
>
> *(Annalisa Rabotti, pedagogista, interview with*
> *Stefania Giamminuti, Reggio Emilia)*

Research as collective experimentation

The qualities of an ethic of research in Reggio Emilia are inseparable from the educational project's tensions towards artful creation, which rely on documentation as an ally. We see enduring parallels between what Manning (2015) terms "research-creation" and *progettazione*-documentation in Reggio Emilia:

> Research-creation […] generates new forms of experience; it situates what often seem like disparate practices, giving them a conduit for collective expression; it hesitantly acknowledges that normative modes of inquiry and containment often are incapable of assessing its value; it generates forms of knowledge that are extralinguistic; it creates operative strategies for a mobile positioning that take these new forms of knowledge into account; it proposes concrete assemblages for rethinking the very question of what is at stake in pedagogy, in practice, and in collective experimentation.
>
> *(Manning, 2015, p. 53)*

Those familiar with *progettazione*-documentation will recognise its potential in being a conduit for collective expression of seemingly disparate practices. They will recall their frustration and despair when the worth of documentation is assessed through the lens of normative modes of inquiry and containment, and thus found wanting. They will understand what it means to generate forms of knowledge that are extralinguistic, they will find themselves in the re-thinking of what is at stake in pedagogy, and they will hail collective experimentation. Collective experimentation is not easy; it is a choice that requires constant daily attentiveness to ways of working that are premised on relationality, reciprocity, and solidarity. In Reggio Emilia, as Paola Cagliari acknowledges, innovation is made possible by constantly keeping all research participants and protagonists "within" the experience:

> An important aspect that characterises our processes and the value we give to research and innovation is that the research protagonists are never ousted at the various levels, but rather they are always included.
>
> *(Paola Cagliari, Director, Preschools and Infant-toddler Centres - Istituzione of the Municipality of Reggio Emilia, Interview with Stefania Giamminuti, Reggio Emilia)*

Both teachers and *pedagogistas* recognise the value of being "within" research, together. Teacher Simona Marani acknowledges the practical support this stance affords in a key aspect of research: synthesising and making choices.

> This has always helped me, the fact that the *pedagogista* is less emotionally involved in the documentation you share. Because often I try to create a synthesis, but I can't choose anything to remove. Perhaps it's her professional background, or her *formazione,* her capacity to read into events. But also, the fact of being less involved, which allows her to support us in abandoning some things. To actually choose, because in the end I wouldn't throw away a thing.
>
> *(Simona Marani, teacher, interview with Stefania Giamminuti, Reggio Emilia)*

Teacher Francesca Forenzi emphasises the relational aspects of researching together, whilst *pedagogista* Paola Strozzi recognises that collective experimentation hinges on generosity:

> This role of teacher as researcher is very true if you live it always. If you live it in relation with the children, with the families, but also with those who are "above" you. Because we should be researching together.
>
> *(Francesca Forenzi, teacher, interview with Stefania Giamminuti, Reggio Emilia)*

Much of the work of the *pedagogista* lies in being close to the schools, to assist this reflexivity. Because the schools offer you very generous traces, documentation, evidence, interpretations, but you have to offer others in exchange, you need to create a synthesis, you have to conceptualise.

> *(Paola Strozzi*, pedagogista, *interview with Stefania Giamminuti, Reggio Emilia)*

FIGURE 7.3 *Pedagogista* Paola Strozzi and *atelierista* Mirella Ruozzi share further interpretations and conceptual links with *atelierista* Alessandro Mainini while viewing a documentation panel in construction, *Scuola dell'infanzia* XXV Aprile.

Furthermore, the value of artfulness which permeates the Reggio Emilia experience makes it impossible to evaluate the worth of its innovation through the lens of conventional research methods. If the experience of Reggio Emilia continues to be mistrusted in traditional academic circles, it may well be because it unsettles the hegemony of quantification on which the academy relies; it does so by keeping theory-practice-research connected, and in its artfulness it threatens to fundamentally disrupt the theory-practice split (Manning, 2015).

In Chapter 5, we referred to master architect Luis Kahn's aspiration towards the "unmeasurable" (Green, 1961) in *progettazione*; in relation to research, Manning (2015) uses the term "unquantifiable" and notes that we can only attend to it "if we begin with a mode of inquiry that refutes initial categorization" (p. 54). Further, she notes that "positing the terms of the account before the exploration of what the account can do results only in stultifying its potential and relegating it to that which already fits within preexisting schemata of knowledge" (Manning, 2015, p. 54). In other words, when you have decided what you will find and how you will find it before you look for it, you will only discover what is already known.

Collective experimentation in Reggio Emilia relies on *pensiero progettuale* and documentation; elsewhere, it is not possible to embrace an ethic of research in dialogue with Reggio Emilia while continuing to privilege method, quantification, categorisation, and pre-existing knowledge. Instead, for those researchers, whether in academia or as teachers working with young children, who encounter Reggio Emilia and recognise themselves, we think that "perhaps they've longed, all along, for difference and different approaches to inquiry-yearned for the not yet, what might be if we could only create it" (Kuntz & St. Pierre, 2021, p. 477). Hence our invitation here is for others to participate in longing for the not yet, and to tend to it through collective experimentation.

Research as thinking in the making

All that we have discussed above leads us back to the question on which this whole chapter hinges: the question of knowledge, how it is crafted, and what it does. As Manning (2015) acknowledges in relation to research-creation:

> The issue here is complex. It not only touches on the question of how art itself activates and constitutes new forms of knowledge in its own right but also, perhaps most importantly, incites us to inquire into the very question of how practices produce knowledge, and whether those forms of knowledge can engagingly be captured within the strictures of methodological ordering.
>
> *(Manning, 2015, p. 52)*

Methodology, with its reliance on obedience and conformity, restricts and confines knowledge creation to the conventional and expected. Method turns knowledge and experience into static and preformed categories, channelling them within disciplinary boundaries and "disciplining the very question of what constitutes knowledge" (Manning, 2015, p. 58). The alternative "against method" (Manning, 2015) is to welcome contamination of knowledge in both thinking and practice, and to re-imagine research in early years settings "as a *practice that thinks*" (Manning, 2015, p. 53 [italics in original]). In so doing, it is imperative to privilege creativity, non-linearity, and inter-disciplinary boundary crossing above order, predictability, and knowledge hegemony. And, as teacher Ethel Carnevali notes, it is also essential that someone is there to ask uncomfortable questions:

> To ask those questions that are a bit uncomfortable, the ones which you as a teacher might not have considered, perhaps because you are fully within the event or because you don't have her experience or because you aren't a *pedagogista*. Such questions help to shift your thinking, and to propel your research forward.
>
> *(Ethel Carnevali, teacher, interview with*
> *Stefania Giamminuti, Reggio Emilia)*

252 The value of culture and an ethic of research

In critiquing conventional ordering and categorising of knowledge, Manning (2015) asks: "but what if the question is tuned towards the issue of what knowledge does?" (p. 56). In Reggio Emilia, the questions of how knowledge is crafted and of what knowledge does have always gone hand in hand, and have been the object of significant debate and responsibility on the part of *pedagogistas* in particular. In fact, in pondering Erin Manning's considerations on the necessary dialogue between philosophy and the arts, and on how knowledge is crafted at the intersections of disciplines and through the correspondence of making and thinking, one can't help but be reminded that such trans-disciplinary readings and doings were privileged by Malaguzzi himself and spilled over into the educational project, becoming an enduring core ethic of the Reggio Emilia experience. Manning (2015) exhorts us to engage in "speculative pragmatism, speculative in the sense that a process remains open to its potential, and pragmatic in the sense that it is rooted in the in-act of its "something doing" (Manning, 2015, p. 56). The experience of Reggio Emilia continues to be speculative (one reason perhaps why it generates mistrust in those enamoured with methodological and pedagogical certainty) and it refuses to be anything but pragmatic. Encounters between *pedagogistas, atelieristas,* teachers, families, children, and others (human and non-human) are events of "thinking in the making" (Manning, 2015, p. 61).

Making and thinking – or, in terms more familiar to pedagogy, theory and practice – give life to an ethic of research to the point that they are inseparable: "making is a thinking in its own right, and conceptualization a practice in its own right" (Manning, 2015, p. 53). Making is also thinking, and conceptualising is also practicing; it is not possible to separate one from the other or to assign one quality or the other (thinker or practictioner) to a particular individual role in educational settings or to a particular time in the learning process (first you think and then you make); such attempts only succeed in fragmenting knowledge and experience. Furthermore, an ethic of research challenges the notion that the thinking and researching can only be done by someone other than the teachers, *pedagogistas, atelieristas,* materials, and children who are fully imbricated in the event. *Pedagogista* Elena Giacopini emphasises this unique quality of the Reggio Emilia experience:

I have participated in many different events and debates on educational topics, witnessing many erudite contributions that narrate what adults believe about childhood. Our distinction, our unique characteristic, is to always bring forth the points of view of the children and of the teachers […] our intention is to speak from within experience, rendering explicit the connection between theory and practice. These are authentic processes of *formazione*, processes of elaboration which also include families, processes that promote transformations within schools' daily life.

(Elena Giacopini, pedagogista, *interview with Stefania Giamminuti, Reggio Emilia)*

Conclusion

In this chapter, we have posed questions of culture, knowledge, research, and innovation. In illuminating Reggio Emilia's value of culture and ethic of research, we have thought with concepts such as: "collective experimentation" (Manning, 2015); "correspondences" (Ingold, 2021); "movement" (Truman & Springgay, 2015); and "thinking-in-the-making" (Manning, 2015). We have drawn parallels with the arts and philosophy, and in aligning the experience of Reggio Emilia with the aspirations of post qualitative inquiry (St. Pierre, 2021c), we have disrupted the primacy of method in conventional pedagogy and research. We have defended an image of all children as knowledge producers, and in so doing we have conveyed the fundamental role of others as knowledge co-producers, disrupting pedagogy's enduring reliance on what is already known. Finally, we have proposed that the experience of Reggio Emilia embodies "affirmative ethics" (Braidotti, 2019), "conceptual creativity" (Braidotti, 2019), and "speculative pragmatism" (Manning, 2015), all of which rely on a collective obligation towards the possible and the not yet.

In conclusion, we contend that those who seek to undermine and silence the experience of Reggio Emilia as "not scientific" (Mantovani, 2017) by reducing it to "good practice" wish to perpetuate the methodological and pedagogical status quo and are fundamentally averse to the ineffable. In fact, as Manning (2015) notes, "methods thus become the safeguard against the ineffable: if something cannot be categorized, it cannot be made to account for itself, and therefore it does not exist" (Manning, 2015, p. 58). Reggio Emilia, ineffable and at the same time very capable of demonstrating its full existence, is "interested in what escapes the order" and "recognizes that knowledge is invented in the escape, in the excess" (Manning, 2015, p. 63). We invite others to seek out those spaces of escape and excess where knowledge is invented and cultures are made.

Notes

1 In many ways this links back to our arguments in Chapter 1 for recognising the teacher as intellectual.
2 In Chapter 3, we illustrated the *confronto* that occurred during this same *aggiornamento.*
3 An ethic of alliances is discussed in Chapter 9.
4 This term is historically significant for the region, as Emilia Romagna was very active in the Resistance against fascism. Today, it could be more loosely translated as "advocates" or "activists", but we prefer to hold onto "partisans", referencing those who sacrificed much in service to the resistance against oppression.
5 The "portrait of yellow daisies" narrated in Chapter 4 is an example of this.
6 This is outlined in detail in Chapter 2.

References

Alaimo, S. (2016). *Environmental politics and pleasures in posthuman times.* University of Minnesota Press.

Anceschi, A., & Maccaferri, E. (Eds.). (2022). *Accorpamenti: Resonances between dance and music.* Reggio Children.

Angosto Ferrandez, L. F. (2013). Ways of living: Tim Ingold on culture, biology and the anthropological task. *Revista De Antropología Iberoamericana, 8*(3), 285–302. https://doi.org/10.11156/aibr.080302e

Bird Rose, D. (2004). *Reports from a wild country: Ethics for decolonisation.* University of New South Wales Press.

Braidotti, R. (2019). *Posthuman knowledge.* Polity Press.

Cagliari, P. (2019). Research notes. In V. Vecchi, S. Bonilauri, I. Meninno, & M. Tedeschi (Eds.), *Bordercrossings: Encounters with living things, digital landscapes* (pp. 10–13). Reggio Children.

Cagliari, P., Castagnetti, M., Giudici, C., Rinaldi, C., Vecchi, V., & Moss, P. (Eds.). (2016). *Loris Malaguzzi and the schools of Reggio Emilia: A selection of his writings and speeches, 1945–1993.* Routledge.

Cavallini, I., & Tedeschi, M. (Eds.). (2008). *The languages of food: Recipes, experiences, thoughts.* Reggio Children.

Chieli, F., Filippini, T., & Maccaferri, E. (2022). Research into children and adults' dialogues on music and dance. Resonances: Daily contexts at infant-toddler centres and preschools. In A. Anceschi, & E. Maccaferri (Eds.), *Accorpamenti: Resonances between dance and music* (pp. 106–111). Reggio Children.

Cipolla, S., & Reverberi, E. (Eds.). (1996). *The little ones of silent movies: Make-believe with children and fish at the infant-toddler centre.* Reggio Children.

Davoli, M., & Ferri, G. (Eds.). (2000). *Reggio tutta: A guide to the city by the children.* Reggio Children.

Filippini, T., & Vecchi, V. (Eds.). (2011). *The wonder of learning: The hundred languages of children.* Reggio Children.

Freire, P. (2005). *Teachers as cultural workers: Letters to those who dare to teach.* Westview Press.

Gandini, L. (2012). History, ideas and basic principles: An interview with Loris Malaguzzi. In C. Edwards, L. Gandini, & G. Forman (Eds.), *The hundred languages of children: The Reggio Emilia experience in transformation* (pp. 27–71). Praeger.

Giamminuti, S., Merewether, J., & Blaise, M. (2022). Pedagogical documentation and the refusal of method: Troubling dogmas and inviting collective obligations. *European Early Childhood Education Research Journal,* 1–14. https://doi.org/10.1080/1350293X.2022.2046834

Giroux, H. (2021). *Race, politics, and pandemic pedagogy: Education in a time of crisis.* Bloomsbury.

Green, W. (1961). Louis I. Kahn, architect: Alfred Newton Richards medical research building. University of Pennsylvania, Philadelphia, 1958-1960. *The Bulletin of the Museum of Modern Art, 28*(1), 2–23.

Ingold, T. (2017). On human correspondence. *The Journal of the Royal Anthropological Institute, 23*(1), 9–27. https://doi.org/10.1111/1467-9655.12541

Ingold, T. (2021). *Correspondences.* Polity Press.

Kuntz, A. M., & St. Pierre, E. A. (2021). Proclaiming the new: An introduction. *Qualitative Inquiry, 27*(5), 475–479. https://doi.org/10.1177/1077800420939125

Lather, P. (2013). Methodology-21: What do we do in the afterward? *International Journal of Qualitative Studies in Education*, 26(6), 634–645. https://doi.org/10.1080/09518398.2013.788753

Malaguzzi, L. (2021). *Design/Progettazione in infant-toddler centres and preschools: Research open to wonder, between the possible, probable, and unpredictable*. Reggio Children.

Manning, E. (2015). Against method. In P. Vannini (Ed.), *Non-representational methodologies: Re-envisioning research* (pp. 52–71). Routledge.

Manning, E., & Massumi, B. (2014). *Thought in the act: Passages in the ecology of experience*. University of Minnesota Press.

Mantovani, S. (2017). Presentazione dell'edizione italiana. In C. Edwards, L. Gandini, & G. Forman (Eds.), *I cento linguaggi dei bambini: L'approccio di Reggio Emilia all'educazione dell'infanzia* (pp. 11–16). Edizioni Junior.

Mucchi, A., Giudici, C., & Vecchi, V. (2021). For children not to be invisible. *Rechild* (December 2021), 1–2.

Reggio Children (1995). *The fountains: From a project for the construction of an amusement park for birds*. Author.

Reggio Children (1996). *The hundred languages of children: Narratives of the possible. New extended exhibit catalogue*. Author.

Reggio Children (2008). *The park is...*. Author.

Reverberi, E. (2021). The voices of teachers and atelieristas. *Rechild* (December 2021), 4.

Rigney, L.-I., & Kelly, S. (2021). Reterritorialising pedagogies of listening: Bringing into dialogue culturally responsive pedagogies with Reggio Emilia principles. *Discourse: Studies in the Cultural Politics of Education*, 1–15. https://doi.org/10.1080/01596306.2021.1961688

Springgay, S., & Truman, S. E. (2018). On the need for methods beyond proceduralism: Speculative middles, (in)tensions, and response-ability in research. *Qualitative Inquiry*, 24(3), 203–214. https://doi.org/10.1177/1077800417704464

St. Pierre, E. A. (2018). Writing post qualitative inquiry. *Qualitative Inquiry*, 24(9), 603–608. https://doi.org/10.1177/1077800417734567

St. Pierre, E. A. (2021a). The lure of the new and the hold of the dogmatic. *Qualitative Inquiry*, 27(5), 480–590. https://doi.org/10.1177/1077800420939133

St. Pierre, E. A. (2021b). Post qualitative inquiry, the refusal of method, and the risk of the new. *Qualitative Inquiry*, 27(1), 3–9. https://doi.org/10.1177/1077800419863005

St. Pierre, E. A. (2021c). Why post qualitative inquiry? *Qualitative Inquiry*, 27(2), 163–166. https://doi.org/10.1177/1077800420931142

Truman, S. E., & Springgay, S. (2015). The primacy of movement in research-creation: New materialist approaches to art research and pedagogy. In T. E. Lewis, & M. J. Laverty (Eds.), *Art's teachings, teaching's art: Philosophical, critical and educational musings* (pp. 151–162). Springer.

Vecchi, V. (Ed.). (2002). *Theatre curtain: The ring of transformations*. Reggio Children.

Vecchi, V., Bonilauri, S., Meninno, I., & Tedeschi, M. (2019). *Bordercrossings: Encounters with living things, digital landscapes*. Reggio Children.

Vecchi, V., & Ruozzi, M. (Eds.). (2015). *Mosaic of marks, words, material*. Reggio Children.

8

EDUCATION COMMONS

History, choices, and tools for rendering a utopia concrete

Claudia Giudici

Translated by Jane McCall

Introduction

In this chapter, we will consider, from a different perspective, themes and key terms that have been central in previous chapters. We will revisit them by inscribing them in an idea of *Education Commons* that offers a framework or horizon within which strategic, organisational, and value-based choices take on more specific meaning. The term "commons" is used to define common agricultural fields, meeting places in towns and villages, or spaces in buildings where people can or could come together to engage in community and social events (Rose, 2020) and in her landmark work *Governing the Commons* (Ostrom, 1990)[1] Elinor Ostrom discusses "the capacity of communities to self-organize and share common-pool resources […] beyond the much travelled paths of the exclusively public or exclusively private management solutions" (Boonen et al., 2019, p. 554). Bollier (2006) also argues that "the commons fills a theoretical void by explaining how significant value can be created and sustained outside of the market system" (p. 29).

Thinking on the commons has explored and interrogated several areas of culture and knowledge including common-pool natural resources,[2] anthropology (Acheson, 2011), feminist politics (Clement et al., 2019), architecture and design (Sanchez, 2020), the arts (the *Creative Commons*, e.g. Miszczynki, 2022), and information, communication and knowledge (the *Knowledge Commons*, e.g. Hess & Ostrom, 2006b; Lemeilleur & Sermage, 2020). Viewed as

DOI: 10.4324/9781003181026-8

an *Education Commons* the concrete experience of Reggio Emilia's municipal *nidi* and *scuole dell'infanzia* is a resource "to be managed, monitored, and protected, to ensure sustainability and preservation" (Hess & Ostrom, 2006a, p. 10).

Following a brief outline of the social, cultural, and historical roots of Reggio Emilia's *nidi* and *scuole dell'infanzia*, the chapter will provide readers with information on different public-private systems created in the city to bring into effect the right to education. In particular: a system of educational services co-ordinated by the Reggio Emilia municipality and guaranteeing a high number of *nidi* and *scuole dell'infanzia*; a plurality of subjects, all tied to the municipal administration, that promote and maintain the vitality of a constant attitude of research, informed by national and international relations; a virtuous economic circle that returns to the system of *nidi* and *scuole dell'infanzia* the income generated by activities of *formazione* requested or proposed by organisations and individuals on all five continents, and whose established quality has been generated by the educational system's momentum towards research and innovation. This ethical economy and cultural enterprise, while replenishing the local experience's resources on the level of thinking and finances, at the same time promotes an attitude of solidarity throughout the world towards childhood and, through childhood, towards all humanity.

In conclusion to the chapter, a deeper reflection on the concept of participation, generative value and strategy within *Education Commons*, offers readers an alternative viewpoint from which to observe the systemic nature of Reggio Emilia's educational project. Participation in fact offers a lens producing a unifying composition, situated in the broader social context, of levels of action that are often theorised and designed separately: the processes of teaching/learning; *formazione* of teachers; relationships with families; and political and organisational decisions related to educational services.

Nidi and scuole dell'infanzia: vital nucleus of a broader educational system

For the city of Reggio Emilia, the *nidi* and *scuole dell'infanzia* constitute an inestimable legacy to be conserved through a constant tension towards innovation, understood as dialogue with changing contexts, and interpretations of social, cultural, scientific, and political changes that affect the lives of children, women, and humanity in general. Seventy years ago, this was a utopia. Today it is a legacy that the city has had the tenacity and volition to construct, care for and evolve, aware of the exceptional circumstances that have made their

258 Education Commons

creation and existence possible: a local administration that is sensitive to the theme of childhood; associations of courageous and persevering women who have gone on to cover significant roles in city administration; and a visionary *pedagogista* like Loris Malaguzzi who was capable of coalescing the pedagogical, political, and civil passions of a multitude – teachers, *pedagogistas*, mothers, fathers, and citizens – around his utopian vision.

The fortunate intersection of these factors made it possible to develop a local experience that has acquired international value, for the city never wanted to keep its experience for itself, and instead, with an innately participatory perspective, offered it up for dialogue with other experiences. This took place first and foremost in Reggio Emilia itself when, alongside the municipal *nidi* and *scuole dell'infanzia*, systems and city bodies discussed in this chapter (the *Preschools and Infant-toddler Centres – Istituzione of the Municipality of Reggio Emilia*, the 0–6 integrated public system, the local pedagogical coordination) were structured to act on the city level, while others (Reggio Children and the International Network, the *Fondazione* Reggio Children, the Loris Malaguzzi International Centre project) have acted as interfaces at national and international levels. However, to better comprehend the roles these different bodies play, and the reasons for their creation, it is important to go back in time, offering readers the historical and evolutionary dimension of what is today an internationally known system.

The city of Reggio Emilia's cultural "revolution"

After the Second World War, the local people, especially the women, gathered important legacies of education and school experience from the Socialist *giunta* or local "parliaments" that had governed Reggio Emilia and other northern and central Italian cities in the interim years between Italy's unification (1861) and the twenty years of Fascist rule, becoming active protagonists, demanding and working directly themselves for the creation of educational places for children under six.

> This large movement had great political and cultural depth. It was the first time women had left the family nucleus and left the home to transfer their commitment, intelligences and hard work outside. Certainly it was a need, and an economic need, but the necessity cloaked an area of rights with a very fine veil: rights that women were acquiring very slowly and which went way beyond the world of work. It was not possible to access the world of work without services[3] behind them. This was not possible – but the services were not there. There was a network of parish schools [for young children] (with all their limits but with all their merits too); there were the little self-managed schools living in great poverty, and living the issues of pedagogy and education in great poverty (the problems were enormous).

At the same time there was this need, to move forward on the subject of guaranteeing services available to families.

(Malaguzzi, 1992, in Cagliari et al., 2016, p. 417)

The commitment of these women was a conscious struggle for rights, equality, emancipation, personal fulfilment outside the family, and recognition of their role in society. They aspired to something that at that time did not yet have the status of a right: emancipation from the conditions of economic, cultural, and social hardship that were characteristic of Italy's post-war years, for themselves and for their children. In Loris Malaguzzi's words, we find images that leave us with vivid impressions of the problems of the time:

When we speak of children we cannot speak as if we were discussing today's children. Children then were extraordinarily poor, extraordinarily thin, and extraordinarily undernourished, from years of war. The signs of rickets were obvious for all to see. The children were dialect speakers, they only spoke dialect and couldn't understand a word of Italian. Their mothers' proposal, their hope, was to entrust them to these miraculous people, people who had been miraculously saved: these were the first teachers. It was as if they, by knowing everything, could guarantee the mothers' aspiration that their children would leave their destiny behind and put themselves in a higher place.

(Malaguzzi, 1992, in Cagliari et al., 2016, p. 415)

In the aftermath of the Second World War, the wounds left behind in northern Italy by Fascist dictatorship and Nazi occupation, and the commitment of men and women in the Resistance movement, fuelled a desire for democracy, participation, and civil passion whose influence was to be felt for several decades. This commitment was not limited to expressing requests and demands but used to create the conditions necessary for effectively realising what the people desired. Speaking of the school in Villa Cella, built between1945 and 1947, Loris Malaguzzi recalls:

I remember the school born in 1945 on the decision of the women, a women's choice, with no invitation, no encouragement, and no [ministerial] circular [...] You have to think these women decided to sell things, objects left by fleeing Germans, and they decided to do it immediately. And they decided immediately because they had the wisdom, yes, the wisdom to foresee that if they left it a little bit later then very probably the delay would become much longer. They had to decide before someone else or something else arrived. The decision was of a spontaneous character: a decision that had to have immediate effect. And this is where we see the birth of an idea that was so anticipatory, of building a school there in the little square

260 Education Commons

of this small village. It was a school made of bricks. They worked all day Saturday: the women worked, the men worked, youngsters worked, children worked. They went to the river and collected sand, and they went to collect old stones from houses ruined by bombing. The women wanted a school that was theirs and that belonged to them. They wanted the school because they were convinced (there was much naivety, but much excitement and much passion too), they wanted it because in their minds owning the premises was directly equivalent to owning the school, and owning the school might mean owning their children's lives and their children's destinies.

(Malaguzzi, 1992, in Cagliari et al., 2016, p. 414)

The project, therefore, was first and foremost a political project, not delegated to the institutions and the experts, but one that everyone wanted to take part in, so as to monitor and promote its fruition: the possibility that every child, whatever their social extraction, could further their own conditions starting out in life through education.

They asked that the school, built with their own hands, be a different school and educate their children differently. It was the women above all who demanded this. The equation was simple: if the children were to have rights and reason on their side they had to be children acknowledged as ready, intelligent and equipped for the success and liberation in which they could not and must not fail. That was their theory. A theory that expresses a universal law of aspiration, a declaration of children's betrayed capacities, and a warning that above all it was necessary to believe in the children. These three arguments would sit well in any good book on education.

(Malaguzzi, 1989–1991, in Gandini, 2017,
p. 61, [translated by Jane McCall])

These small self-managed schools, 7 of which were located in the Reggio Emilia municipality and 60 in the Reggio Emilia province, struggled to stay alive, and even then they only managed thanks to the dedication of the local people. Few survived until the 1960s and these were then municipalised, which is to say they were taken under municipal management. However, the end of the experience of these small schools did not obscure the important values they brought with them; on the contrary, the very fact that some were transferred to municipal management highlighted the values and gave them continuity. Still today these values are the horizons that Reggio Emilia's *nidi* and *scuole dell'infanzia* look towards. Certainly, it was a utopian experience. But it was also a testament to a passion and commitment that represent a warning for us today, unconscious victims of a dominant culture permeated by the incapacity to point to or propose alternatives. As philosopher Roberto Mangabeira Unger (2006) states: "the world suffers under a dictatorship of no alternatives. Although ideas all by themselves are powerless to overthrow this dictatorship, we cannot overthrow it without ideas" (p. 1).

How does the commitment of these women speak to those of us working in education and early childhood today? Firstly, it speaks of encouragement: everything is possible, even things that seem impossible, if there is a will and a consensus. This is a concept we can also find in the words of philosopher Salvatore Veca (2014) who states that "the conservative and inflationist move of converting difficult or even very difficult things, into impossible things is never a good one [...] it is realism, the simple realism of a common [shared] sense that urges us, here and now, to request the impossible" (p. 97, [translated by Jane McCall]). Secondly, it is a reminder to re-position the identity of *nidi* and *scuole dell'infanzia*, from services responding to the economic needs of the market to services built around the centrality of children and their right to education. Even today, in the presence of advanced national laws that are coherent with this premise, it is an achievement that always risks the involutions and back-turns generated by neo-liberal political visions that have shifted *nidi* and *scuole dell'infanzia* in some areas of Italy into the fold of the market and competition. Thirdly, it speaks of an awareness of the project as political and the importance of maintaining a high state of vigilance, of premising education in collective places as a commons and as the right of children and of women, always intrinsically linked, and not the responsibility of State/municipality or market alone, but of citizens together *with* institutions, that is to say, of civil society. A project, therefore, that reflects "the ideal of self-governance of social movements and communities wary of market logic and state hierarchy" (Boonen et al., 2019, p. 570).

Education Commons: policies and actions for realising a utopia

Commons are resources that a community commits to promoting and managing, not only in the immediate interest of the collective, but in order to conserve them, take care of them, develop them, and hand them down to future generations.

A common may be anything a community recognizes as capable of satisfying some real, fundamental need outside of market exchange. In addition to physical public space, this may also include institutional organizations such as cooperatives or commonwealths, trusts in the interest of future generations, village economies, water-sharing devices, and many other arrangements, antique as well as current. Its utility is created by shared community access and diffuse decision making [...] The fundamental organizational principle of commoning everywhere is that of caring, duty, reciprocity, and participation. It is about spending a lot of time together to care for

262 Education Commons

something recognized as a common with high attention and patience. It is a process where individuals sharing a collective purpose institutionalize their collective will to maintain some order and some stability in pursuit of their goals [...] In the current state of affairs, recovering the commons is not the business of lawyers or politicians, whose intellectual and institutional landscape is framed by the ideology of modernity. This process belongs now to plain people who, from choice or necessity, participate in caring for something that they recognize as a common. In doing so, these people engage in an activity that Nobel laureate Elinor Ostrom describes as "communing".
(Capra & Mattei, 2015, p. 150 and 153–154)

With the concept of *Education Commons* we seek a framework that, in Bollier's (2006) words, proposes "a coherent alternative model for bringing economic, social, and ethical concerns into greater alignment" and addresses "the inalienability of certain resources and the value of protecting community interests" (p. 29). The concept of community evoked by the commons requires closer examination. The term "community" sometimes refers to an idea of identity-recognition excluding those who do not identify with that circle of equals. In the name of safeguarding communities and identity, conflicts have been generated, walls have been built, and enemies have been constructed.[4] In the experience of Reggio Emilia, where we prefer to use words like "collective" or "society", considering education as a commons means giving value to the idea that a community is something local, and therefore close to the places where childhood lives and grows in, capable of generating a collective knowledge that measures up against real problems. A community that, as Tim Ingold (2013) states, "rub[s] up against the rough edges of the world" (p. 73), that knows it must take on responsibilities for which it will be directly accountable, a community capable of restoring the quality of human relations through practices inspired by criteria of equality and pluralism.

In the idea of *Education Commons*, key words and values that have accompanied us through this book – dialectics, reciprocity, an ethic of innovation, inclusion, the value of difference, and *pensiero progettuale* as doing and thinking together – find a unifying concept that brings them together. In previous chapters, these values and key words were considered on the level of relations within Reggio Emilia's municipal *nidi* and *scuole dell'infanzia*. In this chapter, we will seek to analyse how the idea of *Education Commons* is made concrete in strategic choices at the city level, and on national and international levels.

The 0–6 integrated public system

We will begin with the local dimension, with Reggio Emilia's constant commitment to developing a system capable of guaranteeing a place for every child whose family applies for one and working towards universal access for children aged

3–6 years old. The women's movements and struggles were premised on this idea of a system of *scuole dell'infanzia* and (after the 1970s) *nidi* capable of responding to all requests and guaranteeing all children their right of access. This aim is still relevant today and has been developed by constructing an integrated public system, in which all providers, public and private, each with their own prerogatives, cooperate by sharing values and collaborating on shared intents, in order to offer all children an experience of education in a collective dimension.

> [Reggio Emilia's] integrated public system interprets the concept of "public" through Conventions that tie the different providers to access criteria and procedures inclusive of every difference of gender, ethnicity, religion, culture and social provenance: the system references parameters for quality that are shared, constructed and expected by the city community, an openness to monitoring the city's representational bodies, and family participation.
>
> *(Scuole e Nidi d'Infanzia - Istituzione del Comune di Reggio Emilia,*
> *2011, p. 3, [translated by Jane McCall])*

These are all characteristics of a commons, as Capra and Mattei (2015) highlight: "it does not matter whether the ultimate legal title on the premises is private or public, a corporation or a municipality, only whether the space fosters generative collective activity or is run on a model of exclusion, extracting profit and rent" (p. 151). The system is co-ordinated by Reggio Emilia's municipal administration, which through its work of directly managing *nidi* and *scuole dell'infanzia*, and by putting together the best experiences from the city's early childhood services, offers references in pedagogy, organisation and management that orient the whole system towards constantly increasing quality. The concept of quality is ambiguous, having been developed within a specific cultural climate, as Gunilla Dahlberg et al. (2007) clearly argue in their interesting work *Beyond Quality in Early Childhood Education and Care*:

> "Quality" itself is not a neutral word. [...] the discourse of quality [...] views the world through a modernist lens, and complements modernist constructions of the young child and early childhood institution. The language of quality is also the language of the early childhood institution as producer of pre-specified outcomes and the child as empty vessel, to be prepared to learn and for school, and to be helped on his or her journey of development. [...] The growing importance of quality in the field of early childhood institutions can be understood in relation to the modernist search for order and certainty grounded in objectivity and quantification. (pp. 87, 89)

264   Education Commons

Aware, therefore, of the risks inherent in using this term, but also of the need for indicating quality as a horizon to pursue in respecting children and their potentials, we felt it necessary to define its meaning in the *Piano Programma*, an annual planning tool of the *Istituzione Scuole* and *Nidi d'Infanzia:*

> The idea of quality that inspires the municipal system of *nidi* and *scuole dell'infanzia* is a local and socially constructed concept that is actuated through the [same] attitude of research that defines the construction of knowledge and therefore our relations with others and with environments. It resides in an idea of human beings, and of children, as bearing the right to freedom, to relations, to happiness and to learning, and an idea of knowledge as the product of a subject in relations with others, as a subjective act of research, curiosity, and creativity. These are the ideas that tie us to choices of organisation and environments, of times and persons.
>
> *(Scuole e Nidi d'Infanzia - Istituzione del Comune di Reggio Emilia, 2011, p. 6, [translated by Jane McCall])*

In a framework of this kind, public and private providers do not act within a logic of competition and profit, but towards the common aim of giving all children a place in quality education services, adopting collaborative modes of cultural and economic solidarity that are upheld in Protocols of Understanding,[5] Concessions for Provision, and Conventions.[6]

The criteria and procedures for families to gain entry into the municipal network of 0–6 services are discussed and evaluated annually in places of public debate that invite representatives of all the City Childhood Councils from *nidi* and *scuole* managed either directly or indirectly by the municipality. This is an example of the diffused decision-making process discussed by Capra and Mattei (2015) whereby deliberating decisions is the task of the *Istituzione's* board of directors, but formulating the proposals they deliberate comes from a dynamic of *confronto* within groups of parents and citizens, representatives of social management bodies, bringing their local issues to bear and constructing a public debate defined by its multiplicity of points of view. This is a significant aspect, as Luigi Bobbio (2010) states:

> A public debate can be considered successful, in terms of participation, not when the number of participants is high, but rather when the positions expressed include all the most relevant points of view on the issue in question. It is not the number that counts, so much as the variety and completeness of the points of view (although there is no guarantee whatsoever that this completeness will actually come about).
>
> *(p. 53, [translated by Jane McCall])*

The Consulta

The *Consulta*[7] is a form of citizen participation and a tool created by the *nidi* and *scuole dell'infanzia* together with the municipal administration, in order for the idea of *Education Commons* to become a lived reality. In fact, the *Consulta* is the institutionalised venue open to all participatory bodies in the city's integrated public system, administrators and citizens, and the moment in which public debate has the greatest possibility of expression, synthesis, and listening on the part of *Istituzione* bodies, the mayor, and the city's *Assessore* for Education. While, for example, the Admissions Criteria Commission is involved in a process that contributes to forming decisions (and corresponding administrative acts) in a specific and limited area, the *Consulta* contributes to decision-making processes that diffuse into the whole of educational policy in the city of Reggio Emilia. Deeper reflections coming from the different local realities of each *nido* and *scuola dell'infanzia,* which bring "more relevant points of view on the issue in question" (Bobbio, 2010, p. 53), are discussed as part of the *confronto* in this institutional venue, producing a bottom-up culture that has shown itself capable of speaking to places far beyond the city confines, to the national and international levels.

Territorial pedagogical coordination

As illustrated in Chapter 2, the *territorial* pedagogical coordination, which groups together *pedagogistas* from a wider net than the municipal area (to include the area of the province), is an organism that witnessed its initial experiences within the Reggio Emilia "territory". It represents a "tool suited to guaranteeing connections between early childhood services in a territory's educational system" (regional law 19/2016, article 33, comma 1). The dialectical exchange, reciprocal knowledge of each other's pedagogical and organisational choices, reflection on *progettazione,* and giving value to differences as a source of learning and self-critique are practices that construct an inclusive and participatory atmosphere, intent on diffusing an ethic of innovation through the whole province of Reggio Emilia and interpreting it in more local communities. The pedagogical coordination cares for *nidi* and *scuole dell'infanzia* present in the local territory by including people with direct knowledge of each reality. This makes the intent of maintaining and raising quality of response practicable on both pedagogical and organisational levels (considering the ratio of offer and demand, demographic changes, different types of functioning educational service in relation to demand, and so on).

The territorial pedagogical coordination also acts as an interlocutor with local administrations, offering them a stimulus to maintain and increase their role in taking responsibility for public policy, something municipalities cannot and must not surrender. It is therefore a tool that promotes continuity and

266 Education Commons

consistency in educational initiatives proposed by both public and private bodies, in neighbouring territories and areas, without losing local stories, realities, issues, and sensibilities, but instead valuing them. With these characteristics we can recognise its crucial role in the local geographical area, for living the experience of education as a commons.

Reggio Children and the International Network; Fondazione Reggio Children; the Loris Malaguzzi International Centre project

The Reggio Emilia Approach system extends and adds potential to the concept of the commons in Reggio Emilia by relaunching it on a national and international level. Each subject that is part of this system has a role to play in pursuing the objective of maintaining, extending, and materially and culturally qualifying the *Education Commons*, which has the *nidi* and *scuole dell'infanzia* at its heart. Reggio Children and the *Fondazione* represent "the market component of the activity [that] can easily support the nonmarket one" (Capra & Mattei, 2015, p. 151), bringing into the system resources that are both economic and cultural, relations, knowledge and interlocutors in deeper research, and a diffused pedagogical system extending well beyond the confines of the *Istituzione* of *nidi* and *scuole dell'infanzia*.

The value of education as a commons, which implies community responsibility for its conservation and growth, has given shape and content to Reggio Emilia's national and international relations, considering them as an extension of the community that cares for this commons. This dialectical dialogue is intent on constructing and re-constructing interpretations of the idea of education and its complementary counterparts: instruction, care, learning, and relations. This reciprocal dialogue has its starting point in the research of Reggio Emilia's *nidi* and *scuole dell'infanzia*, which are the original source of the idea of *Education Commons*, and it enriches the experience of each interlocutor with new gazes and visions. This production of a culture that is at once pedagogical, political, social, and scientific, and which is constructed through a constant attitude of *progettazione,* creates dialogue between geographical and cultural differences and multiple points of view, all held as part of one international debate.

The idea is not to replicate Reggio Emilia's experience in other places or countries, but rather to offer criteria, values, and tools for generating institutions which, each in their own context, are inspired by an ethic of respect for human beings from birth, with their special ways of forming relations, knowing, and self-determining in a community dimension. Institutions, therefore, whose educational intent is not "results" in the sense of standardised measurable performance, but that of knowing how to *be*: human beings capable of putting the opportunities they have enjoyed for growth and learning at the service of their communities, with a constructive and committed attitude of solidarity and care.

Participation: an unrenounceable value and strategy of an *Education Commons*

At this point in the book, after several contributions of knowledge from multiple disciplines, and having offered the reader several experiences, testimonies, and research, we believe it is important to conclude with further reflection on participation as an unrenounceable value and practice of education as a commons. We have previously seen how participation is a particular characteristic of civil society in Reggio Emilia, a way of being a citizen that has roots in the past. Previous chapters, in particular those in which Paola Strozzi recounts experiences from the *nidi* and *scuole dell'infanzia*, have highlighted the ways in which the participation of teachers, *pedagogistas* and *atelieristas* takes place. They do not apply given models, but rather they start from their own observations, developing dialectical and collegial decisional processes to include the point of view of all participants. This active propositional attitude, in the dimension of the collective or working group, is given value and discussed, contributing to shaping the construction of learning contexts that are offered to children for their own research. But the dynamic of participation also includes children.

Why do we consider participation necessary? Is it not enough to have good educational models elaborated by charismatic intellectual figures and validated by authoritative experts, as has always been the case? The question is obviously rhetorical. In fact, this is a way of proposing an authoritarian approach, in contrast with the innately democratic vision of school, society, and science that has always been part of Reggio Emilia's experience and which today is shared by a scientific community increasingly aware that research (in social and medical fields, as well as pure sciences like maths and physics) cannot progress without the active participation of those impacted by its choices, and without the participation of all fields of science. The *confronto* based on each person's narratives, interpretations, and experiences provides a more meaningful endorsement than experimental verification alone. This idea is still unusual in many systems of education. Children are the objects of education invented by adults in ministries or by an academic pedagogical elite. Parents are users, or worse, clients. Teachers, some mediocre or bad, others sufficiently good or even excellent, are the executors of given directives. Schools and education have hardly ever started from the children, the teachers, the parents, their rights, aspirations, and hopes, and their projects for the present and future. Adolphe Ferriere (1947) offers a particularly effective admonishment in this regard:

Schools were created on the devil's indications.
Children love nature: they have been placed in closed rooms. Children love to play; they have been put to work. They love to see that their activities serve some purpose: their activities have been rendered purposeless. They love to

move: they are forced to stay still. They love to manipulate objects: they have been put in contact with ideas. They love to use their hands: only their brains have been put into action. They love to speak: they are asked to remain silent. They love to reason: they are asked to learn by rote. They would like to seek out science: it has been presented to them as already determined. They wish to pursue their imagination: they suffer under the yoke of adults. They love to be enthusiastic: punishments have been invented. They would like to freely make themselves useful: they have been taught to passively obey.

(p. XII)

An echo of these thoughts can be found in the words of Loris Malaguzzi, who cautions: "in these mythic schools the role of their young users is to believe in them, and the role of parents is to delegate their powers and rights to them, and only hold rights that are fake and subordinate" (Malaguzzi, 1975, in Cagliari et al., 2016, p. 231). The tension of Reggio Emilia's project is that of recognising and giving value to children's participation, as their right and capacity, and this comes from a conviction that children's points of view, their research[es] and ways of constructing knowledge are fundamental elements in constructing our educational project, as are those of teachers, parents, and citizens. Therefore, we return to the importance of the diffused decision-making processes discussed by Capra and Mattei (2015), that make the value of education as a commons into an effective reality. Recognising children's participation in constructing knowledge and shaping how we define the educational system's organisational features is the responsibility of teachers and *pedagogistas*. In fact, we are suspicious of transferring forms of adult democracy, such as parliaments and constitutional courts, onto children wholesale, though it is a widespread practice in several western countries. We believe instead that it is respectful towards children, and a right of children, to give them a voice, whether their words are *spoken, drawn, acted on or constructed in a 3-dimensional form*, in places where they naturally speak, draw, act, and construct together, and to make their voices visible through documentation.

This lays an obligation on adults to activate tools in order that listening to children's different learning strategies is not only a personal openness but a professional dimension, enriched by exchange, *confronto,* and shared interpretation, to be capable of closer knowledge of each child's ways of knowing and forming relations, and capable of constructing a dialogue that makes every child's potential for relations and learning more competent.

(Cagliari, 2022, p. 5, [translated by Jane McCall])

Documenting observations is not one of the many possible ways of carrying out the work of an educator, but rather it is the tool for corresponding to children's right to participation, i.e. for them to have a bearing on decisions related to them. Only through the collegial analysis of documentation that has been attentively and competently elaborated, can adults proceed by means of pathways that are neither pre-defined nor *chance* – following the impulse of the moment – but with a constant, recursive, and reflexive *pensiero progettuale*. *Pensiero progettuale* respectfully includes children's contributions to produce elaborations in which children are acknowledged as authors, and which speak to the adult culture of both educators and civil society. This is perhaps the most complex aspect of Reggio Emilia's educational project. As we have seen, the process of interpretation is particularly delicate and not without risks, and the first of these is the instrumental use of children for our own ends. This is why the dialectic between multiple personal and professional points of view acts as an ethical and scientific guarantee of children's propositions.

In this light we can see more clearly the centrality of the *pensiero progettuale* that belongs to experience in Reggio Emilia: experience which, as noted in Chapter 5, pushes the boundaries and invents new ways of thinking and doing not just pedagogically. In this recursive design structure, essential elements are: the construction of contexts that make it possible for children to [re]search their own knowledge paths; the multiple languages children are recognised as having for expressing themselves and dialoguing; documented observation; collegial re-cognition; the recursive procedure of pre-figuration – observation – documentation – re-cognition – new pre-figurations – observations and so on; and the role that scientific and disciplinary knowledge plays in interpretation. The intent of this structure is to favour children's participation in the most authentic way possible, so that education can be a commons, and not a technique that is efficient in terms of time and effective on the level of performance.

Similarly, family and citizen participation does not have the aspiration of forming an uncritical and unconditional adherence to the project, but of offering everyone who may be directly or indirectly interested in the present and future of new generations, the possibility of contributing to decision-making processes. There is nothing romantic or unrealistic in this. We are all aware of the specific roles and responsibilities of teachers, *pedagogistas*, directors, city officers, and mayors. However, what makes the difference, as we have stated several times, is the dialectical process, the *confronto* and dialogue through which we arrive at our decisions.

Parent participation is also based on thinking of a designerly nature, on creating contexts in which parents and/or citizens can examine the hypotheses and issues related to the work we do from their own points of view, contributing with their own knowledge to changing the vision of an issue and forming solutions that can be adopted. Again, with parents and citizens it is important to avoid a ritualisation of standardised rigid procedures empty of the meanings with which they were created, because what is important is the capacity of participatory bodies to stay close to the realities they represent.

> Participation in educational services must have a rigorous processual dynamic, but it cannot be regimented into rigid organisations and bodies that risk having their own preservation and self-reproduction as their only purpose. The vitality of participation is nourished by an open, plural and inclusive dimension, one in which representation is replaced with personal responsibility, collective ties and transparency. The idea of participation we are proposing is of a public space in which we can express ourselves, a piazza that mediates communication, a place of reciprocity.
>
> *(Cagliari, 2015, p. 207, [translated by Jane McCall])*

Participating in the idea of *Education Commons* therefore proposes *nidi* and *scuole dell'infanzia* as public *piazzas* for discussion. It is the idea of a living school, in a social body attentive to all the subjectivities inhabiting it, to their well-being, identities, and life stories. These are public places, where doing things together and discussion between adults, between children, and between children and adults, deepens a knowledge of the world we live in, builds human relations, and makes it possible for us to share values and purpose. This tension of doing and thinking together tends towards making values a lived reality, first and foremost the value of equal rights and respect for all differences, and it safeguards their existence, never giving up the horizon of utopias.

With the help of a brief contribution from philosopher Salvatore Veca (2014), we will now move forward another step on the theme of participation. Veca (2014) affirms: "a public space in a democratic regime includes functions that are alternative to those of the state and institutions. What is made manifest in a public space is the alternative potentials of society" (p. 88, [translated by Jane McCall]). This consideration introduces the issue of change, of dialogue with contemporary life, and the innovation that participation can foster when it is seen as a construction site, a workshop, in which everyone is asked to actively contribute to constructing the educational project, and in which everyone who is part of it contributes to its definition, negotiating intentions, purposes, and desires, and visions of future. In other words, if we see participation as everyone's prerogative, and as a willingness to make our points of view and thinking available in the dialogue, so that they become part of the dialectical play of analysis, *confronto*, and evaluation, it encourages us to be open to the new, to research, to elaborate unexplored thinking and strategies that tend towards greater inclusivity, to recognise the right to subjectivity, to respect differences and everyone's right to a voice, and a re-composition of the fragmentation that is typical of children's and adults' lives. These are specific traits of Reggio Emilia's project, the value of which is not only pedagogical, but above all political and cultural. In 1971, Loris Malaguzzi gave a talk at a conference in Modena on which he had worked tirelessly, on the theme of social management, saying:

> The issues of social management at the centre of our debate do not merely wish to regain a balance or make formal adjustments to school organisation and functions. We want to initiate a movement and grow it, join together the themes of school, education and society, examine and discover their correlations and contradictions. We want to reveal the instrumental and subordinate role of educational philosophy, but also the meaning of struggles taking place in society and their connections with issues of cultural and professional education for children and young people.
>
> *(Malaguzzi, 1971, in Cagliari et al., 2016, p. 176)*

Although participation is necessary, it is not enough in itself to guarantee the generation and maintenance of an inclusive project that tends towards an equality of opportunities: crucial conditions for this are a constant vigilance, a utopian tension that refuses to succumb to the dictatorship of the impossibility of change and of no-alternative to the status quo, and an honest desire to pursue participation itself. It is important for participation never to become the objective we have achieved, but to always ask, with Malaguzzi:

> How much road is there to go before this right to self-management, to working and creating together, to creating democratic education intent on forming happier children and happier humans, people who are more capable of reading the things and issues of the world together, can be realised and no longer be a privilege but the right of all?
>
> *(Malaguzzi, 1973)*

Conclusions

In this chapter we set out to reinforce a concept that runs through the whole book: education, rather than being a field of techniques, methodologies, and quantitative evaluation systems applied in rigid unchanging forms, can, with the same rigour be a dynamic of values, beliefs, dialogues, and *confronto* in which all those involved, in any way, can and must participate – children, teachers, parents, managers, local administrators, and citizens. Only through this involvement, which the idea of commons necessitates, can we generate a project of a future capable of giving dignity to the humanity of the human, the non-human, and the posthuman.

The invitation and aspiration with which we leave the reader, is for each and every one of us, whether educator or citizen, to become capable, by uniting our stories, our experiences, our competences and passions, of changing a culture that, rather than giving each one of us the freedom of shaping

272 Education Commons

ourselves, acts with forms of hidden violence to give pre-defined forms to the present and future dwellers of this planet. It is not true that there are no alternatives, and it is not true that these aspirations are impossible. The stories we have told in this book, of a small city, in a small state in Europe, can be an example of how realising a utopia is possible, inviting us all to hope and take courage.

> Courage is the active reaction to individual or collective danger. It is, therefore, the opposite of indifference, of in-action, of passivity. It is the opposite of resignation. Courage is the virtue of citizens who are aware and, in a wider sense, of those who accept the responsibility of being human [...] If we understand courage to have this meaning then it becomes the result of choices and practices; it is the strength of facing the world, aware of its complexity, but also aware of our capacity for changing it.
>
> *(Carofiglio, 2020, p. 95, [translated by Jane McCall])*

Notes

1 Ostrom's book is a critical response to Garrett Hardin's much cited 1968 article on *The Tragedy of the Commons*.
2 The term "common-pool natural resources" generally refers to oceans, fisheries, freshwater supplies, wildlife, wilderness, and public open spaces.
3 "Services" is a term situated in a precise historical, social, political, and cultural moment, as argued by Malaguzzi. The initial elaboration was that of structures at the service of female emancipation and women's entrance into the world of work. As we have underlined on several occasions in this book the word is still used, and has taken on a specific educational meaning in Reggio Emilia, and more generally on a national level.
4 This choice of terminology has been taken on loan from Umberto Eco, as used in *Costruire il nemico* [*Constructing the enemy*], 2020; English tr. *Inventing The Enemy: Essays*, 2013. We are speaking of a phenomenon that in the absence of enemies leads us to give shape to them by identifying them in professional categories, peoples, and social classes.
5 A Protocol of Understanding is predominantly a political-administrative act defining the terms of a collaboration between public and private subjects who reciprocally commit to achieving common objectives. The act drawn up by the Reggio Emilia municipality with providers of the city's 0–6 educational services, and approved by City Council, is therefore a governance act. Following an introduction on the city's social context and data from the city's *anagrafe* (administrative offices and database recording births, deaths, family status, residence, and so on), the document goes on to establish strategic objectives, the reciprocal commitments between subjects of the protocol listing them in detail, tools for governance (Conventions, Pedagogical Co-ordination, Parity Commission), and economic resources.
6 Conventions are administrative acts that can be of two kinds. The first is related to contracts drawn up with subjects who have participated in public exams or competitions or in tenders, and having arrived in first place owing to the quality of their educational project or the economic conditions they propose, obtain management of a structure that is the property of the municipality (management tender). These educational services [schools] are called "indirectly managed municipal educational

services". These services are among those subject to Protocols of Understanding. The second kind of Convention, directly related to Protocols of Understanding, is an act that commits the municipality to providing a contribution to private providers who, in premises of their own property, contribute to offering the city's families places in a *nido* or *scuola dell'infanzia*.

7 Previously discussed in Chapter 2.

References

Acheson, J. (2011). Ostrom for anthropologists. *International Journal of the Commons*, 5(2), 319–339.

Bobbio, L. (2010). Democrazia e nuove forme di partecipazione. In M. Bovero, & V. Pazè (Eds.), *La democrazia in nove lezioni* (pp. 46–62). Laterza.

Bollier, D. (2006). The growth of the commons paradigm. In C. Hess & E. Ostrom (Eds.), *Understanding knowledge as a commons: From theory to practice* (pp. 27–40). The MIT Press. https://doi.org/Thegrowthofthecommonsparadigm

Boonen, C., Brando, N., Cogolati, S., Hagen, R., Vanstappen, N., & Wouters, J. (2019). Governing as commons or as global public goods: Two tales of power. *International Journal of the Commons*, 13(1), 553–577. https://doi.org/10.18352/ijc.907

Cagliari, P. (2015). La partecipazione politica, sociale e educativa nei servizi per l'infanzia. In M. Guerra, & E. Luciano (Eds.), *Costruire partecipazione: La relazione tra famiglie e servizi per l'infanzia in una prospettiva internazionale* (pp. 199–211). Edizioni Junior/Gruppo Spaggiari.

Cagliari, P. (2022). I diritti delle bambine e dei bambini. *Bambini*, 3, 4–5.

Cagliari, P., Castagnetti, M., Giudici, C., Rinaldi, C., Vecchi, V., & Moss, P. (Eds.). (2016). *Loris Malaguzzi and the schools of Reggio Emilia: A selection of his writings and speeches, 1945–1993*. Routledge.

Capra, F., & Mattei, U. (2015). *The ecology of law: Toward a legal system in tune with nature*. Berrett-Koehler Publishers, Inc.

Carofiglio, G. (2020). *Della gentilezza e del coraggio: Breviario di politica e altre cose*. Feltrinelli.

Clement, F., Harcourt, W. J., Joshi, D., & Sato, C. (2019). Feminist political ecologies of the commons and commoning. *International Journal of the Commons*, 13(1), 1–15. https://doi.org/10.18352/ijc.972

Dahlberg, G., Moss, P., & Pence, A. (2007). *Beyond quality in early childhood education and care: Languages of evaluation*. Routledge.

Ferriere, A. (1947). *Trasformiamo la scuola*. La Nuova Italia.

Gandini, L. (2017). La storia, le idee, La cultura: La voce e il pensiero di Loris Malaguzzi. Interviste a cura di Lella Gandini. In C. Edwards, L. Gandini, & G. Forman (Eds.), *I cento linguaggi dei bambini: L'approccio di Reggio Emilia all'educazione dell'infanzia* (pp. 55–111). Edizioni Junior/Gruppo Spaggiari.

Hess, C., & Ostrom, E. (2006a). Introduction: An overview of the knowledge commons. In C. Hess & E. Ostrom (Eds.), *Understanding knowledge as a commons: From theory to practice* (pp. 3–26). The MIT Press. https://doi.org/10.7551/mitpress/6980.001.0001

Hess, C., & Ostrom, E. (Eds.). (2006b). *Understanding knowledge as a commons: From theory to practice*. The MIT Press. https://doi.org/10.7551/mitpress/6980.001.0001

274 Education Commons

Ingold, T. (2013). *Making: Anthropology, archeology, art and architecture.* Routledge.

Lemeilleur, S., & Sermage, J. (2020). Building a knowledge commons. *International Journal of the Commons, 14*(1), 465–480. https://doi.org/10.2307/27016577

Malaguzzi, L. (1973). With a painted train; children and adults together. *L'Unita.*

Mangabeira Unger, R. (2006). *What should the left propose?* Verso Books.

Miszczynki, M. (2022). *The art of the creative commons: Openness, networked value and peer production in the sound industry.* Brill.

Ostrom, E. (1990). *Governing the commons: The evolution of institutions for collective action.* Cambridge University Press.

Rose, C. M. (2020). Thinking about the commons. *International Journal of the Commons, 14*(1), 557–566. https://doi.org/10.5334/ijc.987

Sanchez, J. (2020). *Architecture for the commons: Participatory systems in the age of platforms.* Routledge. https://doi.org/10.4324/9780429432118

Scuole e Nidi d'Infanzia Istituzione del Comune di Reggio Emilia. (2011). *Piano Programma.* Reggio Emilia. Retrieved from http://www.scuolenidi.re.it/allegati/Piano%20programma%202011.pdf

Veca, S. (2014). *Non c'e' alternativa, FALSO!.* Laterza.

9

THE VALUE OF THE COMMONS AND AN ETHIC OF ALLIANCES[1]

Stefania Giamminuti

> *Education Commons* is a beautiful metaphor for thinking of education to-
> day, with a different perspective and for a different education: education,
> like water, is essential to life and to individual, collective and civic wellbeing.
> (Giudici & Cagliari, 2014, p. 34, our translation)

Introduction

In this chapter, we consider the overtly political stance of the educational project of Reggio Emilia, and we set forth an invitation to privilege the immaterial good that education produces. Drawing on both interview excerpts and
critical theories of philosophy and politics, we examine how the experience
of Reggio Emilia has resisted the "capitalist field" (Massumi, 2017), instead
privileging "affectively-based politics" which "can give rise to radically inclusive forms of direct democracy" (Massumi, 2017, p. 17). We propose that the
experience of Reggio Emilia is an example of "micropolitical flourishing" for
whom "enacting the unimaginable" (Massumi, 2015, p. 82) of the *Education
Commons* continues to be a collective responsibility and care.

In illustrating the meaning and experience of an ethic of alliances, we draw on
the thinking of philosopher, artist, and dancer Erin Manning, specifically her notion of "collective individuation" (Manning, 2013) and the concept of "always
more than one" (Manning, 2013). As explained by Massumi (2015) "a collective individuation is a correlated becoming through which individuals receive a
boost of extra-being from their participation in an event that surpasses them as
individuals" (p. 201); all those who contributed to our research expressed the
value of participating in an educational project that went beyond themselves.

DOI: 10.4324/9781003181026-9

276 The value of the commons and an ethic of alliances

In fact, we dwell on the ethic of alliances in conclusion to our storying because, in many contexts other than Reggio Emilia where neoliberal values and pursuits are privileged, the individual is celebrated and separated from its milieu (Manning, 2013). In such settings, educational leadership often becomes something that converges within the body of an individual, and thus from this point of view the role of the *pedagogista* can be easily misinterpreted and misunderstood, with power seen to be coming from outside (Massumi, 2015).

Instead, an ethic of alliances recognises that "there is no body that isn't already collective, always already active in the relational interweaving of more than one tending, more than one phase, more than one ecology in the making" (Manning, 2013, p. 27). In shadowing Paola Strozzi for this research project, it became evident to me how *pedagogistas* are constantly active in such ways, where multiple tendings, phases, and ecologies emerge constantly and unexpectedly in the space of a day. Interview excerpts convey the complex relational interweaving that animates daily life in the municipal *nidi* and *scuole dell'infanzia* of Reggio Emilia and the "collective platforms for experimentation" (Massumi, 2017, p. 110) that *pedagogistas* constantly create with the participation of teachers, *atelieristas*, children, families, and citizens.

Such pedagogical-social-political-cultural work, in spilling over to multiple relations beyond the city of Reggio Emilia, can be conceived as "a minor gesture" (Manning, 2016). The minor gesture is "a gestural force that opens experience to its potential variation", showing that it is possible to be different, unsettling conventionality and "unmooring [the major key's] structural integrity, problematizing its normative standards" (Manning, 2016, p. 1). As Manning (2016) suggests, "the minor invents new forms of existence, and with them, in them, we come to be" (p. 2). This chapter thus concludes with the exhortation that it is possible to invent new and experimental forms of existence, or "minor gestures" (Manning, 2016) for early childhood education and care elsewhere, and that within such ecologies the role of the *pedagogista* is central to imaginings, thinkings, experimentations, relations, and everyday practices.

Privileging immaterial goods in dangerous times

The commons are all those elements, those conditions that enable the enactment of fundamental human rights and free development of the individual. Education is a right of children and young people, who should all benefit from [education] without limitations due to wealth, income, merit, gender, geographical provenance, etc. But [education] is also a resource for adults, who defend it and enrich it through their participation in the educational project of school – a civil, cultural, pedagogical and social project – and who benefit from the **immaterial good** that [education] produces: civic, cultural, pedagogical and social knowledge.

(Giudici & Cagliari, 2014, p. 34 [bolded
for emphasis], our translation)

As the world emerges from the devastation and despair wrought by the COVID-19 pandemic, it becomes ever more urgent for us to recognise the value of immaterial good. Giroux (2021a) exhorts us to reclaim solidarity, to fulfil the promises and ideals of democracy, and to pay heed to history so that it may "provide insights into imagining alternative forms of social life, solidarity, and the possibility of new political formations" (p. 208). This tension towards imagining alternatives, closely aligned with political thought and action, was felt deeply in post-war Reggio Emilia, when "an unknown era was opening up, a broad horizon where you still could not measure yourself, or measure thoughts and desires. You were in a city that was hoping, and wanted to shout it" (Malaguzzi, in Cagliari et al., 2016, p. 23). This time of liberation from the oppression of fascism was, much like today, a time to "build solidarity among different groups, imagine new forms of social life, make the impossible possible and produce a democratic socialist project in defense of equality, social justice, and popular sovereignty" (Giroux, 2021b, p. 6).

Today, "we are living in dangerous times" (Riddle & Apple, 2019, p. 1); harvesting hope through a re-evaluation of the common good and defence of democratic values may be our way forward. As Riddle and Apple (2019) note, "the act of restoring and strengthening thick forms of democracy is where we can start in education, a project to which so many people throughout the world have devoted their lives in schools, universities, and communities" (p. 7). This includes the citizens and educators of Reggio Emilia, who have coined the term *Education Commons* as a refrain for collective action and civic responsibility. Ostrom and Hess (2006) argue that the effective design of common-pool resource institutions requires "successful collective action and self-governing behaviors; trust and reciprocity; and the continual design and/or evolution of appropriate rules" (p. 43). We have illustrated many instances of such collective action and self-governing behaviours in the experience of Reggio Emilia, whereby the *pedagogista* has a pivotal role in fostering relations of trust and reciprocity and in initiating continual design and evolution of rules and regulatory frameworks.

Education Commons as a concept and as a lived reality therefore requires collective tending of values, policies, and actions that are ultimately capable of realising utopian possibilities, embodying the notion that "democracy should be a way of thinking about education, one that thrives on connecting equity to merit, learning to ethics, and agency to an investment in and strengthening of the public good" (Giroux, 2021a, p. 142). Before we return to dwelling on the possibilities of *Education Commons*,[2] we illustrate the political and cultural scenarios that dominate much of the field of early childhood education and care.

The marketplace and early childhood education as a commodity

The values of civic collectivity, solidarity, and democratic participation foregrounded above are not readily found in the discourse that surrounds early childhood education and care internationally today, particularly in contexts

278 The value of the commons and an ethic of alliances

where neoliberal governments construct their early childhood services as commodities:

> What I would say to Australian families is to make sure you shop around and find a childcare provider that is providing value for money when it comes to early childhood education.
>
> *(Dan Tehan, former Australian Federal Education Minister, cited in Karp, 2020)*

These words are emblematic of a pervasive political discourse that positions families as consumers and clients, distancing them from the possibilities of participation, debate, exploration of cultural alternatives, and construction of a commons that have belonged to the experience of Reggio Emilia from its inception. As Dahlberg (2016) laments, we have transitioned "from the norm of solidarity to the norm of autonomy" (p. 126) and so we find ourselves mired in images of the parent as "autonomous consumer, concerned only with securing the best buy for their child" (Fielding & Moss, 2011, p. 17). This mirage of choice and autonomy, which amplifies a "duty to be free" (Popkewitz & Bloch, 2001, cited in Dahlberg, 2016, p. 127) on the part of citizens for whom early education should instead be a fundamental right, is a motor of exclusion which "qualifies and disqualifies for action, as some children and parents will be brought into active citizenship, while others will not" (Dahlberg, 2016, p. 127).

Not an education system of democracy therefore, not a commons nor a right of all children, but instead an exclusive school-business where teachers are technicians and children are passive, compliant workers of the future. Dahlberg (2016) further contends that "an economic logic, with numbers and quantitative measures, has begun to play a considerable role in legitimising decisions for developing preschools and schools" (p. 125). This is evident in the words of former Australian Prime Minister Scott Morrison, at a time of substantial nationwide early childhood reform where re-imaginings could have been possible:

> We're not trying to run an education system here, we're trying to provide a payment to help people be in work and stay in work [...] which is good for the economy.
>
> *(Scott Morrison, former Minister for Social Services and former Prime Minister of Australia, cited in Morris, 2015)*

The threat from economic rationality is larger than we can conceive, for not only does such a logic determine educational policies and practices, but it limits thought and action and it constrains possibilities, shaping what we hope for (Dahlberg, 2016). The complexities that in Reggio Emilia come from the interweaving of relations, the nurturing of participation, the commitment to research and innovation, and the daily engagement in political debate, are here reduced to education in the service only of economic activity. These are the voices that characterise what Massumi (2017) calls "the neoliberal moment", when "the economy became a regime of power in its own right" (p. 9). It is a frightening time, where humanity is subordinate to the economy and the purpose of education is reduced to producing "capitalized individuals" (Massumi, 2017, p. 13).

> This is the story of the place where we are now – a place in which the fullness of being in the world as a human – Homo sapiens, Homo ludens – is transformed (reduced!) to humanness in relation to economic activity only – Homo economicus.
>
> *(Arndt et al., 2018, p. 100)*

Can we continue to conceive of early childhood education and care settings as *locus economicus*? Dangerously, schools, like other institutions, "must of course bend to the logic of capital. They are fed by capital and under neoliberalism are allowed to prosper only if they in turn feed the capitalist economy, providing something that can be considered an "added value" for it" (Massumi, 2017, p. 23). But, despite what the culture of "inevitabilities" (Riddle & Apple, 2019, p. 8) would lead us to believe, the answers are still open to the questions regarding how we conceptualise childhood, what we conceive as the purpose of education, and how we imagine the roles of those working with young children. The responsibility of critical democracy in education is to continue to challenge the reductive and dangerous discourses of "inevitabilities" and "no alternatives" (Riddle & Apple, 2019). It is possible to choose the common good; it is possible to eschew economic discourses in favour of the immaterial good that education produces. In fact, the Reggio Emilia choice of artfulness and culture, of *progettazione* and documentation as research, is a choice about privileging democracy and ethics. It is far from the *locus economicus* narrative, where services find themselves wilfully avoiding reciprocity in favour of the capitalist economy and the market:

> A key focus of a business venture must be commercial viability. This focus provides little incentive for services to act in socially beneficial ways that encourage reciprocity and information-sharing, particularly if it threatens the commercial viability of the service. For example, it tends to reduce opportunities to share information between services and educators if they are in competition with each other for the market share, particularly if the information to be shared is considered commercial in confidence […] this construction undermines collective action.
>
> *(Press et al., 2018, p. 335)*

Documentation in Reggio Emilia has always promoted democracy and collective action of children and educators; documentation generates *Education*

280 The value of the commons and an ethic of alliances

Commons. Grounded in locality but always looking beyond, documentation is the place for "local micro-politics", or "immanent critique", "active, participatory critique [...] that actively alters conditions of emergence" (Massumi, 2015, pp. 70–71). In contexts that are driven by marketplace values, often educational services will purport to be working with documentation, but then avoid sharing it with others outside of the individual families attending their service, in consideration of protecting their market share. Thus, documentation becomes commercial-in-confidence, or rather it is not documentation at all. This is the place where micro-politics and the *Education Commons* come to die, where the affect gained through collective action is hijacked in the name of profit: "capitalism [...] hijacks affect in order to intensify profit potential. It literally valorizes affect" (Massumi, 2015, pp. 20–21).

As Dahlberg (2016) cautions, in the current logic of consumer choice in early childhood education and care, "the market is now taking over the aesthetic and ethical field – a field where possibilities of alternative practices and resistance against [...] individualistic and competitive subjectivities and predetermined outcomes may be possible" (p. 129). In hijacking and valorising affect, capitalist and neoliberal cultures have conspired to make the commons appear impossible and undesirable. But, "it is critical to be able to think about and experiment with the ways in which affectively-based politics can give rise to radically inclusive forms of direct democracy" (Massumi, 2017, p. 17); this is the experience of Reggio Emilia, where the field of politics is inseparable from the aesthetic, the ethical, the affective; and hence an *Education Commons* is more-than possible.

A political stance: living an *Education Commons*

> This is the point where some of my life choices were born. I would enroll in the Communist Party. I knew nothing about politics, of the October Revolution, of Marx, Lenin, Gramsci, Togliatti. But I was sure I was taking the side of the weakest, of the people who carried most hope.
>
> *(Malaguzzi, in Cagliari et al., 2016, p. 23)*

The end of the Second World War, Reggio Emilia; a time and place where, in the person of Loris Malaguzzi, education, culture, and politics became inextricably interwoven and associated with hope. Only a few days after joining the Communist Party, Malaguzzi would happen upon the citizens of the nearby town of Villa Cella, who had sold trucks, a tank, and some horses left behind by the fleeing Germans and with the precious proceeds of this unusual sale had decided to build a school for young children, brick by brick, in hope and solidarity (Cagliari et al., 2016). As noted by Moss (Cagliari et al., 2016), Malaguzzi's membership of the Communist Party was not exceptional at that time and place, and it was in *Partito Comunista Italiano* [Italian Communist Party]

The value of the commons and an ethic of alliances **281**

led administrations such as the one in Reggio Emilia in the 1960s that the "municipal school revolution" was born (p. xv).

Moss (in Cagliari et al., 2016) contends that Malaguzzi is "a vivid example of the contention that education is, first and foremost, a political practice" (p. xvi) not reduced to particular party leanings, but rather education as political "because it called for making choices between conflicting alternatives, including values, understandings and ways of working; and not only making choices but being prepared to go out and argue the case for them" (p. xvi). The political nature of the educational project would thus not stop at Malaguzzi's membership of the Communist Party, nor would it be put to rest once the darkness of the post war period was replaced by growth and prosperity. The enduring political stance of this experience is unique, and is sustained by its consistent engagement in local and global debate, its unwavering commitment to participation, and by well-considered organisational innovations:

> To create change, Malaguzzi from the start constructed an intelligent organisation by building into the schools different supportive structures, previously unknown in education, for example the roles of "pedagogista" and "atelierista".
>
> *(Dahlberg, in Cagliari et al., 2016, p. x)*

Within this intelligent organisation, notions of power and hierarchy are framed by the value of the commons. The Reggio Emilia experience of hierarchy, or rather the existence of a hierarchical structure within the Preschools and Infant-toddler Centres – Istituzione of the Municipality of Reggio Emilia, was briefly foregrounded in Chapter 2, and the role of the *pedagogista* within this structure was alluded to elsewhere. We have not dwelt on hierarchy because it does not emerge as a defining feature of the educational project, but it is necessary to note here that an intelligent organisation within a commons framework relies on the participation of all those involved in its preservation through "a bottom-up hierarchy in decision-making power" (Boonen et al., 2019, p. 567). To operate an intelligent organisation within a commons framework requires the belief that "people can cooperate and keep credible commitments without there being an external enforcer" (Boonen et al., 2019, p. 560). In Reggio Emilia, *pedagogistas* (and other systemic figures) could be perceived as enacting a somewhat external role because they are not present in *nidi* and *scuole dell'infanzia* on a daily basis; however, they are internal to the system, acting within a shared attitude of *progettazione*, as opposed to operating as enforcers of controls or quantitative standards.

Pedagogistas embody this notion of "power-with" (Arendt, 1970) in their daily work through values of relationality, care, dialectics, and reciprocity. Within a commons framework, "it is held that power originates from the autonomous cooperation within (and among) communities" (Boonen et al.,

282 The value of the commons and an ethic of alliances

2019, p. 571). As such, the *pedagogistas* (Cagliari et al., 2012) speak of balancing concerns and possibilities such as "the inspiring vision of the mayor" or "financial constraints" (p. 145) in their work with teachers and families, and of their engagement in "a continuous exchange of information regarding what is happening within the schools, new advances in theory and practice, and political developments" (Cagliari et al., 2012, pp. 136–137). An image emerges of a profession that is deeply committed to an *Education Commons*, with a responsibility to pursue and defend this value daily and collectively. The *pedagogistas* sustain the *Education Commons* by: sharing and enacting the educational project's enduring political stance; respecting the needs, possibilities, and cultural ferment of the current time; building and making visible a new culture of childhood; and constantly weaving alliances.

Of the many aspects that have emerged out of the enduring experience of Reggio Emilia to irrevocably influence and alter early childhood pedagogy and culture globally, its profoundly political nature and its commons framework have been, perhaps conveniently, generally overlooked. Many reasons for this oversight could be hypothesised, with one perhaps being the visibility the experience garnered in the USA following the naming of *Scuola dell'infanzia* Diana as amongst the 10 best schools in the world in a renowned *Newsweek* article published in December 1991. The international impact and visibility that followed the publication of this article might have otherwise been dimmed by highlighting the Communist and Socialist leanings and origins and the "overtly political stance" (Moss,in Cagliari et al., 2016, p. xvi) of the educational project. Furthermore, to emphasise the collectivist values of the experience would likely have generated mistrust, as Bollier (2006) notes in relation to the exoticism with which the concept and practice of the commons is traditionally greeted in the USA: "perhaps because the Cold War was directed against communism and its cousin, socialism, Americans tend to regard collective-management regimes as morally problematic and destructive of freedom, at least in the abstract" (p. 27).

We might also contend that in many international contexts that have been informed by Reggio Emilia, educational leadership remains traditionally hierarchical and managerial and therefore the absence of the role of *pedagogista* could result in disregard for the more political aspects of the experience and might generate avoidance of political debate. Furthermore, any notion of the commons would likely be resisted within the conventional management structures that pervade educational settings worldwide, with self-regulated modes of governance mistrusted in favour of more "top-down" power systems that are characteristic of a market logic. Hence the Reggio Emilia experience, which inextricably weaves pedagogy, politics, and culture into daily life and organisation of the educational system, has elsewhere frequently been reduced to aspects of pedagogy and curriculum in isolation. To separate the pedagogy from its politics may have made this experience more amenable to becoming known and appreciated in other contexts; however, conversely much of the initial ideals and current struggles of the *nidi* and *scuole dell'infanzia* are lost to the understanding of those worldwide who fail to appreciate, or wilfully repudiate, the enduring connection between education and politics anywhere. It is by practicing politics that we can imagine and invent possibilities for the present and the future; as Massumi (2017) notes, "the politics practiced in the present should prefigure the relational field to come" (p. 63).

We now turn to highlight the political choices that Reggio Emilia made historically and continues to make to this day for an *Education Commons*, making "futurity *in the present* already actionable" (Massumi, 2017, p. 63) by conceiving of education as a collective project for the construction of a new culture of childhood. The voices of its protagonists speak of broad horizons lived every day, in solidarity with a city – a civil, cultural, pedagogical, and social project, and a right of all children.

The value of the commons: micropolitics and the unimaginable

In separating the political from the affective, neoliberal movements demand obedience, undermine critical thought and democratic action, and "manufacture normality" (Massumi, 2015, p. 20). Giroux (2021a) defines neoliberalism as "both a politics and a pedagogy of containment and disappearance" (p. 6) and he bemoans the current historical moment which "supports notions of self-interest that tear up social solidarities in devastating ways" (p. 7). Renzo Bonazzi, mayor of Reggio Emilia from 1962 to 1976 and ardent supporter of the *nidi* and *scuole dell'infanzia*, qualifies the educational project as an experience of democratic resistance and freedom that is inextricably bound to social solidarities:

> Mussolini and the fascists made us understand that obedient human beings are dangerous human beings. When we decided to build a new society after the war, we understood that we needed to have schools in which children dared to think for themselves, and where children got the conditions for becoming active and critical citizens.
>
> *(Bonazzi, R., cited in Cagliari et al., 2016, p. viii)*

As the echoes of fascism and its destructions abound in our present times, it is impossible to ignore the connection between these past aspirations and those expressed by Henry Giroux in 2021:

> In an age where civic culture is collapsing and a culture of compassion gives way to a culture of cruelty, it is all the more crucial to take seriously the notion that a democracy cannot exist or be defended without informed and critically engaged citizens.
>
> *(Giroux, 2021a, p. 127)*

284 The value of the commons and an ethic of alliances

This dedication to building a new society is driven by what Riddle and Apple (2019) call "the principle of a sustainable and collective commitment to civic virtue through education" (p. 3), which they note is "more critically important than ever before" (p. 3). In the words of Renzo Bonazzi, and in the history and present of the experience of Reggio Emilia, we see an enactment of "the public sphere as a site of hope" (Giroux, 2021a, p. 4) and a commitment to defending democracy through minor gestures of resistance that embody the belief that anything is possible. The educational project of Reggio Emilia can thus be conceived as an experience of "micropolitical flourishing" whose continuous aspiration is "enacting the unimaginable" (Massumi, 2015, p. 82). *Pedagogistas* have a key role in enacting the unimaginable in everyday life, and in sustaining the micropolitical milieu of the city itself:

> We have always had a pedagogical coordination, which today is composed of a group of 12 *pedagogistas* who work as a team and meet weekly. The topics of our meetings are diverse, ranging in content from more operational and organisational matters. broader cultural issues, specific concerns in relation to teaching and learning, and formative aspects because we discuss *formazione* and the *formazione project*. Our notion of collegiality is relevant to the pedagogical coordination as well as within the *scuole* and *nidi;* there is a sort of mirroring in fact between the *nidi* and *scuole dell'infanzia* and the structure of the pedagogical coordination. Furthermore, this aspect of collegiality expresses the democratic fabric that is at the heart of the city, a democratic fabric that the pedagogical coordination pursues as its ultimate aim [...] *Nidi* and *scuole dell'infanzia* are places of democracy.
>
> *(Simona Bonilauri,* pedagogista, *interview with Stefania Giamminuti, Reggio Emilia)*

Simona Bonilauri highlights how *pedagogistas* weave the democratic fabric of the city and of its educational system through values of collegiality and participation in quotidian encounters and responsibilities. In so doing, they also convey to teachers the fundamental importance of keeping political thought always alive within the encounters between city, *nidi,* and *scuole dell'infanzia*, and beyond:

> The role of the teacher is a political role, that enables us to grow both personally and professionally. This interweaving with politics is evident here in Reggio Emilia - I had never felt it so strongly in the *nido* where I worked previously, even though it was located in a very small town, where the community truly took care of its children. But there we didn't experience such an interconnected role, such a strong civic sense. I believe that this [interweaving with politics] is determined by the role of the *pedagogista,* for indeed *pedagogistas* bring into the *nidi* and *scuole dell'infanzia* this political thought,

The value of the commons and an ethic of alliances **285**

intended not as belonging to the right or the left, but rather political thought understood as interest towards the community, towards the city's children.

(Ethel Carnevali, teacher, interview with Stefania Giamminuti, Reggio Emilia)

In Reggio Emilia, the value of the commons guides organisational, political, cultural, and pedagogical decisions and safeguards against solitude. The schools in Reggio Emilia are not places that close their gates to each other and to the city that surrounds them; these are instead places where children and adults recognise themselves as belonging to an ever-evolving participatory collective of the human and non-human. It is evident here that privileging a political stance is not to be reduced to party learnings; rather, the ethical position that being overtly political engenders creates the conditions for children to be valued participants in a democratic community. Nurturing political thought and participatory democracy is the responsibility of all families and all professional roles within the schools, but is particularly perceived by the *pedagogistas* themselves as a key responsibility and care:

> We take care of this project, we take care of the participation of families, and we [*pedagogistas*] ourselves participate in encounters and events that are of a public nature. In fact, we often organise them and promote them. Even though participation experiences fatigue and turbulence, it is always a lively phenomenon of our experience, sustained by a city that has always been similarly lively.
>
> *(Simona Bonilauri,* pedagogista, *interview with Stefania Giamminuti, Reggio Emilia)*

These qualities of enduring liveliness and collective participation are key to the flourishing of *Education Commons,* for "in a commons, how the actors interact strongly affects the success or failure of the resource" (Ostrom & Hess, 2006, p. 57) and specifically:

> *Education Commons* finds its strength and its essence in the fundamental and inalienable rights of human beings but also of civil society, in a logic that is not individualistic but rather of civic collectivity, solidarity and innovation that emerges out of the participation of all actors involved within an idea of permanent research.
>
> *(Giudici & Cagliari, 2014, p. 34, [our translation])*

Education Commons is placed at peril where such qualities of participation, civic collectivity, solidarity, and innovation are foregone in favour of individuality, autonomy, normative linearity, quantitative measures, and economic rationalism. The practice of permanently researching and encountering the thinking of others (adults, children, and materials) through documentation

286 The value of the commons and an ethic of alliances

and collective *confronto* is aligned with a democratic stance and with the value of the commons; it would not sit well with a school-business competing for consumers within an individualistic logic, and so in places other than Reggio Emilia the commons is often lost or perceived as impossible. Instead, from this democratic stance of solidarity and participation, one feels part of a collective project that is premised on the notion that education is a right:

> The right to competent teachers and *pedagogistas*, the right to a school. I have always felt like I am part of a project, that I belong to a community, and I have lived this as a civic and political responsibility. My own small part is made of circles connected to others, it is nurtured in *confronto* with others, through the points of view of others and in listening to others. It is as if you give form and content to democracy, no?
>
> *(Marina Castagnetti, teacher, interview with*
> *Stefania Giamminuti, Reggio Emilia)*

> I believe our services have always been experienced as places of life, meaning not simply services that respond to needs, but services that correspond to a right. Therefore, when you assume rights as a priority in your political and educational *progettazione,* you also acquire stories of life, it is inevitable.
>
> *(Annalisa Rabotti, pedagogista, interview with*
> *Stefania Giamminuti, Reggio Emilia)*

These words embody the humanity and affect that is essential to an *Education Commons,* and they reveal what Massumi (2017) refers to as "the state's humanistic aspirations (social welfare, universal rights, and respect of the person)" (p. 10), which are overwhelmingly overlooked in favour of economic rationalism. Attention and care for such humanistic matters shifts power from the economic "monetized, capitalist surplus-value" (Massumi, 2017, p. 27) concept that is derived by the market-driven values of the financial and corporate elite, towards "surplus-value of life" (Massumi, 2017, p. 27), which recognises common humanity and the need for participatory democracy, solidarity, and resistance towards oppression. Educational places everywhere should be constantly striving for "surplus-value of life" (Massumi, 2017, p. 27), as occurs in Reggio Emilia where teachers, *atelieristas, pedagogistas,* and families concur in the understanding that you belong to something larger than yourself: "people feel like they work for a project that is a project of education, but it is a project of community" (Daniela Lanzi, *pedagogista,* interview with Stefania Giamminuti, Reggio Emilia). After 40 years of working in a municipal *nido,* teacher Manuela Pederzoli emphasises the need for participatory democracy in daily life:

> I believe strongly in the values of an educating community. And I also believe that each one of us can offer a personal contribution to these values.

The value of the commons and an ethic of alliances **287**

Perhaps I have, along with my colleagues, contributed to this creation [of an educating community] humbly, through our daily work.

(Manuela Pederzoli, teacher, interview with
Stefania Giamminuti, Reggio Emilia)

Manuela, along with her colleagues, has contributed to creating "surplus-value of life" (Massumi, 2017, p. 27). The Reggio Emilia project of radical public education has endured over an unparalleled period of time due in no small part to its alliances, its commitment to collectivity, its image of children as competent interlocutors, and its capacity to look beyond itself. From the teacher in the *nido*, who sees herself as part of a larger system, contributing to the legacy of knowledge of the system and to its collective voice, to the *pedagogistas* for whom leading means "thinking, dialoguing and arguing about education itself" (Moss, in Cagliari et al., 2016, p. xix). This image stems from Malaguzzi, who saw that his "role as an educational leader was [...] to create and evolve an educational project in his city, but always in relation with others and in a spirit of participation and cooperation" (Moss, in Cagliari et al., 2016, p. xix). This, in contrast to the atomised leader, is the spirit of the democratic educational leader, who rather than controlling teachers "at a distance through a web of procedures, targets and measurements [...] offers an alternative of democratic and participatory management inscribed with an ethos of cooperation and dialogue and practised in close relationship with the frontline" (Moss, in Cagliari et al., 2016, pp. xvii–xviii). This is a leader who operates within a commons framework, bringing the value of the commons to bear in daily encounters and decision-making processes.

Perhaps, for our international early childhood settings, we can envisage places where working with the value of the commons and an ethic of alliances drives a closer encounter between research, theory, and practice, stronger affect and solidarity for and with teachers and children, elevating surplus-value of life to a priority for educational policy and practice. In the hope that the experience of Reggio Emilia will enable us to re-imagine our atomised systems of early education and to truly engage in an ethical encounter with the common good. We now turn to considering more deeply the "collective platforms for experimentation" (Massumi, 2017, p. 110) that *pedagogistas* constantly create with the participation of teachers, children, families, and citizens through an ethic of alliances.

An ethic of alliances: "always more than one"

In these posthuman times, amidst technologically mediated social relations, the negative effects of economic globalization and a fast-decaying environment, in response to the paranoid and racist rhetoric of our post-truth political leaders, how can we labour together to construct affirmative ethical and political practices? How can we work towards socially sustainable horizons of hope, through creative resistance? [...] The answer is in the doing, in the praxis of composing "we, a people", through alliances, transversal connections and in engaging in difficult conversations on what troubles us. In this respect, our posthuman times, with their large inhuman component, are all too human.

(Braidotti, 2019, p. 19)

It may by now be evident, or perhaps mystifying, to the reader that in this book about the role of the *pedagogista* we have resolutely eschewed any conceptualisation of "a leader" or "leadership" as embodied within the individual. Rather, we have dwelt on collectivity, on "the doing, in the praxis of composing 'we, a people'" (Braidotti, 2019, p. 19), for as Malaguzzi (2021) noted "every time we speak of children, every time we speak of ourselves, every time we speak of infant-toddler centres, or of schools, we are speaking of a system" (p. 48). *Pedagogista* Tiziana Filippini notes the contrast between this unique diffused systemic approach and the often atomised and fragmentary reality of educational leadership in other contexts:

This role of the *pedagogista* is still quite unique, in fact when I am in the United States and try to explain what it is and what it isn't ... There you have the person who is responsible for the curriculum, or "curriculum design", the other who is a "coach" and therefore sort of like a formative tutor, the other who is a "principal", and so forth. So, there are a myriad of roles, each quite specialised in their own bit, but in this fragmentation the question arises of: "where do you connect?". And furthermore, there is the problem of who creates the connections, because in the end all the responsibility for connecting can fall to the teacher.

(Tiziana Filippini, pedagogista, *interview with Stefania Giamminuti, Reggio Emilia)*

In sharing the many voices and experiences that participate in the Reggio Emilia system we have, in effect, always emphasised a collective responsibility towards creating connections, thus we have been speaking of and with "more than one" (Manning, 2013). The educational project of Reggio Emilia, named after its city as opposed to any possibly identifiable "I" or leader, has always retained "the collectivity at the heart of its having come-to-be" (Manning, 2013, p. 28). We discussed in Chapter 3 how this occurs through the value of relationality and an ethic of dialectics; here, as we near the conclusion to our storying, we wish to convey how privileging an ethic of alliances ensures the liveliness of an experience that believes deeply in, and determinedly seeks out, the "more-than". By keeping the "more-than" always in sight and mind, experiences, events, and relations in educational settings are never exhausted, contained or definitive, but rather possibilities for learning and relating are expanded, infinite, and connected. As Manning (2013) poetically conveys in relation to the event of sunlight shining on a wall in the early morning, the *nidi* and *scuole dell'infanzia* of Reggio Emilia, and all those who participate within, continue to approach experiences and relations for their potential to be more-than what they seem:

> Each actual occasion is more-than what it seems [...] Any occasion is at once the absoluteness of it-self in the moment of its concrescence and the will-have-become of its tendencies, attunements, and appetitions, both past and future. Take the event of a ray of sunlight that alters the color of the kitchen wall on a sunny early morning. Usually, the wall is light yellow. But this morning the wall is luminous, lighting up the kitchen in a way that exceeds this or that definite color. It is still yellow, but it is also more-than-yellow – how to define it? A yellowness? The musing on color is instantaneous. It is not a reflection on color but an immediate feeling activated by the event of the light.
>
> *(Manning, 2013, pp. 24–25)*

In many educational settings, yellow remains simply yellow, as neither adults nor children are invited to imagine further or differently, or indeed affectively. In Reggio Emilia, where aesthetics, ethics, and affect always participate in pedagogy, yellow is always yellow and more-than yellow. To see events and relations in this way means to forever expand the possibilities for alliances with the human and non-human, to never settle on the already known and already done, but to be alert to potential and curiosity in all encounters.

We now convey, through the words of the protagonists, how in Reggio Emilia "the span of becoming is broader than a being" (Massumi, Prelude, in Manning, 2013, p. xi); in the lives of *pedagogistas*, this means weaving ever-expanding (more-than) connections and relations which ensure the liveliness and enduring nature of the educational project. It can be supposed that the experience of Reggio Emilia has enjoyed its unique visibility, growth, and unparalleled livelihood due in no small part to the alliances it has consistently forged within its *nidi* and *scuole dell'infanzia*, its city, and well beyond.

Collective platforms for experimentation

In considering what it might mean to work daily with an ethic of alliances, we draw on the concept of "collective experimentation" (Manning, 2015, 2016; Massumi, 2017) which we have touched on earlier in this book in relation to *progettazione*. Here we look at how "collective platforms for experimentation" (Massumi, 2017) are created within the system in Reggio Emilia, involving all participants and relying upon broad alliances, individual and

290 The value of the commons and an ethic of alliances

collective curiosities, generosity of thinking, affect, and multiple professional competencies.

> In other words, we can experiment with techniques that bring people together, leaving behind their subject positions, suspending their personal beliefs, their doctrines, but bringing with them what moves them. What forces them to think, what forces them to act, their passions, their techniques, their competencies, all of that brought as a kind of gift, not to others, so much as to their interaction, to the event that's brewing between. A germinal politics.
>
> *(Massumi, 2017, p. 110)*

This experience where people are brought together, suspending personal doctrines but bringing what moves them, sharing their competencies as a gift, is exemplified in teacher Lucia Colla's recollections of joining *Nido d'infanzia* Bellelli in the late 1980s in Reggio Emilia after briefly working in a *nido* in the nearby city of Parma. We share here an extended excerpt from an interview with Lucia for this research project, for it reveals all those elements of "germinal politics" that Massumi (2017) refers to above.

> The most generative aspect of this profession, the one that nurtured my passion and continues to activate my curiosity today, is that here [in Reggio Emilia] I discovered this possibility of working with others, of having a strong social dimension to my work. It is essential to be able to work as a group, to treasure the points of view of others […] I have always been surprised at how in Reggio Emilia I continue to be passionate and curious, and I don't get bored. There are moments of boredom, but they are absolutely irrelevant […]
>
> I owe so much to those early years, and to several opportunities that emerged unexpectedly. Because the *pedagogista* of *Nido* Bellelli then was Tiziana Filippini, who for her own way of working as a *pedagogista* always encouraged people to step outside of the *nido*, of the *scuola dell'infanzia*, creating opportunities so that we could encounter others and dialogue with other *nidi* and *scuole*, to be in relation with the system […] If we didn't understand something she would say: "go and see what they have done over there, why don't you have a look at *Nido* Rodari, they have created some new furniture" or "if you haven't understood this, go visit Vea [Vecchi] and ask her yourself". And maybe you were terrified of Vea because you had just arrived, and you truly understood almost nothing … And so, you would reply "what do you mean, go to Vea, but how?". But eventually you would go, and then you would discover that Tiziana would come too, you would realise that it was not so difficult, and you would discover other pieces of the world. And then other pieces. And so, you discovered the system.

The value of the commons and an ethic of alliances **291**

You discovered a system that with great effort, determination and intelligence has created ways and strategies that we continue to improve on, focus on, and revisit, contextualising them to the present. Because what happened 25 years ago can't and doesn't happen today. But it is evident that the system has always been careful to remain in dialogue, and individual people can contribute greatly to this. In fact, this is a great quality of our educational project: the experience has its premises, its values, and its foundational aspects, through which you can trace the possibilities that the system has created for itself. But as an individual you can also join in this dialogue as part of a collective of a *nido*, or as I do today, after many years, as a teacher educator who feels she is part of the system's resources. Therefore, you are not alone […] This is a system that is truly composed of all its human elements, of all its people, all its subjectivities […] So when you witness a small fragment of thought being created, or a piece of a project being realised, you are absolutely happy, and you are immediately prepared to insert a new piece to connect and combine with the others. And in doing so you experience this feeling of belonging, for yourself and for others, and this for me is extraordinary.

[…] I really don't like working alone. So, from this point of view Reggio Emilia, as an educational experience, is perfect for me because it affords me this possibility, and therefore it keeps me constantly in movement. It also enabled me to grow. For example, when Tiziana would tell me to "go", I went, I was enchanted, I was angry, I wouldn't understand. But something happened within me, and then in an echo effect in my colleagues, with whom I would discuss "Well I haven't understood this, what did you understand?'. This created opportunities for us to construct powerful internal pathways for *formazione* through this play, this exchange. At *Nido Bellelli* I experienced a very fortunate and unique journey of professional growth together with several colleagues. We truly tried to understand how to form ourselves.

(Lucia Colla, teacher, interview with Stefania
Giamminuti, Reggio Emilia)

In her thoughtful reflections on a professional life spent building alliances with others, Lucia conveys the fundamental importance of her *pedagogista*'s encouragement to encounter other participants and other places within the system, to see beyond herself, to reflect beyond her daily work in her own *nido,* and to engage in thinking and doing with others beyond her own working group so that it might spark further experimentation and generate new questions. This practice, which continues today, is a way of creating alliances not just between individuals but indeed between events and competencies so that all converge to become this "gift" that enriches both the people involved and "the event that's brewing between" (Massumi, 2017, p. 110). On a large

292 The value of the commons and an ethic of alliances

scale "the event" is the educational project itself; but in the everyday the event brewing between, where people come together bringing their competencies and what moves them, is documentation and *progettazione:*

> Another significant professional richness is this possibility we are afforded to encounter the thinking of others, and of *pedagogistas* other than your own, when working together with other *nidi* and *scuole dell'infanzia* on areas of research. This is a system of meetings where people bring their own work, they share it and they discuss it.
>
> *(Manuela Pederzoli, teacher, interview with*
> *Stefania Giamminuti, Reggio Emilia)*

Documentation affords unique opportunities for building alliances of thought and action, and encounters such as those as Manuela refers to have a long history in the experience of Reggio Emilia, as outlined by *pedagogista* Elena Giacopini:

> *Formazione,* within a dimension of research, is viewed as an ethical, necessary, and democratic responsibility, because it involves and promotes propositional and critical thinking. This was an idea that Loris Malaguzzi had; in fact, in the 1960s we would organise *aggiornamenti* at the end of the school year, in the Municipal Theatre, and it was the teachers and *pedagogistas* who presented their experiences with the children [...] From this practice emerges an idea of teacher as holder of knowledge that is not dogmatic nor predictable, a subject who designs together with colleagues, proposes experiences to children and is able not only to realise them but also to comment and discuss them, becoming a source of reflection for her working group and for the overall experience of the entire educational system [...] The *pedagogista* promotes re-elaboration and contributes to it, she invites reasoning and discussion on the merits of an experience that has been created, in to highlight important aspects, qualities, and critical issues. These processes of *formazione* are first experienced by the group of teachers of one classroom, then shared with the whole working group of a school, and finally become a legacy that is put into play in other schools and other local, national, and international contexts.
>
> *(Elena Giacopini,* pedagogista, *interview with*
> *Stefania Giamminuti, Reggio Emilia)*

More recently in Reggio Emilia, "the event that's brewing between" (Massumi, 2017, p. 110) is also exemplified in the design of system-wide research projects, also called *centrazioni tematiche* (plural). The term *centrazione* (singular) is an invented term which indicates a centring, or convergence, of thoughts, ideas and actions around questions or topics to be investigated. The root of the term *tematica* (singular) aligns it to the English "theme" or "thematic", which in educational discourse has far more rigid connotations than the Reggio Emilia meaning, and we'd rather avoid translating it literally to avoid misinterpretation. Essentially, a *centrazione tematica* is the convergence of ideas and possibilities for research that bring together different *nidi* and *scuole* in an alliance of thought and action which in turn engenders alliances with diverse fields of knowledge and knowledgeable others, for example the projects on Nature and Digital (Vecchi et al., 2019) or Dance and Music (Anceschi & Maccaferri, 2022). In the words of teacher Simona Marani:

> The *centrazione tematiche* are suggestions that the pedagogical coordination offers us, in the sense that they are part of the *formazione* project and have the great richness of involving several *nidi* and *scuole dell'infanzia*. This distances us even more from that sense of "us" [contained within our school] because it brings you directly into *confronto* with other *nidi* and *scuole dell'infanzia*, focusing on events and data. In the sense that together you view the documentation, and you discuss the thinking that emerged; these might be the most rewarding aspects of the *formazione* project.
> *(Simona Marani, teacher, interview with*
> *Stefania Giamminuti, Reggio Emilia)*

The *pedagogistas*, as part of their yearly design for system-wide *formazione*,[3] propose questions and concepts that tune into broader cultural contemporary concerns and international research but are closely linked to the ideas and events that are constantly brewing within the *nidi* and *scuole dell'infanzia* and more broadly in the city. Such research topics are then offered to working groups as an invitation to engage together in investigations in ways that matter to their own contexts. In the course of these projects, which often last several years, encounters between working groups are frequently promoted so that different points of view can be shared and debated in an attitude of *confronto* and *mettersi in gioco*; Simona in fact identifies this aspect of *confronto* that occurs around documentation as "most enriching". Thus, the *centrazione tematiche* function as an important platform for alliances to be created across the system, connecting working groups of different *nidi* and the *scuole*, as noted by *pedagogista* Annalisa Rabotti:

> The *centrazione tematiche* are the content we use to action this *progettuale* dimension, therefore creating pre-conditions for *pensiero progettuale* to be expressed within continuous and constant daily *formazione*. [They are characterised by] this practice of having *pedagogistas* in project groups, fostering relations between several *nidi* and *scuole*, keeping them connected. Within the different project groups both *nidi* and *scuole* are

294 The value of the commons and an ethic of alliances

always represented, confirming the 0-6 educational project, and reiterating the importance of maintaining children from both *nido* and *scuola* within a continuum of experiences of life and learning. This also enables teachers from the *nido* to truly project themselves, to imagine a future, whilst inviting teachers from the *scuola* to witness young children from the *nido* who are truly competent and who arrive at the *scuola* with a wealth of knowledge. From the point of view of *formazione*, this has been extremely important.

(Annalisa Rabotti, pedagogista, *interview with*
Stefania Giamminuti, Reggio Emilia)

Simona and Annalisa's thoughts illuminate how such events and experiences act as a catalyst for building fruitful alliances between all protagonists – adults, children, materials, and ideas. Furthermore, as *pedagogista* Elena Maccaferri suggests, such diffused projects demand that *pedagogistas* work thoughtfully in building a systemic culture of "more than one" (Manning, 2013):

This has allowed *pedagogistas,* for example from our own *centrazione tematica,* to encounter more frequently those institutions which we did not coordinate directly. I coordinate *Scuola dell'infanzia* Allende and *Nido* Bellelli, and our *centrazione tematica* involved eight institutions; this organisation enabled us to enter within the folds of relations, content, exchanges with other institutions and other *pedagogistas,* and with system resources. A work of weaving that went much further than our own institutions. Therefore, these bridges you constantly practice, which allow you to not simply cross over with other *scuole* and *nidi* but to truly understand, and to enter within.

(Elena Maccaferri, pedagogista, *interview with*
Stefania Giamminuti, Reggio Emilia)

Through these descriptions of the meaning of *centrazioni tematiche* emerges the notion that it is not so much the topic that matters, though of course it is a catalyst for the development and dissemination of significant knowledge, but rather what is most important is the opportunity that is created for building alliances through collective experimentation. As Massumi (2017) notes:

What's important is not coming to supposedly final solutions to general questions. What's important is problematizing – creating singular fields of collective experimentation that make something happen that strikes you as an event, and that offers a relational affordance to others who might want to take up the techniques used, and rework them in their own way, for other situations – a kind of event-variation contagion. That's not about community in the usual sense, but it is about collectivity. It's about collective potentiation that inheres in a fabric of uniquely interwoven events, rather than in any group identity. (pp. 96–97)

Progettazione and documentation, embodied in an ethic of research, enable this kind of "event-variation contagion" (Massumi, 2017, p. 97), understood both as the *confronto* amongst different *nidi* and *scuole* on similar topics, but also as "relational affordance" (Massumi, 2017, p. 96) that is brought to others worldwide who encounter the projects in publicly disseminated documentation. The notion of "collective potentiation" (Massumi, 2017) and the potential for contagion between *nidi* and *scuole dell'infanzia* emerges in the words of teacher Simona Marani, who, like Lucia (above), recognises the contribution of her *pedagogista* in building broad alliances that extend beyond yourself and the place where you work:

I have found the presence of [my *pedagogista*] Daniela Lanzi very precious in this idea of constantly creating connections with her other institutions, but also more broadly with the system. This is a very important role for the *pedagogista* and the pedagogical coordination; [to create connections], also with others who dialogue with us within the region [territory]. And, importantly, [the *pedagogistas* help us] to maintain a gaze that goes beyond ourselves. Because there is always the possibility, when you work within a *scuola* or a *nido*, that you become deeply, very deeply, involved in that *scuola* or *nido,* in the experience that you are living, with the risk (I have experienced this many times) of believing that the world is reduced to the one you are living in. I think that of Daniela's many qualities, she is very skilled in helping you perceive that your value is not lesser, in fact it is strong, but it maintains its strength in this connection you must appreciate, of the "beyond us".

(Simona Marani, teacher, interview with
Stefania Giamminuti, Reggio Emilia)

Daniela Lanzi herself echoes this sensibility, emphasising also how important "collective potentiation" (Massumi, 2017) is to the *pedagogistas* themselves in their collegial work together:

This is a *confronto* on the level of teaching and learning, where your thinking is never in solitude, but always in dialogue. It is a very interesting principle for evaluation, because your work is evaluated by colleagues, and it is thus propelled forward. Our services, beyond the fact that they are coordinated directly by a *pedagogista*, risk far less than other contexts being isolated monads. I don't think it is by chance that ours is a united system, where people feel they belong to a system, beyond individual schools.

(Daniela Lanzi, pedagogista, *interview with*
Stefania Giamminuti, Reggio Emilia)

296 The value of the commons and an ethic of alliances

Ethel Carnevali, a teacher with a comparatively briefer experience to Simona, Manuela, and Lucia, recognises how the system's potential for contagion contributes to the evolution of her knowledge and thinking:

> To have this constant exchange with colleagues, with *pedagogistas*, to be in a network of schools, able to engage in *confronto* with other colleagues, has enabled me to gain an experience that would otherwise not have been possible. I think I have grown on two levels in these few years of experience. On the one hand, from the perspective of pedagogy and *progettazione*, I have become more aware of my choices, of the tools I use and how I use them, and of the strategies of *pensiero progettuale*. On the other hand, I have gained more knowledge about children and childhood.
>
> *(Ethel Carnevali, teacher, interview with*
> *Stefania Giamminuti, Reggio Emilia)*

Collective platforms for experimentation are not only created across *nidi* and *scuole dell'infanzia*, across working groups, and between working groups and *pedagogistas*, but also, crucially, they are designed for the *pedagogistas* to build alliances with each other, so that these alliances may guide thought and action across the system:

> We experience this remarkable context for *formazione* that is the meeting between *pedagogistas*. We also have an extraordinary opportunity, through the *formazione* project, to focus our actions of constant and continuous elaboration at the organisational, educational, and social levels in encounters with the teachers, and to then develop them together daily and for the long term.
>
> *(Annalisa Rabotti, pedagogista, interview with*
> *Stefania Giamminuti, Reggio Emilia)*

We now focus the lens on some of the broader alliances that such collegial work enables and requires, such as those with the city, the region of Emilia Romagna, and the national and international networks, in the spirit of much broader contagion. We conceive of this work as occurring at the "micropolitical level" (Massumi, 2017) which is generally imperceptible and has the quality of resonating with potential.

Expanding alliances and micropolitics

> The capacity [of the *pedagogista*] lies in alighting upon very different contexts, within the space of a day, but to always understand how truly connected these contexts all are to each other.
>
> *(Simona Marani, teacher, interview with*
> *Stefania Giamminuti, Reggio Emilia)*

The *pedagogista* brings the knowledge of other schools, and this is the beauty of a network. Because she acts as a connector, linking the different fragments, and she shares with you what the pedagogical coordination is living and designing at that moment, what is happening in other schools … she acts as a glue, as a link.

(Annalisa Rainieri, teacher, interview with
Stefania Giamminuti, Reggio Emilia)

[As a *pedagogista*] you are in this position that is somewhat privileged, at times uncomfortable if you will, because you have many different observers as a result of the different contexts you inhabit. We always try to create connections, maintaining the axis of values and philosophy within all the contexts we inhabit and all the relationships we nurture – this is the broad mandate of the identity of our educational experience.

(Tiziana Filippini, pedagogista, *interview with*
Stefania Giamminuti, Reggio Emilia)

Simona, Annalisa, and Tiziana emphasise how *pedagogistas* move between different contexts daily, and in doing so they constantly strive to build alliances between these, all the while defending the values of the educational experience; thus, an important alliance is the one that is built not simply with human beings, but rather with the history and values of the educational project itself. As the new millennium gained momentum, Reggio Children acknowledged the generational shift that was occurring within the system, as experienced teachers, *pedagogistas,* and *atelieristas* who had worked in the *nidi* and *scuole dell'infanzia* since the 1970s and 1980s, contributing to building the livelihood and renown of the educational project, neared retirement age. In response to the need for constructing alliances of thought with the "new" members entering working groups of the *nidi* and *scuole dell'infanzia*, and to enhance *formazione*, innovative roles were created in the system, named *insegnanti formatori* [teacher educators]. In the words of *pedagogista* Annalisa Rabotti:

These professional roles, which we call teacher educators, enact *progettazione* within *formazione* in project groups together with *pedagogistas,* but they also execute the definition, prediction, and pre-disposition of contexts in the *nidi* and *scuole dell'infanzia*, thus offering further support to the joint action of teachers and *pedagogistas*. This is another organisational choice that signals the quality of the experience of *formazione* within the system.

(Annalisa Rabotti, pedagogista, *interview with*
Stefania Giamminuti, Reggio Emilia)

298 The value of the commons and an ethic of alliances

These roles have never been intended as "supervisors" or "monitors" overseeing practice with the objective of improving it in linear and hierarchical ways; rather, teacher educators enhance *formazione* by expanding the opportunities for *confronto,* communicating and enacting collective values, activating the wealth of knowledge that all educators possess, problematising-supporting research with children, and pragmatically enabling daily *progettazione.* In so doing, they also facilitate new and unexpected alliances, as teacher Manuela Pederzoli emphasises:

> [In the *nido*] we don't have permanent *atelieristas* like in the *scuola dell'infanzia*, but instead *atelieristas* often accompany us in different design pathways, as Mirella Ruozzi did within the project on narration, colour, or clay. *Atelieristas-resources* who, despite not being with us in the *nido* permanently, generate thinking together with us, creating this thread, this collaboration, this exchange of knowledges.
>
> *(Manuela Pederzoli, teacher, interview with*
> *Stefania Giamminuti, Reggio Emilia)*

A fundamentally important alliance, which often eludes the understanding of those working in contexts where early education and care is perceived more as a commodity than a commons, is that which the *pedagogistas* nurture with the city of Reggio Emilia and its public administration.[4] As Boonen et al. (2019) emphasise, "the consensus is that most commons will need to be formally recognised as autonomous institutions by public authorities in order to survive" (p. 563). Building a culture of childhood that is visible in the city is the responsibility of all those working within the *nidi* and *scuole dell'infanzia*, but the dialogue and reciprocal trust that is sustained with the local administration is in the specific care of *pedagogistas. Pedagogista* Simona Bonilauri qualifies this relationship as a "great alliance":

> We are very fortunate to have a city administration that has always, since the birth of the *nidi* and *scuole dell'infanzia*, invested in services. This, no doubt, is a great alliance.
>
> *(Simona Bonilauri, pedagogista, interview with*
> *Stefania Giamminuti, Reggio Emilia)*

Importantly, this relationship with the public administration is qualified as an alliance because, while everyone enacts their own roles and responsibilities in dialogue with each other as could be the norm elsewhere, in Reggio Emilia this goes beyond, becoming an endeavour of shared *progettazione* or co-design of cultural, pedagogical, and social contexts:

> Along with the existing responsibility of the institutions you follow, many other institutional and cultural aspects that *pedagogistas* care for have

The value of the commons and an ethic of alliances **299**

increased. These are connected to various subjects in the city, with whom we constantly co-design.

(Tiziana Filippini, pedagogista, interview with
Stefania Giamminuti, Reggio Emilia)

This alliance of course is possible because it is located within a broader shared culture of valuing the commons and mutually recognising early childhood education and care as a fundamental right:

Pedagogistas and the pedagogical coordination have always sought to enact a sensitive role of connection between services and issues facing the city. In the 1980s in Reggio Emilia, we were building services for people, not only educational services but also social services and health services. There was in fact the creation of a welfare system, which must remain a right.

(Ivana Soncini, pyschologist and member of the pedagogical coordination,
interview with Stefania Giamminuti, Reggio Emilia)

Pedagogista Daniela Lanzi maintains that "this dynamic of back and forth with our city cannot be lost, because schools are located within a context, within a city" (interview with Stefania Giamminuti, Reggio Emilia). In fact, the *pedagogistas* in their daily work always acknowledge that "this more-than of becoming can never be lost from sight" (Massumi, Prelude, in Manning, 2013, p. xi), whereby educational services are always seen as more-than themselves; this is not the norm elsewhere, where schools and centres generally close their gates to the world, and risk being "isolated monads". While this alliance with the public administration remains stable (but in need of constant tending), new alliances emerge constantly. In recent decades, the establishment of the Loris Malaguzzi International Centre, Reggio Children and the *Fondazione* Reggio Children, the expansion of existing local, regional, and national collaborations, and the formalising of relationships with a diffused international network of allies across the world has led to an "amplifying" of the experience that requires a constant revisiting and broadening of the alliances that *pedagogistas* forge within the system and beyond. As noted by Simona Bonilauri:

This branching out and amplifying of the experience brings a transformation in the role of the *pedagogista*, who somehow decentres herself into all these places, because they are newly created. As *pedagogistas* decentre themselves into all these places, they also assume new duties.

(Simona Bonilauri, pedagogista, interview with
Stefania Giamminuti, Reggio Emilia)

The alliances that *pedagogistas* weave are imperceptible, ever expanding, and resonate with potential. This work occurs at the micropolitical level

300 The value of the commons and an ethic of alliances

(Massumi, 2017), in contrast to the more common macropolitical level (Massumi, 2017) at which educational leadership usually expresses itself, whereby alliances are often foregone in favour of recognisable and bounded structures of power:

> For macropolitics, everything within that field must be well identified and defined, it has to have an assignable position in a structure of power. On the micropolitical level, on the other hand, there is always a surplus of organization, or better, organizability: a surplus-value of life stirring in the between of positioned things, moving to take its own form of expression, self-organizing and self-affirming. Broadly, micropolitics corresponds to what macropolitical discourse dismisses as the pipe-dream of "direct democracy".
>
> *(Massumi, 2017, pp. 104–105)*

The experience of Reggio Emilia, and particularly its stance towards diffused leadership, its collegial organisational structures, and its "power-with" (Arendt, 1970) approach to hierarchy, is easily dismissed as a pipe-dream, not possible in other contexts that are seemingly bound to their linear and well identifiable macropolitical structures of power. From this perspective, the role of the *pedagogista*, dedicated to surplus-value of life and acting at the micropolitical level, can be easily misunderstood and rejected as impossible or irrelevant, lacking true power. It is possible in fact that its many qualities may still elude those who try authentically, from their own places, to dialogue with the experience of Reggio Emilia. However, it is ever more urgent for us to imagine such roles in other places in order to build more direct democracies, where "decision is an emergent property of the coming-together, for becoming-together, of a differential human multiplicity, and not the edict of an individual leader or lead group backed by an existing power structure of whatever stripe" (Massumi, 2015, p. 98). In such contexts where an ethic of alliances guides everyday praxis, decision-making, and relations, "a direct democracy is being improvised. There, resistance is unfolding" (Massumi, 2015, p. 98). Furthermore,

> This is a democracy whose base concept is not the supposed freedom of the individual from the collectivity, but the freedom *of* the collectivity, *for* its becoming. It is the embodied freedom of bodies to come together in thinking-feeling, to participate in differentially attuned becoming, in all the immediacy and with all urgency.
>
> *(Massumi, 2015, pp. 97–98)*

Pedagogistas, in weaving their alliances, construct a lived democracy where the freedom of the collectivity, for its becoming, is a shared value. This is an educational experience that welcomes the more-than of becoming, in pursuit of democracy and the common good. It recognises that "what lives on, that is immanent to life as expressive potential, exceeds this or that body [...] what lives on is never the subject, never the individual. What lives on is affective resonance" (Manning, 2013, p. 30). In the affective, aesthetic, and ethical encounters that guide the work of all participants in the educational project of Reggio Emilia, the experience lives on, grows, and is committed to a just society together with its allies – children, parents, citizens:

> Our pedagogy works so that parents, teachers, people, evaluating together and analysing educational issues, can understand how the history and future of children, and the history and future of schools, are closely linked with events and struggles on several fronts of society; and that their task is to be committed, day by day, to a better understanding of causes and forces threatening to keep this unjust world the way it is. To work for a new world, reflected in schools, reflected in children, who while living the present more fully, have the privilege of choosing and creating their future destiny.
> *(Malaguzzi, 1970, in Cagliari et al., 2016, p. 183)*

Final musings: "the minor gesture"

In this chapter, at the end of our storying, we have opened our reflections more decidedly towards the political. While not exhaustively, we have articulated the many alliances that the experience of Reggio Emilia forges locally, nationally, and internationally. We hope that by welcoming an ethic of alliances elsewhere, more opportunities may be created for educators, parents, citizens, children to work together in defying the many injustices that threaten our world. While the possibility of conceptualising and enacting education from birth as a commons, a public responsibility and a democratic necessity, may appear to be a utopian dream unrealisable elsewhere, it is in fact more-than possible. To those who may feel constrained in situations that are fundamentally and ethically different from the ones we have shared in this book, it may help to consider that this project for an *Education Commons* requires a stance both practical and experimental, expanding potentials and freedoms:

> Maybe if we can take little, practical experimental, strategic measures to expand our emotional register, or limber up our thinking, we can access more of our potential at each step, have more of it actually available. Having more potentials available intensifies our life. We're not enslaved by our situations [...] Our degree of freedom at any one time corresponds to how much of our experimental "depth" we can access towards a next step – how intensely we are living and moving.
> *(Massumi, 2015, pp. 5–6)*

302 The value of the commons and an ethic of alliances

There is always a risk that such unique educational experiences are viewed as purely theoretical and we hope that we have not contributed to such misunderstandings. In fact, the experience of Reggio Emilia is lived fully, it is entirely pragmatic, and it is enduring; it is made of what Erin Manning (2016) calls "minor gestures". The quality of the minor gesture is to displace the normative; as we have extensively argued, the power of the normative and the conventional in educational theory, research and practice is far-reaching. And so, "minor gestures always have to play the major, subverting, perverting, hijacking, or hacking it" (Massumi, 2017, p. 65). In addition, because they subvert the major, such experiences need to be constantly defended; to this end the value of the commons and an ethic of alliances is essential.

Manning (2016) specifies that the minor gesture's "permeability tends to make it ungraspable, and often unrecognizable [...] There is no question that the minor is precarious" (p. 2). Each minor gesture by which the experience of Reggio Emilia draws its livelihood is precarious, however by virtue of its strong values and ethics, and thanks to the alliances forged, it endures. Furthermore, "the minor gesture [...] shifts the field, altering the valence of what comes to be. It is affirmative in its force, emphatic in its belief" (Manning, 2016, p. 6); the experience of Reggio Emilia, empathic in its beliefs, continues to shift the field of possibility for early education culturally, socially, pedagogically, politically. It does so locally, nationally, and internationally by being affirmative, and working "in the mode of speculative pragmatism" (Manning, 2016, p. 2) – the place where much is an utopian possibility but also actual, lived.

Manning (2016) notes that "the minor gesture creates sites of dissonance, staging disturbances that open experience to new modes of expression" (p. 2); this occurs in everyday *progettazione*, where sites of dissonance are often created to displace understandings and generate new knowledge. Furthermore, this practice of offering broader disturbances so that new ways of conceptualising education may emerge elsewhere is also a fundamental quality of the educational experience itself, never method but always provocation to act differently. In creating a site for dissonance in how we think of and actualise education and care, the experience of Reggio Emilia opens up the possibility of inventing new forms of existence and "new modes of life-living" (Manning, 2016, p. 8).

Manning cautions that the minor gesture requires "the prudence of the experimenter" (Manning, 2016, p. 7), and furthermore she notes that "the register of the minor gesture is always political" (Manning, 2016, p. 8). When such experimentation, speculative pragmatism, and political activism are welcomed, the possibility is actualised for "new tendencies to emerge, and in the resonances that are awakened, potential for difference looms" (Manning, 2016, p. 8). Our concern is for this potential for difference to loom large for all those who encounter the experience of Reggio Emilia and hope to transform collective understandings of what early childhood education and care can be. The experience of Reggio Emilia is an example of resistance that has

The value of the commons and an ethic of alliances   303

reverberated potential for difference throughout the world, providing a concrete story to counteract the threat facing the commons and democratic forms of solidarity worldwide. We imagine that the educational project of Reggio Emilia, by virtue of the contributions of all those who participate in its livelihood, has significant power of contagion, gesturing into existence the new in other places of early childhood education and care worldwide and building new horizons of hope. Thank you and farewell.

Notes

1 Some of the thoughts conveyed in this chapter have been previously published: Giamminuti, S. (2021). Childhoods for the common good: The educational project of Reggio Emilia. In N. J. Yelland, L. Peters, N. Fairchild, M. Tesar, & M. Perez (Eds.), *The SAGE handbook of Global Childhoods*. London: Sage.
2 Previously introduced in Chapter 8.
3 Throughout this book, we have referred to this yearly design as the "*formazione* project", a literal translation from the Italian *progetto di formazione*. The terminology highlights how *pensiero progettuale* extends to all systemic aspects, including the design of opportunities for *formazione*.
4 Chapters 2 and 8 have delineated the many levels of complex interaction that characterise the state and municipal education systems.

References

Anceschi, A., & Maccaferri, E. (Eds.). (2022). *Accorpamenti: Resonances between dance and music*. Reggio Children.

Arendt, H. (1970). *On violence*. Harcourt.

Arndt, S., Urban, M., Murray, C., Smith, K., Swadener, B., & Ellegaard, T. (2018). Contesting early childhood professional identities: A cross-national discussion. *Contemporary Issues in Early Childhood*, *19*(2), 97–116. https://doi.org/10.1177/1463949118768356

Bollier, D. (2006). The growth of the commons paradigm. In C. Hess & E. Ostrom (Eds.), *Understanding knowledge as a commons: From theory to practice* (pp. 27–40). The MIT Press.

Boonen, C., Brando, N., Cogolati, S., Hagen, R., Vanstappen, N., & Wouters, J. (2019). Governing as commons or as global public goods: Two tales of power. *International Journal of the Commons*, *13*(1), 553–577. https://doi.org/10.18352/ijc.907

Braidotti, R. (2019). *Posthuman knowledge*. Polity Press.

Cagliari, P., Castagnetti, M., Giudici, C., Rinaldi, C., Vecchi, V., & Moss, P. (Eds.). (2016). *Loris Malaguzzi and the schools of Reggio Emilia: A selection of his writings and speeches, 1945–1993*. Routledge.

Cagliari, P., Filippini, T., Giacopini, E., Bonilauri, S., & Margini, D. (2012). The pedagogical coordinating team and professional development. In C. Edwards, L. Gandini, & G. Forman (Eds.), *The hundred language of children: The Reggio Emilia experience in transformation* (pp. 135–146). Praeger.

Dahlberg, G. (2016). An ethico-aesthetic paradigm as an alternative discourse to the quality assurance discourse. *Contemporary Issues in Early Childhood*, *17*(1), 124–133. https://doi.org/10.1177/1463949115627910

304 The value of the commons and an ethic of alliances

Fielding, M., & Moss, P. (2011). *Radical education and the common school: A democratic alternative*. Routledge.

Giroux, H. (2021a). *Race, politics, and pandemic pedagogy: Education in a time of crisis*. Bloomsbury.

Giroux, H. (2021b). Rethinking neoliberal fascism, racist violence, and the plague of inequality. *Communication Teacher*, 1–7. https://doi.org/10.1080/17404622.2021.1923772

Giudici, C., & Cagliari, P. (2014). I nidi e le scuole d'infanzia a Reggio Emilia. *Bambini, Marzo*(3), 30–35.

Karp, P. (2020). Childcare fees up 3% in last quarter and 34% since Coalition took power in 2013. *The Guardian*. https://www.theguardian.com/australia-news/2020/jan/19/childcare-fees-up-3-in-last-quarter-and-34-since-coalition-took-power-in-2013

Malaguzzi, L. (2021). *Design/Progettazione in infant-toddler centres and preschools: Research open to wonder, between the possible, probable, and unpredictable*. Reggio Children.

Manning, E. (2013). *Always more than one: Individuation's dance*. Duke University Press.

Manning, E. (2015). Against method. In P. Vannini (Ed.), *Non-representational methodologies: Re-envisioning research* (pp. 52–71). Routledge.

Manning, E. (2016). *The minor gesture*. Duke University Press.

Massumi, B. (2015). *Politics of affect*. Polity Press.

Massumi, B. (2017). *The principle of unrest: Activist philosophy in the expanded field*. Open Humanities Press.

Morris, S. (2015). Scott Morrison's kid gloves on upcoming childcare reform. *The Saturday Paper*.

Ostrom, E., & Hess, C. (2006). A framework for analysing the knowledge commons. In C. Hess & E. Ostrom (Eds.), *Understanding the knowledge as a commons: From theory to practice*. The MIT Press.

Press, F., Woodrow, C., Logan, H., & Mitchell, L. (2018). Can we belong in a neoliberal world? Neo-liberalism in early childhood education and care policy in Australia and New Zealand. *Contemporary Issues in Early Childhood*, *19*(4), 328–339. https://doi.org/10.1177/1463949118781909

Riddle, S., & Apple, M. (2019). Education and democracy in dangerous times. In S. Riddle, & M. Apple (Eds.), *Re-imagining education for democracy* (pp. 1–9). Routledge.

Vecchi, V., Bonilauri, S., Meninno, I., & Tedeschi, M. (2019). *Bordercrossings: Encounters with living things, digital landscapes*. Reggio Children.

EPILOGUE

Translated by Jane McCall

Nidi and *scuole dell'infanzia* in Reggio Emilia, a commons

Gigliola Venturini
President, Preschools and Infant-toddler Centres –
Istituzione of the Municipality of Reggio Emilia

It is May, 1945. Villa Cella, a small village outside Reggio Emilia, has paid the highest price for the harshness of war, the bombings, the hunger, the barbarism of Nazi-Fascist massacres. But war is over, and surrounded by the rubble of houses, a community of land-workers and small artisans find themselves discussing how to use funds from the sale of a tank, six horses, and three trucks abandoned by retreating Germans. Some propose building a theatre, and already this says much about their desire for a re-construction that values culture for all; however, the women impose their own point of view. The first priority must be the right of children to education, protection, and care.

So it is that an entire community sets to work, building "brick by brick" the *Asilo del Popolo* later known as the *Scuola dell'infanzia* XXV Aprile. On this day each person understands that the destiny of Cella's children is not only the concern of mothers, and in a rally of industrious solidarity the community takes responsibility for everything: walls, furnishings, food, wood for the stoves, and the extremely modest salary of the teacher and cook. Everyone participates for years in building, from the foundations, not only concrete solidarity but a collective responsibility, a participation and social management. This is the story-symbol that gives meaning and concreteness to the centrality of childhood for the future of every community and the concept of education as a commons.

This is the legacy on which municipal commitment in Reggio Emilia was based, long before the United Nations *Convention on the Rights of the Child*

DOI: 10.4324/9781003181026-10

306 Epilogue

of November 20, 1989 determined that every child has the right to grow in health and safety, fulfil their potential, be listened to, and considered a citizen to all intents and purposes regardless of social, cultural, ethnic, and religious background. In fact the Reggio Emilia municipality, supported by the strong civic participation promoted especially by women's emancipation movements, and guided by Loris Malaguzzi's revolutionary thinking, made qualitative and economic investment in the right to early childhood education its distinctive trait: from 1963 with the *Scuola dell'infanzia* Robinson, and from 1971 with the first *Nido d'infanzia* named after Genoveffa Cervi, it initiated the birth of the 0–6 educational institutions known and appreciated everywhere.

Between the 1960s and the 1980s, a total of 55 educational and school institutions were created, making up the renowned and precious legacy of *nidi* and *scuole dell'infanzia* in the city of Reggio Emilia. Dialogue with the city, the hallmark promoted by Loris Malaguzzi as a founding element of Reggio Emilia's new pedagogical approach, would prove decisive.

Reggio's *scuole dell'infanzia* were not born as a necessary public service limited to satisfying the needs of families, nor as self-sufficient, self-referencing institutions; instead, they were born as educational communities with windows thrown open to their "outside", welcoming, open, and curious, ready to embrace all the stimuli a city can offer on cultural, artistic, scientific, cooperative, and solidarity levels. Participatory places, that through this reciprocal contamination, explore, discover, and interrogate the city, urging it to "think of itself" through the suggestions of children's thinking, in a fertile exchange transforming a service into a true commons, and the city into an educating community. From the first Management Committees to the current City Childhood Councils, democratically elected and open to the citizenry, the alliance between educational services, families, and city would take participation to be the generator of public interest and active civicism. An "incubator" that is capable of promoting collective responsibility in families, institutions, the local area or *territorio*, and educational staff, for researching into coherency, promotion, and constant innovation between the rights of children, daily life in services, and local public policy.

The alliance is constitutive, declaring childhood to be a subject that simply by its existence transforms the possible scenarios of a city's development, whether it is large or small, involving all its actors through the "eye that leaps over the wall", and affirming the "hundred languages" of all children in the world. The guide is the Reggio Emilia Approach, according to which every child is unique, every child is a citizen, every child is competent and curious; researchers, explorers, carriers of universal rights, including the right to quality education that guarantees not only acceptance and inclusion, but above all equality of opportunities. It is an approach that, in line with the principles of the Italian Constitution, aims to favour the full development of each child's

Epilogue **307**

personality, starting with recognition and valorisation of their creative intelligence. It is a democratic approach, at once nourished by and constructor of social cohesion.

Within this framework we believe it can be understood what it means for the city of Reggio Emilia to conceive education from birth as a commons, a good that is never definitive or defined however, but constantly scrutinised by social change. And with precisely this open gaze on the great changes of our times, with awareness of the unacceptable denial of basic rights for a large part of the world's children in a world that must still free itself of the rubble of too many wars, too much poverty, we would like to conclude with a provocation, that for us is a great dream, but not a utopia.

Let childhood itself be the commons for a world capable of building a culture of peace, of living together, of cooperation. Let the eyes and words of children be the compass for re-orienting solidarity, ethical, fair, and ecological thinking. This to our mind is the true challenge of the world to come, a challenge in which, for years, the Reggio Emilia municipality has dedicated energy, projects, and resources, through the daily work of the Preschools and Infant-toddler Centres – Istituzione of the Municipality of Reggio Emilia together with Reggio Children and the *Fondazione* Reggio Children – Centro Loris Malaguzzi, countering educational poverty wherever possible, and promoting a new idea of childhood.

The discourse on education, between pedagogy and politics

Nando Rinaldi
Director, Preschools and Infant-toddler Centres –
Istituzione of the Municipality of Reggio Emilia

This book, with its character of co-participatory research project, makes it possible for us to explore and bring to light the role of the *Coordinamento Pedagogico*, and in particular the role of *pedagogista* in the Reggio Emilia Approach. The Reggio Emilia Approach is a project of Preschools and Infant-toddler Centres – Istituzione of the Municipality of Reggio Emilia that is founded on an idea of secular and democratic education and centred upon a holistic and socio-constructive vision of knowledge and human beings. This project is made concrete each day in the *nidi* and *scuole dell'infanzia* through the competent work of teachers, educators, auxiliaries, cooks, *atelieristas*, and *pedagogistas*, engaged in contexts and environments designed to give value to the learning and knowledge of young children, in which each element, including those of an organizational nature, maintains its own centrality and its own importance.

I am grateful to the authors of this book because through publishing this research, which has its starting point in a gaze that is "other", we can make known certain constituent elements of what the world knows as the

Reggio Emilia Approach, by dwelling on the theme of relations and on the necessity of constructing a deep inter-relatedness between theory, practice and research. Central to this area is the work carried out by the *Coordinamento Pedagogico*, a place in which it is possible to create strong connections between different points of view through dialogue, and through the exercise of a shared reflexivity that listens to others, and is careful to understand, problematise, relaunch, and guarantee the unified nature of the 0–6 educational project. This process takes place through elaborating a culture of childhood permeated with various disciplines, in constant dialogue with the city through the construction of ways of managing services open to the participation of families who are aware – as Loris Malaguzzi underscores – that the discourse of education is also political.

In fact, without this awareness it is true that the *nidi* and *scuole dell'infanzia* would fulfil an important conciliatory function, but they would fail in a task that is essentially political, that has to do with the possibility of constructing conditions for the realisation of article 3 paragraph 2 in the Italian Constitution: "It is the duty of the Republic to remove those obstacles of an economic or social nature which constrain the freedom and equality of citizens, thereby impeding the full development of the human person ..."

Following the Liberation of Italy, the women and men of Reggio Emilia saw *scuole dell'infanzia* directly managed by the municipality as a starting point for constructing an idea of citizenship that was coherent with the new Constitution and antithetical to the cultural asphyxiation typical of the Fascist regime, by offering real opportunities to counter social inequalities. They did this through the image of competent children with a hundred languages at their disposal, and through the construction of a network of *scuole* and *nidi* that placed collegial work and collective responsibility at the centre.

On the threshold of 60 years since the opening of the first municipal *Scuola dell'infanzia* Robinson on November 5, 1963, several challenges have arisen in keeping this history "present", interrogating various areas of public administration, particularly in those Local Authorities that chose to invest substantial human and economic resources in an integrated 0–6 system.

In fact, in a recent book by Stefano Neri (2020) entitled *Servizi di welfare e Comuni*[7] [Welfare Services and Municipalities] the author refers to the European Quality Framework for ECEC underlining how "in municipal services [...] certain characteristics of the organization of work and management of human resources are present to the highest degree, such as to contribute to promoting the quality of educational work [...]. We are referring above all to organizational tools, such as pedagogical coordination" (p. 54).

In this regard it is important to highlight that the reform of the system for integrated education and schooling, approved in 2017 with the passing of decree-law 65, was intended to diffuse this dimension of working collegially, and the role of pedagogical coordination, to all providers throughout the entire country. Pedagogical coordination was a tool created in the 1970s in the form of internal units in municipal services promoting quality in educational contexts by providing fundamental support for cultural design and the construction of staff *formazione* courses. The quality of early childhood services is promoted principally by giving value to the professionalism of staff, and quality to the work of caring.

It is now some years since the decree came into force and was concretely implemented, and several results have been obtained in the direction of consolidating and qualifying the system for integrated education and schooling, in particular through approval of the *Linee pedagogiche per il sistema integrato zerosei* [Pedagogical Guidelines for the 0–6 integrated system], and of the *Orientamenti nazionali per i servizi educativi per l'infanzia* [National Orientations for early childhood educational services]. Documents which work with and develop some of the themes central to this book: the importance of in-service *formazione*, an insistence on educational continuity and pedagogical coordination, to name just a few. Reinforcing awareness and the importance of pre-compulsory schooling, "always, wrongly, considered ancillary to compulsory school".[8]

Frequenting the future in a dimension of community and collegiality

Maddalena Tedeschi

Pedagogista responsible for the Complex Organizational Unit on behalf of The *Coordinamento Pedagogico* of Preschools and Infant-toddler Centres – Istituzione of the Municipality of Reggio Emilia

As we have seen in the previous chapters, the role of pedagogical coordinator has a long history in the experience of the Reggio Emilia Approach, and the epistemological framework that has been created remains as a permanent reference. The trait of working in a dimension of collegiality and a plurality of viewpoints is, we believe, a fundamental condition for inhabiting the complexities of education.

The *pedagogista* in Reggio Emilia is part of a permanent working group called the *Coordinamento Pedagogico* that takes on an identity other than the sum of its single components: moreover, as we have seen emerge in the pages of this book, the *Coordinamento Pedagogico*'s own competences are structured within a diffused system of reciprocal *formazione*. This dimension, of organising collegiality so that it becomes structural, creates a dialogical *forma mentis* with a constant tension towards change and research. The collegiality that is expressed in the group work of the *Coordinamento Pedagogico* does not come about only through frequenting a collective context, but by making this condition structural in our thinking.

310 Epilogue

Among the many traits that characterise the *pedagogista*'s systemic profession, the one that most defines it is the tension towards a permanent elaboration of educational culture that interweaves politics and knowledges – of human sciences, scientific research, the arts, and more. This breathes life into a complex profession that inhabits borders as places of encounter, proposing and informing a social and civil coexistence that is both democratic and emotionally engaging.

We could not walk alone in this complexity: in fact, collectivity and collegiality are antidotes to a prejudicial way of thinking, often defined as "confirmation bias". The essence of the profession is defined by curiosity, openness, and critical thinking: in respecting children's rights a political vision, a perspective of "concrete utopia" is necessary, understood as an ability for reading the relational contexts we move in, deep listening, a way of looking backwards and forwards in history, always with delicate eyes and leaving "doors open".

Work based on *confronto* generates a desire to know more and activate new perspectives and visions: the necessary awareness is that of constantly desiring to be *in*-research in order to elaborate collective thinking and come to a "consciousness of the whole". In our experience in Reggio Emilia, research, which is supported and enhanced by the Pedagogical Coordination, becomes sensitive, passionate, and vital, and is nurtured by certain qualities: the capacity for constructing constant questions, as the driving force that urges intra- and interpersonal reflection; feeling doubt, understood as a dimension of secular scepticism, the desire for finding argumentations and generating discussions so we can look for others, in order to construct new perspectives on theory and experience.

Another key concept for research, as we understand and live it in Reggio Emilia, is the ability to inhabit uncertainty, difficulties, and sometimes fatigue, and seeing them as a structural part of our profession of educating; living with uncertainty and difficulty does not mean we feel them as an additional burden but rather as a constituent element of our profession, seeking to draw aspects of formative gain from them.

The future has always been uncertain but has traits today that are even more difficult to identify, after the pandemic, wars, and environmental catastrophes have traced scenarios that were unimaginable until recent years and lead us toward new questions. However, it is still opportune to maintain a tenacious and optimistic hope: Loris Malaguzzi illustrates this ethical value-based perspective on education when he states that "after all, education must stand on the side of optimism or else it will melt like ice cream in the sun" (Malaguzzi et al., 1996, p. 29).[5]

Together with this reaching towards the future it is also necessary to consciously inhabit the consequences of our choices, starting with the questions that breathe life into research itself: initial geneses are of fundamental importance if we are to succeed in maintaining a gaze that is at once broad and defined. We believe that the art of self-interrogating, of cultivating the "why" questions, is more important than the art of answering. It makes it possible for us to construct a close relation between theory and practice, two concepts connected by a dimension of reciprocity: it is questions that shape our interpretations of experiences, that create a sense of doing education.

There will be an increasing need to generate dynamic, open – and sometimes irreverent and paradoxical – contexts for *confronto* that stretch towards discovery of the future. "Discover" in the sense of "re-finding" how much we knew of what is known but have sometimes forgotten, and in the sense of "inventing" what can be glimpsed of the new: perhaps the vital energy of the *pedagogista*'s profession is that of writing new questions with a new horizon. Children – bearers of future and bearers of humanity – are a compass for research. As Loris Malaguzzi reminds us:

> Our experience also confirms that children need a great deal of freedom: the freedom to investigate and to try, to make mistakes and to correct mistakes, to choose where and with whom to invest their curiosity, intelligence and emotions. [...] As adults, we need the same freedom, as well as much more competence, curiosity, and imagination than we have demonstrated up to now, in order to offer children, and to build with them, the opportunities for learning and knowing.
>
> *(Malaguzzi et al., 1996, p. 36)*[6]

A different and possible way of doing school and education

Cristian Fabbi
President of Reggio Children

The municipal *nidi* and *scuole dell'infanzia* of Reggio Emilia have always loved to weave dialogues with other realities on an international level, in generative exchanges that over the years have led our education system to meet with more than 140 countries, in several cases developing deep and enduring relationships. These collaborations – supported and promoted by Reggio Children, the organisation created by the Municipality of Reggio Emilia in 1994 to safeguard and disseminate the values of the Reggio Emilia Approach at national and international levels – take the form of multiple activities that include journeys of research such as the one conducted by Stefania Giamminuti (Curtin University, Western Australia) on the role of pedagogical coordination, which has led to creating this publishing project together.

The book is dedicated to understanding how the educational experience of Reggio Emilia interprets the figure and professional qualities of the *pedagogista*, a systemic figure who in the weave of theory and practice works every day with the *nidi* and *scuole dell'infanzia*, promoting their openness to the outside world and augmenting their relations in the Reggio Emilia Approach

312 Epilogue

system, with the city of Reggio Emilia, and at national and international levels. Through exploring the role of the *pedagogista*, this book also contributes to an understanding and deeper exploration of a different, possible way of doing school and education, involving a multitude of teachers, *atelieristas*, cooks and auxiliaries in Reggio Emilia every day who are intent, together with children and families, on building and sharing a new culture of childhood.

The *pedagogista*'s role finds meaning and spaces of professional and cultural expression in a hybrid area on the border, or better in the overlap, between pedagogy, culture, and politics, and in the dialogue with disciplines that characterises contemporary discourse. Indeed, it is precisely these hybrid areas that become generative of innovation: in the emergence of a condition of hybridism there lies a secret capable of transforming our world.[1] The *pedagogista*'s professionality is thus expressed through acting on the innovation of practices and research, on support for creativity, on re-definitions of awareness, and on moving from "what" to "how" in learning.[2] In the *pedagogista*'s work the tension towards overcoming habits also becomes extremely important; the habits of education, as in other areas of human expression, are a natural process enacted by the brain as a form of cognitive economy.[3] However, when habits are forced on us, they become enemies both of innovation and of the creative act, understood in all its many variations. The *pedagogista*'s eyes must therefore be capable of going beyond them, restoring spaces of expression to the "becoming" of educating, in forms that can always be new, always innovative.

Therefore, starting with the history of Reggio Emilia, the profession of *pedagogista* becomes one which contributes to an active school[4] around the whole world, a school that self-questions, a school that appreciates the better-formed-questions rather than answers, a school in which children, together with their teachers, become researchers, active and conscious protagonists of their own learning processes. A school that is open, that becomes transparent, diffused, and welcoming, without ever losing its own special traits. A school that becomes a place for developing humanity.

Sixty years on, after the birth of Reggio Emilia's first municipal *scuola dell'infanzia*, we feel it is increasingly important to renew our reflection on the original and authentic nature of the Reggio Emilia Approach, the root of Reggio Children's work, and an essential condition for deep and true dialogue with other educational realities that have relations with this experience of ours. All together, for the future of an education that is competent, and sensitive toward the resources and rights of all human beings.

Notes

1 Chambers, I. (1996). Linguaggio, identità, ibridismo. In AA. & VV. (Eds.), *Identità e differenze: Gli immaginari della differenza. XIX Triennale di Milano* (Vol. 1). Electa.

Epilogue **313**

2 Bruner, J. (1960). *The Process of Education*. Harvard University Press.
3 Duhigg, C. (2014). *The power of habit: Why we do what we do in life and business*. Random House.
4 Dewey, J. (1902). *The child and the curriculum*. The University of Chicago Press.
5 Malaguzzi, L. et al. (1996) *The Hundred Languages of Children*, exhibition catalogue. Reggio Emilia: Reggio Children.
6 Malaguzzi, L. et al. (1996) *The Hundred Languages of Children*, exhibition catalogue. Reggio Emilia: Reggio Children.
7 Neri S. (2020). *Servizi di welfare e Comuni. Nuove politiche e trasformazioni organizzative*, Carocci editore, Roma.
8 Higher Council of Public Education, opinion on the draft decree of the Ministry of Instruction containing the "Adoption of the « Pedagogical lines for the zero-sei integrated system » referred to in article 10, paragraph 4 of legislative decree 13 April 2017, n. 65" p. 1.

INDEX

Note: *Italicized* page numbers refer figures and with "n" notes.

accoglienza 87, 90–91
activity: amateurism 12; continuous 179; economic 279; joint/collective 66, 225, 263; passivity from 59; professionals 35; self-generative 154
administrative decentralisation 22
administrative offices 39, 46, 48, 272n5
aesthetic care 103, 145–147
affect: as differential attunement 66; hierarchical authority 62; humanity and 286; in-between-ness 67; reciprocity and 57, 58–68; value of relationality 58–68
affirmative alternatives 239
affirmative ethics 57, 78, 227, 238–241, 253, 287
Agazzi, Carolina 29
Agazzi, Rosa 29
aggiornamento 17n3, 42, 60–62, 74, 161, 176, 292; children's mark-making artefacts *60*; class 210–217, 220n5; collective 50, 173–212; *confronto* 77, *80*, 138, 253n2; inter-collective 49; *mettersi in gioco* 157; monthly planning of 42; mutual capacity 60; at *Nido-scuola dell'infanzia 63*; professional profile's working

week 36; at *scuola dell'infanzia 61, 62, 65, 76, 77, 80, 81, 92, 103, 140–141, 228, 229, 231;* working group 50
alliances 296–301; cultural 233; ethic of 12, 275, 276, 287–301; for individuals and collective 232; micropolitics and 296–301; in struggles 231
amateurism 7, 8, 12, 14
amateur scholarship 6–12
ambientamento (to "acclimatize" or "settle in") 90
Aporti, Ferrante 27
Apple, Michael 277, 284
architecture 150–155
artfulness 15, 127–164; architecture 150–155; documentation and 130–131, 137–146; ethic of making 155–163; pedagogy 150–155; *pensiero progettuale* and 130–131; potential of constraints 150–155; *Progettazione* 128–142; *programmazione* and 132–137; in Reggio Emilia 146–149, 279
asili nido 23, 30, 36, 37
assessore 22, 36, 42, 46, 265
atelieristas 17n3, 25–26, 36, 41, 64, 65, 71, 76, 77, 87, 92, 97,

Index **315**

110, 117, 122, 123, 128, 131, 134, 145, 146, 172, 173, 230–231, 233, 234, *237, 250*, 276, 286, 297, 298, 307, 312; class *aggiornamento* 183–184, 210–212; co-teacher and 107; experience 48; ideas for designing a door 96; *mettersi in gioco* 9; *pedagogistas* and 67, 90, 91, 99, 100, 125, 155, 183–184, 267; tiny plants made by *106*
authoritativeness 43, 44, 88
auxiliary colleague 175, 176, 177, 182, 210–212
auxiliary staff 25, 26, 41, 42, 45, 52n7, 53n20, 63, 172, 179, 190, 220n4

Ball, Stephen: "terrors of performativity" 150–151
Barbiero, Federica *63*
Beltrami, Barbara 76, *77*, 227, *228*
Bianchi, Lorenza 172, 178, 182, 186, 187, 193, 211, 220n13
Bird Rose, Deborah 15–16
Bobbio, Luigi 264
Bollier, David 256, 262, 282
Bonazzi, Renzo 283, 284
Boncinelli, Edoardo 105
Bondioli, Anna 31–32, 53n14
Bonilauri, Simona 7, 40, 62, 73, 76, *77*, 78, 92, 93, 94, 97, 99, 101–105, 134, *140*, 145, *162*, 227, *228*, 229, 234, 235, 284, 285, 298, 299
Boonen, Christiaan 256, 261, 281, 298
Braidotti, Rosi 1, 57, 59, 78, 225, 227, 231, 240, 241; on affirmative ethics 238, 239; disruption of disciplinary purity 238; "killing our freedom softly" 239; on negativity 239

caged-in experience 135
Cameron, Claire 6, 74
Camorani, Barbara *63*
Capra, Fritjof 262–264, 268
care *see* collective care
Carnevali, Ethel *61–62*, 79, *80, 160*, 232, 251, 285, 296
Castagnetti, Marina 11, 82, 138, 139, 156, 230, 232, 286
Castrico, Federica *140, 162*

Cattozzo, Simonetta 172, 211
centrazione tematiche 293
Cerini, Giancarlo 28
Cervi, Genoveffa 306
Ciari, Bruno 28, 244
Cipollone, Laura 30
City Childhood Councils 44–46, 54n21, 264, 306; *Consiglio* (Council) 40; *Consiglio Infanzia Città* 39
City Intercouncil 44–46
class meetings 39, 44, 54n21, 136
Colla, Lucia 10, 230, 290, 291
collective *aggiornamento* 50, 173–212
collective care 6–15; amateur scholarship 6–12; collective response 12–15; obligation to care 12–15; teachers as intellectuals 6–12
collective experimentation 63, 147, 248–251, 253, 289–296
collective potentiation 295
collective practice 78, 87, 128, 226, 238, 240, 246
collective response 12–15, 57
collegiality 90, 92, 284; administrative offices 48; community and 309–311; *Indications* Rulebook 39; *sistema pedagogico diffuso* 56
Collegio Docenti (Teachers' Board) 23
Common Core Standards 150
common-pool natural resources 272n2
commons 305–307; *see also Education Commons*; value of the commons
community 78, 262; affirmative ethics 239; collegiality and 309–311; defined 262; democratic 285; education 286–287; of land-workers and small artisans 305; local 148; scientific 267; shared 261; value of education 266
competent systems 4, 22, 41
compulsory schooling, Italy 22–23
conceptual creativity 238–241, 253
confronto 29, 34, *62*, 82, 87, 102, 103, 125, 131, 177, 182, 190, 230, 242, 244, 264, 265, 295, 310; during an *aggiornamento 80*; by the classroom door *97*; collective 138, 286; constructive 76; dialectics and 46, 88, 109; ethic of dialectics 76–84; *progettazione* from 116
Constitution 22, 25, 306, 308
constraints 150–155; employment 25–26

316 Index

Consulta 17, 36, 53n19, 265–266
continuous professional development 9
conventions 27, 31, 48, 49, 52n6, 264,
    272n6
Coordinamento Pedagogico 35, 40,
    307–309
copying 111, 112, 195, 212, 213
co-responsibility 38–40, 41, 43, 63, 64,
    184
correspondence 17, 253; in culture
    241–243; defined 225;
    relational 71
courage 91, 108, 272
COVID-19 6, 234, 239
Crispiani, Piero 26, 32
culture, valuing of 223–243; affirmative
    ethics and conceptual
    creativity 238–241; children
    as knowing subjects 227–235;
    as correspondence 241–243;
    posthuman convergence and
    226–227; thinking that takes
    place in the world 235–238
culture of dialectics 108

Dahlberg, Gunilla 128, 137, 278, 280
decentralisation, administrative 22
Declaration of Intents 172
Delrio, Graziano 12
democracy 68, 129, 278; adult 268;
    ethic of 164n4; participatory
    286; value of relationality 72–76
"democratic deficit" 74
Dewey, John 29
dialectics 86–126; municipal *nidi* 87–90;
    perspective 78; portrait of yellow
    daisies 108–125; *progettazione*
    (*progettualità*) 125–126; *scuole
    dell'infanzia* 87–90; three-year-
    old children 90–108
diffused pedagogical system 40–51
discourse: cultural 239; early childhood
    curriculum policy and 57; on
    education 9, 129, 147, 307–309;
    hegemonical 231; of masculinity
    and power 4; neoliberal 6, 132;
    political 3
documentation 10, *61*, 63, *65*, 72,
    130–131, 159, *160*, 161, 164n4,
    228, 233, 245, 246, 250,
    268–269, 279, 280, 292;
    in-process 183; internal
    172; pedagogical 60;
    pensiero progettuale and 156;

progettazione and 66, 71, 72, 75,
    130–131, 137–142, 152, 159,
    173, 248; *scuola dell'infanzia* 83;
    selection of 64; theory-practice-
    research 137–142
Documentation and Educational
    Research Centre 47, 130
Dolci, Mariano 47

early childhood education 8, 11, 15, 28,
    29, 57, 70, 147, 302, 303; care
    and 70, 143, 303; marketplace
    and 277–280; praxis-theory-
    research 58; relationality and
    affect 67
early childhood services 28–29, 31, 33,
    263, 265, 278, 309
Eco, Umberto 272n4
educational services, 0–3 years 23–26
Education Commons 256–272, 275;
    0–6 integrated public system
    262–264; *consulta* 265–266;
    cultural revolution 258–266;
    ethic of alliances 287–301;
    micropolitics and 283–287; *nidi*
    and *scuole dell'infanzia* 257–258;
    participation 267–271; policies and
    actions for realising utopia 261–
    262; political stance and 280–283;
    territorial pedagogical coordination
    265–266; unimaginable and
    283–287; unrenounceable value
    and strategy 267–271; value of the
    commons 283–287
educator professionalism 1, 2
Emilia Romagna region 28, 29, 31, 33,
    34, 53n15
enchanted animism 105
enthusiasm 75, 192, 203
équipe allargata 39, 49
équipe pedagogico-didattica 35, 36, 37,
    46–47
ethic: of alliances 276, 287–301; of
    dialectics 76–84, 288; of making
    155–163; of research 243–252
everyday contexts and routines 170
experimentation 156, 224; aesthetics
    and 132; collective 63, 248–
    251, 289–296; innovation 31;
    transformation and 131

Fabbi, Cristian 311–312
Fadda, Rosanna *63*
Ferriere, Adolphe 267–268

Filippini, Tiziana 40, 108, 111–112, 115, 118, 121–122, 133, 137, 142, 172, 174–176, 182, 184, 185, 187, 199, 203, 204, 210–212, 229, 233, 243, 288, 290, 297, 299
"folding-in" architecture 154
Fondazione Reggio Children – Centro Loris Malaguzzi 47, 49, 266
Forenzi, Francesca 70, 80, 132, 160, 238, 249
formazione 4, 5, 80, 99, 130–134, 136, 141, 156, 169, 184, 229, 232, 249, 257, 284, 292–294, 296; amateur scholarship and teachers as intellectuals 6–12; defined 9, 10; geographies and compositions 49–50; in-service 23; reciprocity and 78; *see also* reciprocal *formazione*
formazione permanente (permanent lifelong learning) 21
Forni, Maura 32, 53n15
four-year-olds: classroom 94, 177; how to set the table to 185–197; presenting billboard to *218*; *see also* three-year-old
freedom, value of relationality 72–76
Freinet, Célestin 29
Freire, Paulo 7
Fröbel, Friedrich 27, 29

Gallerani, Paola 237
Garofalo, Loredana 9, 11, 62, 74, 136, 141–142, 149, 152, 161, 221n18
Giacopini, Elena 8, 11, 67, 75, 83, 137–138, 157, 159, 244, 252, 292
Gianni Rodari Theatre Laboratory 47
Giaroni, Loretta 36
Giroux, Henry 5, 11, 78, 80, 81, 82, 83, 87, 239, 240, 277, 283
Giudici, Claudia 129, 150, 242
giunta (cabinet) 22
Gobetti, Ada 29, 53n12
Harvard Project Zero 137
"horizontal" relationships 56
Hundred Languages of Children exhibition 246

I Cento Linguaggi dei Bambini (The Hundred Languages of Children) 40
immanent obligation 14
immaterial goods 276–277
in-betweenness *(in-between-ness)* 66–67, 241
Incerti, Cinzia 92, 93, 100, 101, *140, 162*
Indications (the new Rulebook) 38–40
Indicazioni nazionali per il curricolo della scuola dell'infanzia e del primo ciclo di istruzione [National Indications for *scuola dell'infanzia* and primary education curriculum] 173
individualist autonomy 68
"in-folding" approach 154
Ingold, Tim 1, 3, 4, 7, 8, 155, 156, 157, 159, 160, 161, 163, 164, 223, 225, 226, 241, 242, 243, 262
innovation and research 50–51
inserimento (introduce into) 90
institutional identity 44, 46, 51
Integrated System of Education and Instruction 34–35
Interconsiglio Cittadino [City Intercouncil] 39, 45, 54n22
interested schools 224
Iotti, Daniela 233
Iotti, Nilde *63*
Italy: 0–3 educational services 23–26; 3–6 *scuole dell'infanzia* 23–26; administrative de-centralisation 22; compulsory schooling 22–23; post-war years 259; unification 258
Itard, Jean-Marc Gaspard 27

Kahn, Louis 152, 153, 250
Karmiloff-Smith, Annette 185

Lanzi, Daniela 13, *63*, 73, 82, 139, 141, 295
Lather, Patti 136, 224
"Learning to Be" Report 21
Levinas, Emmanuel 16
Linee pedagogiche per il sistema integrato zerosei [Pedagogical Guidelines for the 0–6 integrated system] 309
lively ethography 2, 126n8

318 Index

Lorenzani, Marika 13, 80, 142–143, 154, 155
Loris Malaguzzi International Centre 48–49, 266

Maccaferri, Elena 130, 294
Magnani, Palazzo: *Somersaults of Thoughts* 240
Mainini, Alessandro *65, 250*
making and thinking 252
Making Learning Visible 137
Malaguzzi, Loris 5, 7, 10, 11, 26–28, 35, 37, 38, 39, 41, 42, 43, 45, 52n8, 72–74, 78, 130, 134, 135, 136, 138, 139, 148, 164, 168–169, 180–181, 233, 242, 244, 258, 259–260, 268, 270–271, 288, 292, 307–308, 310–311; approach of "listening to children" 57; "pedagogy of relations" 56; prophetic pedagogy 150–151; systemic theory 132
Manning, Erin 68, 128, 135, 147, 149, 245, 247, 248, 250, 251, 252, 253, 276, 289, 302
Mantovani, Susanna 224
Marani, Simona 75, 82, 144, 148, 242, 249, 293, 295, 296
marketplace 277–280
Massumi, Brian 59, 66, 67, 68, 75, 154, 155, 247, 275, 283, 286, 294; "event-care" 72; "the neoliberal moment" 279
"material doings" 70
Mattei, Ugo 262–264, 268
Mayer, Susanna 29–30, 33
McCall, Jane 86, 90, 91, 169, 173, 181, 191, 260–261, 263–264, 268, 270, 272, 305–312
McTighe, Jay 150, 151
measurable means 152–153
Meninno, Isabella 172, 184, 184, 185, 186, 187, 189, 194, 195, 202, 211, 216
Merewether, Jane 105, 132
"messy worldliness" 69
mettersi in gioco 9, 74, 75; excitement and discovery 10
micropolitics 283–287, 296–301
Ministry of Instruction 30
minor gesture 301–303
Montessori, Maria 27, 29

Mori, Marina 108, 111, 112, 113, 114, 117–121, 172, 177, 178, 181–184, 186–189, 193, 194, 196, 198, 199, 203, 205, 211–212, 214–216
Morrison, Scott 278
Moss, Peter 4, 6, 9, 11, 14, 74, 76, 128, 129, 150, 280–281
multi-body situations 67
Munari, Bruno 76, *77*, 227, *228*
municipalities 31, 37, 38, 52n1; 0–3 educational services managed by 25–26; 3–6 *scuole dell'infanzia* managed by 25–26; early childhood educational services by 28; pedagogical coordination 29
municipal *nidi* 16, 47, 48, 53n20, 76, 87–90, 147, 167, 257, 258, 262, 276. *see also nido d'infanzia/nido*
Musatti, Tullia 29–30, 33

narcissistic singularity 235
neoliberalism 5, 14, 15, 67, 81, 129, 132, 239, 279, 283
Neri, Sergio 244
Neri, Stefano: *Servizi di welfare e Comuni* [Welfare Services and Municipalities] 308
nido d'infanzia/nido 10, 12, 24, 29, 31, 38, 41–44, 45, 46, 51, 64, 67, 70, 73, 80, 87, 89, 112, 143, 149, 169–170, *171*, 172, 230, 290, 291, 294–295, 298, 306; *aggiornamento 63*; *asili/asilo* 23, 28, 36, 37, 53n13; municipal 16, 47, 48, 53n20, 76, 87–90, 147, 167, 257, 258, 262, 276; regional law 26, 30; research 50; teachers 25; tiptoeing 74
normative appropriation 14

obligation to care 12–15
organisational process 87
organisms of participation 38–40
Orientamenti nazionali per i servizi educativi per l'infanzia [National Orientations for early childhood educational services] 309
Ostrom, Elinor 262, 277; *Governing the Commons* 256
Ovi, Giulia 11, *63*, 79, 156, 157

Palmisano, Tiziana *63*
participation 76–84, 267–271
Partito Comunista Italiano (Italian
  Communist Party) Federation of
  Reggio Emilia 11, 233, 280–281
pedagogical coordinations 7, 13, 22,
  29–35, 38, 40, 46, 50, 82, 90,
  97, 233, 234, 242, 245, 295,
  297, 299, 308–311; *centrazione
  tematiche* 293; recognition
  and support 34; responsibility
  towards *formazione* 66, 284; in
  scuole dell'infanzia 34, 73; team
  39, 133; territorial 265–266;
  theoretical support to educators
  155
pedagogical coordinator 28–29, 32–35,
  40, 46, 82, 97, 155, 233, 234,
  242, 245, 265–266, 284, 293,
  299, 309
pedagogical coordinators 32–35; Article
  34, the tasks of 33; of early
  childhood services 28–29; role of
  29–32
pedagogy 26–27, 150–155; defined 37;
  documentation 60, 137, 164n3;
  politics and 307–309; psychology
  and 78
Pederzoli, Manuela 12, 73, 74, 76, 147,
  149, 157, 226, 232, 247, 286–
  287, 292, 298
pensiero progettuale 10, 70, 75, 88, 127,
  128, 130–131, 134, 149, 152,
  167–220; appointment with
  the children 212–214; *collective
  aggiornamento* 173–212; in daily
  life 142–146; everyday contexts
  and routines 170; following
  day after appointment with
  children 214–217; and research
  in everyday contexts 168–170;
  setting the table 170–173, *171*;
  unexpected relaunch 218–219
photo reportages *214*
Piano della Offerta Formativa
  (Educational Offer Plan) 23
policies and actions for realising utopia
  261–262
politics: beyond the self-interest 68;
  pedagogy and 307–309
portrait of yellow daisies 108–125
posthuman convergence 225, 226–227
Preschools and Infant-toddler Centres -
  Istituzione of the Municipality of

Reggio Emilia 2, 17n1, 38–40,
  44–45, 54n21, 56, 67, 78, 129,
  136, 242, 244, 245, 249, 258,
  281, 305–311
professional development 5, 9
professional learning 5, 60
profession of *pedagogista* 27–28
progettazione (progettualità) 8, 50, 63,
  90, 125–126, 130–131; as an
  elusive concept 128–130; defined
  136; theory-practice-research
  137–142; welcoming complexity
  and participation 132–137
programmazione (programming) 127,
  131; defined 132; welcoming
  complexity and participation
  132–137
Protocol of Understanding 272n5
Provincial Pedagogical Coordination 34
psychology 26, 28, 37, 78, 173
Psycho-Pedagogical Medical 35
Public Administration Reform of 1993
  31
public space 261, 270
Puig de la Bellacasa, Maria 14, 69, 70,
  71, 84

Quinti, Barbara 76, *77*, 227, *228*

Rabotti, Annalisa 74, 75, 247, 248, 286,
  294, 296, 297
Rainieri, Annalisa 10, 11, *60–62*, 79, *80*,
  82, 158, 159, *237*, 297
reciprocal *formazione* 1, 21–52;
  collective care and 6–15;
  experience of 0–6 services 35–40;
  genesis of profession 28–29;
  pedagogical coordinations 29–35;
  pedagogical coordinator 28–29,
  32–35; pedagogical system
  40–51; profession of *pedagogista*
  27–28; schooling in Italy 22–27;
  system for education 22–27
reciprocity, value of relationality 58–68
Reggio Emilia Approach system 48–49
Reggionarra (annual city initiative)
  47
Regolamento 35, 36, 54n22
relational affordance 294, 295
relationships 58, 66, 233, 297, 299;
  environmental 158; international
  educational policy 58; local
  community 148; pedagogy of
  57

320 Index

relaunching 17, 107, 123, 161, 167, 168, 178, 181, 189, 194, 195, 203, 205, 207, 218–219, 221n19, 242, 266
representation 246; internal and external 185; of setting the table 185–186
representational redescription/ re-description 185
research, ethic of *see* ethic of research
research-creation 245, 248, 251
research in everyday contexts 168–170
Reverberi, Evelina 234
Riddle, Stewart 277, 284
Rigney, Lester-Irabinna 231
Rinaldi, Carla 35, 72; pedagogy of relationships and listening 57
Rinaldi, Nando 307–309
Robert-Holmes, Guy 129, 150
Rodari, Gianni 29, 53n11, *171*
Romanazzo, Mariagrazia *140*, *162*
Ronchelli, Giuseppina *140*, *162*; sharing documentation and children's artefacts in clay *141*
Rubizzi, Laura 76, *77*, 92, 93, 94, 96–97, 103, 104, 105, 107, 227, *228*
Ruozzi, Mirella 64, *65*, 71, 72, 134, 230, *250*, 298

Sahlberg, Pasi 150
Said, Edward 6, 9, 12
Santarini, Duilio 28
schooling in Italy 22–27
scuola materna (motherly school) 59
scuole dell'infanzia/scuola 9, 11, 21, 22, 25, 45, 46, 47, 50, 51, 59, 64, 67, 70, 74–76, 87, 89, 91–92, 94, 99, 102, 103, 109, 112, 117, 138, 145, 164n5, 169–173, 185, 227, 229, 231, *237*, 241, *250*, 265, 282, 290, 294, 295, 298, 305, 306, 307, 308, 312; 3–6 years 23–26; *aggiornamento* at *60–63*, *65*, *77*, *80*, *81*, *92*, *140*, *141*, *160*, *162*, *228*; hypothesis 74; in Italy 24; *nido* and 38, 41–44, 87, *171*, *172*; three-year-olds 91
Second World War 258, 259, 280
Seguin, Edouard 27
Serra, Michele 103
Servizi di welfare e Comuni [Welfare Services and Municipalities] (Neri) 308

setting the table 170–173, *171*, 178–183, *208–210*; drawing of *191–192*; to the four-year-old children 186–197; instructions for *206*, *217*, *218*; to representations of setting the table 185–186
Sims, Margaret 5
sistema pedagogico diffuso 56, 59, 66, 68, 69, 71, 75, 78, 84
social management 57, 264, 271, 305
social quality 29
solidarity, value of relationality 72–76
Somersaults of Thoughts (Magnani) 240
Soncini, Ivana 63, 93, 133, 232–233, 245, 299
Spaggiari, Simona 92, 93, 96, 97, 100, 101, 102, 103, 105, *106*, 107
speculative middle 247–248
speculative pragmatism 253
Spuybroek, Luys 163
Squarza, Annetta 65
St. Pierre, Elizabeth Adams 2, 134, 135, 245–247
Strozzi, Paola 60, *60–62*, 64, *65*, 69, 74, *80*, 103, *106*, 107, 108, 111–116, 118, 119, 122, 138, 145, 153, *160*, 172, 175–179, 181–183, 185–189, 192–199, 202, 204–205, 211–212, 215–216, 237, 242, 249, *250*, 267, 276
system for education 22–27
system resources 47–48, 294
systems governance 31, 32

Tamburini, Anna 76, 227, *228*
Tanzi, Viviana 34, 53n16
teacher educator 176, 183–184, 210–212
Tedeschi, Maddalena 309–311
territorial pedagogical coordination 265–266
The City and the Rain project 134
theory fatigue 225
theory-practice-research 16, 130, 137–142, 155, 250
thinking-in-the-making 253
thinking that takes place in the world 235–238
"totalitarianism of the same" 128

UNESCO 21
Unger, Roberto Mangabeira 260–261

unimaginable 283–287
United Nations: Convention on the
  Rights of the Child 305
unquantifiable 250
unrenounceable value and strategy
  267–271
Urban, Mathias 3, 4

value of artfulness *see* artfulness
value of artistry 147
value of complexity 114
value of *confronto* 108
value of co-responsibility 43
value of culture 17, 223–253; *see also*
  culture, valuing of
value of design 147
value of relationality 16, 56–58; affect
  and reciprocity 58–68; solidarity,
  freedom, and democracy 72–76;
  worlds seen through care 68–72
value of the commons 12, 17, 275–303;
  ethic of alliances 287–301;
  immaterial goods 276–277; living

an *Education Commons* 280–283;
  marketplace and early childhood
  education as a commodity
  277–280; micropolitics and the
  unimaginable 283–287
van Dooren, Thom 14
Veca, Salvatore 261, 270
Vecchi, Vea 102–103, 108, 111, 113–
  116, 118–122, 124–125, 145,
  147, 290
Venturini, Gigliola 305–307

the welcome 87, 91–93, 96
whole school working group 173–176;
  collective aggiornamento
  177–178
Wiggins, Grant 150, 151
Wittgenstein, Ludwig 90

Zagnoli, Olimpia 240
0–6 integrated public system 262–264
Zoebeli, Margherita 29, 53n10
Zumthor, Peter 152

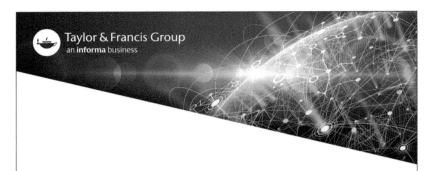